To the thousands of students who have given me the opportunity to smile each day the moment I enter the classroom.

THE ESSENTIALS OF WINE

with Food-Pairing Techniques

A straightforward approach to understanding wine and providing a framework
for making intelligent food-pairing decisions

John Peter Laloganes

The International Culinary School at the Illinois Institute of Art-Chicago
and
International Sommelier Guild

Prentice Hall
Upper Saddle River, New Jersey
Columbus, Ohio

Library of Congress Cataloging-in-Publication Data

Laloganes, John P.
  The essentials of wine with food pairing techniques : a
straightforward approach to understanding wine and providing a framework
for making intelligent food pairing decisions / John P. Laloganes.
     p. cm.
  Includes index.
  ISBN-13: 978-0-13-235172-0
  ISBN-10: 0-13-235172-2
  1. Wine and wine making—Analysis.   2. Wine tasting.   I. Title
  TP548.5.A5L35 2010
  641.2′2–dc22   2008053838

Editor in Chief: Vernon Anthony
Acquisitions Editor: William Lawrensen
Editorial Assistant: Lara Dimmick
Production Coordination: Aptara®, Inc.
Project Manager: Kris Roach
AV Project Manager: Janet Portisch
Operations Specialist: Deidra Schwartz
Art Credits: Thomas Moore
Art Director: Diane Ernsberger
Cover Designer: Candace Rowley
Cover Image(s): Getty One
Manager, Rights and Permissions: Zina Arabia
Image Permission Coordinator: Nancy Seise
Director of Marketing: David Gesell
Marketing Manager: Leigh Ann Sims
Marketing Coordinator: Les Roberts

All chapter opening photos are from SuperStock with the exception of chapters 5 (Ian O'Leary ©Dorling
Kindersley) and 14 (Ian O'Leary ©Dorling Kindersley) and chapter 11 (Collection CIVC; photographer:
LECOMTE Jean-Marle).

This book was set in TradeGothic 9.5/13.5 by Aptara®, Inc., and was printed and bound by Courier
Kendallville. The cover was printed by Lehigh-Phoenix Color/Hagerstown.

Pearson Education Ltd., London
Pearson Education Singapore Pte. Ltd.
Pearson Education Canada, Inc.
Pearson Education—Japan

Pearson Education Australia Pty. Limited
Pearson Education North Asia, Ltd., Hong Kong
Pearson Educación de Mexico, S.A. de C.V.
Pearson Education Malaysia Pte. Ltd.

Prentice Hall
is an imprint of

www.pearsonhighered.com

10 9 8 7 6 5 4 3
ISBN-13: 978-0-13-235172-0

CONTENTS

PREFACE

HOW THIS TEXTBOOK IS ORGANIZED

The Essentials of Wine with Food-Pairing Techniques is a straightforward approach to understanding wine and provides a framework for making intelligent food-pairing decisions. The units (and the chapters within the units) in this book have been arranged by a **building-block** approach that was developed through trial and error over a period of several years of classroom testing. The units and chapters build upon one another (particularly Units 1 and 2) until a certain point when the textbook allows for **flexibility** if the instructor desires, in order to adjust and adapt the order of units presented according to the skill level of the learners or the appropriateness of the curriculum. The units also allow teachers to utilize the text in a single course or multiple courses, either as a main textbook or as a supplement in conjunction with other wine, culinary, or pastry books. The book can work in single classes such as "Introduction to Wine," "Wine Appreciation," "Wine and Food Pairing," or "Food and Beverage Operations." It can also be used as a supplementary text in "Culinary 101," "Baking 101," "Guest Service," and "Hospitality Marketing and Retail Sales" courses.

Unit 1—**The Basics of Wine** introduces the learner to fundamental wine concepts, professional tasting, and the process of how grapes are grown and wine is made. *Unit 2*—**Wine and Food Compatibility** outlines the most significant and common grape varietals and then proceeds to the foundations and advanced information about wine- and food-pairing concepts. *Unit 3*—**Wines of the New World** introduces the learner to the major New World wine-producing countries and the most notable regions within them. *Unit 4*—**Wines of the Old World** introduces the learner to the major Old World wine-producing countries and the most notable regions within them. *Unit 5*—**Other Types of Wine** provides vital information that exposes the learner to sparkling, fortified, and dessert wines. Not all culinary, pastry, and hospitality management programs have the classes or allowance for advanced wine content in their programs. Unit 5 allows instructors to forego such content or to manipulate the order of the chapters to suit their situation. *Unit 6*—**Wine Management** provides some necessary techniques for managing wine successfully. Discussed here are the processes controlling the flow of wine, cost control, and the development of a wine menu. This material can be useful either in a wine course, cost control, or in a menu-planning course.

To get the maximum benefit and depth of information out of the book, follow the units and chapters in order while periodically flipping through the **Appendix, Wine Glossary: From A to Z.** This appendix acts to support the other chapters and should be used as a reference throughout the textbook. The six units into which the book is broken down are described in more detail as follows:

- *Unit 1*—**The Basics of Wine:** The student is exposed to the fundamentals of wine, beginning with what wine is, how grapes are grown, how wine is made, and the three main categories of wine. The differences between Old World and New World wine is analyzed, and bottle shapes and labelling are then discussed.
- *Unit 2*—**Wine and Food Compatibility:** The significant white and red wine grape varietals are discussed, with an eye toward gaining a strong analytical understanding of how to pair wine and food together. This unit is fairly "culinary heavy" as a means of providing a solid foundation or review of cookery. The culinary

information affords a bridge for the student by reinforcing techniques learned in order to truly understand the analytical approach to pairing wine with food.

- *Unit 3*—**Wines of the New World:** The student is introduced to the major wine-producing areas of the United States (California, New York, Washington, and Oregon) and Canada. Also explored are other New World wine-producing countries, such as Chile, Argentina, Australia, New Zealand, and South Africa.
- *Unit 4*—**Wines of the Old World:** The student is introduced to the major wine-producing areas of France, Italy, Germany, and Spain.
- *Unit 5*—**Other Types of Wines:** The student is introduced to the various production methods and different styles of sparkling wines, fortified wines, and dessert wines.
- *Unit 6*—**Wine Management:** This unit provides a solid foundation for the new or already working beverage manager.
- **The Appendix** is a comprehensive glossary complete with the pronunciations of difficult or foreign wine terms.

MAJOR COMPETENCIES

Upon completion of this textbook, the reader should be able to do all of the following:

- ☑ Classify wines according to type, and recognize their distinguishing styles and classification methods. (Chapter 1—Introduction to Wine)
- ☑ Apply wine-tasting assessment techniques for table, fortified, and sparkling wines. (Chapter 2—Wine Tasting)
- ☑ Identify the major elements within the grape-growing and winemaking processes. (Chapter 3—Viticulture and Enology)
- ☑ Distinguish between different grape varietals, their major locations of production, and their unique personalities. (Chapter 4—Performance Factors of Grape Varietals)
- ☑ Apply the analytical approach to wine and food pairing. (Chapter 5—Foundations to Wine and Food Pairing)
- ☑ Comprehend specific food types with their respective pairing strategies. (Chapter 6—Advanced Wine and Food Pairing)
- ☑ Discover the wine philosophies and major wine-producing areas of American and Canadian wines. (Chapter 7—Wines of the United States and Canada)
- ☑ Discover the wine philosophies and major wine-producing areas of Chile, Argentina, Australia, New Zealand, and South Africa. (Chapter 8—Other New World Wine Countries)
- ☑ Discover the wine philosophies and major wine-producing areas of France and the notable wines that are produced in those areas. (Chapter 9—Wines of France)
- ☑ Discover the wine philosophies and major wine-producing areas of Italy, Germany, and Spain. (Chapter 10—Other Old World Wine Countries)
- ☑ Distinguish between the different production methods and major styles of "other wines" (sparkling wines, fortified wines, and dessert wines). (Chapter 11—BUBBLES: Sparkling Wine, Chapter 12—BOLD: Fortified Wine, Chapter 13—NECTAR: Dessert Wines)
- ☑ Identify the elements within each control point throughout the flow of wine. (Chapter 14—The Flow of Wine)

☑ Demonstrate fundamental wine opening and serving techniques. (Chapter 14—The Flow of Wine)

☑ Comprehend different variables needed to arrange and compile an effective wine menu. (Chapter 15—Developing a Wine Menu)

☑ Acquire a comprehensive vocabulary of wine terminology. (Appendix, Wine Glossary: From A to Z)

ADDITIONAL TOOLS

Practice Quizzes—At the end of each chapter, there are "Check Your Knowledge" quizzes that include a combination of 20–30 multiple choice, true/false, matching, and short answer essay questions. Unit 2, "Wine and Food Compatibility," offers several worksheets at the end of each chapter to assist the learner with gaining a solid understanding and practice of pairing guidelines and principles.

Key Words—These terms have been set in italics throughout each chapter within the book. Most words can also be found in the Glossary for quick reference if a definition or pronunciation is needed.

Colorful maps—Maps of key grape/wine production areas help to illustrate terroir in a general sense. Certainly, it is helpful to have a sense of place, particularly an understanding of where regions or countries are in relation to one another. Each winemaking region has its own character and heritage, and its wines represent both the unique properties of the land and local winemaking practices. The climates and topographies within a country or even a wine region can vary dramatically, so knowing where the wine is made gives clues as to the grape varieties and flavors one can expect.

Pronunciation Guides and Glossary—Some wine terms can be challenging to articulate, because they are taken from French, Italian, German, or Spanish (or even, in some cases, from Portuguese or Hungarian). The first time a "foreign term" appears and is expanded upon within the text, a phonetic guide is included for English speakers. The guide provides an approximate pronunciation in English and does not necessarily reflect the nuances or specific dialects that may be apparent with the use of these terms in the country or wine region of origin. Certainly, a French word will sound best as said by a French-speaking person, but the guides provide a close approximation that would be acceptable to use throughout the world.

Vocabulary that is used throughout the book is summarized in a Glossary at the back of the book. The reader is encouraged to reference the Glossary throughout the text upon encountering a term whose meaning he or she does not know. Unit 4, "Wines of the Old World," presents easy-to-locate wine bottle labelling terminology at the beginning of each chapter.

INTRODUCTION BY THE AUTHOR

The GOAL of This Textbook

The Essentials of Wine with Food-Pairing Techniques is a resource that educates the reader through the presentation of a practical and straightforward approach to understanding wine and by providing a framework for making intelligent, well-informed wine- and food-pairing decisions.

The textbook provides both a foundational wine education and guidelines and principles for pairing wine and food. Of course, the book discusses the "typical" classic wine and food combinations that are in all wine books; yet it emphasizes the necessity of understanding the pairing strategies for "World Cuisine" that is prevalent around us today and for food found in everyday types of restaurants.

Throughout the book, broad-brush strokes will be used to present information in a user-friendly format. Sometimes, however, a fine brush will be applied to emphasize areas that are foundational concepts in the text. The writing style and format of the book have been designed in a way that allows simplicity to guide the student through the maze of wine information by keeping it on a level that learners can relate to.

This textbook strives to provide relevant, to-the-point information that saves the reader from personal or long-winded stories. There are other books for that. This book and all of its contents (study quizzes, tasting sheets, etc.) have been designed and tested in a classroom environment for a period of several years. While things aren't perfect, they hopefully will ensure greater success of the transition of the content from the book into a classroom or training environment.

The Current State of Wine Textbooks

Currently, many wine and wine-and-food-pairing textbooks fall short of effectively delivering information that will train and educate students in the essentials of both topics. Some of the books discuss only wine pairing and veer towards being more of a cookbook or "coffee-table" type of book, rather than a "cut to the chase" wine-and-food book. Other books are extensively researched treatises on wine and devote a meager page or two to the subject of wine pairing—and that only out of obligation.

Many of these books are written at two extremes of imparting information about wine. At one extreme, the books that are available are incredibly basic, often written in a first-person narrative and even comedic style and not very academic for an educational institution. At the other extreme are books written by wine experts for other wine experts, without regard to the level of comprehension or to whether they can give the reader a foundation of wine knowledge to build upon. These books, while certainly informative, are written at such a complex level that they require the novice wine reader to read and speak several foreign languages as he or she sifts through and pronounces foreign terms and relevant concepts. Also, such books sometimes require the reader to be an expert in geography and decipher maps detailing the most obscure wine-producing areas and vineyards in, for example, Burgundy, France. These books often leave the novice to intermediate wine reader confused or overwhelmed. The Essentials of Wine With Food Pairing Techniques doesn't contain all the information one needs to know about the topic of wine. There are many advanced books available for enhanced knowledge, but this text provides a solid foundation that will prepare the reader for those other books.

Whom This Book Is for . . .

The Essentials of Wine with Food-Pairing Techniques is ideal for anyone who desires a strong, solid foundation to understanding wine, as well as wine and food pairing. The book is targeted not only at students who are presently enrolled in culinary or hospitality management programs, but also for individuals working within the restaurant industry and salespeople in wine retail. The book will be useful to the novice cook, but also to the culinary student and the seasoned chef. The Essentials of Wine with Food-Pairing Techniques will be most valuable (though, not necessary) to those who have some initial foundation in a basic culinary training because of the pervasive theme of wine and food pairing throughout.

The book strives to demystify wine and food pairing. A difficulty of many wine textbooks is their inadequate coverage of information about food, while food textbooks don't cover enough about wine. This leaves a large gap in wine and food education, but also an opportunity to bridge that gap.

There appears to be a dichotomy of wine perspectives out there in the world. Certain people espouse the idea that wine shouldn't be a routine drink: In drinking wine, rituals and customs go with the wine experience. Other wine drinkers champion the notion that wine is simply another beverage for enjoyment, and barriers that limit access and consumption should be avoided as much as possible. As an avid wine drinker, I value both approaches and see no right or wrong with either as the motivation and meaning of wine is different for every individual who consumes it. If I could make one suggestion, it would be the following: Pour a glass of your favorite wine to sip as you read these pages. Allow this book to uncover all the intrigue, seduction, and complexity that wine has to offer. If it hasn't already, it is my hope that you permit wine to enrich your life as it has mine.

ABOUT THE AUTHOR

John Peter Laloganes

John has worked in the restaurant industry since the mid-1980s and works avidly with Chicago restaurants and related establishments in assisting them to become more successful.

He has taken extensive coursework in culinary arts, earned a bachelor's degree in hospitality and tourism management from the University of Wisconsin–Stout and a master's degree from the University of Minnesota. John was an associate professor at the Cooking and Hospitality Institute of Chicago–Le Cordon Bleu schools, he earned the "Educator of the Year" award in 2004 and the "Customer Service Award" from North American Le Cordon Bleu Schools in 2005. John also was awarded the distinctive Sommelier Diploma (level III) through the International Sommelier Guild (ISG) in 2007.

John is currently a sommelier/management instructor at the International Culinary School at the Illinois Institute of Art–Chicago and, in addition, teaches wine fundamentals, levels I and II, for the International Sommelier Guild.

John is a current member of the Society of Wine Educators (SWE), the American Culinary Federation (ACF), and the National Restaurant Association (NRA). Feel free to visit John's web-site at www.johnlaloganes.com or blog-site at www.laloganes.blogspot.com for additional informational resources and services.

ACKNOWLEDGMENTS

The construction of any textbook is the result of dozens, if not hundreds, of different people pulling together. This book is a collection of efforts from so many different individuals through the years, some of whom I have never met and some of whom I have had the pleasure of meeting at different points throughout my life. For those who have assisted me through this project, but whom I may have failed to mention, I thank you, too.

I would like to acknowledge the following individuals (not in any particular order) for their assistance:

Cheryl Kabb, for initially getting this project rolling and to Bill Lawrensen, for making it all happen. This book would never have been possible if not for your seeing the need for an accessible, user-friendly text about wine and food pairing.

Sharon Hughes, for your guidance and support throughout the review process. Your encouraging nature and helpful advice were always beneficial.

Julie Mason, for your assistance with image procurement. Thanks for adding a dimension to the textbook that would not have occurred without you.

Thomas Moore, for your excellent and speedy development of some fantastic maps.

Janel Syron, for providing me with the opportunity to have intelligent wine conversations on a regular basis.

Kerri Williams—a huge thanks—for your assistance with providing feedback on the dessert chapter and for the development of some support materials.

Tara Jobe, for your dedication in helping me complete the initial draft, oh so long ago!

Chef Mark Facklam, Chef Alisa Sattler, and Mr. Bert Lindstrom, for your support and encouragement that help me balance all the crazy stuff in life and allow me to do what I do best in the classroom.

Jamie Kluz, for your always inspiring approach to living life and your memorable quote, ". . .such a sexy, challenging and complex thing wine is!"

Peter D'Souza (from University of Wisconsin-Stout), Evan Saviolidis (from WineSavvy Consultants (www.winesavvy.ca), and Wayne Gotts (from International Sommelier Guild) for being inspiring and knowledgable wine educators.

Denise and Martin Cody, for providing me an additional opportunity to educate consumers about wine. You both continue to work to demystify wine for the public—and you do it with such tireless enthusiasm.

Thanks to the reviewers for all of their insightful comments. They are Marc DeMarchena, *Johnson & Wales University;* Brian Hay, *Austin Community College;* Dr. William Jaffe, *Purdue University;* Ken Jarvis, *Anne Arundel Community College;* Dr. Joe LaVilla, *Art Institute of Phoenix;* Greg Lemaire, *Manchester Community College;* Joe McCully, *Lane Community College;* Robert Pierson, *W. Delaware Valley College* and Sue Slater, *Cabrillo College.*

Edyta and Amelia, for your patience and support. I missed way too many trips to the park :)

Mrs. Cooney (my eighth-grade math teacher). Your prediction was obviously incorrect.

WEB RESOURCES

All Purpose

www.state.il.us/lcc/

The Alcohol and Tobacco Tax and Trade Bureau (TTB)

http://www.ttb.gov/appellation/index.shtml

Wine Institute of California

www.wineinstitute.org

Local wine events that can be searched internationally, by individual state or city.

http://www.localwineevents.com

Grape Radio

http://www.graperadio.com/

UNIT 1—The Basics of Wine

Riedel Stemware Company

http://www.riedel.com

UNIT 2—Wine and Food Compatibility

Food recipes from *Bon Appetit* and *Gourmet* magazines

http://www.epicurious.com/

UNIT 3—Wines of the New World

Wine Trade Group

http://www.wineinstitute.org/

American Wine Trade Group

http://www.wineamerica.org/

Wines of Napa Valley

http://www.napavintners.com/

Wine Appellation

http://wine.appellationamerica.com/wine-region-index.aspx

Wines of Monterey

http://www.montereywines.org

Wines of Sonoma

http://www.sonomawine.com

Wines of Washington State

http://www.washingtonwine.org/

Wines of New York State

http://www.newyorkwines.org/

Wines of Oregon State

http://www.oregonwine.org

Wines of Canada

http://www.canadianvintners.com/woc/index.html

Wines of British Columbia

http://www.winebc.com/

Wines of South Africa

http://www.wosa.co.za/

Wines of Chile

http://www.winesofchile.org/

http://www.chileinfo.com

Wines of Argentina

http://www.winesofargentina.org/

Wines of Australia

http://www.wineaustralia.com/australia/

Wines of New Zealand

http://www.nzwine.com/

UNIT 4—Wines of the Old World

Wines of France

http://www.frenchwinesfood.com/

Wines of Alsace

http://www.vinsalsace.com/en/index.html

Wines of Loire Valley

http://www.loirevalleywine.com/

Wines of Bordeaux

http://www.bordeaux.com/

Wines of Beaujolais

http://www.beaujolais.com/eng/page.htm

Wines of Rhône Valley

http://www.rhone-wines.com/pages/home-en.asp

Wines of Provence

http://www.provenceweb.fr/e/mag/terroir/vin/

Wines of Banyuls and Collioure

http://www.banyuls.com/banyuls/

Wines of Spain

http://www.winesfromspainusa.com

http://www.winesfromspain.com

Wines of Germany

http://www.germanwineusa.org/

Wines of Portugal

http://www.vinhoverde.pt/en/default.asp

Wines of Austria

http://www.winesfromaustria.com/eindex.php

UNIT 5—Other Types of Wine

The official website for Champagne

http://www.champagne.com/en_indx.html

Office of Champagne, USA

http://www.champagne.us/

The Port and Douro Institute (IVDP)

http://www.ivp.pt/index.asp?idioma=1&

http://www.infoportwine.com/

Consejo Regulador de las denominaciones de Origen

http://www.sherry.org/en/intro.cfm?CFID=144672&
CFTOKEN=71113649

http://www.enjoysherry.com/sherry/index.html

Chocolate

http://www.fieldmuseum.org/Chocolate/exhibits.html

http://www.scharffenberger.com/

Wine Publications

Decanter magazine

http://www.decanter.com/

Wine Spectator magazine

www.winespectator.com

Wine X magazine

www.winexmagazine.com/

Food and Wine magazine

www.foodandwine.com

Wine Enthusiast magazine

http://www.winemag.com/homepage/index.asp

Wine and Spirits magazine

www.wineandspiritsmagazine.com

Unit 1
THE BASICS OF WINE

"...from so simple a beginning endless forms most beautiful and most
wonderful have been, and are being, evolved".
—Charles Darwin

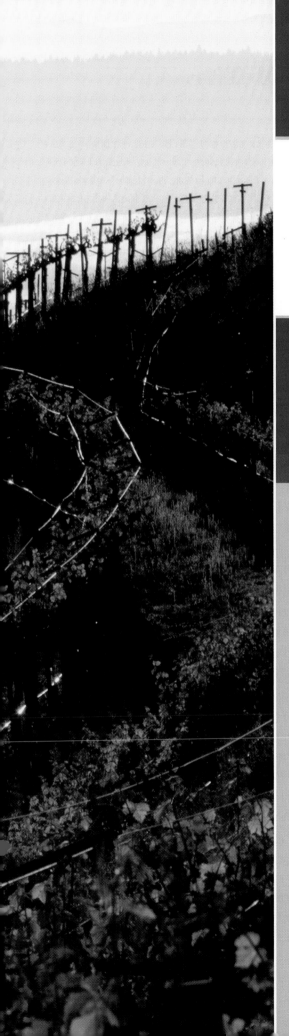

1

Introduction to Wine

Whether a wine is modest or distinguished, it's intended for pleasure; yet somehow, it unfortunately has developed a mystique and pretentious image that many people find intimidating.

LEARNING OBJECTIVES

Upon completion of this chapter, the learner will be able to:

- Understand the basic composition of a grape and its contributions to a wine.
- Identify each of the three distinctive categories and several styles of wine.
- Comprehend the broad distinctions between the Old and New Worlds.
- Discern clues about a wine through various bottle shapes and colors.
- Identify common wine closures as well as advantages and disadvantages of each.
- Recognize the distinctions between glassware for the different categories and types of wine.
- Identify the four approaches for labelling table wine.
- Discover the five most significant components of information found on wine labels.

THEN AND NOW OF THE WINE INDUSTRY

There is evidence that, originally, wine was made as early as 6000 BC and is thought to have originated in the Middle East. It is believed that the Greeks were making wine around 4500 BC and that they eventually influenced the Romans. The Roman Empire is, in turn, largely responsible for influencing the spread of the grapevine throughout Europe and the Mediterranean.

Some 8000 years later, the popularity and consumption of wine throughout the world and, in particular, the United States has reached new heights. This success is evident in the overall upward demand for wine in the United States and certain other countries throughout the world. In 2005, U.S. wine sales reached a record $26 billion, a 115% increase since 1995 (according to the Wine Institute). The American wine industry has maintained 14 years of consecutive sales growth, with over 304 million cases consumed in 2007 (according to Wine Impact Group) (see Figure 1–1).

The food wholesaler COSTCO, which operates a chain of international warehouses, is currently the nation's largest retailer of wine, with over $700 million in wine sales. This upward consumption of wine is becoming more evident, and current data indicate that America will overtake France as the world's largest consumer of wine by volume in 2015. In all likelihood, by that year France will still have the United States beat in per-capita wine consumption, as it does today: The average French person outdrinks the average American by nearly eight to one.

The United States is home to over 5,000 wineries spread through all 50 states. This state of affairs is dramatic, considering that the U.S. government implemented prohibition from 1920 to 1933, making it illegal to produce, distribute, or consume any alcohol (with a few exceptions) in the nation. The wine industry was near dead, with only a handful of wineries surviving to produce wine for sacramental purposes.

It wasn't until 1975 that the industry started to gain back some growth; that year, there were 579 wineries in the United States. With this slight revival of U.S. wine, France and Italy ruled the market, and the majority of American wine states and New World countries and regions were unknown. Then, in the course of 20 years, the wine industry experienced explosive growth and vast changes. As the eighties approached, wine consumption increased with the coming of age of the new wine consumer known as the *"Baby Boomer"*. The popularity carried throughout the nineties, but the dominant American wine consumed was low-quality jug wine named after classic European wine regions such as Burgundy or Chianti. Then wine consumption saw another explosion in 1991 after the CBS news program *60 Minutes* reported on the "French Paradox," an inconsistency of lifestyles and rates of heart disease among people in America and France. This report provided evidence of medical benefits derived from the moderate consumption of wine. These newly discovered advantages have led people to drink wine more now than ever before. As the new millennium approached and the industry matured, the majority of wine consumed became grape name or "varietally" labelled and newly evolved wine cultures from countries such as New Zealand, Australia, Chile, Argentina, and South Africa, together with the United States, had an impressive impact on the wine industry, setting new standards and styles for the wine-drinking public.

The New Wine Consumer

A 2006 Gallup poll study from several different age groups named "wine" as America's most preferred alcoholic beverage. The study identified 39% of respondents claiming wine as their alcoholic beverage of choice, compared with 36% for beer and 21% for

In 2005, U.S. wine sales reached a record $26 billion, a 115% increase 1995 (according to the Wine Institute).

2005

1995

FIGURE 1–1 Increase in U.S. wine sales
(Thomas Moore)

spirits. Unfortunately, these results were short lived as the study has been repeated to only have beer regain its "number one" status. The study does illustrate the ground that wine has gained in reputation. Wine's popularity is partly propelled by a nontraditional wine consumer: individuals in their twenties and thirties known as the "*Millennials.*" These young adults are showing the same interest in wine as their baby boomer parents, who originally fueled a previous wine explosion in the early eighties. The Millennials have become a significant growth factor in the wine industry, as the popularity of wine has trickled down to this new generation of wine drinkers. The millenials acquire approximately 25% of total wine purchases and are more likely to spend an average of $20 and even more substantially on bottles of wine, particularly if they are living at home with parents (as many of them are), allowing them greater disposable income without sacrificing quality of life.

User-Friendly Approach

The popularity of wine is owed to numerous factors. To a large extent, it has been fueled by the accessibility of wine retail stores and restaurants that increasingly focus on hiring and training intelligent salespeople to help guide the consumer to an enjoyable wine selection and one that can enhance their dining experience. Some progressive restaurants and wine stores have designed wine menus in user-friendly formats, listing wines by "style" as opposed to "geographical origins". Some adventurous beverage managers have even coordinated the wine list with the food menu, offering useful recommendations after each description of food, to enhance the guest's experience.

New Styles of Wine

Other factors that contribute to increased acceptance and consumption of wine include the process of making wine in fruit-forward style. Many New World wines contain aromas and flavors that make them easy to drink, with or without food. Most of this wine is being produced to encourage a "drink it now" mentality. It's no longer necessary to bottle-age a wine and hold it for 5 or 10 years, as has been the tradition associated with old world wines.

Reasonably Priced, Yet Good Quality, Options

Many wine countries, such as Australia, Chile, New Zealand, and the United States, are making wines of good value that encourage consumption on a daily basis. This notion is illustrated by some of the successful brands, such as Charles Shaw (California) or Yellow Tail (Australia), which retail anywhere from $3 to $10 a bottle. Wine options at this price point dismiss the mentality that consumers should wait and drink wine only for special occasions; instead, they encourage buyers to consume as often as they desire.

A new breed of wine stores has exploded with popularity, offering value wine largely near or below the $25 price point. The international wine chain "WineStyles" has been designed to be user friendly in the staging of their wine. The customer is greeted with wines categorized according to eight styles that describe the basic personality and characteristics of the wine.

Packaging and Closures

Wine is being bottled with easy-to-read and eye-catching colorful labelling. Some producers have redesigned the bottle in an effort to make it easy to open, store, and transport. Screw-cap closures, single-serve bottles, and better quality bag-in-box allow consumers to drink wine in nontraditional situations and places, such as the beach, park, and sporting events, without the concerns of breaking a glass bottle or having to aquire a special tool to open

This photo represents wine having gained considerable popularity, allowing it to be viewed as more of an everyday beverage around the world instead of one only being reserved for the fine-dining restaurant.
(Lluís Real/AGE Fotostock America, Inc.)

the container. Screw–cap closures have gained considerable popularity, allowing wine to be viewed as more of an everyday beverage, but have also been criticized by some wine aficionados as an abomination to tradition.

Direct Shipping

Direct-shipping laws allow wineries to ship wines to consumers, though not in all states. This is important because many small wineries do not have the means to market or sell their wines in any other way. The Internet has provided greater accessibility and a venue for consumers to scout out small producers, who then legally can ship the product directly to customers at their front door.

Changing Eating Habits

Throughout thousands of years, wine has evolved with cuisine, and at one time in our modern world, classical French cuisine was the rage. The idea of matching wine with food had mostly been tied to a natural connection of evolution of regional cuisines. However, over the last decade, American eating patterns changed dramatically, with globalization exerting an ever-growing influence on contemporary cuisine. Americans have turned food into a hobby. With the success of restaurant and food television shows and the heightened status of *chef* as a profession, people have become more experienced in terms of restaurant usage, menu items, ingredients, seasonings, and spices. More Americans are growing up with ethnic flavors and are well traveled, which makes the world a much smaller place. In fact, salsa surpassed ketchup as the "number-one" condiment in America back in 1991. The culinary landscape has been rapidly expanding as new cuisines, flavors, and ingredients (such as North African, Peruvian, Indian, etc.) evolve and become more mainstream in the United States.

In 2008, "world cuisine" was available to most Americans on television without their ever having to leave home to experience it. In any medium-sized to large city, we are likely to walk down the street and find a Thai restaurant next door to an Italian restaurant, and a few doors down is a hot dog stand. The influx of immigrant food ingredients and cuisines, and Americans' diverse experiences, are contributing to more discerning tastes and to not only an understanding of food, but also a desire to drink wine and find wine that pairs well with the food. Diners are becoming more adventurous, and American palates more knowledgeable, than ever before. Food and wine pairing has become less about the classical combinations and more about matching a type and style of wine with what is being eaten at the moment.

World Wine Producers

As of 2006, the top five wine-producing countries—France, Italy, Spain, the United States, and Argentina—produced over 178,133 hectoliters, representing 62.8% of the world's wine production.

2006 COUNTRY RANK	HECTOLITERS	PERCENTAGE OF MARKET
1. ITALY	52,036	18.3
2. FRANCE	51,700	18.2
3. SPAIN	39,301	13.9
4. UNITED STATES	19,700	6.9
5. ARGENTINA	15,396	5.4
World Production	283,600	100.0

Source: International Organisation of Vine and Wine, *OIV State of the Vitiviniculture World Report*, March 2007.

♦ In Europe, Canada, and the South American countries, wine production figures are commonly expressed in hectoliters (hl), equal to 100 liters, or 26.418 U.S. gallons.

World Wine Consumers

As of 2006, the top five wine-consuming countries—France, Italy, the United States, Germany, and Spain—consumed over 119,500 hectoliters, representing 49.6% of the world's wine consumption. A study conducted by VINEXPO (the largest wine trade organization), in conjunction with IWSR (a leading London-based beverage research organization), forecasts that by 2015, the United States will overtake France and Italy as the world's largest wine consumer.

2006 COUNTRY RANK	HECTOLITERS	PERCENTAGE OF MARKET
1. FRANCE	32,800	13.6
2. ITALY	27,300	11.3
3. UNITED STATES	25,900	10.8
4. GERMANY	19,850	8.2
5. SPAIN	13,650	5.7
Forecasted World Consumption	240,800	100.0

Source: International Organisation of Vine and Wine, *OIV State of the Vitiviniculture World Report*, March 2007.

Summary

Many factors are contributing to the continued increased growth of wine, including the perception and acceptance of wine as a part of everyday life. Indeed, wine is becoming a part of mainstream society in America, something that for decades has been a part of everyday life in European wine countries such as France, Italy, and Spain.

THE NOVICE WINE CONSUMER

Whether a wine is modest or distinguished, it's intended for pleasure; yet somehow, it unfortunately has developed a mystique and pretentious image that many people find intimidating. The world of wine can be frightening for restaurant and retail customers, employees, and students of wine. The common belief is that one has to be an expert or connoisseur to appreciate wine. Ultimately, as with all matters of taste (music, food, or clothing, for example), wine is a matter of preference, but appreciating wine takes experience. To truly understand wine and, even more, to comprehend how it can integrate with food (this is the good news), one must continue to experiment and taste it. With enough patience and practice, it's possible for a wine drinker to develop a palate and truly identify and differentiate the subtle or significant nuances associated with wine. Presented next are some perspectives that may be useful for the novice and intermediate wine drinker to reference in beginning or continuing his or her exploration in understanding the somewhat complex world of wine.

Perspective 1: There Is No Bad Wine

Take comfort in knowing that there is no one ideal wine or style of wine for everyone. This truism is evident in the thousands of different wines produced around the world that individuals enjoy or appreciate. Culture can influence adult taste preferences, and Americans raised over the last 40 years have typically been raised on milk, juice, or soda drinks at mealtime and throughout the day. Therefore, it's likely and quite common for beginning wine drinkers to gravitate and appreciate wines with greater sweetness and little complexity associated with them. Even if there is a wine that one may find too simple or too sweet for personal tastes, know that someone, somewhere, is drinking it. Also, wine still has other applications other than drinking. Wine can be a very important culinary ingredient. Ultimately, people have a right to like what they like, whether or not it's a style that is preferred by the mass wine consumers and collectors around the world.

Perspective 2: There Is a Wine for Every Purpose

In some situations, a wine may not pair well with food items as presented on a menu, but it may still have some application in the kitchen or as a part of another beverage. For example, it's possible to use a wine as an ingredient in a food marinade, as part of a cooking liquid, or in a sauce to accompany a food item. For Friday evening a Chardonnay can be combined with cassis to create a wine cocktail called "Kir" or Sunday mornings, sparkling wine can be added to orange juice to create a Mimosa.

Perspective 3: The Wine Drinker's Palate Is the Only One That Matters

Wine ratings conducted by professional evaluators may be considered a useful tool; however, they should not necessarily be the defining influence. A wine rating may be the equivalent of a film critic rating a new movie release. The critic may declare, "Thumbs up"; however, the movie might not be enjoyed and held in the same opinion by the average moviegoer. Similarly, if a wine critic declared a particular wine "excellent" or "90+ points," this doesn't necessarily guarantee enjoyment by every wine consumer. Wine ratings have played a role in facilitating wine purchases for some people, but caution is advised when using them as the only source to make wine decisions.

In 2006, the results of a survey of 869 wine drinkers were published in *Nation's Restaurant News,* offering some interesting statistics about the views and preferences of these wine consumers (See Figure 1–2). An important objective of this textbook is to address many of the issues and to demystify wine in order to help the reader more effectively understand, comprehend, and communicate the story of wine to others. The communication can happen in multiple ways, depending on the situation. It could occur in a classroom with a teacher and a student, in a restaurant or store with a server or retail salesperson and a customer, at the workplace with a manager and an employee, or just about

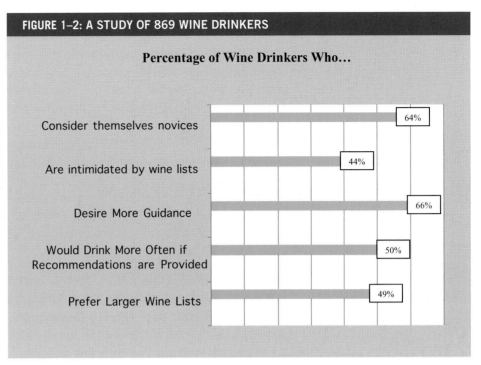

FIGURE 1-2: A STUDY OF 869 WINE DRINKERS

Percentage of Wine Drinkers Who...

Consider themselves novices — 64%

Are intimidated by wine lists — 44%

Desire More Guidance — 66%

Would Drink More Often if Recommendations are Provided — 50%

Prefer Larger Wine Lists — 49%

(Russel Research, New York)

anywhere between friends. Presented next is a bit of perspective on the results of this study that may provide insight into the state of wine being sold and consumed in restaurants and retail stores. Hopefully, it raises some cautionary flags to the saleperson who is directly assisting the consumer in making wine decisions and to the manager who is accountable for producing wine revenue.

"64% of 869 Wine Drinkers Classified Themselves as Novices When It Comes to Their Wine Knowledge"—This statistic should identify some of the challenges for the frontline service employees who suggest and/or sell wine to others. It points to the fact that many consumers desire guidance on some level when selecting wine. Here are some relevant questions that can be used by the salesperson making decisions about which wines to sell to customers:

- Are you looking for a wine to pair with dinner or to drink by itself? If with dinner, what will you be ordering for dinner? Do you have a certain price parameter in mind? What kind of wine do you usually enjoy?

Once a salesperson can discover the type and style of wine a consumer enjoys, it's possible to now suggest different producers, regions, or comparable grape varietals, just as it's possible to seek out new variations on a genre in art, film, or music. It's an effective way for a wine drinker to develop the palate and gain a sense of stylistic differences. For example, someone who enjoys the rock group the Rolling Stones may also appreciate the sounds of Pete Townsend and The Who.

Encouraging a salesperson to ask wine drinkers the appropriate set of questions allows the salesperson to determine an adequate and sometimes even a great wine selection. The goal of the saleperson is to identify a wine selection that can suit the personal taste preferences and meal selection of the customer.

"44% of These Wine Drinkers Indicated That They Often Feel Intimidated by Wine Lists at Restaurants"—It's amazing how the novice wine consumer can make any sort of intelligent wine decision based on the wine lists or, in some cases, wine catalogues offered in some restaurants. Most wine stores are filled with endless aisles of shelves that may be labelled merely by a country, offering little helpful information about the style or type of wine. How are consumers supposed to be able to comprehend a wine list and the entire geographical mystique, foreign languages, and unfamiliar words that are necessary in order to identify many of the wines? Some progressive restaurants and wine shops are beginning to address this concern with user-friendly wine lists that have been organized by either wine styles or food-pairing recommendations. But the vast majority seem to expect the wine consumer to have taken wine courses or to have a degree in geography, French, or Italian. The paradigm has been designed to confuse the novice wine drinker and discourage future purchases. Whether a customer is in a wine shop or a restaurant, the goal, of course, should be to sell wine to make money, but also to ensure that the customer is satisfied with his or her selection and, hopefully, with the least amount of pain in the attempt to select a wine.

"66% of Customers Wish More Restaurants Would Provide More Guidance in Choosing Wine to Go with Their Meals," and "50% of Respondents Said They Would Drink More Often if Restaurants Provided Recommendations"—Wine (or, indeed, any beverage) can be one of the biggest moneymakers for a restaurant. It has become imperative for chefs and managers—but most importantly, the frontline worker who is selling and making suggestions—to understand what wine is and how it can enhance a diner's experience. Unfortunately, in some restaurants and wine stores it's difficult for managers and chefs to provide guidance and training to their staff. Common reasons for this are that they don't understand wine or they lack the ability to effectively communicate and provide training to the people who sell wine.

There is a famous saying in the hospitality industry: "If you are not serving the customer, then serve the person who is." By learning more about wine, the manager is equipped to assist others with well-informed and satisfying wine-related decisions. Also, chefs and managers may be accountable for the revenue and cost control of wine or other beverages within the wine store or restaurant. These individuals may be responsible for creating wine lists, purchasing wine, storing and issuing wine, training staff on wine, pairing wine with the daily specials, conducting wine seminars, designing wine dinners, etc. For many restaurants, these are opportunities to attract new customers and stimulate sales through understanding and promoting wine.

"49% of Participants Said They Would Prefer Restaurants with Large Wine Selections"—This particular statistic is a bit baffling, considering that a large percentage of consumers (according to this study) are confused with the current state of wine programs. If one is confused, why desire to add more confusion by having a larger wine selection? Perhaps what wine drinkers are referencing (and this is purely speculative) is their preference that a restaurant or wine store offer ample options to more effectively suit their particular needs. It's unfortunate, but many wine stores stock shelves with wines that are enjoyed by the manager and only minimally alter or adapt to consumer trends or up-and-coming wine-producing regions or producers. And similarly, restaurants may develop wine lists that are never changed again. A stagnant wine selection that doesn't evolve or adapt can create a waning guest. Increasing options should include having a wine-by-the-glass program, offering half-bottle selections, providing a sample taste, and so on. A wine selection should keep up with the times and evolve with that of the customer base.

Final Comments on This Study—Perhaps the insight of this study speaks to us about current practices of how wine is marketed and sold across America. Possibly, the current approaches and practices should be rethought. Granted, U.S. wine sales are increasing, as are the number of wine stores and restaurants. But could wine sales and customer satisfaction be increased? By taking a new approach, wine sellers can educate and guide the consumer without embarrassment and intimidation, and that can demystify wine's sometimes pretentious image. Ultimately, this more "suitable" approach can provide the consumer with a more enjoyable experience, and in the process, the beverage operation can produce more revenue.

WHAT IS WINE?

Wine is, very simply, an agricultural product produced from the fermented juice of fruit. It's almost always the fermented juice of grapes (legally, unless otherwise specified), although apples, blackberries, rhubarb, and other fruits can be substituted. On the surface, grapes are no different from tomatoes or olives. Taking a step further, all fruits, including grapes, have several varieties or types that can yield a multitude of different personalities. A wine's personality is derived from several different stages throughout the production process, wherein thousands of different compounds influence aromas, flavors, body, and more. This is what makes each grape unique, with its own set of performance factors. Some of the personality-influencing compounds are inherent in the original grape and its juice; others are created during fermentation or through processing or aging methods.

Wine Defined

Wine grapes, in some ways, are just like people. Some individuals grow up in the suburbs, others in the city. Depending on where grapes grow up, they can be influenced and molded the same way a person can be, according to their surroundings. On the surface, people are all the same: human beings. However, as one learns more about them, it becomes obvious that individuals are different. The same holds true for wine grapes: On the surface they contain skins, pulp, seeds, and stems, and like people, they have been influenced partially by their environment. Grapes deliver their distinctiveness in many ways: their color (red, white, or rosé), body (lightness to fullness), aroma and flavor (fruit, to vegetables, to tobacco shop), and texture (acidity, sweetness, spiciness and bitterness). Wine can be made from a single grape varietal or a blend of different complementary grapes. The grape variety, or blend of grapes, will impart a specific style or personality into a wine. *Table grapes* are a basic agricultural product that yields about $1.50 per pound, but *wine grapes* can deliver a complexity that can yield anywhere from $3.00 to $16,000 a bottle, and sometimes even more.

Wine grapes are generally described as either white or red. White wine grapes are not actually white, but any shade between green and an amber-yellow. White wine can also be made from red grapes that have had the skins removed from the juice and pulp before fermentation begins.

Red wine grapes are generally not actually red, but instead can range from blue to deep purple-black. Red wine can also be made from a blend of red and white wine grapes. The red grape skins remain with the juice and pulp during fermentation and provide color.

Rosé wine is made either from a blend of red and white wine or from the more common process known as the French "Saignée" (san-YAY) method, allowing some of the color from red grape skins to bleed into the fermenting juice, creating a pinkish color.

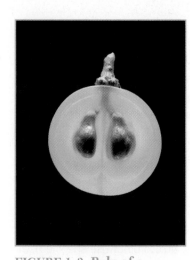

FIGURE 1–3 Pulp of a Chardonnay grape

(Collection CIVC. Photographer: CORNU Alain)

FIGURE 1–4 Pulp of a Pinot Noir grape

(Collection CIVC. Photographer: CORNU Alain)

The grape is made of three major components: pulp, skin, and seeds/stems. Figure 1–3 and 1–4 are sample cross sections of a white wine grape and red wine grape.

Pulp—(Pulp is found on the inside of the grape, where the juice, acid, sugar, and flavor can be found.) Pulp makes up approximately 75% of a grape by weight. It plays a major role in providing acid, which is present in the juice, and is pivotal to giving both red and white wine good structure. A wine without acid falls flat on the palate and has a difficult time standing up to food when they are paired together. When a wine has inadequate acid, it is frequently referred to as *flat* or *flabby*. A flabby wine is often lost when paired with an otherwise compatible food item.

Skin—(Skin is on the outside of the grape, where the tannin, flavor, and color can be found.) Skin makes up approximately 20% of the grape by weight. Skin plays a greater influence on the style and structure of a red wine, which are achieved when the skins are allowed to ferment with the juice. Anthocyanins (ann-thoa-SY-ann-inns) and other natural pigment chemicals found in the skins of red wine grapes are responsible for contributing the color to a wine.

Grape skins also contribute tannin to a red wine. The tannin is pivotal to providing a red wine with good structure and aging potential. Tannin is a compound that causes the same dry feeling on the tongue and around the gum line that one feels after drinking black, heavily steeped tea. Tannin content varies with grape variety and wine style. Like a wine with insufficient acid, a red wine without adequate tannin falls flat on the palate and is often referred to as *flat* or *flabby*. (Tannin is discussed in greater detail in Chapter 2, "Wine Tasting". The contribution of grape skins in the winemaking process is discussed in greater detail in Chapter 3, "Viticulture and Enology.")

Seeds and Stems—(Seeds are found on inside and stems are found on the outside of the grape and may contribute a bitter component if crushed or used in excess.) Stems and seeds contribute approximately 5% of the grape by weight. In most cases, they are a minor component of a wine, but can have a pronounced negative influence if handled poorly. Seeds and stems can yield an undesirable bitterness to the finished wine if the grapes have been handled too harshly in the harvesting and production process.

CATEGORIES OF WINE

Wine may be broadly divided into three groups (see Figure 1–5):

1. **Table Wine**—This category of wine gets its name because it's made to be drunk at the table with meals. The alcoholic content of table wine generally is between 8% and 15%. Table wines are white, pink, or red wines that can be dry, sweet, or somewhere in between.

2. **Sparkling Wine**—This category of wine consists of a table wine as the base, with the addition of large amounts of CO_2 for carbonation. Sparkling wine typically contains between 10% and 13% alcohol. The most prestigious of all sparkling wines is Champagne. However, many other sparkling wines of varying quality are produced throughout the world and can rival the excellence of Champagne.

   Sparkling wine can be made into white, pink, or red wine that can be dry, sweet, or somewhere in between. However, the majority of sparkling wines are white and made into a dry style. It's possible to find options of varying levels of sweetness, particularly from Italian and German sparkling wines.

3. **Fortified Wines**—This category of wine consists of table wine as the base, with additional alcohol (in the form of a distilled spirit—often an unaged brandy) added.

Fortified wine typically contains between 17% and 22% alcohol, and it's possible to have white or red options that can be made into dry, sweet, or somewhere in between.

Dry—Drier fortified wines are commonly consumed prior to a meal as an aperitif to help stimulate the appetite and cleanse the palate.

Sweet—Sweeter fortified wines are commonly consumed after a meal for satiety or fullness.

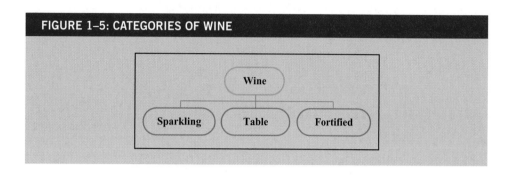

FIGURE 1–5: CATEGORIES OF WINE

All wine categories have specific production methods that will be discussed and expanded upon throughout this book.

WINES OF THE OLD WORLD VS. WINES OF THE NEW WORLD

The world of wine has expanded from its origins in Europe to new possibilities in the far west. For the grapes to truly flourish and ripen appropriately, they need warmth, sunshine, and water, but not too much of any one. These conditions are located primarily between the latitudes of 30° and 50° north, and 30° and 50° south, of the equator. In some cases, grapes are found in areas that don't normally grow a quality wine grape; however, these areas will have mitigating influences such as varying elevation levels, coastal waters, and rivers that all help moderate temperature extremes. Figure 1–6 highlights the significant wine-producing countries throughout the world.

There are two broad schools of thought and practice in the wine world, and they are identified by broad geographic concepts: Old World and New World. These designations separate the wines by geography, but also by a perspective that stylistically will affect the wines. What follows are generalizations between the two worlds; however, drawing similarities and differences between the two assists in the broad understanding of wine concepts.

Old World: Primarily Inside Europe

The Old World references the long-established tradition of winemaking within the European countries of France, Italy, Germany, and Spain. These countries have nurtured and developed many of the vines and winemaking techniques that form the foundation for modern practices of wine throughout the world. The Old World generally believes in the terroir (tehr-WHAR) concept. *Terroir* loosely translates to the connection to the land. Since grapes are the product of the earth (or soil), they will have characteristic aromas and flavors tying them to the land in which they are grown. In Europe, the region also often predetermines how the wine must be made.

FIGURE 1–6 Wine producing areas of the world
(Berry Bros & Rudd)

New World: Primarily Outside Europe

The New World is a concept used primarily to reference the wine-producing countries of America, Canada, Australia, Argentina, Chile, South Africa, and New Zealand, which have a relatively brief history and culture associated with grape growing and wine production. These countries were settled within the last 500 years or so and are known as some of the most significant New World wine-producing countries. The grapevines and some techniques were transported into them by European settlers and through trade and wars. In the New World, producers aren't bound by tradition, instead they can utilize different techniques and can radically alter the style of wine from one vintage to the next or as they see fit.

Climate Influences

Climates within both the Old and New Worlds have a large influence on the development of grapes. (The topic of climate's influence on wine grapes is discussed in greater detail in Chapter 3, "Viticulture and Enology.") Aroma, flavor, and textural components (acid, tannin, sugar and, ultimately, after fermentation, alcohol) are dependent to some extent on the area where the grapes are grown, because vines are very sensitive to climate and soil.

COOL/WARM CLIMATES Cooler to warmer climates can suggest inconsistently ripened grapes that have not seen adequate warmth and/or sunshine throughout the growing season. The more slowly the grapes ripen, the richer is their aroma. Grapes grown farthest from the equator in both hemispheres are the most fragrant. Wines produced in this climate are often incredibly food friendly because of their substantial acidity and freshness.

In cool/warm climates, **GRAPES** are less pigmented, less consistently ripe, low in sugar, and high in acid, compared with identical grapes found in a warm/hot climates.

In cool/warm climates, **WINES** have the following characteristics compared with identical wines found in a warm/hot climates:

Sight. Pale to light in intensity, green tint to straw yellow in hue for white wines.
Smell/taste. Muted to highly aromatic; lighter, more subtle citrus; tree fruit, vegetables, herbs, and mineral aromas and flavors. These wines are often stainless steel aged or lightly oaked and are high in acidity and low in alcohol content.

WARM/HOT CLIMATES Warmer and hotter climates can suggest a ripe grape that has seen ample sunshine and/or heat during the growing season. Wines produced in this climate are often *easy drinking wines* and work well with or without the consumption of food.

In warm/hot climates, **GRAPES** are more pigmented, very ripe, higher in sugar, and lower in acid, compared with identical grapes found in cool/warm climates.

In warm/hot climates, **WINES** have the following characteristics compared with identical wines found in a cool/warm climate:

Sight. Medium in intensity, high straw to golden yellow in hue for white wines.
Smell/taste. Flavors that predominate with riper fruit and that suggest cooked or dried fruit rather than fresh-off-the-vine fruit. These wines are often oak aged and are lower in acidity with high alcohol content.

The following table summarizes the broad distinctions between Old World and New World wines:

CHARACTERISTICS	OLD WORLD	NEW WORLD
MAJOR COUNTRIES	France, Italy, Germany, and Spain	United States, Australia, New Zealand, Argentina, Chile, and South Africa
CLASSIC EXAMPLE	France	United States
VITICULTURE PERSPECTIVE	Strict laws define acceptable viticultural practices, depending on level of classification. Grape growing areas can be small and relatively fixed.	Limited laws regarding viticultural practices. Grape growing areas can be large and relatively flexible.
TERM FOR GEOGRAPHIC LOCATIONS	Appellations	American Viticultural Areas
WINEMAKING HISTORY	Thousands of years	Hundreds of years
WINEMAKING PHILOSOPHY	Traditional wines are made to reflect the local style. Intervene as little as possible.	Experimental wines are made to reflect an international style. Control the winemaking process in order to produce the best wine possible, given the raw material.
GRAPE DESIGNATIONS	Legally defined on the basis of appellations	Not legally defined
GENERAL STYLE	Subtle; more about finesse and complexity. Lower to medium alcohol levels. Expression of the individual terroir through the fruit.	Bolder, rich, and oaky, with great expression of fruit. Often made with medium to higher levels of alcohol—around 13% or more.
LABELLING PRACTICES	Primarily labels according to place of origin (or appellation)	Primarily labels according to the dominant grape found within the bottle
PRIMARY AROMAS / FLAVORS	Earth, barnyard, vegetable, mineral	Fruit

FIGURE 1–7 The anatomy of a wine bottle

1. Lip
2. Neck
3. Shoulders
4. Label
5. Base

WINE BOTTLE SHAPES

During the Greek and Roman periods, wine was originally transported in a two-handled vessel called an *amphorae* (ahm-FOR-uh). Possible evidence suggests that this was not only a crude form of a wine bottle, but also part of an early appellation system. The shape of the container could indicate the city or region, winemaker, and vintage of the wine. During the 1700s and 1800s, the glass bottle was invented. Once it became more durable, it was evident that wine could be aged in glass bottles to mature in flavor. Eventually, various bottles shapes were developed to hold different types of wine. The shapes of the bottles made it easy to identify the type or style of wine that was within each bottle. This became particularly useful if it wasn't possible to read the label. Today, the wine bottle can assist in the same way. Recognizing the bottle shape can quite possibly lead a wine drinker in the general direction of understanding the grapes or particular style of wine that might be found within.

Even before reading a wine label, it's possible to learn a large amount of information about a wine by examining the color and shape of a wine bottle that the wine is stored in. The shape and color of the bottle can provide some basic information about the region or country of origin and grape varietal within the bottle. Many wine regions have their traditional bottle shapes, and winemakers throughout the world typically respect the traditions of those wine regions and the grapes that are produced in them. Winemakers can choose any bottle shapes, but for recognition purposes, when winemakers anywhere in the world produce a wine from a grape from a particular traditional place, the bottle that the wine is sold in is usually consistent with the wine region.

Wine bottles have been used for centuries and appear in a variety of shapes and sizes, but have been standardized to generally contain 25.4 oz (750 ml) of liquid. The half-bottle (contains 12.7 oz/375 ml) has become popular over the last decade as an alternative to provide a source of high-quality wine for single diners. Figure 1–7 is an example of the anatomy of the bottle.

Bordeaux Wine Bottle

FIGURE 1–8 Bordeaux wine bottle
(Thomas Moore)

The Bordeaux bottle, shown in Figure 1–8, has straight sides with steep, tall, shoulders. It's an excellent shape for wines that tend to exude sediment (typically, old red wines and Bordeaux reds are known to age well) because the steep shoulders can serve to hold back the sediment as the wine is poured. This can be particularly useful if a decanter is not available.

RED WINE: The Bordeaux shape is the most common shape used for red wine around the world and is often found in dark green or black glass. Red wine grapes commonly found in this style of bottle include *Cabernet Sauvignon* (KAB-er-nay SOH-vin-NYOHN), *Merlot* (mehr-LOH), and *Zinfandel* (ZIN-fun-del).

WHITE WINE (Dry or Sweet): The Bordeaux shape can also be used for white wine in a light green or clear glass bottle. White wine grapes commonly found in this style of bottle include *Sauvignon Blanc* (SOH-vihn-YOHN BLAHNK), particularly if the wine is from Bordeaux or California, *Semillon* (seh-mee-YOHN) and Pinot Grigio (PEE-noh GREE-joh) when it comes from Italy.

Burgundy Wine Bottle

FIGURE 1–9 Burgundy wine bottle
(Thomas Moore)

The Burgundy bottle, shown in Figure 1–9, typically is sturdy and heavy, with shallow, gentle sloping shoulders.

RED WINE: The Burgundy shape can be used for red wine in a light green or black glass. Wine grapes found in this bottle include *Pinot Noir* (PEE-noh-NWAHR), *Gamay* (gah-MAY) and *Syrah* (SEAR-ah) and *Syrah blends.*

FIGURE 1–10 German wine bottle

(Thomas Moore)

FIGURE 1–11 Sparkling wine bottle

(Thomas Moore)

FIGURE 1–12 Fortified wine bottle

(Thomas Moore)

WHITE WINE: The Burgundy shape can also be used for white wine in a light green or clear glass bottle. Wines commonly found in this bottle include *Chardonnay* (SHAR-duh-nay) and *Sauvignon Blanc* (SOH-vihn-YOHN BLAHNK) when the bottle comes from New Zealand or Loire Valley France.

German Wine Bottle

This narrow, thin, tall bottle, shown in Figure 1–10, has a very gently sloping shoulder and is typically light green or brown in color. Some have brown glass for wine produced from the Rhine (RINE) region in Germany, and green glass for wine from the Mosel-Saar-Ruwer (MOH-zel sahr ROO-vayr) region in Germany.

WHITE WINE (Dry or Sweet): Wine grapes commonly found in this bottle include *Riesling* (REEZ-ling), *Gewurztraminer* (guh-VERTZ-trah-mean-er), and *Pinot Gris* (PEE-noh GREE) when it comes from Alsace, France.

Sparkling Wine Bottle

This bottle, shown in Figure 1–11, is made from a very thick glass, with gently sloping shoulders and a long neck. The sparkling wine bottle also contains a rather large *punt,* or indentation in the bottom of the bottle, to assist in durability. The punt is needed to help reduce the pressure felt along the bottom of the bottle.

Classic Champagne uses a blend of three grapes, including Chardonnay, Pinot Noir, and Pinot Meunier (muh-NYAY). Other sparkling wines from around the world may use the same or similar grapes.

Champagne bottles are designed with thick glass because of the need to withstand the high pressures exerted by the carbonation development after bottling. Pressures can yield 80–120 lbs per square inch (psi), approximately two to three times the pressure of a car tire.

Fortified Wine Bottle

Fortified wines such as Port, Madeira, and Sherry typically use sturdy bottles, as shown in Figure 1–12. Vintage Port may often have tall shoulders and a larger bulge in the neck to help capture the sediment when it is decanted. Often, these are wines that need many years to properly age and tend to contain some sediment.

With the exception of vintage or late-bottled vintage port, these bottles usually have a cork stopper rather than the traditional larger corks typically used for other wines. The cork stoppers allow easy opening and closing of a bottle after each serving.

WINE CLOSURES

There are various types of closures or stoppers available for a winemaker to seal a bottle of wine. There are advantages and disadvantages for all, but each one must perform the essential function of preserving the wine and, if necessary, promote conditions conducive to appropriate development.

Most wines are produced for early consumption shortly after purchase. Only a small percentage of wines are created to benefit from and to be enhanced by bottle development through long-term aging. Bottle development occurs when a wine closure allows the optimal amount of oxygen (too much air can lead to oxidation) to positively affect the wine. The type of wine closure can affect the outcome of the finished wine by determining the personality and overall quality of the finished wine. Ultimately, a winemaker's vision of the finished product will determine the appropriate wine closure.

Cork

Cork has been used since the 18th century to seal bottles and has been the primary closure ever since. Wine corks come from the bark of the cork oak, a tree found in Portugal, Spain, North Africa, and other Mediterranean countries. After the tree reaches maturity (16 to 25 years), it is harvested by hand every 9 years in a labor-intensive process that strips the bark, only for it to regenerate throughout the coming centuries.

Corks are flexible, lightweight, and natural, and when the cork is wet, it swells to form a tight seal within the neck of the bottle. Therefore, wine bottles closed with corks must be stored either upside down or on their sides in order to keep the cork wet and the bottle tightly sealed. If a wine bottle closed with a cork is stored upright for too long, then the cork can dry out and contract over time, allowing air to enter the bottle, causing a darkening of the wine and a loss of aroma and flavor.

Besides proper storage, another concern is the development of an off-flavor from tainted corks. During the corks' preparation for use as wine closures, they are bleached, and if a certain mold is present in the cork, a highly aromatic compound called *2,4,6-Trichloroanisole* (try-clore-AN-iss-all), or TCA, is formed. This TCA has a disagreeable smell that is detectable in very low concentrations and will destroy a bottle of wine by imparting a "wet cardboard" character to wine. Winemakers refer to a wine having detectable levels of TCA as being *corked*. It has been estimated that between 3% and 5% of the corks are tainted with TCA, and unfortunately, there is no efficient way to determine whether a cork is tainted until a bottle of wine is opened.

Screw Caps or Twist Offs

New World (largely in New Zealand) winemakers are leading a campaign to replace the traditional wine cork with a high-tech aluminum screw cap, named the *Stelvin* after the company that created it. Screw caps first appeared in the 1970s; however, the connotation that they were "cheap" didn't help their success. More recently, there has been a renewed push for screw caps for short-term aging of wines because they are inexpensive, easy to open (not requiring a special tool—the corkscrew), and easily resealable and because they limit the passage of oxygen.

Philosophically, it seems natural to use the screw cap, particularly if the wine has been stored only in stainless steel prior to bottling and is destined to be consumed early. This carries on the intended style of the winemaker of pure essentials of fruit and preservation of acid and youthfulness of the wine that oak aging and a cork would otherwise alter.

Wine traditionalists find it difficult to accept the screw cap because the lost romance surrounding the opening of a corked bottle is now replaced by twisting the cap off of the bottle. Because of the tradition and mystique that are pervasive in the wine industry, wine drinkers still tend to associate a screw cap with inexpensive wines of low quality. Nonetheless, the more adventurous winemakers in Australia and California, and even some Old World producers, have begun to bottle some of their prestigious wines with a high-quality screw top. Ultimately, the biggest test will be the acceptance by the consumer.

Synthetic

The popularity of artificial or plastic corks for early-drinking wines has been on the upswing in response to the problem of cork taint in natural corks. But synthetic corks are not without problems of their own and have not been widely embraced by the industry. For long-term storage, the biggest problem has been the quick passage of oxygen, which, after a period of time, can result in oxidized wines that exhibit symptoms of aging sooner than if sealed with other closures. Others are hesitant to put their wines in contact with the elastic polymers that make up a synthetic cork for fear that some undesirable compounds may be extracted from the corks.

Technicals, or Composites

Technicals, or composites, are formed with pieces of natural cork and bonding materials and usually incorporate disks of natural cork at each end.

Glass Stopper

The glass stopper is a recent creation that can be made out of either glass or Plexiglas.

WINE GLASS SELECTION

Wine glasses are often referred to as *stemware* or *glassware*. They are generally composed of three parts: (1) bowl, (2) stem, and (3) foot. It's generally believed that the construction and shape of a glass can significantly improve the aromas and flavors of a wine. Some companies go as far as to create particular shapes suited for specific grape varietals, in addition to making several different price points based on what the glass is made out of. Stemware can be made out of glass or crystal. Glass provides a more durable and inexpensive alternative to crystal stemware, which is delicate and expensive, but viewed as better quality. In handling stemware, it's important to hold the glass by the stem to avoid smearing the glass with fingerprints and to avoid warming the wine.

Two of the most common types of glassware are a white and red wine glass used for table wine. In addition, two more glasses are used: the sparkling (flute) and fortified wine glasses.

Table Wine Glassware

White Wine

FIGURE 1–13 White wine glass
(Thomas Moore)

Many restaurants utilize an all-purpose wine glass that can be used for both white and red wine. For those restaurants that choose a more extensive wine list or have the budget to allow for better glassware, they can opt for the minimum white wine and red wine glasses.

Some high-end restaurants with extensive wine budgets carry several different styles of stemware for individual grapes or types of table wine. Not only is there a variety of various shaped glassware, but consisting of various quality levels as well. *Crystal stemware* is often (but not always) made with lead to provide a higher index of refraction than normal glass affords. It gives the wine a greater "sparkle" at a more expensive price.

Red Wine

FIGURE 1–14 Red wine glass
(Thomas Moore)

An effective size for wine glassware should be large enough (about 10–12 ounces) to allow for the standard portion size of wine (about 4–5 ounces) to be swirled in the glass without being spilled.

White wine glasses are tulip shaped, with a small bowl, generally narrow, and with a slightly inverted lip, which allows the concentration of the wine's aromas to the nose after being swirled. The narrow surface area also allows the wine to retain its chilled temperature by reducing surface area. Figure 1–13 shows a sample white wine glass.

Red wine glasses usually are larger in size, with a bigger bowl and wider surface area, which allows the wine to have greater air contact to cause the softening of tannin and integration of aromas. Figure 1–14 shows a sample red wine glass.

Stemless

FIGURE 1–15 Stemless wine glass
(Thomas Moore)

The Austrian glass company Riedel (ree-DEL) created a "*stemless*" line of glassware for the more casual and trendy wine drinker. The stemless glassware comes in a variety of shapes and sizes. Figure 1–15 shows a sample stemless wine glass.

Flute

FIGURE 1-16 Flute
(Thomas Moore)

Saucer

FIGURE 1-17 Saucer
(Thomas Moore)

Fortified Wine

FIGURE 1-18 Fortified wine glass
(Thomas Moore)

Sparkling Wine Glassware

Sparkling wine glassware should be designed to maximize the idea of what a sparkling wine is about: bubbles. The *flutes* are the most suitable stemware for all types of sparkling wine, as they are tall, thin, and designed to bring the delicate aromas toward the nose. The length of the flute allows the preservation of carbonation as it slowly rises to the surface. Figure 1–16 shows a sample flute glass.

The *saucer glass* (sometimes called *coups*) is an inferior option (and still sometimes used) because it causes the dissipation of effervescence at a fast rate. In addition, it has a large surface area that makes it difficult to drink from without spilling the wine. Figure 1–17 shows a saucer glass.

Fortified Wine Glassware

Fortified wine is enhanced with additional alcohol. Therefore, the portion size (about 2 ounces) is much smaller than other types of wine. Since the portion size is more reserved, the glassware size corresponds to the amount of wine—generally small and capable of holding about 2 ounces. Figure 1–18 shows a sample fortified wine glass.

TABLE WINE CLASSIFICATION

Varietal Labelled Wine

Varietal based wine is a concept applied to most non-European wine labels, including those from Australia, New Zealand, South Africa, South America, Canada, and the United States. The names of wines in this category are derived from their predominant grape variety. A grape variety is like an ice cream. At a basic level, ice cream is ice cream no matter how it's made, and you may say the same thing about wine. On the other hand, chocolate ice cream tastes quite different from vanilla, and likewise, Cabernet Sauvignon tastes very different from Chardonnay. The greatest distinction from one variety to the next is in the aroma, taste, and texture of the resulting wine. If wine is made from predominantly one grape variety, it can be called a *varietal* wine.

Serious wine-producing countries and states regulate the amount of a particular grape that must be present as an ingredient before the wine can be identified by that grape's name. Throughout the United States, any wine with a designated grape varietal must contain at least 75% of that grape within the bottle. Each state within the United States can choose to be stricter with this rule. For example, most varietals in Oregon must contain a minimum of 90% (for most varietals) of the grape identified on the label.

Geographically Labelled Wine

Geographically based wine is a concept applied to most European (Old World) wine labels, where the wines are named after the place they come from. Europe's wines are intimately linked to their terroir concept rather than to the name of the grape variety. Geographically based wines refer to wines that are labelled and produced from strictly regulated areas of the wine-growing country. For example, the bottle may read "Burgundy" (a French region that specializes in Pinot Noir) rather than identifying the name of the grape. Over the past 200 years, the Europeans have used trial and error to understand which varieties will make the best wines possible in each region. *Terroir* is a sense of place with special characteristics that can't be duplicated elsewhere. It's a sort of thumbprint that contributes to a particular "personality" for a given wine.

The following table lists some renowned wine-producing areas and the wines named after them:

THE MOST RENOWNED WINE-PRODUCING PLACES AND THE WINES NAMED AFTER THEM	
PLACES/NAME OF WINE	COUNTRY
Barbaresco	ITALY
Barolo	ITALY
Beaujolais	FRANCE
Bordeaux　　　　　→	FRANCE
Burgundy	FRANCE
Chablis	FRANCE
Champagne	FRANCE
Chianti	ITALY
Port	PORTUGAL
Rioja	SPAIN
Sauternes	FRANCE

All European wine-producing countries have their own regulations controlling labelling. To further complicate the labeling, regions are divided into districts (subregions), subdistricts (sub-subregions), villages (communes or neighborhoods), and localities as specific as a vineyard (someone's house). For example, Burgundy has five significant districts, several subdistricts, dozens of villages, and hundreds of vineyards. A general rule that can assist with reading and understanding a label is to identify how much specificity is given on that label. A broader place on the label generally indicates less quality; the more specific label indicates better quality. (View the Place chart at the end of this section.)

Currently, winemakers around the new world are showing more interest in this kind of regional and local specialization. As non-European countries establish reputations for the wines of certain regions, they often add the region's name to the varietal name. Examples are Napa Valley Cabernet Sauvignon and Russian River Pinot Noir.

The following table shows some labelling conventions:

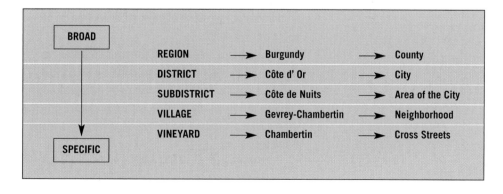

BROAD			
REGION	→ Burgundy	→ County
DISTRICT	→ Côte d' Or	→ City
SUBDISTRICT	→ Côte de Nuits	→ Area of the City
VILLAGE	→ Gevrey-Chambertin	→ Neighborhood
VINEYARD	→ Chambertin	→ Cross Streets
SPECIFIC			

FIGURE 1–19 Jug wine
(Thomas Moore)

Generic Labelled Wine

Generic wines were widely popular in the early 1900s and up until the 1980s, but are still available today. Throughout the United States, these wines have been commonly referred to as jug or generic wine because they were often purchased in a jug or box, shown in Figure 1–19.

Generic wines generally consist of a blend of different grapes that often are of lower quality than grapes that compose varietal labelled wines. The grapes used are often high-yielding varieties that can be grown and produced at low cost. In many cases, the grape is not even known to the consumer, because these wines may be labelled so vaguely.

Up until the 1990s, it was quite common for California winemakers to freely borrow the names of European wines and regions to label their jug or generic wines, rather than give them grape varietal names, as is the common current practice in the rest of the United States. The common practice in America was to use names such as "Burgundy," "Chablis," or "Champagne" (names based on famous wine-growing regions where the grapes were produced), even though the wines were not from those areas. This sort of imitation irritated the wine growers of Europe, who argued that these names had very specific meanings in terms of local origin, grape types, vineyards, and cellar practices. The American winemakers, however, felt that if a red wine tasted similar to the red wine of Burgundy, France, it seemed perfectly reasonable to call it as such. The names of American wines in this category are unrelated to the geographic or varietal origin associated with European wines using the same designation.

Proprietary Blends/Trademark Labelled Wines

The types and kinds of proprietary blends are endless. Many wineries have opted to create opportunities by blending various complementary grape varietals to distinguish their wines from the traditional varietal-based wines that are most prominent in the New World.

Many (but not all) of the proprietary-based wines are respectable high-quality American versions of the classic red or white Bordeaux (bohr-DOH) style. These wines (as in Bordeaux) are a blend of several complementary grape varietals.

Back in 1988, a few Napa Valley winemakers started their own association and devised an official name for this style of wines: Meritage (rhymes with the word "heritage"). The name *Meritage* is a combination of two words, "merit" and "heritage," to symbolize the quality and history associated with the origination of these wines made in a Bordeaux style. These wines tend to be the best a particular winery produces.

According to the Meritage Association, the wine must contain at least two of the approved grapes (classic to Bordeaux), with no single variety containing more than 90% of the blend. The approved varietals for red Meritage are Cabernet Sauvignon, Merlot, Cabernet Franc, Petit Verdot, and Malbec. The combination and proportions of these grapes are completely determined by the individual producer. However, most often, the wines tend to be dominated by either Cabernet Sauvignon or Merlot, with smaller amounts of the other approved varietals.

Throughout California, other winemakers produce red Bordeaux-styled wines, but choose not to use the Meritage name. Instead, they have chosen to create and market alternative names that sound fancy or unique to the particular winery without being confined to the rules associated with Meritage. Some producers have identified their wines variously as *Affinity, Opus One, Rubicon,* and *Insignia;* or they call them simply *Reserve Bottlings.*

These blends in many cases are a winery's flagship option, and prices often start at around $50 to $100 a bottle. In addition to possessing fancy names, they have stylish labels and tall-shouldered heavy glass bottles. Craig Williams, winemaker at Joseph Phelps Vineyard, was the first winemaker in California to produce a proprietary red—Insignia—in 1974.

Many winemakers have also opted for other blends. The popularity of white and red Rhône-style wines has increased dramatically. These wines tend to be dominated with Syrah and other varietals.

READING A TYPICAL WINE LABEL

What does a wine label tell us? In addition to a bottle informing us about the shape and color, a wine label can provide a great deal of information as to the contents within the bottle. Law mandates most of the information offered on a label, but additional information is sometimes provided to assist the consumer with making a well-informed decision. Every wine-producing country has its own set of government wine laws that regulate grape growing, winemaking, and labelling. The following are five categories of wine label information:

1. **WHO:**—The producer (winery or estate or negociant)
2. **WHAT:**—The grape variety (not always listed, particularly in Europe)
3. **WHERE:**—The geographic location (where the grapes are grown)
4. **WHEN:**—The vintage year (the year the grapes were picked and the wine was made)
5. **HOW:**—The level of quality or some other classification. Whereas these are not always listed or known, there may be clues that imply (but do not necessarily guarantee) quality, such as the specific geographical location of the vineyard(s), whether the wine came from a single vineyard, and, in the case of many French vineyards, the rating or quality classification of a particular vineyard.

Typical New World Wine Label

A sample of a common United States wine label is pictured in Figure 1–20. The most prominent items on a U.S. wine label are the following:

1. The name of the winery or vintner that produced the wine. The producer's name usually is the largest text on the label and the easiest element to identify. In the example, the producer is St. Supéry.
2. The identification of the wine grape(s). A wine predominantly from a single grape varietal identified on the label means that at least 75% of that varietal is used in the wine. When the wine is blended from several varieties or regions, it will not be labelled as a varietal wine. In the example, the grape is predominately Cabernet Sauvignon.
3. The geographical location where the grapes were grown. In the United States, these are legally defined as American Viticultural Areas (AVAs). Some are as broad as "California," whereas others are narrowly defined as a section of a river valley. In the United States, vineyards can be named if a minimum of 95% of the grapes came from that vineyard. If a region is identified on the label, 85% or more of the grapes must come from that specific locality. In the example, the location is predominately Napa Valley.
4. The vintage is the "year" in which the grapes were harvested and the wine was made. If a vintage year is displayed, it means that at least 95% or more of the wine was produced from grapes grown in the stated year. In the example, the vintage date is 2003.

Wine labels can be particularly confusing, because they are loaded with foreign terms. The remainder of this book attempts to illuminate some of this mystery. Key label terms for France, Italy, Germany, and Spain are discussed within their individual chapters, "Wines of France," in Chapter 9, and "Other Old World Wine Countries," in Chapter 10.

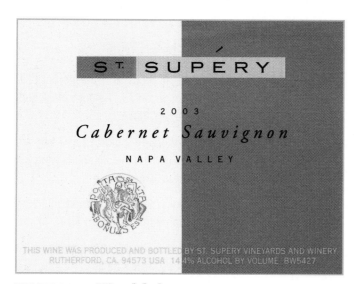

FIGURE 1–20 Wine label
(St Supery Winery)

INTRODUCTION TO WINE

NAME: _____ Score out of 20 points_____.

Use these questions to test your knowledge and understanding of the concepts presented in the chapter.

I. MULTIPLE CHOICE: Select the best possible answer from the options available.

1. A disadvantage of using screw caps as closures is
   a. the ability to easily reseal the cap.
   b. the cost is high, compared with that of corks.
   c. the perception of low quality.
   d. the ease of opening the caps.

2. The number one country producing the most table wine is
   a. the United States.
   b. Australia.
   c. Italy.
   d. France.

3. The number one country consuming the most table wine is
   a. the United States.
   b. Australia.
   c. Italy.
   d. France.

4. Which of the following are among the disadvantages of using corks as closures?
   a. the perception of low-quality and cheap wines
   b. having to store wines on their side for extended storage periods
   c. TCA/cork taint
   d. All of the above
   e. Answers b and c

5. A broader geographic label on a wine label usually indicates that the grapes are
   a. of less quality.
   b. of better quality.
   c. of undetermined quality.
   d. Not enough information is given to answer the question.

6. Jug and generic wines take their names (such as Chablis) from
   a. the grapes.
   b. famous Old World regions.
   c. where the wine was produced.
   d. where the grapes were grown.

II. TRUE / FALSE: Circle the best possible answer.

7. Old World wines tend to be made in a fruit-forward style. **True / False**

8. Grape skins contribute to the color in a wine. **True / False**

9. The three categories of wine are table wine, sparkling wine, and dessert wine. **True / False**

10. A purpose of a wider bowl for red wine glassware is to assist in aeration of the wine. **True / False**

11. Fortified wine glassware generally is smaller in size in order to accommodate a smaller portion size. **True / False**

12. The amount of sugar present in the grape juice can have an influence on the amount of alcohol that is produced. **True / False**

13. If fermentation is stopped before the yeast has had a chance to ferment all the sugar, the wine will have some sweetness. **True / False**

14. In Europe, the wines often are named after the place the grapes come from. **True / False**

15. Proprietary blends are styled after either red or white Bordeaux wines. **True / False**

16. The "Old World" refers to the long-established tradition of winemaking within the European countries of France, Italy, Germany, and Spain.
True / False

17. Wine bottles have been used for centuries and appear in a variety of shapes and sizes, but have been standardized to generally contain 33.8 oz.
True / False

III. IDENTIFY:

18. Given a typical wine label as shown, draw an arrow to the most prominent items that may be found on them.

    - Name of winery
    - Varietal
    - Location
    - Vintage date

19. For each bottle, identify the name of the bottle and the common grapes found in them.

    a. _____

       _____

    b. _____

       _____

    c. _____

       _____

IV. SHORT-ANSWER ESSAY / DISCUSSION QUESTION: Use a separate sheet of paper if necessary.

20. List at least two reasons for increased popularity and consumption of wine in America. Explain.

2

Wine Tasting

Tasting wine (as opposed to just drinking it) adds an extra dimension to the basic routines of eating and drinking; it turns obligation into pleasure.

LEARNING OBJECTIVES

Upon completion of this chapter, the learner will be able to:

- Exercise the professional four-step tasting technique used to assess and evaluate wine.
- Understand and communicate using key wine-tasting terminology.

THE TASTING RITUAL

Drinking wine is easy, but tasting wine can be more of a challenge, as it involves a concentrated sensory approach. Wine tasting is a technique used to determine the *performance factors* of wine by the senses of sight, smell, and taste. It is an attempt to capture a sensory experience in order to understand the unique personality of a given wine and, possibly, communicate it in simple terms to others.

Tasting wine (as opposed to just drinking it) adds an extra dimension to the basic routines of eating and drinking; it turns obligation into pleasure. Tasting wine can be as simple as "I like it" or "I don't like it" or as complicated as "Is it good or poor quality?" There are four essential steps in tasting: (1) looking at the wine (sight), (2) smelling the wine (smell), (3) tasting the wine (taste), and (4) spitting or swallowing the wine.

The ability to isolate and identify specific aromas and smells can be challenging, but will develop through experience. "Practice" is the most important advice for any wine drinker, as it can improve the ability to identify a wine's obvious and subtle clues through the tasting process.

FIGURE 2–1 Wine tasting
(Getty Images-Stockbyte, Royalty Free)

Wine tasting is a sensory evaluation of a particular wine or grouping of wines in a formal or informal arrangement. A wine tasting can be conducted blind (without seeing the labels) or in full view (seeing the labels). Blind tasting ensures zero influence by a wine's reputation and allows the taster to establish both an uncontaminated objective assessment and a subjective opinion about the wine. A wine's color, smell, and taste all offer insight into its origin of production and distinctive personality. Figure 2–1 shows an arrangement of wines prepared for a blind tasting.

Beyond producing enjoyment of the senses, the object of a wine tasting is to deduce the characteristics (or performance factors) of the wine, such as the type of grape, the region of origin, grape growing and winemaking methods, and maybe even the vintage date. In a competitive tasting where a wine may be compared with another wine, such as Cabernet Sauvignon from California against Cabernet Sauvignon from Bordeaux, the tasting is done blind to ensure a fair outcome so that, for example, the more established reputation of the Bordeaux region doesn't yield more clout than it may deserve.

1. Looking at the Wine

The appearance of a wine can create initial expectations, as the personality can be assessed partly by sight. The first impression can provide clues to a wine's grape variety, climate it was grown in, age of the wine, the winemaking methods, and potential faults. The visual aspects can also provide valuable clues to what the wine may smell and taste like just as the color of an avocado or a banana may suggest its level of ripeness, taste, and texture.

In the majority of grapes (except for a handful of obscure ones), we know that only the grape skins contain pigment responsible for a wine's color. Therefore, smaller grape berries contain a higher ratio of skin to juice, yielding a deeper, more concentrated color pigment. In contrast, a larger grape has a lower proportion of skin in relation to juice, yielding a wine with a lower color pigment. For example, a pale or lighter white wine with a greenish-to-straw yellow appearance may suggest a youthful wine grape (possibly larger berries) that was grown in a cooler area and possibly aged in stainless steel to preserve color (as opposed to oak aging, which may contribute color). If any of the clues are accurate, the wine will have a fresh, youthful smell and contain low to moderate alcohol to yield a light- to medium-bodied wine with ample acidity.

Unlike a white wine with medium intensity, wine with a golden yellow hue may be older and more evolved—a wine that was made from grapes (possibly smaller berries) grown in a warmer to hotter area and perhaps picked later in the season, suggesting that they had reached ample ripeness and sugar content and were aged in oak. If any of the clues are accurate, the wine will have an evolved smell containing several secondary aromas and flavor characteristics indicating moderate to high alcohol that yields a medium- to full-bodied wine with moderate to low acidity and slight to heavy residual sugar.

Process of Sight—Ensure that there is only a small amount of wine in the glass (about 1–2 ounces). This allows for better assessment of color and, later on, helps to detect aroma. Hold the stem of the glass between the thumb on one side and the index finger and middle finger on the other side. Tilt the wine glass and hold it over an opaque white background (such as a placemat or tablecloth) in a well-lit area. This is the best way to observe and assess the *clarity* (freedom from particles), *depth* or *intensity* (its level of concentration), and *hue* (shade of color). It is more accurate to judge hue by viewing the wine as the glass is tilted. View the wine from its deepest color for *intensity* (located in the core, or center of the glass) to its very thinnest and lightest color for *hue* (located at the rim, or edge of the glass), which is the first place to show signs of either youth or age.

> **WHITE WINES COLOR SCALE:** White wine can range in color from a greenish tint, to pale straw yellow (both are a possible sign of cool climate, youth, bone dryness, and stainless steel aging), to deep golden yellow (probably indicating a warmer climate, well-aged wine, exposure to oak barrels, or, possibly, some level of residual sugar). brown-amber (showing signs of possible death or spoilage).
>
> **RED WINES COLOR SCALE:** Red wine may appear any color from purple to ruby red (both of which may indicate a youthful wine) to red and brick red (indicating an evolved, more mellow wine), showing signs of age then finally to brown (showing signs of death or spoilage).

Swirl the wine in the glass, and notice how quickly or slowly the wine filters down after it has stopped moving. The patterns and viscosity of the wine remaining on the glass are together referred to as *legs* or *tears*, which provide a visual measurement of the wine's body. Slower moving and more viscous legs indicate a higher alcohol content, extract, or a high volume of sugar, all of which are characteristic of a wine with a fuller body. Quickly moving legs may indicate a wine low in alcohol or low in sugar, signifying a wine with a lighter body.

2. Smelling the Wine

Smell is probably the most important and certainly the most evocative sense we have. This is our key sensory tool for wine tasting because the nose can detect and distinguish an estimated 10,000 different odors, depending on the training of the individual. Even those lacking the ability to smell and detect specific odors can often be prompted to learn them by repeated exposure. The focus of initial training for wine tasters is the repetition of the common grape varietals for the purpose of building both a memory base for subsequent recognition of a wine and a solid foundation of common odor associations.

When smelling wine, it's possible to detect some of the same smells that might be associated with other food ingredients, the farm, or even a forest. The smells associated with a particular variety of grape have been influenced by that grape's cultivation under certain environmental conditions throughout the growing season. The actual scents associated with the grape (and all its environmental effects) are known as the *primary aromas*. These smells are combined with additional, more complex ones (known as *secondary* or *tertiary* aromas) that emerge from chemical changes of fermentation, from barrel and bottle aging, and through various winemaking techniques, to culminate in what is known as the wine's *bouquet*. Whether they are primary or secondary, the most common and detectable aromas associated with wine are broken down into *common wine aroma/flavor categories*. (See charts of the wine flavor categories in Chapter 4, "Performance Factors of Grape Varietals.")

Winemaking and maturation or aging techniques create and impart aromas often associated with bakery, cigar shop, and coffee shop smells and flavors. For example, the smell of butter or cloves may suggest that the wine has been adulterated with butter or cloves when it hasn't. Many of the aroma compounds we find in other places and food items that are actually derived from the same aroma compounds found in wine. The aroma in butter is actually derived from a chemical compound called *diacetyl* (die-ASS-ih-tahl), which is a by-product of malolactic fermentation. (This technique is discussed in Chapter 3, "Viticulture and Enology.") The smell of cloves is really caused by the chemical compound *eugenol* (u-jen-ahl), extracted in wine through aging in oak barrels.

The tasting experienced can be enhanced by learning aroma and flavor terms (see Chapter 4, "Performance Factors of Grape Varietals") in order to communicate better with others and, most importantly, to develop a memory of their likes and dislikes.

Perception of Aroma and Taste—We perceive the aroma of a wine in two ways and in two areas: by actively smelling the odors on the outside through the nose, and by holding the wine in the mouth to taste its flavor on the inside, through the *retronasal passage*. We differentiate the two kinds of odors by referring to the external odor as *smell* or *aroma*, and the internal odor as *flavor* or *taste*. These terms are commonly confused and used interchangeably, but are actually two different elements in wine tasting. Often, we taste more flavors than we smell aromas, because once the wine is in the mouth, it warms up as well as react with saliva to release more odor components.

When smelling a wine, we can also determine its level of *intensity*. The level of intensity provides an impression whether a wine has a somewhat diluted aroma or a concentrated one, which can be an association of its quality of production but of course, also the typicity of a particular grape varietal.

Process of Smell—To get a strong sense of the wine's smell, use the proper glass in order to concentrate the aroma molecules in the wine. Fill the glass only about one-third full or less to allow space for the wine's vapors to be released.

Next, swirl the wine to release and intensify the aroma of the wine. Then immediately bring the glass up to the nose and take several small whiffs. As the wine clings to the inside of the glass, the alcohol evaporates and carries with it the aromas of the wine.

The first impression of aroma is important, as the nose is at its freshest point and maintains the ability to identify subtle nuances. Concentrate on the smell in order to form an initial description of the wine's aroma personality. The longer a particular wine is smelled, the more the nose fatigues and loses its keen sense of discerning subtle aromas.

One of the most effective methods employed to develop the palate is to keep notes or tasting sheets of the wines tasted. This allows us to record connections between different styles and kinds of wines. Write down impressions and associations to help establish an aroma memory. Different wine tasters will have different sets of associations with which to identify a wine's aroma personality; however, there are some common smells associated with each particular grape variety that should be universal. In describing the aromas and flavors, the terms should be objective, not subjective. For example, *floral* is a more specific descriptive term and more useful to record than "It tastes good," which is a subjective opinion.

Fatigue and Adaptation—Smell is the most easily stimulated sense, but it is also the most fragile. The nose will *fatigue* after a short period of smelling (primary olfaction) something and will become temporarily unable to detect additional aromas. Simultaneously, *adaptation* sets in, which is the self-adjustment to a constant level of stimulus in an environment. For example, most of us, from time to time, have applied a noticeable amount of cologne or perfume to our bodies. After a short time, however, the odors may no longer be noticeable to us. This experience of fatigue and adaptation is no different when one is sniffing wine and will certainly influence the tasting process. A solution is to use quick sniffs, make an assessment, and move on, rather than sniffing a single wine for an extended period.

3. Tasting the Wine

When we taste a wine, our palates can break down different characteristics within the wine. The tastes that the tongue senses in wine are four *taste components*: (1) sweet, (2) sour, (3) bitter, and (4) salty. The palate can also detect texture (a combination of weight, tannin, and alcohol) associated with a wine.

When wine drinkers order and describe wine, they often refer to the flavor components they desire in their wine, whether they are aware that they are doing so or not. In many cases, it will be necessary to interpret their preference for components, because the thresholds of perceptible levels of sweetness, alcohol, tannin, and acidity can vary significantly among individuals. It's important to understand that perceived sweetness can be affected by levels of alcohol and acidity in a wine as well as perceived tannin can be affected by the level of fruit concentration.

Taste Components

Body can be light, medium, or full and can be comparable to skim milk, 2% milk, or whole milk.
- Light Body ⟶ Skim Milk
- Medium Body ⟶ 2% Milk
- Full Body ⟶ Whole Milk

Tasting a wine also involves detecting a wine's body. *Body* can be thought of as the boldness, thickness, or viscosity of a wine. The body of a wine can be felt as light, medium, or full-bodied, which is merely the impression of the weight and size of the wine in the mouth. The description *full bodied* is frequently applied to wines that are high in alcohol, sugar, extract, or tannin.

These elements (alcohol, sugar, extract, or tannin) are distinguishable, with each simultaneously influencing the other. If one element is dominant, a proficient taster will still be able to identify the other elements and possibly predict the effects of further aging. For example, a young red wine might be overly tannic, but have definite fruitiness and acidity, suggesting that in a few years the tannin will have softened, while the fruit will have become more complex.

The Process of Tasting—Place approximately one-half ounce of the wine in your mouth, suck in some oxygen (in order to aerate and open the wine's aromas and flavors), and swish the wine around in your mouth to ensure sure that as large an area of the tongue as possible has a chance to judge the wine's components (acid, sweetness, tannin, and salt). While doing this, simultaneously sense the body, flavors, and effects of other components.

The Purpose of Sucking Oxygen—Sucking oxygen volatilizes the wine and sends it to the back of the nasal cavity, then up into an interior nasal passage in the back of the mouth called the retronasal passage. The smell and flavor are now intensified. This could be referred to as *smelling the wine on the inside,* which we often associate with the term *flavors*.

The Four Taste Zones on the Tongue—Tastes are sensed by nerve receptors called buds, and there are about 9,000 of them on the average tongue. Combinations of

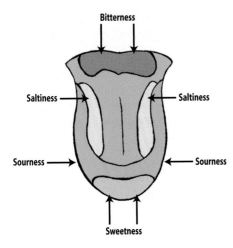

FIGURE 2–2 Tasting zones
(Thomas Moore)

tastes, along with the accompanying combined aromas (smelling from the inside), account for different flavors. Sensitivity to specific tastes varies considerably among individuals. Figure 2–2 is a visual representation of the taste zones on the tongue.

While there may be a vast array of aromas, historically only four taste components have been considered: sweet, sour, bitter, and salty. These four building blocks differentiate and describe common taste sensations.

Sugar—(Perceived as Fruit) Sugar is derived from the grape pulp and juice that contain equal amounts of both glucose and fructose. Sugar is the needed catalyst for yeast to produce alcohol and create wine. The amount of sugar fermented determines the wine's alcohol level. If yeast consumes most or all of the sugar present in the grape juice, the wine will be dry. If yeast consumes some but not most of the sugar, the remaining sugar after fermentation, is known as *residual sugar* or *RS*, the wine may have some detectible level of sweetness.

Sugar is sensed throughout the palate, but it is concentrated at the tip of the tongue. Most wine (particularly, red wine with some exceptions) is intended to be dry. Often, wine drinkers associate a fruit-concentrated wine with sweetness. Fruit is a smell and flavor through the nasal passage, and sweetness is a taste component. The effects of sweetness may be perceived more or less on the basis of varying amounts of other components such as acidity, fruit, and alcohol. For example, a wine with ample acidity may convey less sugar onto the palate.

If a wine is described as dry, there is no perceptible sugar. An off-dry wine may be described as having a hint of residual sugar, and a sweet wine has noticeable amounts of residual sugar.

Terms used to describe sweetness: *Sweet, ripe, luscious.*

Acid—(Perceived as Sourness) Acid derives primarily from the grape pulp and juice, but may also come from skins. Acid is best perceived as sourness and is a vital and fundamental structural component of both white and red wines. Without an adequate level of acid, a white wine is considered *flabby*, or falls *flat*, when paired with a food. Acid is sensed throughout the palate, but it is concentrated on the sides of the tongue and causes salivation. Sourness derives from various kinds of acids that are all found in wine in varying degrees such as tartaric (one of the main acids in wine), citric (also prevalent in lemon and grapefruit), malic (also found in apples and pears), lactic (also prevalent in dairy products), and acetic (also prevalent in vinegar). Collectively, these acids also acts as preservatives, but unlike tannin, they add a fresh, crisp sensation to the wine.

Terms used to describe acids: *Bright, lively, crisp, firm, zesty, fresh, and sharp.*

Tannin—(Perceived as Bitterness) Tannin originates primarily from grape skins, seeds, and stems (through the fermentation process) and also in part by the amount of contact with oak aging. Large oak casks impart less oak flavor and less tannin than smaller oak barrels do. Tannin is a vital structural component of a red wine and is, for the most part, undetectable in white wines. Fundamental to a red wine are its acid and tannin. Without an adequate level of either tannin or acid, a red wine becomes *flabby*, or *flat* and will fall flat when paired with food. Tannin is sensed throughout the palate, but it is concentrated toward the back of the tongue and around the gum line of the mouth. It causes a drying sensation that creates a "puckery" feeling and acts to cancel out the salivation caused by acid. In young red wine, tannin is most apparent and perceived as astringent and rough.

Tannins vary in type, strength, and character, depending on grape type and aging methods. The longer the maceration (juice and skin contact) period, the more tannin will be extracted. Tannin, therefore, helps wine age by acting as a natural preservative and suppressing oxidation throughout the aging process. Over time, tannin (in combination with color pigment) will *polymerize* (Puh-LYM-err-ize) (separate or fall out of the liquid solution) and form sediment in the wine bottle.

While there are several sources of tannin, not all tannin is created equal. The tannin present in skins, and particularly that found in seeds and stems, is known as *condensed tannin* (or unripe tannin). This type of tannin tends to taste slightly harsh on the palate, particularly if the grapes were harvested too soon before they had an adequate chance to ripen. Wines with condensed tannin are less likely to benefit and soften from aeration associated with aging and decanting. The type of tannin extracted through oak barrels is a *hydrolyzable tannin* (or ripe tannin). Hydrolyzable tannin benefits the wine by softening it from aeration during the aging process.

Tannin can significantly effect the texture and body of a wine. Low tannin usually is associated with light-bodied red wines, medium tannin with medium- to full-bodied red wines, and high tannin with full-bodied red wines.

Terms used to describe tannin: *Chewy, rough, gritty, dry, firm, rich, and puckery.*

Salty—(Perceived as Tangy) It is commonly believed that salt is not detected or sensed when tasting wine (with the exception of Manzanilla Sherry). Salt is more often associated with food items such as smoked meats or fish, baked goods, and canned or processed foods. Salt becomes integral to our understanding of wine when wine is paired with a food item that has a noticeable salt content. (This topic will be discussed in greater detail in Chapter 5, "Foundations to Wine and Food Pairing.")

Other Factors That Influence Taste, Flavor, and Texture—Texture in reference to wine is the feel of the wine on the palate. It is driven by a combination of factors, such as *tannin* (level of smoothness or roughness), *alcohol level* (feel of burn or lack of burn in the back of the mouth and down the throat), *extract* (number of particles of fruit suspended in the finished wine), amount of *residual sugar* (which creates a more weighty feel and viscous consistency), and impact of *temperature*.

Terms used to describe body: *Weight, richness, fullness, and intensity.*

Alcohol—(Perceived as a burning or spicy sensation) Alcohol is produced through the fermentation process of yeast consuming sugar. Alcohol plays a large role in the style, body, structure, and taste of wine. The level of alcohol in the finished wine is most often related directly to how much sugar the grapes contained at the harvest.

Alcohol is perceived as fullness or body in a wine. It frequently can be detected through a warming sensation that is largely noticed by a slight burn or spiciness toward the back of the mouth and throat. Alcohol can act somewhat similarly to the way acid is sensed, by assisting with cleansing the palate and having the ability to cut through rich types of foods and sauces. When the proportion of alcohol is too high for the other flavor elements, alcohol may give a burning sensation in the nose as well as a hot feeling in the back of the throat or the roof of the mouth. Sometimes, alcohol can be perceived as sweetness.

Fruitiness—(Perceived as sweetness) *Fruitiness* means the aroma and taste of the character of fruits (such as strawberry, blueberry, pineapple, etc.); it does not mean sweet. Although some fruity wines may be sweet, fruity wines more often are dry. Keep in mind that fruitiness and sweetness are two different things and that real sweetness is detected on the tongue, not in the nose.

Temperature—(Influences the perceptions of the other components) The temperature of a wine can affect the other components of wine (acid, tannin, sugar, fruit, and alcohol) by either emphasizing or de-emphasizing their sensations. A white wine served very cold gives a taste impression that is less fruity and more acidic than the same wine at a warmer temperature. A red wine served too warm yields more perception of alcohol than the same wine served cooler. (The topic of proper serving temperatures is discussed in greater detail in Chapter 14, "The Flow of Wine.")

The Theory of Umami—In the early 1900s, a Japanese scientist identified a fifth basic taste on the human tongue: *Umami*, which describes a savory sensation of foods high in glutamate. Such foods include meat, milk, mushrooms, and walnuts. The sensation creates a fullness or completeness of flavor upon tasting.

4. Spit or Swallow the Wine

After spitting or swallowing, notice which flavors and sensations are left and how long they linger in order to determine the *finish* or *persistence* (how long the aftertaste lasts in your mouth after you spit or swallow) of the wine. Many associate a longer finish with a better quality wine. However, this is not always the case. Some wines are not meant to have a longer finish, as they were created to be simple and perhaps one dimensional. The best measure is to understand that if a wine (such as Cabernet Sauvignon) typically has a long, lingering finish, and, during a tasting, it has been observed a glass of that wine has a short finish, then the quality of that particular wine should be called into question. The following chart approximates how to judge the persistence of a wine:

11 or more seconds	Long Finish
6–10 Seconds	Medium Finish
0–5 Seconds	Short Finish

Wine Flaws and Faults

A wine flaw is a minor error that still allows the wine to be drinkable, whereas a wine fault is a major error rendering the wine undrinkable. Both wine flaws and wine faults are defects and are generally considered undesirable and unpleasant characteristics of a wine, often caused by poor winemaking practices or storage conditions that lead to wine spoilage. Flawed and faulty wines are inevitable, and many of the flaws are undetectable until the bottle is opened and the tasting process begins.

Many of the compounds that cause flaws and faults are naturally found at insignificant levels in wine. Depending upon the perception of the drinker, the concentrations of the compounds may impart positive characteristics to a wine. However, when these compounds are at significant, noticeably perceptible levels, they adversely influence the wine by overpowering desirable aromas, flavors, and other pleasing components.

In 2006, the London-based International Wine Challenge (IWC), the largest wine competition in the world, revealed that some 13,000-plus wines (7% of all wines) tasted were identified as faulty. If a wine fault is detected, most credible suppliers, restaurants, or wine stores will allow the tainted product to be exchanged.

Six Common Flaws in Wine

1. **VOLATILE ACIDITY**—This encompasses both compounds of *acetic* acid and *ethyl* acetate. Acetic acid often is referred to as *vinegar taint,* and ethyl acetate in large doses contributes to the smell of fingernail-polish remover in a wine.
2. **CORK TAINT**—Often referred to as a wine being *corked,* a wine with *cork taint* is not to be confused with a wine being enclosed by a cork. Cork taint is caused by the compound *2,4,6-trichloranisole* (try-clore-AN-iss-all), or TCA, which originates from

mold present on cork or barrels when they are treated with chlorine for preparation. This is one of the more common wine flaws, and evidence suggests that it occurs in 2% to 4% of wines. Wine that displays this fault is characterized by an aroma reminiscent of wet cardboard or wet dog.

3. **HEAT DAMAGE**—Often referred to as *maderized*, heat-damaged wine contains a cooked aroma, flavor, and color. Visually, the cork may be pushed partially out of the bottle, the wine will look brick colored or brownish around the edges of the glass (whether red or white), and it may have an aroma and a flavor of caramel.

4. **SULFUR**—Sulfur is a naturally produced compound derived from the winemaking process. It is also a common additive used as an antioxidant (to stop oxidation) and as a preservative (to prevent undesirable microorganisms). If an excessive amount of sulfur is used, the perception is reminiscent of rotten eggs or burnt matches. The perception of sulfur may also cause a prickly sensation in the nose of the drinker smelling the wine. A closely related compound called *mercaptans* (mer-KAP-tuhns) is associated with a strong cabbage or onion-skin smell.

   U.S. federal regulations require any alcoholic beverage that contains more than 10 parts per million (ppm) of sulfites to print the phrase, "contains sulfites" on the label. The absence of the term on a label does not mean that the product is sulfite free, however; rather, it means that it has from 0 to 10 ppm of sulfites.

5. **ACETALDEHYDE (ass-ah-TAHL-duh-hide)**—This is a compound that causes a wine to have oxidized qualities, caused by the unintentional and undesirable effect of oxygen. Visually, an oxidized wine has a darkening or browning appearance, similar to an apple that turns color when cut open and not eaten right away. In table wines, acetaldehyde is generally considered a fault. However, an exception is made in the case of certain styles of fortified wines, in which such an aroma is desired.

6. **BRETTANOMYCES (breht-tan-uh-MY-sees)**—Often referred to as *brett*, this is a spoilage yeast that can grow on grapes and be present in wineries to affect a wine during processing. Brett can add a horse-saddle aroma and flavor to a wine.

DETAILED TASTING SHEET

WINE
Producer, varietals, location, vintage, etc.

SIGHT

CLARITY → Clear—sediment   **INTENSITY →** Watery — pale — medium — deep — opaque

COLOR

White Wine ——→ Greenish — straw yellow — golden yellow — Brown amber

Red Wine ——→ Purple — ruby red — red — brick red — brown

SMELL

HEALTHY → Yes – No   **INTENSITY →** Muted — lightly aromatic — fairly aromatic — highly aromatic

WHITE WINE AROMA CHARACTERISTICS

1. FRUIT

TREE → Apricot, peach, pear, apple, cherry

CITRUS → Lemon, lime, grapefruit, orange, tangerine

TROPICAL → Melon, banana, lychee, coconut, pineapple, passion fruit, fruit salad, mango

DRIED → Raisins, figs, apricots

BERRY → Strawberry, blueberry, raspberry, blackberry

2. BAKESHOP

NUTS → Toasted hazelnut, walnuts, almond, nutmeg

SAUCES → Caramel, vanilla, butterscotch, honey, cream, butter, custard

SPICES → Cinnamon, cloves, orange peel, anise, ginger

BREAD → Yeast, toast, biscuit, dough

3. MINERAL/CHEMICAL → Chalk, flint, petrol, ammonia, rubber, steel

4. BARNYARD/HERBACEOUS → Grass, hay, straw, tomato vine, dill, fresh chives, Earl Grey

5. FLORAL → Rosé, peonies, orange blossom, honeysuckle, violets

6. VEGETABLES → Olive, asparagus, bell pepper, cucumber

RED WINE AROMA CHARACTERISTICS

1. FRUIT

FRESH FRUIT → Cherry, black cherry, raspberry, blackberry, blueberry, plum, cranberry, strawberry, banana

BAKED/DRIED FRUIT → Prune, raisin, jam, baked/dried cherry, baked/dried raspberry, baked/dried blackberry, currants, fig

2. COFFEE SHOP → Cinnamon, cloves, black pepper, orange peel, chocolate, vanilla, coffee, tea, black tea, licorice/anise, bubblegum, toffee

3. GARDEN → Green pepper, green olive, black olive, mushroom, eucalyptus, mint

4. FLORAL → Rosé, rosehips, violet, geranium, orange blossom

5. EARTH → Forest, mud, dirt, chalk, manure, dust

6. TOBACCO SHOP → Pine, cigar, cigarettes, leather, cedar, tar

TASTE

DRYNESS/SWEETNESS → Dry — off dry — sweet

TANNIN LEVEL → Low — medium — high

ALCOHOL LEVEL → Low (11% or below) medium (11%–13.5%) high (13.5%–15%)

ACID → Low — medium — high

BODY → Light — medium — full

Did the palate confirm the nose? YES or NO. If no, then identify _____

FINISH → Short — medium — long

CONCLUSION

PRICE CATEGORY → Budget friendly ($15 or less) — moderate ($16–$30) — expensive ($30+) PRICE $_____

QUALITY → Poor — acceptable — good – outstanding

READINESS → Drink now (within the year) — could age (a couple of years) — definitely needs aging — tired

COMMENTS: _____

WINE TASTING

NAME: _____ Score out of 20 points_____.

Use these questions to test your knowledge and understanding of the concepts presented in the chapter.

I. MULTIPLE CHOICE: Select the best possible answer from the options available.

1. What term would apply when a white wine is lacking in adequate acidity or a red wine is lacking in acid and/or tannin?

   a. flat
   b. dry
   c. sweet
   d. tart

2. The first step of the tasting process begins with

   a. smell.
   b. taste.
   c. sight.
   d. spit or swallow.

3. The second step of the tasting process begins with

   a. smell.
   b. taste.
   c. sight.
   d. spit or swallow.

4. The third step of the tasting process is

   a. smell.
   b. taste.
   c. sight.
   d. spit or swallow.

5. The fourth step of the tasting process is

   a. smell.
   b. taste.
   c. sight.
   d. spit or swallow.

6. A white wine with a green-to-straw-yellow color may mean that the wine is

   a. youthful.
   b. aged in stainless steel.

   c. made from grapes grown in a cool climate.
   d. all of the above.

7. When looking at the wine, the best place to view youth or age is in the wine's

   a. core.
   b. rim.
   c. center.
   d. all of the above.

8. A wine's acidity causes

   a. salivation.
   b. dryness.
   c. spiciness.
   d. none of the above.

9. A wine's tannin causes

   a. salivation.
   b. dryness.
   c. spiciness.
   d. none of the above.

10. The purpose of decanting a wine is

   a. to aerate a young red wine in order to soften tannin and integrate aromas and flavors.
   b. to remove liquid from the sediment in an older red wine.
   c. to soften acid in a white wine.
   d. none of the above.
   e. all of the above.
   f. only answers a and b.

II. TRUE / FALSE: Circle the best possible answer.

11. White wine color ranges from green yellow, to straw yellow, to golden yellow, to amber, to brown. **True / False**

12. Red wine color ranges from purple, to ruby red, to brick red, to red, and then to brown. **True / False**

13. The best way to remember a wine's personality is to make an association of the aromas and flavors. **True / False**

14. The purpose of sucking oxygen into the mouth when tasting is to open up the wine's aromas and flavors. **True / False**

15. Smelling wine through the nose (on the outside) is done to perceive what is known as flavor. **True / False**

16. Smelling the wine in the mouth (on the inside) is done to perceive what is known as flavor. **True / False**

17. If a wine's alcohol content is relatively high, it generally can be sensed from a slight burn in the back of the throat. **True / False**

18. We have the ability to detect thousands of smells. **True / False**

III. SHORT-ANSWER ESSAY / DISCUSSION QUESTIONS: Use a separate sheet of paper if necessary.

19. Explain the difference between drinking wine and tasting wine.

20. Explain the four-step tasting process.

3

Viticulture and Enology

The wine in a glass is a product of nature, guided by the human hand from its initial conception in the vineyard, to its adolescence in the winery and, finally, to its maturity in the bottle.

LEARNING OBJECTIVES

Upon completion of this chapter, the learner will be able to:

- Learn how grape growing and winemaking can influence a type and style of wine.
- Discover how terroir can influence a wine's style.
- Understand the impact of key viticultural decisions and techniques on the flavors and style of a wine.
- Understand the impact of key enological decisions and techniques on the flavors and style of a wine.

FROM GRAPES TO GLASS

The wine in a glass is a product of nature, guided by the human hand from its initial conception in the vineyard, to its adolescence in the winery and, finally, to its maturity in the bottle. To produce a first-rate wine, the process must begin with the nurturing development of quality grapes, as the overall excellence initially comes from the combination of vine, grape, climate, and soil found within the vineyard. Figure 3–1 shows the two significant elements needed to create a wine.

The common phrase "Great wine is made in the vineyard" illustrates how a grape's personality is influenced much in the same way that a child is raised and nurtured. The upbringing in the vineyard can determine how the grapes behave later in life as they are transformed into wine. Once in the winery, the grapes are influenced by the numerous decisions made by the winemaker. The multiple factors in the winemaking process work collectively to alter grapes into a beverage that is desirable to drink from a glass (or for some, directly out of the bottle).

Producing wine involves two major steps typically done by two different individuals (or two different teams of individuals). The first person, responsible for growing the grapes, is called the *viticulturist* or simply, *farmer*. The second person, the specialist in creating the wine, is called the *enologist* or *winemaker*.

VITICULTURE

The science and practice of growing grapes in the vineyard

Viticulture (from the Latin word for *vine*) refers to the cultivation of grapes. When the grapes are used for winemaking, the practice is known as *viniculture*. Viticulture is the science, production, and study of grapes and deals with the series of events that occur in the vineyard.

A *vineyard* is a grape-growing area characterized by its *terroir*, a French term loosely translated as "a sense of place" and used widely throughout the wine world to distinguish one grape-growing area over another. All the nonhuman factors present in a vineyard area, such as soil, altitude, terrain, and microclimate (rain, wind, temperature, humidity, and so on), can identify the charecteristics of a vineyard and an approriate grape to be planted. Each vineyard around the world is distinct and unique in its own way, whether it is geographically or geologically based. Every varying element of a vineyard can impart its characteristics into the grape varietal. Even though the differences may be indetectable at times, no two vineyards in the world have the exact same terroir.

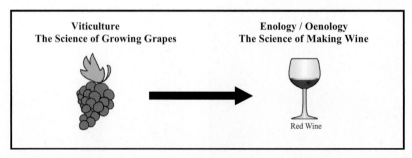

FIGURE 3–1 Viticulture and enology
(Thomas Moore)

Factors That Influence the Grape

In the vineyard, the personality of a wine is initially affected by the age of the grapevines, how they have been raised, and the soil composition (types of soil the vines are grown in). Later, the grape is influenced all the way through the growing season by exposure to sunlight, rainfall, temperature, pruning methods, and time of harvest.

The Viticulturalist

The vineyard manager commonly is responsible for monitoring and controlling pests and diseases, for fertilization and irrigation, for monitoring fruit development, for vine pruning throughout the season, and, finally, for determining when to harvest the grapes.

The most influential factor in determining the taste of wine is the grape. Therefore, viticulturalists often are intimately involved with the vision of the winemaker, because vineyard management and the resulting characteristics of the grape provide the basis from which winemaking can begin.

The Life Span of the Grapes

The grapevine is a deciduous plant that loses its leaves in the fall, becomes *dormant* (below a temperature of 50°F) in the winter, and follows the basic process of *bud break, flowering, fruit set, summer pruning, and véraison* throughout the spring and summer. Grapevines follow a growing season based on the combination of sunlight and weather. In the Northern Hemisphere, grapes usually are harvested in the late summer or early fall (September or October). In the Southern Hemisphere, harvest time (six months behind that of the Northern Hemisphere) occurs in the late winter to early spring (February or March).

FIGURE 3–2 Dormancy
(Photo by Jason Tomczak. Knudsen Vineyard, Dundee Hills AVA, Argyle Winery.com)

Dormancy—The dried vines are cut back during winter pruning to assist in conserving their energy throughout the season. Winter pruning will also train the vine for the approaching growing season. Figure 3–2 shows grape vines in dormancy.

Budbreak—In spring, the vines emerge from dormancy as sap begins to rise. As daytime temperatures warm, the emergence of green buds, or *budbreak*, occurs, where shoots begin to swell and open. At this point, growers watch the weather with concern, as the buds are extremely sensitive to frost and can easily be killed, significantly reducing or even destroying an entire crop. Figure 3–3 shows a vine at budbreak.

FIGURE 3–3 Budbreak
(Photo by Jason Tomczak. Knudsen Vineyard, Dundee Hills AVA, Argyle Winery.com)

FIGURE 3–4 Flowering

(Photo by Jason Tomczak. Knudsen Vineyard, Dundee Hills AVA, Argyle Winery.com)

FIGURE 3–5 Fruit set

(Photo by Jason Tomczak. Knudsen Vineyard, Dundee Hills AVA, Argyle Winery.com)

Flowering—When temperatures begin to reach into the mid-60s (May in the Northern Hemisphere and November in the Southern Hemisphere), the buds bloom and *flowering* occurs. It is during this phase that self-pollination and fertilization of the grapevine take place. At this point, excessive rain or hail can prevent flowering, and a significant amount of potential crop may be lost. Figure 3–4 shows a bud flowering.

The flowering stage can be of concern if the spring climate is unusually cool, rainy, or windy. Either of those conditions can cause *coulure* (coo-LYUR). Coulure occurs when the flowers have been improperly pollinated, resulting in insufficient fruit set and causing berries to abort or fall off the clusters. Another vineyard concern is *millerandage* (mill-lehr-AHN-dahj), in which grape bunches contain berries of varying sizes and maturity levels.

Fruit Set—*Fruit set* will occur during summer as the flowers form into green, hard berries. The berries continue to gain sugar and ripen throughout the summer. Figure 3–5 identifies fruit set.

Summer Pruning—Pruning is the process of removing excessive grapes and foliage from the grapevine for the purpose of influencing yield, which affects flavor development in the grapes. Pruning forces a vine to exert more energy into its fruit rather than its foiliage.

Véraison—Near the middle to end of summer, *véraison* (vehr-ray-ZOHN) occurs, where the green berries begin to change color and become recognizable as grapes. Toward the end of the summer to early fall (depending on grape varietal and climate), the grapes are at the optimal level of ripeness (level of sugar and acid) and flavor content to begin the harvest. Figure 3–6 identifies some grapes going through véraison.

FIGURE 3–6 Véraison

(del Amo, Tomas/Photolibrary.com)

1. THE GRAPEVINE

Grapevines are fairly adaptable, growing in a wide range of soils and temperature range. The most successful wine grapes are grown in temperate climate bands in the range from 30° to 50° north of the equator and from 30° to 50° south of the equator. The areas located in the temperate climate bands generally provide the right combination of sun, rain, and temperature.

As the grapes grow throughout the growing season, they gradually lose acid, and sugar levels increase through photosynthesis. The grapes also gain color and take on flavor as they begin to ripen. The grape grower's challenge is to ensure that there is enough acid in the juice to balance the sugar content, while simultaneously making certain that the grapes are neither underripe, nor overripe with sugar and flavor.

The first step in producing a quality wine is to select a grape variety best suited to the particular growing environment. Some varieties can tolerate more winter cold than others; some, more summer rain. Some varieties ripen earlier than others, making them desirable for areas with short growing seasons, whereas some mature later and are ideal for a location with a long growing season. Once the grower has decided which grape varieties to plant, a process begins that will take several years to bear fruit.

The types of grapes used to make a wine probably are the single most important factor in the taste and style of wine. Indeed, at the dinner table, the grapes and the style of wine are the dominant consideration in deciding which food items eventually are paired with a wine.

There are about 20 different species of grapevines, but only one of them, *Vitis vinifera,* the European species, produces all the grapes used in high-quality wine.

The native North American *Vitis labrusca* is another grape-growing species used by some winemakers, mainly in challenging climates. The labrusca is a hardier vine able to withstand extreme cold temperatures, but its musky off flavors tend to rule it out as a serious wine producer. Labrusca possibly is most famous for its Concord grape used in the production of jams, jellies, and grape juice.

Within the *vinifera* species, there is estimated to be as many as 10,000 strains, clones, and hybrids of different variations of grapes. Most of the wine world depends on perhaps 30 to 40 grapes, of which an even smaller number are considered *classics*, or Noble grape varietals.

Clones are grapes that are produced through the replication of an original vine that may arise over time through natural evolution or manipulated intentionally through grafting vines (referred to as, scions) onto rootstocks. Either method may allow the clone to become modified due to climatic effects. Cloned grapes may develop characteristics that differ from the parent as the grapevines evolve and mutate with changes in their surroundings. The differences in the flavor profile can range from being very pronounced to being extremely difficult to discriminate on the palate. For example, the Sangiovese grape that is prevalent throughout central Italy varies significantly enough with its location that it is commonly identified by different names to point out the various distinctions.

Cross-pollination occurs between two different grapes of the same vine species, either naturally through evolution or intentionally within a vine nursery. For example, current evidence suggests that the Cabernet Sauvignon grape varietal is derived from the natural crossing of the Cabernet Franc and Sauvignon Blanc varietals.

Hybrid grapes are created from cross-pollinating two different vine species, such as American vine (to obtain hardiness) and European vine (to obtain complexity) varieties. Some notable hybrids are Seyval (say-VEL) Blanc and Vidal (vee-DAHL) Blanc, which are both prevalent in New York State and Canada.

This textbook will concentrate on *the Big Six grapes produced from the* vinifera *vine species*—Riesling, Sauvignon Blanc, Chardonnay, Pinot Noir, Merlot, and Cabernet Sauvignon—but will also discuss other important grapes grown throughout the world. The list easily could include so many more magnificent grape varieties, but the Big Six grapes are selected because of their adaptability in multiple locations to produce quality wines throughout the world.

FIGURE 3–7 Vineyard rows

♦ Exact figures vary greatly from vineyard to vineyard, according to the variety of grape, desired yields, the planting formation, the age of the vines, and so on.

(Ron Redfern © Dorling Kindersley)

The Vineyard

Vineyards can vary in size and in spacing between individual vines. Varying quantities of grapes can be grown, depending on the age of the vine, the variety of grape, the amount of rainfall, and various viticulture practices. In addition, different grape varieties have the ability to yield larger or smaller amounts of juice per pound. Figure 3–7 depicts the orderly arrangment of a vineyard.

As a rough guideline, one vineyard acre can contain 900 to 1300 vines, which collectively can yield from 2 to 12 tons of grapes, equal to about 300-plus cases of wine bottles. A single vine can produce between 15 and 45 clusters of grapes, which collectively can produce somewhere between 40 and 75 grapes. A single vine can produce about four to six bottles of wine annually. In Europe, Canada, and South America, vineyard size is commonly measured in hectares (ha), as opposed to acres in the United States. (For reference, 1 hectare is equivalent to 2.47 acres.)

2. CLIMATE

Weather and location

The geographical location and related climate significantly dictate the type of grapes a vineyard is able to successfully grow. A producer selects varieties specifically for their style and their suitability to a particular site—varieties that will perform best under the climatic conditions within the producer's specific vineyards. Through hundreds of years of trial and error, the French invented and perfected this system of matching varietal to location.

Today's winemakers have many methods for manipulating wine; however, the basic climatic influence will always be one of the most significant factors affecting the personality of a given wine. Grapevines do not tolerate extended periods below freezing, nor can they take tropical heat. Therefore, wine grapes grow best in temperate climates associated with both the Northern and Southern Hemispheres. The length of the growing season, daily temperatures, and amount of sun and rain all influence the sugar–acid balance and flavor development.

Climate factors are important considerations in wine and often may influence the appropriateness of a food pairing. Climate can affect a wine's fruit ripeness, acidity level, alcohol level, tannin, and aromas and flavors. White wines from cool climates have aromas and flavors associated with cool-climate tree fruits such as apples and pears. Warm climates give aromas and flavors associated with warm-climate trees and tropical fruit such as mango, banana, and pineapple. Cool-climate red wines promote fresh fruits such as cranberries and red cherries, whereas warm climates encourage dried and stewed fruits such as figs, plums, and dried cherries. These examples highlight aroma and flavor differences between grapes grown in different climates, but certainly also will influence other variables such as acidity and alcohol content. The aroma and flavor difference (as well as other factors) can be used as a basis for establishing and justifying a particular wine and food pairing (discussed in greater detail in Chapters 4, 5, and 6).

In warm climates such as in California, grapes maintain high sugar levels because of their magnified exposure to sun and excessive heat throughout the growing season. In addition, as the grapes sugar content rises, the acid level drops. This can result in a wine with low acid and high alcohol. In a warm climate, sugar development is automatic, but if the climate is too hot, the grapes will not ripen fast enough. In some warm wine-growing areas, winemakers are allowed to add acid (a method known as acidification) during the winemaking process to balance the drop in acid due to the increased sugar content.

In cool climates such as in Germany, grapes maintain higher acid levels because the cooling influence limits the production of sugar and maintains the grapes' natural crispness. This climate produces grapes with lower natural sugar levels because the grapes have not been exposed to the sun and warmth consistently for a long enough period. The result may be a wine with low alcohol content and, possibly, slightly underripe flavors.

In some wine-growing regions such as Germany, as well as Champagne, Burgundy, and Alsace, in France, winemakers may be allowed to manipulate the ripening process to make up for the limitations imposed by the climate. Depending on the classification level, some winemakers may add sugar in the process known as *chaptalization* (shap-tuh-luh-ZAY-shuhn) or reserve grape juice during the winemaking process to make up for the lack of sugar that was not naturally produced in the grapes. This sugar is necessary in some cases in order to eventually ferment the grapes and turn the juice into alcohol.

Climates can be broadly classified for the purpose of understanding grapes that may grow and prosper. Four major types of climates (often referred to as *macroclimates*) are found throughout the major wine-producing areas:

1. **Maritime Climates** have large bodies of water that moderate the temperatures throughout the year by keeping summers cool and winters mild and, overall, the environment moist. Examples are New Zealand and Bordeaux.
2. **Continental Climates** have four distinct seasons with short, hot summers and cold winters. Examples are Champagne and Burgundy.
3. **Mediterranean Climates** have long warm-to-hot growing seasons with mild winters, low moisture, and low rainfall. Examples are Rhone, Provence, and Southern Spain.
4. **Alpine Climates** have influences of altitude from vineyards being perched upon mountainous areas. Examples are parts of Northern Spain, Argentina, and Southeastern France.

Within the macroclimate, there are smaller growing areas that may have different weather or climate patterns. Growing areas can be influenced by such local factors as lakes or rivers, or even hillsides with greater or lesser sun exposure. This type of smaller climate pattern, known as a *microclimate,* has the ability to alter the personality of a given grape or even influence the growth of a grape variety completely different from those that might be found in the larger, broader climate area.

3. SOIL

Soil is the medium necessary for a grapevine to grow, as it supports the root structure and controls drainage levels and amounts of minerals and nutrients that the vine is exposed to. Grapes have the ability to extract flavors and attributes from the geological conditions that they are partnered with.

These conditions include soil and all of the other non-human factors (or terroir) that contribute to the personality of a wine. Terroir is a guiding principle behind most of European winemaking, apparent from the practice of labelling the wines according to their location of origin. The Europeans, and certainly the French, believe that the place influences the personality and distinction of the grapes in its own unique way that cannot be duplicated elsewhere, similar to the unique and distinguishing mark of a fingerprint.

Influence of the Soil

Soil is a mixture of minerals, organic matter, and particles that are of different sizes and textures. Grapevines grow in a combination of *topsoil* and *subsoil* with varying particles. The sizes of the particles determine the texture of the soil, which influences a grapevine's root structure, water drainage, temperature, and absorbtion levels of minerals and nutrients. Essentially, the best soils for grape growing are lightly textured soils because they allow for good drainage, have a good capacity to hold nutrients, and are relatively infertile. Ideally, well-drained infertile soils force the vine to struggle for its nutrients, which results in a good concentration of flavor characteristics in the grapes.

Different types of soil are available in different geographic wine-growing areas. High importance is placed on matching the correct or suitable soil type with the appropriate type of grapes. However, soil is highly variable even in individual vineyards. Soils can affect vines in several ways:

1. Soils can influence the temperature of the vineyard. Darker soils retain heat well, whereas light-colored soils reflect sunlight either toward or away from the vines.
2. Soils can influence water management. Free-draining soils force roots to grow downward to reach nutrients and water.
3. Soils can affect flavor development. In cooler climates such as Champagne, where grapes ripen slowly, the strong mineral content of the soil influences the flavor profile of the wine.

Figure 3–8 shows the chalky soil that is highly prevalent in the Champagne region of France.

Topsoil and subsoils are extremely important to vine development and consequently influence the personality of the grapes. In rich topsoil, the vine does not need to dig hard because its nutrients are found close to the surface. Thus, yields are likely to be high and quality may be low. However, if the vines are given poor, low-nutrient soil, the roots are forced to dip deep, and this results in better grapes, according to the *struggling vine philosophy*. This philosophy theorizes that the farther the vine's roots must dig to find nutrients, the fewer, but better-quality, grapes will be produced, with thicker skins and more concentrated flavor. In order for the vine and the grapes to retrieve their nutritional requirements, the vines grow slowly and thus produce fewer grapes, but with greater flavor development. Ultimately, a better wine may be produced because of a better-quality ingredient. The chart shown in Figure 3–9 lists some general characteristics associated with how various types of soil may function.

Classic Soil Types

In some famous wine regions, the soils produce certain varieties of grape that are considered almost legendary in the manner that they are expressed. This is not to say that the same grapes can't be grown in alternative soil types and still produce high quality. But in the wine world, the degree of distinction associated with something such as soil that can't be duplicated by humans carries a certain romance and desirability. The following table lists some legendary kinds of grapes grown in their respective soil types and regions:

FIGURE 3–8 Chalk cliff in the Champagne vineyard
(Collection CIVC.
CIV Photographer: SPAANS ERIK)

FAMOUS SOIL TYPES				
GRAPE		**SOIL**		**REGION**
Chardonnay	➤	Chalk	➤	Champagne, France
Cabernet Sauvignon	➤	Gravel	➤	Bordeaux, France
Pinot Noir	➤	Limestone	➤	Burgundy, France
Riesling	➤	Slate	➤	Mosel, Germany

Appellations

The French term *appellation* refers to a viticulture region distinguished by geographical features that produce wines with shared characteristics. In simple terms, an appellation is a place where the grapes are grown. Though the term has a specific meaning to European grape growers, most wine-producing countries use it loosely. The idea of appellation is that the soil, climate, sun, and water quality of a region combine to produce a style of wine that cannot be duplicated elsewhere. The size of an appellation can range from very small plots of land to huge areas that cover hundreds of miles.

In 1935, France founded the Institut National des Appellations d' Origine (an-stee-TYOO nah-syaw-NAHL dayz ah-pehl-lah-SYOHN daw-ree-ZHEEN), or INAO, becoming the first nation to set up a countrywide system based on geography for controlling the origin and quality of wine. The *Appellation Controlee* system, or AC, is a French term meaning "controlled appellation of origin" and is applied to standards of production for various kinds and types of products such as wine, cheese, butter, and so on. The designation is given and controlled by the French government, and it guarantees that the products have been held to a set of rigorous production standards.

This plan originated during the Great Depression as a preventative measure to protect French winemakers and consumers from fraudulent and inferior wine-blending methods practiced by some unethical French wine brokers.

INFLUENCE OF COMMON SOIL				
Stones >	**Gravel** >	**Sand** >	**Silt** >	**Clay**
Larger Particles				Smaller Particles
Poor Nutrients				Rich Nutrients
High Drainage				Low Drainage
Warmer Soils				Colder Soils
Retains Heat				Reflects Heat
Heat of Minerals				Retains Minerals
Early Ripening				Late Ripening

FIGURE 3–9 The influence of common soil types in Southern Rhone Valley

(Vineyards Domaine de la Mordoreé)

The system is based on several levels, with the highest and most stringent tier called the *Appellation d' Origin Controlee* (AOC). This top category is reserved for wines meeting quality criteria in seven areas: (1) land, (2) grape varieties used, (3) viticulture practices, (4) permissible yield, (5) alcohol content, (6) winemaking practices, and (7) official tasting.

The system is the model in the wine industry and parallels other systems throughout the world, such as the Denominazione Di Origine Controllata Garantita (DOCG) in Italy and the Denominacion De Origen Calificada (DOCa) in Spain. Outside of France, the systems may or may not be as strict or as comprehensive.

The European Union (EU)

The European Union (EU) has registered place names called appellations of origin. Each EU country defines the specifics of its appellations of origin in terms of standards for type of grapes grown, processes for grape growing, and wine-making methods. Each appellation serves as a definition of the wine, as well as the wine's name. The EU regulates the wine appellations. The chart on the left identifies the quality levels of top classifications for France, Italy, Spain and Germany.

In the United States, appellations are known as *American viticulture areas*, or AVAs. In simple terms, a viticulture area is a place where the grapes are grown. However, the American viticulture areas carry a different connotation than the French appellations of origin. American labels may identify a wine's AVA or location when a minimum of 85% of the grapes used for the wine come from the AVA specified on the label. The French AOC regulations have stricter guidelines, which include standards regulating vineyard location, grape varietal, growing technique, crop yield, grape ripeness, ensuing alcohol content, and winemaking practices.

Generally, the French rely more on topography and the effect of nature upon grapes than do Americans. It is the basis on which the entire French wine classification and terroir concept are built. However, American winemakers do recognize what important elements regional flavors and style characteristics are to wine identification and classification. To illustrate, a wine labelled simply "California Chardonnay" could originate from anywhere in California, rather than only from the Sonoma-Napa County wine region or even the more specific, "Carneros" AVA that is within Napa and Sonoma.

Sustainable Agriculture and Biodynamics

The sustainable, or "green," concept is gaining momemtum as the world becomes more aware of and concerned not only about its food supply and other resources, but also about the environment in general. Sustainable viticulture is known to be ecologically sound. With today's more educated customers, the wine world has started to implement a bit of green philosophy. This trend not only benefits the earth's natural resources, but, many believe, results in better-tasting grapes and, thus, more flavorful wine that can reflect the distinctiveness of the land.

Biodynamics is a view of the land as a living system and of the vineyards as an ecological self-sustaining whole. Biodynamics takes organic farming to a new level. The concept was developed by Austrian philosopher Rudolph Steiner in 1924 as a way to express the authenticity of the vineyard in which the produce (grapes, in this case) has been grown. It bans pesticides and artificial additives and strives for a self-contained sustainable farming system in which water and organic materials are recycled to regenerate the land.

As of 2007, there are over 20 certified biodynamic wineries in the United States and 200 more throughout the world; however, this number is growing each day.

QUALITY WINE CATEGORIES WITHIN FAMOUS WINE-PRODUCING COUNTRIES

☐ France ➝ AOC, VDQS
☐ Italy ➝ DOCG, DOC
☐ Spain ➝ DOCa, DO
☐ Germany ➝ QMP, QbA

---

4. GRAPEVINE MAINTENANCE

Grapevine maintenance is a lot like nurturing a child going through adolescence. We attempt to raise children with values and principles and to help them create futures filled with an excellent quality of life. As parents, we attempt to keep children away from predators and other elements that may do them harm and stifle their development. With grapes, the goals are similar as the grape grower attempts to guide them, provide nourishment, nurture them to develop excellent qualities, and keep them protected from predators.

Pruning

Crop control involves the adjustment of grapevines by *pruning*—an important factor in determining the quality of the grapes and, ultimately, of the wine. Pruning is the process of removing excessive grapes and foliage from the vine for the purpose of affecting yield, which influences flavor development in the grapes. It forces a vine to exert more energy into its fruit rather than its foiliage.

If pruning is limited, the results will be a high yield of grapes per vine with less intense flavors and reduced concentration. Alternatively, if high pruning is conducted, the result will be lower quantity, but higher-quality, concentrated grapes. Theoretically, the fewer grapes there are on a vine, the more concentrated is the juice of the grape.

Pruning requires a delicate balance. The answer is neither to always prune excessively nor not to prune at all. In both situations, the grapes can be prone to viticultural and financial hazards. Too much pruning can cause the grape crop to be uneconomical, as it creates an expensive wine, whereas too little pruning can cause diluted grapes, creating a low-quality wine.

Typically, high-quality vineyards produce around two tons of grapes per acre or less, whereas vineyards of lower quality levels may produce in excess of 12 to 14 tons of grapes per acre.

In many vineyards, the method of *dropping crop* is practiced, according to which some of the grape bunches are picked and dropped on the soil next to the vines. This practice has two benefits:

1. The flavors are more strongly concentrated in the remaining grapes left on the vine.
2. The dropped crop gets absorbed back into the topsoil, adding nutrients to the grapevine.

Canopy Management

Canopy management is the practice of adjusting or positioning the vine's leaves, shoots, and fruit as the vine grows, in order to gain such beneficial advantages as increased sunlight exposure and air movement. Canopy management improves varietal character and decreases problems with fungal rot and insects.

COMMON HAZARDS IN THE VINEYARDS

There are numerous microorganisms, pests, and disease that can attack and kill grapes and vines. Both temporary and permanent solutions have been developed to combat these viticultural challenges.

Microorganisms

Fungal Disease—Managing fungal diseases such as odium, mildew, grey rot, and so on is a constant concern in the vineyard. Fungal disease is often associated with vineyard locations with excessive rain or with constantly moist climates without adequate sunshine. In some cases, wind can assist in drying the vines and helping to prevent some fungal disease.

Widespread control methods to lessen fungal disease have included chemical sprays such as *bouillie bordelaise* (Bwee-YEE Bor-duh-LEZZ) (a solution of copper sulfate, lime, and water) and better knowledge of canopy management.

Glassy Winged Sharpshooter—These pests are named after the glassy or transparent appearance of their wings. The sharpshooters have caused widespread disease by passing on the bacterial infection known as *Pierce's disease*. Insecticides have been used to deter the ailment, but have not worked as a complete solution. Currently, experimentation with biological control by natural enemies is underway.

Animals/Pests

Phylloxera (fil-LOX-er-uh)—This aphid feeds on the roots of grapevines (especially on the highly vulnerable Vinifera roostock species), causing the vine to starve and thus preventing fruit development.

In the 1800s, phylloxera was unknowingly transported from hardy Native American vine species (which are resistant to phylloxera) in the United States to the Vinifera species in Europe. Over the next 100 years, the vineyards of France, Spain, and other countries were nearly devastated. It took Bordeaux over three generations to recover.

The solution was to graft Vinifera vines to the American rootstock. *Grafting* in the vineyard is the technique of securing a vine to a rootstock. In most Vinifera vineyards (except for those in Chile and vinyards in some parts of Australia), cuttings of the desired varieties are grafted onto rootstocks of Native American varieties that are resistant to phylloxera.

Birds—Birds eat grapes as a source of nourishment. Large nets are often placed across the vineyards in order to deter birds. Other animals such as deer and raccoons have been known to consume fruit and cause vineyard damage.

Weather

Wind—Wind may prevent pollination of the flowers during the early part of the season. Later in the season, the winds can knock fruit off the vine and heavier winds can knock vines over. Some of the heaviest winds occur in Southern France (the Mistral) where they have been known to rip vines right out of the ground.

Frost—Frost is a serious danger in many vineyards, especially those located on the valley floors where the coldest air settles on frosty nights. Sprayers, burners, and wind machines can all be used collectively or separately where frost is a constant danger to the buds, flowers, or berries. Wind machines are used to distribute heat from a central heat source, such as a fire or chaufferettes (gas heaters), that warms the grapes (or vines) to keep them free of frost. (See Figure 3–10, which depicts "Chaufferettes" in a Champagne vineyard protecting the vines against the frost.)

FIGURE 3–10 "Chaufferettes," protection against the frosts

(Collection CIVC.
Photographer: DIVERS)

FIGURE 3–11 Sprinklers
(Collection CIVC.
Photographer: HODDER JOHN)

FIGURE 3–12 Against the frosts: a bud wrapped by ice to protect it from the frosts
(Collection CIVC.
Photographer: HODDER JOHN)

Many grape growers located in cold climates (particularly with early budding grapes) may also use *aspersion*, which involves sprayers that release water into the air. The water that lands on the grapes (or buds) forms an outer ice shell, but a warm, protected state is maintained on the inside. Figures 3–11 and 3–12 show water spraying on grapevines to form a protective coating around a bud to protect it from damage due to frost.

Rain—Heavy rains are a concern both in early spring and at harvest time. Too much rain can prevent pollination of flowers in the spring. If it rains near harvest time, the fruit may be over-saturated and the flavors, sugars, and acid that have been developing throughout the growing season may be diluted.

In locations such as Argentina and Australia, where lack of rain is a consistent problem, select vineyard areas may be allowed to use irrigation systems created to feed off nearby rivers or lakes.

5. HARVESTING

Picking the grapes

All grapes start out as unripe, hard, green berries. Finally, after the grapes have been exposed to enough sun and heat, the white wine grapes change to yellow and the red wine grapes to purple in a process known as *véraison* (vehr-ray-ZOHN). This is part of the ripening process, when grapes change color, acid decreases, and sugar content, or *brix,* increases. Véraison is an indicator that the grapes are evolving along their path, eventually to be harvested.

In the Northern Hemisphere, grapes ripen in late summer or early fall, depending on both the varietal and the climate. As the growing season progresses, the winemakers ultimately decide when the grapes will be ready for harvest on the basis of sugar ripeness and flavor development. The winemakers' concern is to pick grapes at the correct level of ripeness and near the harvest; grapes are often measured multiple times throughout the day. There is a small window of time when the grapes (depending upon the climate and the type of grape) should be picked, because if picked too early, the grapes will be underripe, and if picked too late, they will be overripe.

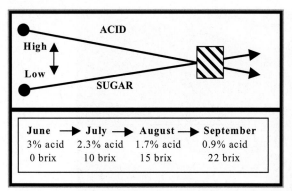

FIGURE 3-13 Acid/sugar ratio

(John Laloganes)

June	→	July	→	August	→	September
3% acid		2.3% acid		1.7% acid		0.9% acid
0 brix		10 brix		15 brix		22 brix

The ability to evaluate grape ripeness is vital for determining the suitable time of harvest. The evaluation should involve both an objective approach, by measuring grape sugars (through the use of a refractometer), and a subjective one, by measuring flavor through the use of taste. Flavor ripeness (otherwise known as phenolic ripeness) is represented by a group of compounds that contribute color, aroma, flavor, and tannin to a grape. This kind of ripeness allows the tannins to become softer as the growing season progresses. Phenolic ripeness often trails sugar ripeness, but is important for allowing the maximum flavor of the grape to be obtained. Grape ripeness can be compared with teenagers in this regard; Often, their bodies (a grape's sugar content) mature faster than their minds (a grape's flavor development), leading the teens to believe that they are older and more mature than they really may be.

A recent 10- to 15-year trend has been to extend the "hang time" (the delay of harvest) of the grapes, with the expectation of increasing flavor development. This practice produces very ripe fruit that yields a "jammy" quality in the finished wine. In some cases, certain producers have been criticized for too much hang time, allowing the grapes to become overripe with a surplus of sugars to yield a wine that is higher in alcohol and can be excessively out of balance.

There has to be sufficient sugar in the juice of wine grapes for yeast to feed on and convert into alcohol. When there is too much sugar, the wine becomes cloyingly sweet, or flabby; when there is too little sugar, the wine becomes thin and unsatisfying. Figure 3–13 offers a perspective on sugar and acid balance throughout the growing season.

In warm-to-hot climates, sugar/acid ripeness is almost automatic, but it presents a problem. Phenolic ripeness and sugar ripeness don't happen simultaneously, and the concern is when sugars develop too quickly before phenolic ripeness has caught up. In this environment, the grower is forced to harvest grapes earlier than desired or risk losing the grapes' acid. Unfortunately, at this time, the flavor of the wine may not have developed as fast as the sugar, leaving somewhat of an underripe flavor in the wine.

In cool climates, both types of ripeness are a concern because each will inhibit the ability of a vine to produce sugar and develop flavor. Most often, grapes are planted at various angles on hillsides for the maximum exposure to sunlight, to assist in the development of sugars and flavors. In these environments, the vines develop at a slower rate, and the greater concern tends to be frost striking in early fall, damaging the grapes before they are ready to be picked.

ENOLOGY

The science of making wine in the winery

Methods of production can vary greatly from country to country, region to region, and even grower to grower. Among the influential factors that shape the quality and style of a wine are the grower's philosophy and whether it is based on tradition or innovation. Figure 3–14 shows the common steps in white and red wine production.

Making Wine

In the winery, personality of the wine is influenced by how the grapes are handled and fermented, the types of yeast used, and whether the wine is aged in wood or stainless steel.

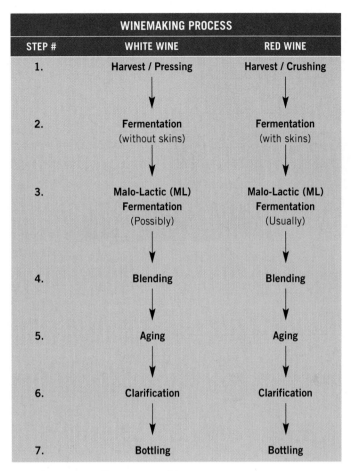

WINEMAKING PROCESS		
STEP #	WHITE WINE	RED WINE
1.	Harvest / Pressing	Harvest / Crushing
2.	Fermentation (without skins)	Fermentation (with skins)
3.	Malo-Lactic (ML) Fermentation (Possibly)	Malo-Lactic (ML) Fermentation (Usually)
4.	Blending	Blending
5.	Aging	Aging
6.	Clarification	Clarification
7.	Bottling	Bottling

FIGURE 3–14 The winemaking process
(John Laloganes)

♦ It is important to note that some of the winemaking process steps outlined here may occur in practice in a slightly different order, and/or some steps may occur multiple times throughout the winemaking process.

FIGURE 3–15 The harvest time in Champagne
(Collection CIVC.
Photographer: HODDER JOHN)

Therefore, the same grape varietals can be grown in France, Italy, Australia, and California, but various factors will result in wines with differing flavors and aromas.

The winemaker is similar to the chef, as they both create something out of raw ingredients according to a preliminary vision. Both require specialized skills and have been taught the best manner to bring out the maximum potential from the ingredients they are using to create their finished product. Initially, the winemaker has to envision the type and style of wine he or she wishes to create. A winemaker's goal is to make the best-tasting wine possible from the raw product available. Ultimately, however, as the philosophy goes, great wine is made in the vineyard.

1. HARVESTING AND PRESSING/CRUSHING—Great care is taken to ensure that grapes are picked at the right time and in the correct manner. At harvest time, the quality of the grapes represents the greatest potential of any wine that can be created. Just as a chef takes painstaking efforts to select the best-quality ingredients to produce a dish, winemakers search for the most excellent grapes to make the greatest wine possible. Pictured in Figure 3–15 are Champagne vineyards ready for harvesting.

The harvest and crush typically will take two to three weeks before all desirable grapes are obtained. Freshly picked bunches of grapes are put into mechanical crushing

FIGURE 3–16 Crushing grapes
(Alice Grulich-Jones/Omni-Photo Communications, Inc.)

and destemming machines. The higher-quality wines are made from the first pressing of grape juice, known as *free run*, while lower-quality wines are made from progressive pressings called *press wine*. With olive oil, the first pressing of the olives yields what is known as extra virgin oil because of its purity. It is the same with wine grapes: Secondary pressings release additional juice, harsh and not as pure as the free run. Figure 3–16 illustrates the destemming process that is necessary prior to crushing red wine grapes.

The remains of the grapes after the juice has been pressed out are known as *pomace* (PUHM-ess) which is a dry mass of pulp, skins, and grape seeds. The pomace can be used to fertilize the vineyard or sold to spirit producers to distill and make into brandy. As the grapes are being pressed or crushed, until fermentation is complete the grape juice is known as *must*.

Yeast consumes sugar and releases by-products of:
1) Alcohol 2) Carbon Dioxide 3) Heat

Alcohol
CO2
Heat

Yeast   **Grapes**

FIGURE 3–17 Fermentation process
(Thomas Moore)

2. FERMENTATION—The *bloom*, or white powdery film on the grape skin that gives the grapes their dusty look, contains millions of *wild yeast* cells. The problem with wild yeasts is that the effects of their fermentation are difficult to understand and predict. In most cases, winemakers use *sulfur dioxide* to destroy the wild yeasts (and, in the process, also kill bacteria and mold) so that the wild yeasts cannot interfere with the *cultured yeasts* which are universally chosen because they are more predictable and understood.

Some winemaking purists produce wine with wild yeasts because they believe that wild yeasts are indigenous to the origin of the grape's vineyard and winery. They believe that natural yeasts are an essential aspect to the terroir, as they provide a wine with personality derived from a specific place.

The diagram in Figure 3–17 illustrates the fermentation process.

Yeast is eventually added to the grape must, where it gradually breaks down the sugar into carbon dioxide, alcohol, and heat. The alcohol will be in the flavor or personality of the grape used. As the grape juice (or must) is fermenting and converting into wine, the carbon dioxide is allowed to escape (except in the case of sparkling wine) and the release of heat is controlled through refrigeration.

The level of alcohol produced during fermentation depends primarily on the sugar content of the grapes and the point at which the winemaker decides to stop fermentation. In most situations, the winemaker allows the yeast to consume all or most of the grape sugar (particularly for red wine), yielding a dry wine with higher alcohol. If the winemaker halts fermentation prior to the yeast consuming all or most of the sugar, then unfermented sugar known as *residual sugar* or RS will remain and leave a sweet wine with lower alcohol.

The amount of alcohol produced from fermentation depends largely on the amount of sugar that is available for yeast consumption. Of course, there are ways to manipulate this equation, but it is not always legal or advantageous to participate in them.

Fermentation takes place in large containers called *vats*. For red wines, the skins are present; white wines are fermented without the skins; and for rosés, the skins are left on for a portion of the time. This is referred to as *maceration* or juice and skin contact time.

SACCHAROMYCES CEREVISIAE

(sack-row-MY-ceese)

This is the common and famous yeast used in the production of various wines and beers, with more than 700 catalogued strains. Wild yeast was beginning to be understood in the 1850s through the work of Louis Pasteur. Currently, winemakers can purchase specific strains of cultured yeasts that are suited for particular tasks. Some strains can ferment high amounts of grape sugar, while others can highlight specific flavor profiles.

Climate's Effects on Winemaking Methods   In warm-to-hot climates, winemakers are sometimes allowed to add acid in a process known as *acidification* to make up for what was lost throughout the long growing season.

In cool climates, winemakers are sometimes allowed to add sugar in a process known as *chaptalization* to make up for the lack of sugar developed throughout the short growing season.

White Wine Fermentation   As the grapes are pressed, the clear juice is fermented on its own without skins. This is not only because the skins are not needed for color, but also because any potential tannin extracted from skins may detract from the subtle flavor nuances associated with a white wine.

Because of the heat produced during fermentation, most delicate white wines are fermented in stainless steel or temperature-controlled vats to preserve the delicate fruit aromatics. Control of temperature during fermentation is critical: Too high of a temperature will burn out any fruit aromas and flavors. If the wine is fermented at too low of a temperature, not enough alcohol will be created.

White wine is usually fermented and maintained within a range of 45 to 70°F. Because of the low temperature, the fermentation time for white wine often takes several weeks. During this process or after it has been completed, the wine is often held in stainless steel vats or wood barrels for a few months.

Red Wine Fermentation   When the grapes are crushed, the juice is allowed to remain in contact, or macerate, with the skins and seeds for a period during red or rosé wine fermentation. The longer the maceration period, the more certain it is that components such as tannin, color, and aromas/flavors will be extracted from the skins. To ferment red wine, the temperature of the must is brought between 70 to 90°F. The fermentation time for red wines is somewhere between several days to a few weeks. For most fuller-bodied red wines, this process takes about four weeks for extended maceration in order to extract more color, flavor, and tannin.

The Relation of Skins to Juice and Tannin

Some grape varietals such as Cabernet Sauvignon have small berries with a larger proportion of skin and seeds compared with pulp. The thicker skins not only minimize the evaporation of water from inside the grape during hot weather, but also give the wine its characteristic deep color. The skin and seeds (possibly along with the stems) contribute to tannin that acts as a natural preservative, but also adds a desired dryness to wine. In comparison, grapes such as Pinot Noir have thin skins and tend to produce lighter-colored wine.

The amount of tannin varies significantly within wine. Tannin levels depend on many factors: grape variety, growing season, winemaking methods, and so on. Tannins can add a desirable, tactile, dry complexity to the wine. It is important that winemakers not add too much (by longer extraction time or by too many stems or seeds), because excess tannin (in addition to being underripe phenolics) will give an undesirable astringent quality to the finished wine.

The thin skins also allow more evaporation from within the grapes, which makes Pinot Noir more difficult to grow successfully in hot climates. Wines made from thin-skinned grapes also tend to have less color pigment, low tannin, and less structure compared with those made from thicker-skinned varieties.

Other Fermentation Techniques

Carbonic Fermentation   *Carbonic fermentation,* also called "whole-berry fermentation," is a popular technique for producing light, fruity, red wines. The purpose is to make a red wine that accentuates its youthful fruitiness and avoids excessive, unwanted tannin.

METHODS OF CAP MANAGEMENT

Since the red wine grape juice is allowed to ferment with the grape skins, carbon dioxide produced during fermentation pushes a thick layer of the purple skins, stems, and seeds to the surface of the fermenting vessel, forming a *cap*. It is necessary to submerge the cap within the must; otherwise, it will be exposed to oxygen and subject to bacterial growth. As the cap is pushed back into the must, greater color and flavor extraction occur.

1. **Punching Down**—The gentle process of pushing the cap down into the wine as it is fermenting is common in Burgundy, France. This method is used to minimize air contact and allow for minimal extract of excessive tannins.
2. **Pumping Over**—The aggressive process of pumping and circulating the juice (with a giant hose) over the cap during fermentation is commonly used in Bordeaux in order to extract maximum color, juice, and tannin from skins.
3. **Rotary Fermenters** — A large mechanical device periodically rotates the juice and skin in order to maintain contact between them. The process is similar to that of a cement mixer.

REASONS FOR BLENDING

✓ Adjust or fine-tune the aromas/flavors.
✓ Adjust the components of acid, tannin, alcohol, or fruit.
✓ Adjust the color.
✓ Adjust the price.
✓ Add greater dimension or complexity.

Carbonic maceration is a quick process that takes about one to two weeks and produces a simple, one-dimensional type of wine. This fermentation technique is indigenous to the Beaujolais subregion of Burgundy, France.

Barrel Fermentation   *Barrel fermentation* means that the unfermented grape juice was converted to wine in wood barrels. The term typically applies only to white wine.

Micro-Oxygenation   *Micro-oxygenation* is a winemaking technique that introduces small amounts of controlled oxygen into the barrels of a red wine as it ages. This method produces a young red wine that tastes older than it is, by softening tannins and speeding the aging process.

3. *MALOLACTIC FERMENTATION*

Also called "secondary fermentation"   Winemakers sometimes use a secondary technique based on a biochemical reaction. Malolactic fermentation (ML) transforms crisp, sharp *malic acid* into softer, creamier *lactic acid*. The result is a reduction of tartness and added buttery aromas and flavors, along with added texture. The release of the butter-like flavor derives from a natural chemical known as *diacetyl* (die-ASS-ih-tahl).

This effect of ML is similar to the difference between the taste of a tart Granny Smith apple, which contains malic acid, and the taste of creamy milk, which contains lactic acid. The winemaker may perform malolactic fermentation on all of the wine or on only a portion, depending on how much acid is desired to be converted.

Malolactic fermentation is applied to most red wines and a select few white wines. For white wine, the winemaker typically uses this process for Chardonnay, particularly from California and Australia, and generally, in smaller doses throughout the rest of the world.

4. *BLENDING*—Blending can take place during various stages of the winemaking process. In some cases, it can take place immediately after fermentation or just before clarification. It truly depends on the training and vision of the winemaker.

Some of the most famous wines in the world consist of a blend of complementary grape varietals. For example, Champagne contains a combination of Pinot Noir, Chardonnay, and Pinot Meunier. Bordeaux is another classic blended wine that consists of varying quantities of Cabernet Sauvignon, Merlot, Cabernet Franc, and others. A wine blended from several grapes may often be more complex than one which is not. For example, a blend of Cabernet Sauvignon and Merlot is often more complex than a wine that is solely 100% Cabernet Sauvignon. This is not to say that a predominant single varietal wine is inferior to a blended wine, some grape varieties have the ability to provide enough dimension (such as Pinot Noir or Riesling) on their own without the assistance of other grapes. Ultimately, blending is a matter of the style of wine that is desired and the grapes that typically make that style.

There are different methods and reasons for blending wine, depending on the winemaker's vision of the finished product.

To achieve these objectives, it is possible to blend several complementary grapes from the same or different appellations or to blend the same grape from different appellations. For example, a winemaker may blend 75% of a Cabernet Sauvignon grape with 25% of a Merlot grape. This approach can adjust or fine-tune components and add complexity or dimension to the wine.

Some wines are blended for the purpose of maintaining a certain cost parameter, by incorporating into the blend a small percentage of either an inexpensive grape or the same grape that has been harvested from a less desirable appellation. An example is blending 85% of the Chardonnay grape from Russian River with 15% of the Chardonnay from the larger Sonoma County. This approach allows the winemaker to incorporate grapes from locations where the cost of land (ultimately, the cost of the grape) is less expensive.

Other wines may skip the blending process; it depends on the style chosen by the winemaker. In some cases, laws or tradition prohibit the blending of different grapes or grapes from different locations.

Natural Grape Partnerships   Some grapes are considered natural or compatible partners. The grapes of origin of wines are not always obvious when grapes are blended together, particularly if a wine is dominant with one varietal and has a tiny percentage of others.

Within each box in the following is a list of grape varietals that are commonly blended together in various parts of the world:

COMMON BLENDING PARTNERS	
Cabernet Sauvignon and Merlot	Syrah and Grenache
Sauvignon Blanc and Semillon	Shiraz and Cabernet Sauvignon
Chardonnay and Pinot Blanc	Sangiovese and Merlot or Cabernet Sauvignon

5. *AGING*—The aging process significantly influences the style and body of the wine. Think of the aging process as if the wine is going to etiquette school to lose its rough edges. The winemaker's vision of the finished wine is the determining factor as to whether and, if so, how it will be aged.

The aging process can be conducted in one of two ways: "*oxidative* or *reductive*". If the wine is aged by an oxidative technique, then it is wood aged. If the wine is aged by a reductive approach, then the wine is aged (or, more accurately, preserved) in stainless steel.

Stainless Steel   *Stainless steel tanks* are used primarily for white aromatic wines whose primary flavors and crisp acidity need to be preserved. Stainless steel doesn't truly age the wine; rather, it preserves the wine and prevents the passage of oxygen that would otherwise alter the wine's personality. The preserving process allows the wine's flavors to integrate fully before the wine is bottled. Most tanks are double-jacketed, circulating cold water between the inner and outer walls in order to adjust and maintain the temperature throughout fermentation and the aging process.

Wood Barrels   *Wood barrels,* a centuries-old tradition, are vessels used to store and age most red wines and many full-bodied white wines. The industy standard is to use French or American oak as the preferred wood. Oak from other places, such as Slovenian oak, is sometimes still used. In the past, different wine regions have used different kinds of wood, such as mahogany, chestnut, and pine. For the most part, use of these wood barrels have been disregarded over time due to their distinguishable flavors overpowering the aromas and flavors of the wine. Figure 3–18 shows some wood barrels used to age wine.

A *cooper* is someone who constructs the barrels—an age-old profession. The barrels are made from various types and sizes of wood and various levels of *toast* (the effect of exposure of the wood to varying degrees of fire and varying lengths of time during which the fire burned). *Barrel aging* is the process of holding the wine in wood barrels for a maturation period of months to years, whereby various components present in the wine slowly combine to create complexity and finesse.

The Barrel's Influence on Wine Personality   A wood (typically oak) barrel's porous nature allows for the slow passage of oxygen and a small amount of evaporation, which is a beneficial interaction between the wine and the air. Wood barrels contribute their own flavor of complex chemical compounds, each of which lends its own flavor to wine.

FIGURE 3–18 Wood barrels called "pièces" in Champagne
(Collection CIVC.
Photographer: CORNU Alain)

Typical flavor characters are in the category of *bakeshop/coffee shop* (coffee, chocolate, caramel, vanilla, almond, and toasted nut), *cigar shop* (tea and tobacco), and *bakeshop spice* (nutmeg, cinnamon, and allspice).

The Barrel's Influence on a Wine's Personality   Wood can soften a wine's texture, alter the wine's color (from more golden-yellow, depending on the length of aging), and assist in creating a more complex beverage.

Factors that affect the ability of barrels to impart flavor and that influence the extent of the aging process include (1) type of wood (2) the size of the barrel, (3) age of the barrel, (4) the level of toast, and (5) the aging time.

Type of Wood   Winemakers select wood for their wine barrels from different forests, for the effect on the finished wine. American and French oak are the standards. Barrels made from American oak typically cost less than half the price of French oak barrels. The most prestigious and expensive barrels derive from white oak trees that come from several French forests and that are hundreds of years old, such as *Limousin* (lee-moo-ZAHN) and others whose wood has distinctive characteristics.

The type of wood can have a dramatic influence on the wine through the aging process. American oak has bigger grains that allow greater passage of oxygen and so contributes stronger, more significant aromas and flavors. French oak has smaller grains to permit less flow of oxygen and thus maintains more subtle aromas and flavors than American oak.

Typical Barrel Size   The size of the barrel influences the flavor of the wine as well. A smaller barrel contributes stronger and faster flavor because more wine is in contact with greater surface area. The typical wine barrel holds 225 liters (almost 60 U.S. gallons) and is commonly called a *barrique* (ba-REEK) or the *piece* (pee-YESS). One wine barrel can yield roughly 20 cases of wine. Between wine regions, barrel names and capacities will vary. Other barrel sizes include the *butt,* which is an English term for Spanish cooperage that consists of 151 U.S. gallons.

Age of the Barrel   The flavor distinction and prominence of wood tannin is most pronounced in new, unused barrels and becomes less significant with older barrels that have been previously used. By the time a barrel is about five years old, it is virtually neutral as far as its influence on the taste of the wine. Every time that a barrel is reused (for each yearly vintage), it contributes less flavor and fewer components and becomes more of a holding vessel rather than a contributor to the quality of the wine. A barrel can be thought of as a tea bag. The first use of a tea bag yields the most flavor and components. It is possible to reuse the tea bag and still extract benefits, but the effects are less intense and become somewhat diluted.

Level of Toast   The amount or degree of toast (or seasoning, as it's sometimes called) in the barrel has an affect on the flavor profile of the aging wine. Barrels can be ordered with varying levels of toast: Light toast contributes subtle aromas and flavors to the wine, and medium toast and heavy toast both contribute greater intensity of aromas and flavors to the wine. The toast decision will be made on the basis of the variety of grape to be used and the style of wine to be produced.

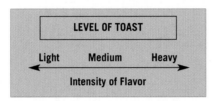

Length of Aging   Wines are aged anywhere from a few months, to several years in cases where small amounts of evaporation occur through the aging process. Lengthy aging assists to soften harsh tannins and allow desirable flavors to develop. As red wine ages, its tannins and color compounds *polymerize* (PUH-lym-err-ize), forming a larger molecule until they eventually fall out of the suspended wine solution, becoming sediment in the bottom of the barrel.

Shortcuts have been created to gain the benefits of oak flavor without actually going through the time or expense of traditional oak barrel aging. Such methods include using oak chips or oak shavings in a large "tea bag" placed inside stainless steel tanks or flavorless barriques. Using barrels in winemaking (though not appropriate for all grapes) can be compared with a chef's use of salt and pepper to enhance and bring out the natural flavors of a food. Without the seasonings, the dish may be bland, but the correct amount adds a certain something to the food. With the appropriate use and application of barrel aging, a wine can be enhanced to better showcase itself.

Sur Lie Aging   The French term *sur lie* (soor-LEE) *aging* refers to the process of aging the wine *on the lees*. Lees are the yeast deposits that add a toasty quality, making the wine rich, smooth, and complex.

Examples of Typical Unoaked and/or Lightly Oak Aged and Oaked Wines

COMMON UNOAKED LIGHTLY OAKED AND OAKED WINES		
	WHITE WINE	**RED WINE**
Stainless Steel and/or Lightly Oak Aged	Riesling, Chardonnay (from Chablis, New Zealand), Sauvignon Blanc, Pinot Grigio, Gewürztraminer, Grüner Veltliner, Pinot Blanc	Gamay, Dolcetto, Rioja (Joven or Crianza), Barbera, Pinot Noir, Cabernet Franc
Oak Aged	Pinot Gris (Oregon or California), Chardonnay, Fume Blanc, Viognier	Shiraz, Syrah, Syrah blends, Merlot, Cabernet Sauvignon, Nebbiolo, Rioja (Reserva and Gran Reserva)

6. *CLARIFICATION*—Clarification is the process of removing undesirable particles and making a wine more stable. The methods are similar for both red and white wine; however, the particles may be more obvious in a white wine because of its lack of color pigment as associated with a red wine. After fermentation is complete, new wines appear cloudy, so the wines are allowed to rest. Over time, residues settle out and the wines will become more stable. All methods of clarification remove undesirable particles from wine and assist with stabilization (preventing the chance for refermentation) until the bottle is purchased and opened by the consumer.

Clarification is a major concern because of the potential risk of stripping the wine of desirable aromas, flavors, body, color, and other components. Therefore, most quality-oriented winemakers opt for the softest, gentlest method and least amount of clarification. At some point during this stage—and truly, all throughout the winemaking process—sulfites are added to stop oxidation (browning) of the wine in order to preserve the wine during the aging process and during distribution.

The clarification process can be carried out by several different methods and, possibly, in combination with one another, depending on the grapes or the traditions associated with a particular winemaking region. The five common methods are *racking, cold stabilization, centrifuge, fining,* and *filtering.*

1. Racking   The racking method is considered one of the gentlest methods for limiting the loss of desirable components in the wine. Racking involves periodically draining the sediment, or dead yeast cells, called *lees,* by transferring the wine from one container to another, leaving sediment behind in the original container. Racking is a natural method because it relies on gravity to pull the unwanted particles to the bottom of the original container. Racking can be conducted once or several times before bottling, for greater clarification.

2. Cold Stabilization   This clarification process removes excess tartaric acid that would otherwise later form potassium *bitartrate crystals,* or *tartrates.* Tartrates have the appearance of shards of glass, but are completely safe and edible. Although a common practice is to remove this type of sediment, not all producers do so, and it seems more common in producers who believe in a "hands-off" type winemaking philosophy. Cold stabilization is accomplished through chilling a wine down to 40°F, causing the tartaric acid to crystallize, which allows the wine to then be racked, leaving the crystals behind.

3. Centrifuge   The wine is spun at very high speeds to pull out the impurities by centrifugal force.

4. Fining   This is a clarification method that incorporates a *fining agent* which forms a chemical bond with the undesirable particles, causing them to precipitate out to the bottom of the vessel. Then the wine is racked, leaving the particles behind in the original container. Some fining agents can include egg whites, blood, bentonite clay, bull's blood, gelatin, and isinglass (an extract from fish bladders). In addition to clarification, this process can soften harsh astringent tannins and allow desirable flavors to develop.

5. Filtering   This method passes the wine through a fine mesh filter with small holes that are smaller than the particles to be removed. Thus, the particles are collected and disposed of.

6. Bottling   Small quantities of sulfur dioxide (SO_2) are added to the bottle in order to limit oxidation and inhibit any further yeast activity. Ascorbic acid and antioxidants may be added as well.

Freshly bottled wines are usually held in stock for a few weeks to recover from *bottle shock,* a condition that causes a temporary loss of delicate aromatics due to the excessive agitation during the bottling process. The bottle will be sealed with either a cork or screw cap to prevent any oxygen from entering and destroying the wine.

If desired, the wine will be bottle-aged in order to integrate the wine components and add extra complexity. The fruit characteristics in white table wine tend to slowly develop into more complex characteristics (often described as "toasty" or "kerosene–like") with time in the bottle. These changes may take between six months and five years to become noticeable. In addition to influencing flavor changes, bottle aging has a softening and mellowing effect on the wine and integrates the oak and fruit flavors if the wine has been matured in barrels. A quality red wine will almost certainly be aged in the bottle before being released for sale.

Sulfur Dioxide   Sulfur is a compound found within most bottles of wine. It is created naturally in small quantities during the fermentation process, and the winemaker may also add it throughout the winemaking process.

Sulfur's antimicrobial and antioxidant properties assist in preventing a wine from refermenting within a bottle and prohibit oxygen exposure throughout the winemaking and bottling processes.

Producers are required to write "Contains Sulfites" (meaning sulfur dioxide) on the label of every bottle of wine in the United States if it contains 10 parts per million or more. Almost every bottle will contain this amount, whether the winemaker has added sulfur or not, because 10–20 parts per million may occur naturally. Levels of sulfur can range from 100 to 150 parts per million, but the U.S. allowable maximum is 350 within a single bottle of wine.

VITICULTURE AND ENOLOGY

NAME: _____ Score out of 20 points_____.

Use these questions to test your knowledge and understanding of the concepts presented in the chapter.

I. MULTIPLE CHOICE: Select the best possible answer from the options available.

1. Enology is the science of

    a. making wine.

    b. growing grapes.

    c. growing wine.

    d. making oak barrels.

2. The personality of a wine is *initially* affected by

    a. the type of grape.

    b. the winemaking techniques.

    c. whether the wine had malolactic fermentation or not.

    d. the amount of oak aging.

3. The major grapevine species that produces world-class quality wine grapes is

    a. Vitis labrusca.

    b. Vitis rotunda.

    c. Vitis vinisca.

    d. Vitis vinifera.

4. Chaptalization is the process of adding

    a. sugar to the finished wine.

    b. sugar to the grape juice prior to and/or during fermentation.

    c. acid to the finished wine.

    d. acid to the grape juice.

5. Pruning grapevines can produce

    a. higher quality grapes with higher yield.

    b. higher quality grapes with lower yield.

    c. lower quality grapes with higher yield.

    d. lower quality grapes with higher yield.

6. Grapes are harvested

    a. when the sugar has reached the desirable level.

    b. always in September.

    c. when the grape flavors are present.

    d. when a combination of sugar content and flavor development has reached the desirable level.

7. Large bodies of water (oceans, lakes and rivers) have the ability to moderate climate by

    a. regulating temperature extremes.

    b. regulating rainfall.

    c. regulating soil drainage.

    d. b and c

8. Grapevines grow best between the latitudes of

    a. 20–40 degrees.

    b. 30–60 degrees.

    c. 45–65 degrees.

    d. 30–50 degrees.

9. Terroir refers to

    a. the soil.

    b. the winemaker's influence.

    c. all environmental effects on the vine.

    d. the weather.

10. Viticulture is the science of

    a. making wine.

    b. growing grapes.

    c. growing wine.

    d. making oak barrels.

11. The most commonly used yeast for wine production is

    a. cultured yeast.

    b. wild yeast.

    c. a combination of both.

    d. none of the above.

12. Red wines are fermented with their skins in order to extract

    a. flavor.

    b. color.

    c. tannin.

    d. all of the above.

13. Racking refers to a method of clarification in which the wine is

    a. transferred into a series of new containers, leaving the dead yeast behind.

    b. incorporated with a protein such as egg whites.

    c. put through a centrifuge.

    d. passed through a fine mesh filter.

II. TRUE / FALSE: Circle the best possible answer.

14. A grape's sugar levels are the only factors that determine when the grapes should be harvested. **True / False**

15. Stainless steel aging is conducted in order to impart additional flavors into the wine. **True / False**

16. A winemaker may blend different grapes together for the purpose of reducing cost and increasing complexity. **True / False**

17. Malolactic fermentation is performed on most white wines when crisp fruit acids want to be preserved. **True / False**

18. The amount of sugar present in the grape juice can have an influence on the amount of alcohol that is produced. **True / False**

19. If fermentation is stopped before the yeast has had a chance to ferment all the sugar, the wine will have some sweetness. **True / False**

III. SHORT-ANSWER ESSAY / DISCUSSION QUESTION: Use a separate sheet of paper if necessary.

20. What are two types of aging? What does each do to the finished wine?

Unit 2
WINE AND FOOD COMPATIBILITY

"Beauty of whatever kind, in its supreme development, invariably excites the sensitive soul to tears."

—*Edgar Allan Poe*

4

Performance Factors of Grape Varietals

"Performance factors" identify the distinguishable defining elements of color, aroma, flavor, body, style, and common locations associated with particular grape types produced around the world by varying viticulture and winemaking techniques.

LEARNING OBJECTIVES

Upon completion of this chapter, the learner will be able to:

- Understand the effects of how viticulture and enology and age can influence color, aroma, flavor, style, and body of a wine.
- Explore the performance factors (aromas, flavors, styles, and body) of the Big Six grape varietals and other common wine grapes.
- Realize the significant growing locations of the Big Six grape varietals and other common wine grapes.
- Discover wine pairing strategies and potential food partners of the Big Six grape varietals and other common wine grapes.
- Recognize wine styles and identify potential food pairings on the basis of classification.

PERFORMANCE FACTORS OF GRAPE VARIETALS

This chapter explores the more popular and significant grape varietals and the related *performance factors* associated with each one. Performance factors are a combination of aspects (color, aroma, flavor, acid, alcohol, tannin, body level, and so on) that cumulatively create the distinctive personality of a particular grape varietal. They can be used to identify the distinguishable defining elements linked with a particular grape as it has been produced around the world by varying viticulture and winemaking techniques. Once the performance factors are understood, it is then possible to seek out different producers, vintages, and regions, just as it is possible to seek out a new genre in art, film, or music. Understanding the performance factors of each grape and the variations they can produce can be an effective means of developing the palate and gaining a sense of the distinctive styles between the grape varietals as they are produced in different places around the world.

The Big Six grapes are arguably the most noble, as they are adaptable and produced around the world. Riesling, Sauvignon Blanc, Chardonnay, Pinot Noir, Merlot, and Cabernet Sauvignon are examined in detail here. Other notable grapes are discussed in lesser detail, not because they are any less important, but because they are outside the scope of this textbook. Figure 4–1 shows the famed Pinot Noir grape varietal.

Understanding the performance factors of each grape makes it easier to understand suitable pairings with food, as identified by the detailed pairing strategies offered here for each of the Big Six grapes. In this chapter, there are terms and concepts that may be foreign to some readers. The reader is strongly encouraged to reference the glossary in the back of the book A until he or she reaches those chapters in which the concepts are expanded upon.

FIGURE 4–1 Close-up of Pinot Noir grapes

(Collection CIVC. Photographer: CORNU Alain)

WHITE WINE GRAPE VARIETALS

White wine is made primarily from green and amber-yellow grapes, but can also be made from red, purple, and black grapes.

There are 50 major white-wine grapes grown in the world today, but the three most significant for producing high-quality wine are Riesling, Sauvignon Blanc, and Chardonnay. Other distinguishable white-wine grapes renowned for producing great wine in select locations include Albariño, Chenin Blanc, Gewürztraminer, Grüner Veltliner, Muscat, Pinot Blanc, Pinot Gris/Grigio, Sémillon, and Viognier.

The Colors Progression of White Wine

As white wines age, many factors affect their color progression. They can range from a slight green tint, straw yellow, golden yellow, and brown amber. This progression of a wine's color is very similar to a banana ripening from green to brown as sugars are converted.

Some factors that influence color are (1) the type of grape—some grapes contribute greater color just because smaller berries have greater skin-to-juice ratios, yielding greater color pigment; (2) oak aging, which can heighten the color; (3) residual sugar, which also may provide heightened color; (4) the age of the wine, which can enhance the color; and

(5) improper storage conditions (such as exposure to direct light for an excessive period), which, too, may heighten the color).

As whites wines mature, they gain color. However, as identified in the last paragraph there are numerous other variables that can also influence color:

- **GREEN TINT**—In young fruity wines about six months to one year from harvest, green tint is possible evidence of a cool climate and stainless steel aging.
- **STRAW YELLOW**—In the majority of white wines one to three years from harvest, this color is possible evidence of a cool climate and stainless steel aging or the subtle use of oak aging.
- **GOLDEN YELLOW**—In mature white wine two to five years from harvest, the golden yellow color is possible evidence of a warm climate, oak aging, or considerable residual sugar.
- **BROWN AMBER**—This color may indicate that the wine is past its useful life and likely to be oxidized.

Once a white wine has progressed to a brown amber color, the wine is generally considered undrinkable. Some white wines might progress to this color somewhat rapidly (within a few years); others may take as long as 20 years. The goal in consuming wine is to drink it when it is at its peak; for most wines, that means within months to a few years of its vintage date.

Aromas and Flavors of White Wine

Aroma and flavor categories are a means to create an association with a wine's smells and tastes and link it to memory. Associations can be used as memory "anchors" the same way that a ship or boat uses an anchor in the ocean to provide stability and foundation. Anchors help individuals remember the personality of a wine. There are six broad white-wine aroma/flavor categories and several smaller defined aromas/flavors. Once the general smell has been identified (which is often the easier aroma to identify), the specific, more defined aromas (which tend to be more difficult to identify) can be pinpointed. In some cases, it is possible to make an association between an aroma and flavor of a wine and an everyday type of item. For example, some Sauvignon Blancs have aromas and flavors that may be associated with hay, grass, herbs, or even cat urine (actually an ammonium smell associated with underripe grapes that have been shielded from the sun).

Climatic Influence

Hotter/Warmer Climates—In warm-to-hot climates, grapes are often more ripe and contain greater sugar, yielding a wine with a more pronounced deep-yellow color, rich overripe tropical fruit aromas, and flavors with lower acid. Because of the high sugar content, these wines provide more food for the yeast consumption and create greater levels of alcohol content. The increased alcohol may detract from the enjoyment of some wine consumers, but it replaces a somewhat desirable dimension that was lost with the acidity.

Cooler/Warmer Climates—In cool-to-warm climates, grapes are often less consistently ripe and contain less sugar, yielding a grape with less color pigment and therefore a wine with a lighter-yellow color. The wines also maintain lighter, more subtle aromas and flavors of citrus, tree fruit, vegetables, herbs, and minerals. Because of the lower sugar content, these wines provide less food for yeast consumption, resulting in a lower alcohol content. The cooler climate acts to preserve acidity and youthfulness; therefore, the wines are typically left un-oaked by aging in stainless steel for only a short period.

WHITE WINE AROMA/FLAVOR CATEGORIES

Common Aroma/Flavor Families Associated with White Wine

WHITE WINE AROMA/FLAVOR FAMILIES		
GENERAL AROMAS/FLAVORS	SPECIFIC AROMAS/FLAVORS	VERY SPECIFIC AROMAS/FLAVORS
1. FRUIT	Citrus	Lemon, lime, grapefruit, orange, tangerine
	Tree	Apple, pear, peach, apricot, cherry
➝	Berry	Strawberry, blueberry, raspberry, blackberry
	Tropical	Melon, banana, coconut, pineapple, passion fruit, lychee
	Dried	Raisin, figs, apricots
2. BAKESHOP	Nuts	Toasted or untoasted (hazelnuts, walnuts, almonds)
	Sauces	Caramel, vanilla, butterscotch, honey, cream, butter, custard
➝	Spices	Cinnamon, cloves, nutmeg, anise/fennel, ginger, orange peel
	Bread	Yeast, dough, toast, biscuit
3. MINERAL/ CHEMICAL	Mineral	Chalk, flint
➝	Chemical	Petroleum, ammonia, steel
4. Barnyard/ Herbaceous	Barnyard	Grass, hay, straw
➝	Herb Garden	Tomato vine, dill, basil, chives, Earl Grey tea
5. FLORAL	Floral	Rosé, peonies, orange blossom, honeysuckle, violets
6. VEGETABLES	Vegetables	Asparagus, cucumber, bell pepper, olives

THE BODY OF A WHITE WINE

A wine's *body* refers to how the wine feels in terms of weight or viscosity inside the mouth. White wine can range from light to medium to full bodied. Certainly, there are levels in between that a taster may describe by saying, "I give this wine a light body (but on the high side)" or "I give this wine a medium body (but on the low side)." However, describing a wine's body more precisely than low, medium, or full may only confuse the novice wine consumer.

An effective analogy is to think of the body of wine in terms of the weight or mouth feel of milk. For example, skim milk can be compared to a light-bodied wine, 2% milk to a medium-bodied wine, and whole milk to a full-bodied wine.

Some factors that can influence a white wine's body are as follows: (1) The size of the berries can alter the impact of acid, tannin, and overall extract. Large berries have more juice and less skin; smaller berries have less juice and more skin. (2) The level of alcohol affects body in that higher alcohol content can provide more body, while lower alcohol content can provide a lighter body. (3) Residual sugar yields a fuller mouth feel, while a wine that has been fermented dry can yield a lighter body. (4) *Extract* is a term used to indicate the level of concentration of several components (such as acid, alcohol, and fruit concentration) working together to create an impression of greater concentration. (5) Oak aging can influence body partly through the amount of evaporation of water content of the wine during the barrel aging process. Also, the addition of flavors associated with wood aging may add to the intensity of the wine.

Contributors to a White Wine's Body

CONTRIBUTORS TO A WHITE WINE'S BODY		
VARIABLES	LIGHTER BODY	FULLER BODY
Size of Berries	Larger berries with less skin-to-juice ratio	Smaller berries with greater skin-to-juice ratio
Level of Alcohol	11% or less	13% or more; sometimes as high as 14%
Dryness/Sweetness	Fermented dry	Fermented with allowing some varying amount of residual sugar.
Extract (concentration of fruit and other components suspended within the wine)	Lower	Higher
Oak Aging	None to light	Medium to heavy

♦ Generally, a fuller bodied wine is 13% alcohol or above, and a lighter bodied wine is low in alcohol, at 11% or below.

♦ Tannin is present in all wines, but is thought to be perceptible only in red wine.

Although there are many exceptions, understanding the relative weights and bodies of some common wines provides a good foundational beginning. On occasion, some wines can overlap in weight and body, depending on country or region of origin, or stylistic differences of producers. For example, Chardonnay can often be described as a light- to medium-bodied wine when it is produced in Chablis. In some cases, because of increased alcohol content, malolactic fermentation, sur lie, and oak aging (as with most California versions), Chardonnays become more medium to full bodied.

RIESLING (REEZ-ling)

Riesling is native to Germany, where it is the most significant white wine grape and has been cultivated for hundreds (possibly thousands) of years. Though often consumed young, Riesling's substantial acidity, aromatic aromas, and concentration of flavors are suitable for extended aging, particularly of wines that have a high sugar content. It prefers to be a "stand-alone" varietal, as it is very rarely blended with other grapes. Riesling produces a range of wines from dry to sweet and from light- to full-body, largely dependent on the amount of residual sugar and tradition associated with area of production. Figure 4–2 shows the Riesling grape varietal.

Over the years, Riesling has become unfashionable because of the often oversweet versions with inadequate levels of acid created by some non-quality-oriented winemakers.

FIGURE 4–2 Close-up of Riesling grapes

(Ian O'Leary © Dorling Kindersley)

This has led many serious wine drinkers to consider that Riesling is reserved for the novice wine drinker. Riesling may be experiencing a bit of a renaissance, as producers are providing drier or sweeter options that balance the components that Riesling has to offer.

Aromas/Flavors

Riesling is a highly aromatic grape variety with concentrated aromas and flavors. Listed are some frequent (though not exclusive) aromas and flavors associated with Riesling:

- **Fruit**—tree fruit (peach, apricot), tropical fruit (pineapple), dried fruit (raisin)
- **Citrus**—grapefruit, lemon, lime, orange
- **Bakeshop Sauces**—honey
- **Mineral**—petroleum, flint, steel

The petroleum (or rubber band) aroma/flavor is associated less often with youthful wines and becomes more predominant with aged ones.

Body/Style

Rieslings can range from dry, to sweet and light, to full bodied, largely depending on the level of residual sugar left over in the wine after fermentation. Well-made Rieslings are high in tartaric and malic acids, which are necessary (although sometimes going unnoticed) to balance the wine's varying levels of sugar content and intense fruit aromatics. The acid also acts as a preservative for long aging capabilities. Rieslings are often left un-oaked (or at minimum, stored in old oaked barrels) in order to maintain the concentrated aromatic fruit and high acidity levels.

Riesling can often be seen in two differing styles. Winemakers either will ferment the wine dry, achieving higher alcohol levels, as in Alsace, France, or will leave considerable residual sugar (RS) through partial fermentation, leaving the wine with varying levels of sweetness, as in many German styles. The density and body increase with greater levels of sweetness, providing an effective pairing with more robust, fatty food items. Low-alcohol sweeter versions hover near 11% alcohol or less, and high-alcohol drier versions can be found at 12% or higher.

Riesling is also known for producing some of the world's most celebrated dessert wines. These wines can be made in a combination of methods. Three of the most well known dessert wines are *Late Harvest* (the grapes remain on the vine and gain additional sugar content), *Rot wine* (the grapes are attacked by a friendly fungus that concentrates the aromas, flavors, and sugar and causes evaporation), and *Ice wine* (where the grapes are frozen on the vine in order to extract water content). ♦ Riesling is discussed in greater detail in Chapter 10, "Other Old World Wine Countries," and in Chapter 13, "Nectar: Dessert Wines."

Significant Locations

Riesling is a late-ripening varietal which tends to prefer cooler climates that allow longer ripening periods.

Rieslings are capable of performing well in various types of soil, but some of the best examples of quality Riesling grapes derive from slate- or clay-based soils.

- **OLD WORLD**—Riesling wines come from Germany (Mosel and Rhingau), France (Alsace), Austria (Wachau), and Italy (Alto Adige, Friuli).
- **NEW WORLD**—Riesling wines also come from Washington (Columbia Valley), California (Central Coast), Australia (Clare and Eden Valleys), New Zealand (Marlborough, Martinborough, Nelson, Wairarapa), New York (Finger Lakes), and Canada (Niagara).

STYLE #1: German Style—German-style Rieslings have good concentration of fruit aromas and flavors, with some level of residual sugar. The sweetness creates a somewhat weighty palate and, coupled with lower alcohol (11% or less), allows the wine to be fairly food friendly.

Pairing Strategies

1. Riesling can pair well with salty, spicy, fatty, smoky, and sweet food items.
2. Riesling's varying level of residual sugar allows it to work well with cuisines that have some spicy or salty components, such as Asian food, including Chinese, Thai, and Japanese food.
3. Riesling's intense concentration of aromas and flavors increase the density of the wine, which allows it to work with fatty poultry (duck, goose), pork (pork loin, barbecued ribs), and game birds (quail).
4. Rieslings can couple with several dessert options such as fruit-based dishes (fruit tart, cobbler, pie, crisps, fruit mousse cake), chocolate-based desserts (white chocolate and varying types of nuts), pastry-based desserts (blueberry muffins, cranberry orange muffins, pineapple upside-down cake).
5. Rieslings that have considerable sweetness and density (such as German Auslese) work well with blue-vein cheese (Bleu, Gorgonzola, Stilton).

STYLE #2: Alsatian Style—These Rieslings also have a good concentration of fruit aromas and flavors and from having been fermented more fully, the resulting wine is drier and leaner with higher levels of alcohol (12% or higher). Thus, they work well with more delicate, lighter, and simpler dishes.

Pairing Strategies

1. Riesling can work well with lighter seafood preparations such as sushi and steamed, poached, or sautéed lean and fatty fish.
2. Riesling can pair with leaner poultry and pork that have been prepared by light to medium cooking methods.
3. This style of Riesling has substantial and detectable acidity that works well with food items (as mentioned previously) that are served with béchamel, hollandaise, and cream-based sauces.
4. Riesling pairs well with fresh/soft cheeses (goat, feta, and Neufchatel cheese).

FIGURE 4–3 Close-up of Sauvignon Blanc grapes
(Wines of Argentina)

SAUVIGNON BLANC (SOH-vihn-YOHN BLAHNK)

Sauvignon Blanc is native to France and is found widely throughout the wine world. Sauvignon Blanc is one of the most versatile grapes and is known for producing food-friendly wines. This grape expresses its personality most effectively when aged in stainless steel or when a subtle use of oak has been used for aging. Sauvignon Blanc goes by various other names when found around the world. It is referred to as *Blanc Fumé* (few-MAY) in some areas of the Loire Valley, or it may be named after one of its two famous appellations within the Loire Valley: *Sancerre* (sahn-SEHR) and *Pouilly Fumé* (poo-YEE few-MAY). Figure 4–3 shows the Sauvignon Blanc grape varietal.

Oak aging can also be applied successfully to add an alternative dimension, such as in Bordeaux and California. Back in the 1980s, Robert Mondavi called his Sauvignon Blanc *Fumé Blanc* ("Fumé" is French for smoked) because he aged it in wood that would yield a smoky aroma to the wine. In the Loire Valley, the wines have a smokiness that comes from the minerality in the soil. In California, the wine may be called Fumé Blanc (particularly if it has been aged in oak); it is also known as white Bordeaux in Bordeaux, France.

Aromas/Flavors

Depending on the climate and growing methods, Sauvignon Blanc can range from grassy to tropical. When grapes lack sun exposure or are harvested underripe, aromas and flavors veer toward citrus, herbal and vegetable. If Sauvignon Blanc experiences lower yields and warmer, longer sun exposure, the grape expresses greater ripe fruit and tropical fruit elements.

- **Fruit**—tree fruit (peach, apricot), tropical fruit (gooseberry, pineapple), dried fruit (raisin)
- **Citrus**—grapefruit, lemon, lime
- **Herbs**—dill, cilantro, basil, thyme, fresh-cut grass, tomato vine
- **Vegetables**—bell pepper, jalapeno pepper, asparagus

Body/Style

Sauvignon Blanc is made in a variety of styles and can range from light- to medium-bodied and from dry to sweet. Either way, Sauvignon Blanc is always a crisp, highly acidic wine typically left un-oaked and drunk young to capture its youthful zesty acidity.

In Bordeaux's left bank, in and near the appellation of Sauternes (soh-TERN), the Sauvignon Blanc and Semillon grapes are allowed to obtain the desirable rot, or *Botrytis Cinerea*, producing some of the best sweet wines in the world.

Significant Locations

- **OLD WORLD**—France (Loire Valley and Bordeaux) and Italy (Northeastern) are notable.
- **NEW WORLD**—New Zealand (Marlborough, Martinborough), California (North Coast), Chile (Casablanca Valley), Australia, and South Africa are significant.

STYLE #1: The Loire Style—This style has become very popular as showcased in the Loire Valley and New Zealand, which arguably are now the world's leading producers of excellent Sauvignon Blanc. The Loire style creates a subtle to no oak influence in an effort to capture the pure essence of the grape varietals. These styles tend to be highly acidic and veer toward light- to medium-body. The high levels of acids maintained in this style allow the wine to work with other high-acid foods. Sauvignon Blanc's high acidity acts like a spark plug to the food and amplifies the food's flavors. Within this style, Sauvignon Blanc from Loire Valley and Sauvignon Blanc from New Zealand are actually quite different. Loire Sauvignon Blanc tends to emphasize herbal and vegetal qualities, whereas New Zealand Sauvignon Blancs tend to offer greater ripeness, with red grapefruit and gooseberry aromas and flavors.

Pairing Strategies

1. The dryness and acidity help to accentuate appetizers (artichoke dip, shrimp cocktail, oysters), salads (Caesar, seafood salad, Greek salad, Antipasto), and soups.
2. The light- to medium-body pairs well with similar body levels of protein, such as lean poultry (with or without skin) and seafood (lean to fatty fin fish, seviche, sushi, seafood brochettes).
3. Vegetarian friendly, it can work well with pasta and grains with or without any combination of seafood or poultry, with oil- or cream-based sauces.
4. This style pairs well with fresh/soft cheese (herbed or pepper-crusted goat cheese, feta cheese) and pasta filata cheese (Buffalo Mozzarella and provolone).

STYLE #2: The Bordeaux Style—This Sauvignon Blanc style is often blended with the compatible Semillon grape that adds richness and weight while calming some of the natural acidity. This dry (or even sweet) style has often seen a liberal use of oak aging. The Bordeaux style (often referred to as a white Bordeaux) derives from Bordeaux France, but has been also produced in California and may go by the name *Fumé Blanc*.

Pairing Strategies

1. The added weight of this Bordeaux allows it to work more effectively with cream- or milk-based sauces such as Alfredo or Béchamel sauce.
2. The grapes that produce this style are susceptible to botrytis and can create a sweet, luscious full-bodied dessert wine.
3. Pairs well with soft or rind cheese (Brie and Camembert) and semi-soft cheese (Edam, Gouda).

**CHARDONNAY
(SHAR-dun-nay)**

FIGURE 4–4 Close-up of Chardonnay grapes
(Collection CIVC.
Photographer: CORNU Alain)

Chardonnay is one of the most popular and widely planted grapes in the world. It is extremely adaptable to different climates and winemaking techniques. It has been said that virtually anywhere that there are vineyards, Chardonnay can be found.

Chardonnay is believed to have originated in the *Mâconnaise* (mah-kawn-NEH) region of Burgundy, France, where *Pouillly-Fuisse* (poo-YEE fwee-SAY) is currently produced. Chardonnay is vitally important in Champagne, France, where it is blended with Pinot Noir and Pinot Meunier to make the Champagne quartet. Some Champagne styles are even labelled *Blanc de Blanc* (white from white), where Chardonnay is made as a stand-alone varietal. Figure 4–4 shows the Chardonnay grape varietal.

A California Chardonnay wine was responsible for bringing great fame to California (and overall the new world) when a "Chateau Montelena Chardonnay" won the top place over French counterparts in the famous 1976 Paris wine tasting (discussed in greater detail in Chapter 7, "Wines of the United States and Canada").

Aromas/Flavors

Chardonnay is a fairly neutral grape that is quite adaptable both to its surroundings and to winemaking techniques. It is sometimes thought of as a painter's "blank canvas," as the grape is quite moldable and has the ability to be influenced greatly by the winemaker. The primary flavors include tree and citrus fruit, and in cool climates, mineral. Secondary flavors derived from winemaking techniques are commonly associated with bakeshop-type elements.

- **Fruit**—tree fruit (apple, pear, figs), tropical fruit (pineapple, banana, mango), citrus (lemon)
- **Mineral**—chalky
- **Bakeshop Spice/Sauces**—butter, toast, toasted nuts, caramel, vanilla, butterscotch, and honey

Body/Style

Chardonnay is medium bodied when aged in stainless steel or old oak barrels and full bodied when aged in new oak. Chardonnay grows well in many different regions and can be produced with various winemaking techniques.

Significant Locations

- **OLD WORLD**—Chardonnay is grown and made into wine in France (Burgundy, Champagne, and the un-oaked versions are found primarily in Chablis) or Italy (Alto Adige, Friuli).
- **NEW WORLD**—Chardonnay is also produced in California (Carneros, Russian River, Sonoma Coast, Monterey), Australia, New Zealand, and Chile (Casablanca Valley and Maipó).

STYLE 1: The Chablis Style—The Chablis style is a lighter Chardonnay that has gained renewed interest in the wine world. A classic "Chablis" is a Chardonnay produced in France's Burgundy region within the subregion of Chablis. Countries such as New Zealand and Australia have begun to model some of their Chardonnays in this style. The Chablis style is often left un-oaked or lightly oaked to showcase not only the subtle aromas and flavors of the grape, but also the expression of the type of soil and the high levels of acidity that are present.

Pairing Strategies

1. This version can work well with appetizers, soups, and salads.
2. Lean poultry, seafood (fin fish or shellfish), and pasta dishes prepared with either oil- or cream-based sauces are a good match.
3. The style works well as a vegetarian-friendly wine because of its leanness and ability to pair well with grains, pasta, and vegetables.
4. It pairs well with fresh/soft cheese (goat, feta, and Neufchatel).

STYLE 2: The Burgundian Style—In Burgundy, France oak is used as a seasoning to enhance the Chardonnay grape. California Chardonnay (and, to some degree, Australian versions) is Burgundian style, but with more overt and dominant oak influence. California versions can be tricky to pair because the riper fruit, high alcohol (from the warmer climate) and oak tend to be overpowering elements in the wine. Caution is advised when pairing with spicy foods, as spices can intensify the perception of alcohol.

Pairing Strategies

1. Burgundian style Chardonnays pair well with richer meats such as veal and pork and fatty poultry such as pheasant, hen, duck, and goose.
2. This style works well with richer fish and shellfish such as crustaceans (shrimp, scallops, crab, and lobster) and with fatty and meaty finfish (halibut, sea bass, monkfish, snapper, swordfish, salmon, shark, and tuna).
3. Chardonnay also works with leaner poultry (chicken and turkey), seafood, or pasta that use more robust cooking methods and/or incorporate butter or cream-based sauces.
4. Cream-based soups and chowders as well as dairy-based salad dressings go well with this style.
5. This wine pairs well with richer soft ripened or rind cheese (Brie, Camembert), fresh/soft cheese (feta or cream cheese), and semi-soft cheese (Edam, Gouda).

Other White Wine Grapes

Albariño (ahl-bah-REE-nyoh)

Considered by many to be Spain's premier quality white wine, Albariño is labelled according to the grape varietal. Albariño is also known as Portugal's leading white wine in the Vinho Verde region known as Alvarinho (ahl-vah-REE-nyoh), where it is often labelled after the location.

- **AROMAS/FLAVORS**—Typically, wines made from Albariño are very aromatic, (because of its thick skins) often described as having the intense aroma of nuts (almonds), tree fruit (apricots, peaches, apples), and citrus.
- **BODY/STYLES**—The wine produced is unusually light to medium bodied, with high acidity and often with a slight "spritz" in Portugal.
- **SIGNIFICANT LOCATIONS**—Spain in the Rias Baixes (REE-ahs BY-shehs) region and sections of the Galicia (gah-LEE-thee-ah) region of Northwestern Spain produce this wine. The Portuguese region of Vinho Verde is also a producer.

Chenin Blanc (SHEN-ihn BLAHNK)

Chenin Blanc is arguably the most versatile of all grape varieties. It can successfully produce dry table wines, sparkling wines, and off-dry and sweet dessert wines.

- **AROMAS/FLAVORS**—Honey, tropical fruit (melon), tree fruit (pear, peaches), exotic scents (Bergamot, Earl Grey tea), and mineral (wet stone).
- **BODY/STYLE**—Chenin Blanc can be made in a full range of styles, from dry and crisp to semi-sweet and fruity, and from sparkling wine to full-blown late-harvest dessert wines. Any style contains certain floral, honeyed aromas and flavors with zesty acidity, which are the trademarks of a Chenin Blanc. This grape can stand up to modest oak aging and is occasionally blended with Chardonnay and other varietals to add fruitiness and acidity.
- **SIGNIFICANT LOCATIONS**—The Loire Valley (several areas that will be discussed in greater detail in Chapter 9, "French Wine"), California (Central Coast), and South Africa.

Gewürztraminer is a German word for "spicy grape." Sometimes the grape is referred to as *Gewürz* or *Traminer*. It is known for its spicy characteristics and high aromatics, often with some slight spritz on the tongue.

- **AROMAS/FLAVORS**—A distinctive wine, it can have citrus fruit (grapefruit), bakeshop spice (spicy cinnamon), tropical fruit (lychee), and flowers (rosé).
- **BODY/STYLES**—Gewürztraminer can be made light, dry, and crisp (Alsatian selections) to slightly full, sweet, and slightly flabby (California selections). It can also make luscious, honeyed sweet dessert wines.
- **SIGNIFICANT LOCATIONS**—This grape performs best in cooler climates such as France (Alsace), Germany, New York, Canada, California, Italy (Trentino and Friuli), and Washington State (Columbia Valley).

Grüner Veltliner is indigenous to Austria, where it accounts for the most dominant grape varietal throughout every Austrian wine-growing region.

- **AROMAS/FLAVORS**—This style carries intense concentrated aromatics of citrus fruit (lime, grapefruit), tropical fruit, and bakeshop spice (white pepper).
- **BODY/STYLES**—Grüner typically produces a highly acidic wine that is medium in body.
- **SIGNIFICANT LOCATIONS**—Austria (Wachau) is a significant producer.

Muscat goes by several different names and styles. In Italy's Veneto area, this grape is known as *Moscato*, where it makes the sparkling wine *Spumante* and a lightly carbonated version called *Moscato d'Asti*. In white France, Muscat makes sweet wine in Alsace and is considered most famous for the white Vin doux Naturals (VDN) sweet fortified wines produced in Southern France.

- **AROMAS/FLAVORS**—Musky, tropical fruit, tree fruit (peach and apricot), and citrus fruit (orange peel).
- **BODY/STYLES**—Muscat can range from dry wine (with occasional spritz) to sparkling wine and sweet wines.
- **SIGNIFICANT LOCATIONS**—Italy (Piedmont), France (Alsace and Provence), California, and Australia are significant producers.

This grape is grown primarily in northernmost wine regions throughout the world. It is called *Pinot Bianco* in Northern Italy (where it is produced in the Trentino-Alto-Adige, Veneto and Friuli areas) and *Weissburgunder* (VICE-buhr-gun-dehr) in Germany and Austria.

- **AROMAS/FLAVORS**—Subtle aromas and flavors of bakeshop (nuts, spice, yeast) and tree fruit (apple).

Gewürztraminer
(guh-VERTZ-trah-mean-er)

Grüner Veltliner
(GROO-ner FELT-lih-ner)

Muscat
(MOO-scott)

Pinot Blanc
(PEE-noh-BLAHNK)

- **BODY/STYLES**—Pinot Blanc is part of the Pinot family (Noir, Gris, Grigio). It produces dry, light-to-medium-bodied wines with high acidity.
- **SIGNIFICANT LOCATIONS**—France (Alsace), Italy (Trentino-Alto-Adige, Friuli, Veneto) California, Germany, and Austria are significant winemaking locations for Pinot Blanc.

Pinot Gris is a darkly colored white wine grape that evolved from the Pinot Noir. *Gris* means grey, the color that comes from the grape skins' unique pinkish-gray hue.

Pinot Gris goes by different names, depending upon where it is produced. It is called *Pinot Gris* in France and the United States and is referred to as *Pinot Grigio* in Italy.

- **AROMAS/FLAVORS**—Has subtle aromas and flavors: citrus fruit (lemon), tree fruit (pear, apricot), bakeshop sauces and spice (almonds and honey), and mineral.
- **BODY/STYLES**—Pinot Grigio is often made in a crisp medium-to-high acid that is light to medium body. These wines are commonly aged in either stainless steel or old oak barrels, although some winemakers practice suble new oak aging to provide a touch of richness and increase complexity.
- **SIGNIFICANT LOCATIONS**—This grape thrives in cooler regions—France (Alsace), Italy (Trentino-Alto-Adige, Veneto, Friuli), and Oregon (Willamette Valley)—which assist in preserving its high acidity. In the New World, Pinot Gris receives greater sun and heat exposure, allowing more ripeness and concentration to be expressed, compared with many old world versions.

**Sémillon
(seh-mee-YOHN)**

A well-known grape variety grown in Bordeaux, France, Sémillon is often blended in varying quantities with Sauvignon Blanc to produce a range of dry to sweet wines. It is often used to produce famous dessert wines from the Bordeaux appellation of Sauternes.

- **AROMAS/FLAVORS**—Dried fruit (figs), tree fruit (ripe apricots), citrus fruit (lemon), vegetables (grass), and bakeshop (honey).
- **BODY/STYLE**—Sémillon can be made in a dry or sweet style, producing a medium to full body. Sémillon is often a brilliant gold-colored wine with a soft, full, and sometimes even oily texture and low acidity. Sometimes this grape is used to fill out the leaner and highly acidic Sauvignon Blanc.
- **SIGNIFICANT LOCATIONS**—France (Bordeaux) and Australia (Hunter Valley, Margaret River) are significant producers.

**Viognier
(VEE-oh-NYAY)**

Viognier has become one of the more "fashionable" white wine grape varietals throughout the wine world. Viognier is a highly intense aromatic grape varietal, often producing a distinctive deep golden-yellow wine with a rich full body.

Although often a stand-alone varietal, Viognier is unknowingly blended in small amounts in the red wines of France's Northern Rhône Valley and to create a white *Côtes du Rhône* in Southern Rhône.

- **AROMAS/FLAVORS**—Viognier has an aromatic, rich, and intense smell.
  If fermented in stainless steel tanks, it can produce an aromatic wine that shows off the fruit tree (peach), tropical (tangerine, pineapple, mango, and apricot), bakeshop sauce (honey), and floral.
  If Viognier is oak aged, the wood barrels add further complexity by contributing elements of bakeshop spice (anise, vanilla).

- **BODY/STYLES**—This grape is fairly low in acidity and is medium bodied when un-oaked and full bodied when aged in oak. Viognier is usually high in alcohol, which can compensate for the occasional limited acidity.
- **SIGNIFICANT LOCATIONS**—France (Rhône Valley, Languedoc-Roussillon), California (Central Coast), and Australia (Eden Valley, Adelaide Hills) are significant locations for making this wine.

ROSÉ/BLUSH WINE

Rosé (roh-ZAY) is French for "pink" and is named after its color that can range in shade from light pink to orange. The pink color identifies the fact that the wine was made from some type of black-to-purple grape varietals that bleed a small amount of red color into the juice when the grapes are pressed. Rosé combines the fruitiness of a red wine with the crispness and lightness of a white wine that are generally an appropriate warm-to-hot-weather drinking option and work very well with spicy or full-flavored foods.

Many rosés are created from a blend of grapes (Syrah, Grenache, Mourvèdre, and others), while others are made from a single grape varietal (Zinfandel, Merlot, or Cabernet Sauvignon).

Rosés are packed with berry fruit and occasional floral aromas and flavors, while producing a light- to medium-bodied wine (but it can be fuller if there is significant residual sugar) with low to medium in alcohol content. Most rosés are not oak aged, and if they are, it is only for a short period. Most rosés are released less than a year after they are made, as they are meant to be consumed to showcase their youth and fruity personality.

Some of the best-known rosés are made in Provence (praw-VAHNSS) and Tavel (ta-VEHL) in the Rhône region of Southern France. These wines are rarely complex and never aged in oak. Rosés are typically dry—at most, barely sweet, tart, and fruity. They gain their charm from their freshness, and most are served chilled. The United States and South Africa generally make their Rosé sweet in style, although there are increasingly dryer options to be found.

White Zinfandel was introduced in the United States in the late 1970s and filled a niche in the early 1980s as the desire and interest in white wine started gaining momentum. White Zinfandel is an American twist on rosé that is engineered to be sweet (with various amounts of residual sugar). White Zinfandels are made from Zinfandel red wine grapes and, during fermentation, have minimal skin contact, so they pick up a touch of the red color from the grape skins. Sutter Home Winery (located in Napa Valley) was one of the first wineries to promote White Zinfandels. Some consumers and wine experts frown upon sweet wines, particularly the White Zinfandel, not because it is sweet, but because it has an amount of acidity and alcohol that is inadequate to balance the sweetness in order to provide some element of structure to the wine.

Although Rosés are not complex, they do have a place for matching with some more difficult food items. They can work well with spicy Asian, Latin American, or Cajun foods and lemon sorbet, and they are enjoyed for sipping on the beach or with a splash of soda water.

Pink Wine Styles

1. **FRUITY AND DRY**—Typically called rosé wine, this style is produced primarily in Southern France or throughout Spain, although it is increasingly being produced around the world.
2. **FRUITY AND SWEET**—Typically, these pink wines are made in California. Their names sometimes begin with the term *white*, such as *White Zinfandel* or *White Merlot*.

RED WINE GRAPE VARIETALS

Made from red, purple, or black grapes that typically make red wine, but can also make pink or even white wine.

There are about 40 primary red wine grape varietals grown in the world today, but the 3 most significant for producing high-quality wine throughout the world are *Pinot Noir, Merlot,* and *Cabernet Sauvignon.* These primary varietals are listed and are ranked from typical light- to full-bodied, low to high in tannin level, lighter to deeper in color density (which generally corresponds to the perceived tannin level), and younger to older in ageability. There are many exceptions to the typical body of these wines. It is possible to find Pinot Noirs that are light or medium bodied, as well as some Cabernet Sauvignon based wines that range fom medium to full bodied. A lot of the determining factors are involved that influence variations of grape varietals such as climate, grape growing, and winemaking differences.

There are other red wine grapes famously known for producing great quality wine in select locations such as Barbera, Cabernet Franc, Carménère, Dolcetto, Gamay, Grenache, Malbec, Mourvèdre, Nebbiolo, Nero d' Avola, Pinotage, Sangiovese, Syrah/Shiraz, Tempranillo, Touriga Nacional, and Zinfandel.

The Color Progression of a Red Wine

As red wines age, many factors affect their color progression. They can range from a youthful purple to ruby red, red, brick red and, ultimately, a brown amber. Some factors that influence color are as follows: (1) Type of grape—some grapes contribute deeper color because smaller berries have a greater skin-to-juice ratio, yielding greater color pigment. (2) Oak aging can de-emphasize the color because of oxidation. (3) The age of the wine can also decrease the color because of loss of color pigment when pigmented particles fall out as sediment. (4) Improper storage conditions—exposure to direct light for an excessive period may cause the wine to lose color. (5) The degree of extraction (suspended particles in the wine) of color from the skins through the maceration period also affects the color.

- **PURPLE**—Young, fruity wines are ready about six months to one year from harvest. This is a possible indication of a cool to warm climate, minimal to no oak aging, or the application of carbonic maceration.
- **RUBY**—Slightly aged, these wines are ready about one to three years from harvest. This is a possible indication of a cool to warm climate, minimal to no oak aging, or the application of carbonic maceration.
- **RED**—These wines are ready only after several years of barrel aging, about three to five years from harvest.
- **BRICK RED**—These mature wines are ready about 5 to 10 years from harvest and often indicate extensive aging.
- **BROWN AMBER**—Definite signs of age, likely to be oxidized.

Over time, red wines lose their bright, youthful color shading because the color pigment particles (anthocyanins), in conjunction with tannin, fall out of the wine solution and form a sediment on the bottom of the bottle.

Once a red wine has progressed to a brown amber color, the wine is generally considered undrinkable. Some red wines might progress to this color rather rapidly (within a few years), and others may take as long as 20 or more years to reach brown amber. Factors that influence this color change are mostly the type and quality of the grapes. The goal in consuming wine is to drink it when it is at its peak or, of course, to satisfy the wine consumer.

Aromas and Flavors of a Red Wine

Aroma and flavor categories are a means of associating the way a wine smells and tastes with one's memory. We can use these associations as a sort of anchor to remember the personality of a wine. There are six broad general red wine aroma/flavor categories, with several smaller defined aromas/flavors. Once the general smell (which is often the easier aroma to recognize) has been identified, we proceed to identify smaller, more defined aromas (which tend to be more difficult to recognize). In some cases, it is possible to make an association between an aroma flavor of a wine and some everyday item, such as Beaujolais Noveau having an aroma/flavor of pear, cherry, and bubblegum.

Climatic Influence

Hotter/Warmer Climates—Hotter/warmer-climate grapes ripen with high sugar content and lower acid. They produce aromas and flavors of baked and dried jammy fruits. They can produce greater concentration of color with the possibility of high alcohol content and fuller body and texture that will provide a greater mouth-feel, with a slight or significant burn in the back of the throat.

Cooler/Warmer Climates—Cooler-climate grapes tend to preserve their natural acidity. Their color intensity tends to be lighter, and the grapes do not produce an abundance of sugar. Therefore, they tend to produce wines that are lower to moderate in alcohol levels. Aromas and flavors may be more pronounced—of fresh fruit berries or of mineral and vegetation associated with limited heat or sun exposure throughout the growing season.

RED WINE AROMA/FLAVOR CATEGORIES

Common Aroma/Flavor Families Associated with Red Wine

RED WINE AROMA/FLAVOR FAMILIES		
GENERAL AROMAS/FLAVORS	**SPECIFIC AROMAS/FLAVORS**	**VERY SPECIFIC AROMAS/FLAVORS**
1. FRUIT	Fresh fruit	Cherry, black cherry, raspberry, blackberry, blueberry, plum, cranberry, strawberry, banana
	Baked/Dried Fruit	Prune, raisin, jam, cherry, raspberry, black cherry, currant, fig
2. COFFEE SHOP		Cinnamon, cloves, black pepper, orange peel, chocolate, vanilla, coffee, tea, black tea, licorice, anise, bubblegum, toffee, caramel
3. GARDEN	Vegetables	Green pepper, green olive, mushroom, black olive
	Herbs	Eucalyptus, mint
4. FLORAL		Rosé, violets, geranium, orange blossom, lanolin
5. EARTH		Forest, mud, pine, dirt, chalk, manure, dust
6. TOBACCO SHOP		Cigar, cigarettes, pipe, leather, cedar, tar

The Body of a Red Wine

A wine's *body* is the way it feels in terms of weight or viscosity inside the mouth. Red wine can range from light, medium, or full bodied. Certainly, there are levels in between that one arguably can say, "I give this wine a light, but on the high side or a medium, but on the low side." However, being so precise when describing a wine can sometimes contribute to more confusion for the novice wine consumer.

An effective analogy in describing wine is to think of the body of wine in terms of the weight or mouth feel of milk. For example, skim milk can be compared to a light-bodied wine, 2% milk to medium bodied, and whole milk to a full-bodied wine.

Some factors that can influence a red wine's body are as follows: (1) The size of the berries can alter the impact of acid, tannin, and overall extract because large berries have more juice and less skin (and vice versa). (2) The level of alcohol can be a factor because higher alcohol can provide a bigger body while lower alcohol content can provide a lighter body. (3) The level of tannin can influence the wine's body because higher tannin can provide a bigger mouth feel with substantial texture while lower tannin can yield a lower body. (4) Residual sugar can affect the body in that higher residual sugar yields a fuller mouth feel, while a wine that has been fermented dry can yield a lighter body. (5) *Extract* is a term used to indicate the level of concentration of several components (such as acid, alcohol, and fruit concentration) working together to create an impression of greater concentration. (6) Oak aging can influence body partly through the amount of evaporation of water content of the wine during the barrel aging process.

Contributors to a Red Wine's Body

CONTRIBUTORS TO A RED WINE'S BODY		
VARIABLES	**LIGHTER BODY**	**FULLER BODY**
Size of Berries	Larger berries with less skin-to-juice ratio	Smaller berries with greater skin-to-juice ratio
Level of Alcohol	11% or less	13% or more; sometimes as high as 14%
Level of Tannin	Lower	Higher
Dryness/Sweetness	Fermented dry	Fermented with allowing some varying amount of residual sugar.
Extract (concentration of fruit and other components)	Lower	Higher
Oak Aging	None to light	Medium to heavy

♦ Generally, a fuller bodied wine is usually 13% alcohol or above and a lighter bodied wine is low in alcohol, at 11% or below.

♦ Tannin is present in all wines, but is perceptible only in red wine.

PINOT NOIR (PEE-noh-NWAHR)

FIGURE 4–5 Close-up of Pinot Noir grapes
(Collection CIVC. Photographer: CORNU Alain)

The cultivation of Pinot Noir (or *Pinot*, as it is often coined) dates back over 2000 years and arguably produces some of the finest wines in the world. The grape is largely associated with the Burgundy and Champagne regions of France, where it originally gained its fame. Pinot Noir thrives in France's Burgundy region, particularly in the subregion of Côte d'OR (koht-d-OR). Figure 4–5 shows the Pinot Noir grape varietal.

Pinot is a difficult variety to cultivate and generally produces fairly low yields, which ultimately affects the selling price. With such limited production, good Pinots, when found, tend to be fairly expensive.

The name *Pinot* is used in the names of many different grapes because Pinot Noir is very prone to mutation. The widely used varieties Pinot Gris, Pinot Blanc, and Pinot Menieur are relatives of the Pinot Noir varietal.

Aromas/Flavors

- **Fruit**—tree fruit (cherry, cranberry, black cherry, raspberry, candied fruit)
- **Earth**—mushrooms, dust, dirt, wet leaves
- **Coffee Shop**—espresso, butterscotch, vanilla, cinnamon, clove, nutmeg, anise

Body/Style

Pinot Noir tends to be of light to medium body, with low tannin and medium to high acidity. The wine's color is often light and transparent in intensity because Pinot Noir is a thin-skinned grape that ends up contributing less color concentration (through anthocyanins) than other red wine grapes.

Significant Locations

Some of the best quality Pinot Noir is grown in cooler climates that allow the grapes to mature slowly.

- **OLD WORLD**—France grows, arguably, the best Pinot Noir in the world, especially in Burgundy and specifically in the areas of Côte d' Nuits (koht duh NWEE) and Côte'd Beaune (koht duh BOHN), and in Chamagne.
- **NEW WORLD**—California (Sonoma, Sonoma Coast, Carneros, and Central Coast), Oregon (Willamette Valley), and New Zealand (Central Otago, Marlborough, Martinborough, and Waipara) are significant producers.

STYLE #1: The Burgundian Style—Burgundy has always produced the classic Pinot Noir style that has been so widely imitated around the world. These wines typically offer medium body, with medium to high acid and medium tannin. The Burgundian style offers a wine that is harmonious and elegant. The alcohol content is typically found hovering around 13.5%. Oregon is another significant Pinot Noir producer that has traditionally been compared to Burgundian style.

STYLE #2: The California Style—In trying to mimic the Burgundian style, California and New Zealand have instead created something different. The Pinot from California generally offers a greater richness of fruit, with a bit more spice sensation coming from the often higher alcohol content hovering around 14% or higher. The high alcohol content can affect the type of food that is successfully paired with the wine, compared with Burgundian Pinots, which have a traditionally lower alcohol content.

Pairing Strategies

1. Pinot Noir is one of the most adaptable red wines and can pair well with roasted and braised preparations of lamb, pheasant, and duck. It works with meats such as poultry with skin; stewed or braised chicken such as Coq au Vin (chicken cooked in red wine); and other game birds such as quail and turkey; veal; and pork.
2. Pinot Noir pairs excellently with fatty fish prepared by robust cooking methods, such as tuna, salmon, shark, and swordfish. It is important that these fish be wild, as they contain greater flavor and fat content than farm-raised versions.
3. Pinot works excellently with coagulated beef such as Boeuf Bourguignon (beef stew), roast beef sandwiches, beef stroganoff, or any beef that is cooked medium well or greater. Because California style Pinot Noirs are often higher in alcohol, they have the ability to work with some steaks (Filet Mignon) that have been uncoagulated (that are rare to medium in level of doneness).
4. Pinot Noir can pair with some vegetarian dishes that have heightened flavors, such as mushroom risotto enriched with a touch of cream or butter.
5. Some Pinots that offer an intense concentration of fruit (common in the Sonoma Coast Pinots) can pair well with chocolate-based and nut-based desserts that offer some elements of caramel or toffee.

MERLOT
(mehr-LOH)

Merlot is the leading varietal consumed by Americans. It can be made as a stand-alone grape-varietal-based wine from California's Napa Valley or from Washington State. In Bordeaux, France, Merlot has been quite famous, blended in varying quantities with its natural

FIGURE 4–6 Close-up of Merlot grapes
(Chad Ehlers/Stock Connection)

companion, Cabernet Sauvignon, along with other varietals. This grape varietal is a great complement to Cabernet Sauvignon because it can assist in lightening the tannins and contributing greater fruit qualities, therefore making the wine a bit more approachable and adding a dimension of complexity at the same time. Figure 4–6 shows the Merlot grape varietal.

Aromas/Flavors

- **Fruit**—tree fruit (cherry, plum), tropical fruit (pineapple, banana, mango), citrus (lemon).
- **Vegetables**—green olives, bell pepper
- **Coffee Shop**—chocolate or cocoa, coffee
- **Tobacco Shop**—cigar or pipe

Body/Style

Merlot is medium bodied and deep in color intensity and can be fairly high in alcohol, with medium tannin (from thinner-skinned grapes) and medium acid.

Significant Locations

- **OLD WORLD**—France (Bordeaux), specifically in the areas of Pomerol (POAM-ehr-all) and Saint-Émilion (sahn-eh-meel-YOHN), and the northern regions of Italy are significant producers.
- **NEW WORLD**—Washington State (Columbia Valley), California (Napa Valley), and Chile also produce significant amounts of Merlot.

Pairing Strategies

1. Since Merlot often has less tannin than Cabernet Sauvignon, the wine can be paired with skin-on grilled and roasted poultry and game birds (including duck).
2. Roasted or grilled meats such as pork tenderloin, venison, veal, and lamb go well with Merlot. Grilled steaks with less texture and flavor such as beef tenderloin and steaks with minimal degrees of marbling such as skirt steak are also excellent partners.
3. Fruit-forward new world Merlots can pair well with pizza and burgers. Also, suitable Latin and Tex-Mex dishes such as chicken or steak fajitas and beef quesadillas are delicious with Merlot.
4. Some Merlots that offer an intense concentration of fruit (common in Washington) pair well with dark-chocolate-based desserts.

Often called just *Cab* or *Cab Sauv*, this is one of the most widely planted grapes throughout the world. It is frequently referred to as the king of red wine grapes and is often viewed as a winery's benchmark wine. Cabernet is a stand-alone varietal (though seldom 100%) but more often blended in a *Bordeaux style* (where it is a dominant grape, but blended with numerous others) as a *Super Tuscan* (blended with Sangiovese), where it has been the backbone of some of the world's most renowned wines.

A California Cabernet Sauvignon wine was responsible for bringing great fame to California (and overall the new world) when a "Stag's Leap, Napa Valley, Cabernet Sauvignon" won the top place over French counterparts in the famous 1976 Paris wine tasting (discussed in greater detail in Chapter 7, "Wines of the United States and Canada"). Figure 4–7 shows the Cabernet Sauvignon grape varietal.

Aromas/Flavors

Intense aromas and flavors of

- **Fruit**—tree fruit (cherry, plum) dried fruit (black currents)
- **Garden**—black olives, bell pepper, eucalyptus
- **Coffee Shop**—chocolate or cocoa, coffee, black tea
- **Tobacco Shop**—cedar, clove, cigar or pipe

**CABERNET SAUVIGNON
(KAB-er-nay SOH-vin-NYOHN)**

FIGURE 4–7 Close-up of Cabernet Sauvignon grapes
(Michele/Tom Grimm/Creative Eye/MIRA.com)

Body/Style

This deeply colored grape can produce medium-bodied wine (particularly when yields are high), but is often fuller bodied due to its thick skin. It is highly concentrated, rather high in tannin (smaller berry with thicker skin) and alcohol with medium acidity.

Cabernet Sauvignon is often blended with "fleshy" yielding grapes such as Merlot or Shiraz in order to lower tannin and balance flavors (by contributing a bit more fruit qualities). Cabernets are almost always aged in oak for at least 1–2 years from harvest, and are more likely bottle aged for years to decades to soften its tannin and to allow flavors and other components to integrate. World Class examples of Cabernet Sauvignon can often improve and be aged for decades.

Significant Locations

- **OLD WORLD**—France (Bordeaux), specifically in the areas of the Médoc (may-DAWK), Pessac-Léognan (peh-SAK leh-oh-NYAHN) and Graves (GRAHV) and Italy (Tuscany) are significant producers of Cabernet Sauvignon.
- **NEW WORLD**—California (Napa Valley), Australia (Barossa and Coonawarra), Chile, and Washington State (Columbia Valley) are significant producers.

Pairing Strategies

1. The firm tannins that are often present in Cabernet can be tempered in food pairing with robust cooking methods and uncoagulated meat protein found in beef, particularly steaks.
2. Cabernet Sauvignon can partner well with other meats such as lamb or veal shank.
3. As a Cabernet Sauvignon ages, it becomes less intense as the tannins soften and flavors come together. An aged Cab can alter a pairing and require meat that is less fatty as a successful partner.
4. Cabernet can pair with dark chocolate that has a high cocoa content.
5. Cabernet Sauvignon can pair with blue-vein-type cheese.

Other Popular Red Wine Grapes

**Barbera
(bar-BEHR-ah)**

Barbera is one of the grapes most commonly planted throughout Italy. It is generally regarded as producing simple and inexpensive wine though there are some excellent high quality examples. Because of Barbera's high acid and lower tannin, it tends to be highly versatile with food. ♦ For a more extensive discussion of Barbera, refer to Chapter 10, "Other Old World Wine Countries."

- **AROMAS/FLAVORS**—Fruit (bright to sour cherry and berries) and light tobacco shop.
- **BODY/STYLE**—Barbera is a deep-ruby-colored, light- to medium-bodied wine with low to medium levels of tannin and high levels of acidity.
- **SIGNIFICANT LOCATIONS**—Italy (Piedmont) is a significant producer, and the wine is most recognizable in the areas of Asti and Alba, where they are known as Barbera d' Asti and Barbera d' Alba.

**Cabernet Franc
(ka-behr-NAY FRAHNK)**

Cabernet Franc is widely used as a blending grape in the famous *Bordeaux Blend*. But Cabernet Franc is also famous as a stand-alone varietal in Loire Valley, France. ♦ For a more in-depth discussion of Cabernet Franc, see Chapter 9, "Wines of France."

- **AROMAS/FLAVORS**—Fruit (strawberry or berry fruit), garden (vegetables and herbs), cigar shop (slightly cedar and tobacco).
- **BODY/STYLE**—Cabernet Franc has low to medium tannin and tends to be light- to medium-bodied with high acidity.
- **SIGNIFICANT LOCATIONS**—France (Bordeaux, Loire Valley) is the significant producer in the Old World; California, Canada (Niagara Peninsula, and Okanagan Valley), and New York (Finger Lakes) in the New World.

Carménère (car-men-YHER)	In Chile, Carménère was originally thought to be Merlot, but its identity has been clarified as a separate, distinctive varietal. Carménère has since been rediscovered in Chile as a leading red grape capable of stand-alone single varietals wines. ♦ For a more thorough discussion of Carménère, refer to Chapter 8, "Other New World Wine Countries."

- **AROMAS/FLAVORS**—Fruit (fresh berries), bakeshop spice (cardamom, clove, nutmeg), vegetables (green pepper).
- **BODY/STYLE**—Medium bodied with low to medium tannin and medium acid.
- **SIGNIFICANT LOCATIONS**—Chile (Rapel Valley and Maipó).

Dolcetto (dohl-CHET-toe)	Dolcetto means "little sweet one," in reference to its early ripening, which allows the wine to be drunk sooner than other varietals. ♦ For further discussion of Dolcetto, see Chapter 10, "Other Old World Wine Countries."

- **AROMAS/FLAVORS**—Bakeshop (licorice), nuts (almonds), fruit (plums, blackberries).
- **BODY/STYLE**—Dolcetto produces a medium-bodied wine with low-acid and medium tannin.
- **SIGNIFICANT LOCATIONS**—Italy (Piedmont) is a significant producer, and the wine is most recognizable in the area of Alba, where it's known as Dolcetto d' Alba.

Gamay (gah-MAY)	Gamay is a French varietal most recognizable and dominant in Southern Burgundy in the area of Beaujolais, France. It produces the popular, simple, and highly fruity Beaujolais Nouveau and the more serious, complex, and well-structured *Crus* of Beaujolais. ♦ For a deeper discussion of Gamay, refer to Chapter 9, "Wines of France."

- **AROMAS/FLAVORS**—Gamay produces a highly aromatic wine with fruit (berries such as raspberry and cherry), tropical bakeshop (chocolate) in older vintages.
- **BODY/STYLE**—Most Beaujolais (Beaujolais and Beaujolais Village levels) are light bodied, low in tannin, and medium to high in acid. Many of the Crus of Beaujolais are heartier, with deeper, more intense fruit, and offer greater structure that can benefit from a short period of aging.
- **SIGNIFICANT LOCATIONS**—France (Beaujolais and Loire Valley).

Grenache (Gren-AHSH)	Grenache is a vigorously growing grape that has the ability to produce simple fruity rosés or powerful age-worthy reds. It is almost always blended (often with Syrah and Mourvèdre) and may even be a dominant grape in many of the blends. The Spanish call this grape *Garnacha* (gahrr-NAH-chah), or it is known as *Cannonau* (cahn-AH-now) in Sardinia, Italy. This varietal produces the famous French red based fortified wines called *Vin doux naturel* (VDN) in Southern France, specifically in the areas of Banyuls and Maury. ♦ For further discussion of Grenache, see Chapter 9, "Wines of France."

- **AROMAS/FLAVORS**—Fruit (fresh strawberries), bakeshop (chocolate), spice, earth (wet leaves) and tobacco shop
- **BODY/STYLE**—This grape produces a medium-bodied to full-bodied wine with medium acid and tannin.
- **SIGNIFICANT LOCATIONS**—France (Rhône Valley, Provence, Languedoc-Roussillon), Spain (Priorat and Rioja) is also a significant producer.

Malbec (mahl-BEHK)	Malbec has traditionally been a blending grape in red Bordeaux, but over the last decade, it has become the leading red wine grape as a stand-alone varietal in South America. Malbec goes by many synonyms, depending on the growing area. It is known as *Auxerrois* in Cahors (Southwestern France) or *Cot* in the Loire Valley. ♦ For a more in-depth discussion of Malbec, refer to Chapter 8, "Wines of the New World" or Chapter 9, "Wines of France."

- **AROMAS/FLAVORS**—Floral (violets, rosé), fruit (loganberries, black cherry, blackcurrant, plums), bakeshop (toffee, cinnamon, chocolate, coffee, anise), tobacco shop.
- **BODY/STYLE**—This deeply colored grape can range from medium to full bodied, with medium tannin and medium to high acid.
- **SIGNIFICANT LOCATIONS**—Argentina (Mendoza), France (Bordeaux, where it is blended in varying amounts in the famous *Bordeaux blend*; Loire Valley; and Southwest France) and California (North Coast, where it is blended in the *Bordeaux blend,* often called a *Meritage*) are the significant producers.

Mourvèdre (moor-VEH-druh)

Mourvèdre is traditionally used as a blending grape in the famous Côtes du Rhône and Châteauneuf-du-Pape. But it is becoming extremely popular as a stand-alone varietal, as it is primarily this grape that produces a *Bandol* in Southern France's Provence. Mourvèdre is said to have originated in Spain, where it still remains very popular and is known as Monastrel (mahn-ah-STRELL). ♦ For further discussion of Mourvèdre, see Chapter 9, "Wines of France."

- **AROMAS/FLAVORS**—Tree fruit (cherries), berry fruit (blackberries), spicy, cigar shop (animal, leather).
- **BODY/STYLE**—Medium bodied, with medium to high acid and tannin.
- **SIGNIFICANT LOCATIONS**—France (Rhône Valley, Provence, Languedoc-Roussillon), Spain (Jumilla) and California are the major producers.

Nebbiolo (neh-b'YOH-loh)

The name derives from the word *nebbia*, Italian for "fog," which is known to encase the Nebbiolo vineyards in Piedmont during the harvest time. Nebbiolo produces one of the most ageable and long-lived wines available. ♦ For more on Nebbiolo, refer to Chapter 10, "Other Old World Wine Countries."

- **AROMAS/FLAVORS**—Dried fruit raspberries and cherries, plums, prunes), earth (soil, mushrooms, tar), floral (rosés, violets), cigar shop (tobacco, licorice, leather), bakeshop (bitter chocolate).
- **BODY/STYLE**—Nebbiolo is generally full bodied, with high tannins and acids. It often needs several years of bottle aging before it is ready to drink.
- **SIGNIFICANT LOCATIONS**—Nebbiolo's main producer is Italy (Piedmont), where it is most famous in the appellations of Barolo, Barbaresco, and Gattinara.

Nero d'Avola (neh-ROH dah-voe-lah)

This grape, indigenous to Southern Italy, is known for producing a simple, rustic style wine that has similarities to wines made from the Zinfandel and Syrah varietals. ♦ For further discussion of Nero d'Avola, refer to Chapter 10, "Other Old World Wine Countries."

- **AROMAS/FLAVORS**—Fruit, dried fruit (berries, cherries), earth (soil), tobacco shop.
- **BODY/STYLE**—Nero d'Avola produces a medium-bodied wine with high acidity and medium tannin.
- **SIGNIFICANT LOCATIONS**—Italy (Sicily and Puglia) is the dominant producer.

Pinotage (pee-noh-TAHJ)

Pinotage is a grape unique to South Africa, where it was created in 1925 as a cross between Pinot Noir and Cinsault (SAHN-so) varietals. ♦ For further discussion of Pinotage, see Chapter 8, "Other New World Wine Countries."

- **AROMAS/FLAVORS**—Dried fruit, earth, animal (leather), tobacco shop (smoke), chemical (acetone).
- **BODY/STYLE**—Medium bodied with low to medium tannin and acid.
- **SIGNIFICANT LOCATIONS**—South Africa is this wine's major producer.

Sangiovese (san-joh-VAY-zeh)

Sangiovese is a famous and significant grape found throughout central Italy, primarily within Tuscany where the famous Chianti region is located. This grape varietal goes by various names, depending on the type of clone, such as *Sangioveto* in Chianti, *Brunello* in Montalcino and *Prugnolo* in Vino Nobile di Montepulciano.

Sangiovese is often a stand-alone varietal, as in Brunello di Montalcino, but is more often blended with small amounts of indigenous Italian grapes in Chianti or Vino Nobile di Montepulciano. It has also been blended with greater amounts of international varietals such as Cabernet Sauvignon and Merlot to create the Super-Tuscan wines of Tuscany. ♦ For further discussion of Sangiovese, refer to Chapter 10, "Wines of the Old World."

- **AROMAS/FLAVORS**—Fruit (cherry, black cherry), bakeshop (spice, nuts), cigar shop (tobacco, tea leaves, leather), floral (violet, rosé).
- **BODY/STYLE**—Sangiovese-based wines can range from medium to full bodied, with medium to high acid and tannin.

  Lighter versions may be labelled Chianti, Rosso di Montalcino; while medium versions may be labelled Chianti Classico and full-bodied versions Chianti Classico Riserva, Brunello di Montalcino, and Vino Nobile di Montepulciano.
- **SIGNIFICANT LOCATIONS**—Italy (Tuscany), and more specifically the area of and surrounding Chianti, boasts being the predominant producer of this wine.

**Shiraz/Syrah
(shih-RAHZZ)/(SEAR-ah)**

The grape is called *Syrah* in France and California. In Australia, it is referred to as *Shiraz*. This grape is possibly the most significant of the emerging varietals throughout the entire wine world. It is beginning to play an important role in many wine areas and in some cases is being showcased as a particular country's calling card.

There appear to be two distinct styles of this grape. Syrah (and Syrah blends) tends more toward a spicy, rustic, or earthy style that can be medium to full bodied. Shiraz, on the other hand, is created in a bolder style that is intensely fruit forward.

Syrah or Shiraz is often created as a stand-alone varietal, but is also adaptable to blend with other grapes such as Grenache, Mourvedre, Cabernet Sauvignon, and Viognier. ♦ For further discussion of Shiraz/Syrah, refer to Chapter 8, "Wines of the New World," and Chapter 9, "Wines of France."

- **AROMAS/FLAVORS**—bakeshop spice (pepper), dried/baked fruit (jam and blackberry), animal (leather, wild game, tar).
- **BODY/STYLE**—A dense, dark red wine with a rich, full body, medium tannin and acid, with high alcohol content.

  Syrah blends tend to be a bit softer and with less tannin than Syrah, and with less alcohol than Shiraz.
- **SIGNIFICANT LOCATIONS**—In France (Rhône Valley), such as Cote Rotie or Crozes-Hermitage in Northern Rhône. California (Central Coast), Washington (Columbia Valley), Australia (Barossa Valley, Coonawarra), Chile (Colchagua and Maipó), and South Africa (Cape) are the main producers.

**Tempranillo
(tem-prah-NEE-yoh)**

Tempranillo is often described as Spain's *Noble* grape. It can be produced as a stand-alone varietal, but shows more complexity when blended with grapes such as Garnacha (Grenache), Cabernet Sauvignon, and Merlot. Tempranillo is capable of producing deeply colored and concentrated fruity wines for early consumption, or richly flavored and age-worthy wine for later consumption. ♦ For further discussion of Tempranillo, see Chapter 10, "Wines of the Old World," and Chapter 12, "BOLD: Fortified Wines."

- **AROMAS/FLAVORS**—Fruit (dark cherry, strawberry), earth, bakeshop (spice), tobacco, floral.
- **BODY/STYLE**—Richly colored, Tempranillo is fairly low in acid and alcohol levels and medium to high in tannin levels (from thick-skinned grapes).

- **SIGNIFICANT LOCATIONS**—Spain (Rioja, Ribera del Duero, and parts of Penendes), Portugal, and Argentina are this wine's most significant producers.

Touriga Nacional
(too-REE-gah Nah-syon-AL)

Classically, Touriga Nacional has served as one of the most significant grapes used to produce the fortified wine, Port. Currently, this grape has gained renewed interest and popularity as a stand-alone varietal in an unfortified wine style.

- **AROMAS/FLAVORS**—This grape maintains the deep, concentrated flavor and aroma of the exotic spices of baked/dried fruit (blackberry, black cherry), floral (violets), bakeshop spice (black pepper, all spice, cinnamon), and cigar shop (smoke).
- **BODY/STYLE**—Touriga Nacional creates a wine with substantial concentrated color, with medium to high tannin (from thick-skinned grapes), medium acid levels, and medium-to-full body.
- **SIGNIFICANT LOCATIONS**—Portugal (Duoro and Dão Valleys) is the main producer.

Zinfandel
(ZIN-fun-dehl)

The Zinfandel grape is native to Croatia and for centuries has made wine in Italy's Puglia region (where the grape is known as *Primitivo*).

In the United States, the Zinfandel grape has made resurgence after suffering from an image problem in the 1980s when people associated it mostly with its white counterpart, White Zinfandel.

- **AROMAS/FLAVORS**—Maintains a deep, concentrated flavor and aroma of exotic spices of fresh/dried fruit (jam, berry, currants, cherry, blackberry), bakeshop spice (black pepper, cinnamon), cigar shop (smoke), and vegetables (herbs, bell pepper).
- **BODY/STYLE**—Ranges from medium to full bodied and intense. Offering medium acid and tannin, with high alcohol.
- **SIGNIFICANT LOCATIONS**—California (Sonoma and Central Coast) and Italy (Puglia) are significant producers of this wine.

FRUIT WINES

A *fruit wine* is generally any wine fermented from a fruit other than grapes. There are many different types of fruit wines, but some of the most popular include red raspberry, blackberry, and cherry. These wines are big in flavor and intense in their fruit character, as it typically takes over 10 pounds of fruit to produce 1 gallon of premium fruit wine.

Fermentation techniques vary with the specific winemaker, but often the fermentation takes place under cold conditions to maximize the retention of fruit character. Well-made fruit wines are a delicate balance between the fruit's natural acidity and residual sugar. If the finished wine is too sweet, it tends to be cloying on the palate. If it is too dry, it tends to be sharp and astringent.

Well-made fruit wines come from the finest growing regions for that particular fruit. These include Willamette red raspberries and Marion blackberries from the Pacific Northwest and Montmorency cherries from Michigan. As in grape wine, optimal fruit quality translates into spectacular fruit wines.

Fruit wines have a multitude of uses. They are often consumed slightly chilled (55° F) with a dessert course. For example, blackberry and red raspberry wines are a delightful accompaniment to dense chocolate desserts, as the wine cleanses the palate of the sweet chocolate. Blueberry and cherry have a similar effect on cheesecake. Fruit wines can also be used in the sauté pan to make reductions or on roasts to create a glaze.

PERFORMANCE FACTORS OF GRAPE VARIETALS

NAME: _____ Score out of 20 points_____.

Use these quesetions to test your knowledge and understanding of the concepts presented in the chapter.

I. MULTIPLE CHOICE: Select the best possible answer from the options available.

1. Which is *not* a prominent location for high-quality Pinot Noir?

   a. Bordeaux, France
   b. Central Otago, New Zealand
   c. Willamette Valley, Oregon
   d. Burgundy, France

2. Which is *not* a prominent location for high-quality Cabernet Sauvignon?

   a. Napa Valley, California
   b. Chile
   c. Bordeaux, France
   d. Germany

3. Which is *not* a prominent location for Sauvignon Blanc?

   a. Germany
   b. Loire Valley, France
   c. Bordeaux, France
   d. New Zealand

4. Which is *not* a prominent location for Riesling?

   a. Germany
   b. Alsace, France
   c. Washington State
   d. Chile

5. Where is the *Gamay* grape grown?

   a. Bordeaux, France
   b. Beaujolais
   c. Napa Valley, California
   d. New Zealand

6. Which one of the following colors in white wine is a sign that the wine has been exposed to too much oxygen or has been bottled too long?

   a. very pale yellow with a hint of green
   b. straw yellow
   c. golden yellow
   d. brown

7. Which one of the following colors in white wine is a sign that the wine has been aged in oak?

   a. very pale yellow with a hint of green
   b. straw yellow
   c. golden yellow
   d. brown

8. Which one of the following colors in a red wine is associated with a wine that has been aged for a considerable period?

   a. purple
   b. ruby red
   c. red
   d. brick red

II. MATCHING: Match the correct grape varietal with its common aromas and flavors.

9. _____ Honey, raisin, petroleum, peach

10. _____ Earth (mushrooms, soil), bakeshop spice (anise, clove, cinnamon), fruit (berries)

11. _____ Black tea, tobacco, plum, cedar, black olive

12. _____ Bakeshop (cocoa, coffee), berries (cherries), green olive

13. _____ Bakeshop (vanilla, butter, toasted nuts), apple, pear

14. ____Citrus (grapefruit), barnyard (hay, fresh cut grass)

    a. Riesling

    b. Sauvignon Blanc

    c. Chardonnay

    d. Pinot Noir

    e. Merlot

    f. Cabernet Sauvignon

III. TRUE / FALSE: Circle the best possible answer.

15. Chardonnay is often known as a "moldable" grape varietal. **True / False**

16. Pinot Noir often produces a light- to medium-bodied red wine that is easy to grow, as seen in numerous growing locations around the world. **True / False**

17. Cabernet Sauvignon and Merlot are often blended together in varying amounts. **True / False**

18. Fumé Blanc is a white wine grape varietal. **True / False**

IV. SHORT-ANSWER ESSAY / DISCUSSION QUESTIONS: Use a separate sheet of paper if necessary.

19. List and briefly explain four factors that can influence the body of a wine.

20. List and briefly describe four factors that can influence the color in a red wine.

5

Foundations to Wine and Food Pairing

A large part of our daily food and beverage rituals involve our seeking some sort of balance, whether consciously or subconsciously, that we perceive as ideal for our palate, given the time of day, occasion, or mood. Pairing a glass of wine (whether extravagant or humble) with a food can elevate a meal and the dining experience from mundane to special occasion.

LEARNING OBJECTIVES

Upon completion of this chapter, the learner will be able to:

- Provide a framework for wine and food pairing choices by developing analytical and decision-making skills.
- Examine how various taste components can influence successful wine and food pairings.
- Discover the concept of bridge flavors and recognize how to reinforce a successful wine and food pairing.
- Describe the effects that moist- and dry-heat cooking techniques have on food and wine pairing.
- Discover how to select a wine on the basis of an analytical approach to pairing.
- Explore the effects that various cooking techniques have on the subsequent success of a wine and food match.

CUISINES AND HOW THEY AFFECT WINE PAIRING

Classical, or French, cooking is the foundation to most other cuisines. French cuisine became known as *haute cuisine* (OHT-kwih-ZEEN), which translates to "high cuisine" and identifies food prepared in an elegant or elaborate manner. Haute cuisine has maintained great influence because for many years France was one of the most important political forces in the world. Currently, European cooking methods and ingredients are still the foundation for modern-day cuisines the world over.

> As European influence spread through travels and trade, the Europeans left their thumbprint of food and beverage knowledge, as well as ingredients and techniques, throughout most modern-day cultures. Over time, changing eating and dining habits redefined cooking and *nouvelle cuisine* (NOO-vehl) eventually became the new healthy cooking philosophy. Popularized in the 1970s, nouvelle cuisine rose up in reaction to the rich and supposedly unhealthy nature of classic French cookery.

Creation of a Cuisine

A cuisine's foundation is a specific set of cooking traditions, techniques, and ingredients associated with a specific culture within a geographical area. Throughout the world, the diversity of cuisines is a reflection of the cultural dynamics derived from various factors that are particular to that specific area: geography, immigration, economics, trade, politics, religion and ethnicity. These factors act collectively to affect ingredients, traditions, and styles, which in turn affect our eating habits, flavor preferences, recipes, and dining etiquette. They are the primary drivers that sustain the distinction of a particular cuisine.

Throughout thousands of years, wine has evolved with cuisine. Traditionally, there has been a *classical* perspective on wine and food pairing that matches the regional cuisine to the local wine. This approach is still evident, and many wine drinkers live by it.

Currently, cookery has been modernized to create what is known as a *world cuisine*. Quite different from classical cuisine, it does not have defined geographic boundaries, but instead is rooted in the creation of food that incorporates aspects, ingredients, and techniques from around the world. Hence, a new approach to wine and food pairing has been established. The *contemporary* perspective is more appropriate for this new cuisine than the alternative, classical approach to wine and food pairing.

Classical Cuisine and the Classical Approach to Wine and Food Pairing

Classical cuisine is rooted in and produced according to tradition. Each culture around the world has its own unique culinary identity. The specifics of climate, politics, history, and geography all collectively influence the types of food that are readily available and that have evolved together.

With classical pairings, the idea of wine and food matching is tied to a natural connection of regional cuisines. These types of pairings are associated with Old World countries such as France, Italy, Spain, and Germany, where there is a strong sense of regionality that has taken hundreds and thousands of years for a cuisine to evolve. This is a somewhat romantic notion, to partake in a ritual of eating food and drinking wine that has a sense of time and place.

Sample of Classical Wine and Food Pairings

- Aged Tawny Port → Stilton Cheese
- Red Burgundy → Coq au Vin
- Chianti Classico → Bistecca Fiorentina

World Cuisine and the Contemporary Approach to Wine and Food Pairing

World cuisine in the broadest sense is food that has been created in the present day and that may incorporate a combination of modern or classical practices, ingredients, and techniques. Globalization has dramatically influenced contemporary cuisine, bringing to people the possibility to obtain almost any kind of wine and food ingredient at any time of the year. In addition, the fusion cuisine movement blends two or more cuisines collectively to create a new one. The World Cuisine movement began in the late 1980s and has now become pivotal in the United States, as a result of immigration, greater accessibility to foreign travel, and the renewed popularity of cooking. Professional and home cooks have been exposed to different cultures and the practice of combining different ingredients and techniques. As Americans' eating patterns have changed, so has the way wine is paired with food. Globally, cooking has been liberated and has led wine drinkers to rethink how wine is paired with food.

With contemporary matching, the idea of wine and food pairing is more about freedom—freedom from the evolution of food and beverage combinations that have been traditionally tied together because of culture. Instead, the contemporary approach is about finding a wine that is compatible no matter the origin of the food or cuisine. This notion may seem less romantic than a classical pairing; however, the world has become such a small place that it is not uncommon to find two or three different cuisines integrated together on a single plate.

Samples of Contemporary Wine and Food Pairings

- German Riesling → Roasted Honey and Ginger Glazed Pork Tenderloin Stuffed with Dried Fruits
- California Chardonnay → Corn Fritters with Dungeness Crab and Crème Fraiche
- Oregon Pinot Noir → Grilled Copper River King Salmon with Garlic Mashed Potatoes

FOUNDATIONS TO WINE AND FOOD MATCHING

"Wine is both a garnish and a condiment for food, changing and enhancing the way the diner tastes the finished product."
—Danny Meyer, Restaurant Owner

The Integration of Wine and Food

People pair wine and food out of tradition, for personal enjoyment, and for hedonistic reasons, by achieving a union between the two. When attempting to pair a wine with a food, it may help to think of wine as a condiment or just another ingredient to season the food. Wine can act much the same way that relish enhances the flavor of a hot dog, cream provides richness in coffee, and salsa adds dimension to tortilla chips. All these combinations are meant to enhance or alter the food item that is being consumed. Pairing a wine with food can be somewhat subjective because of personal tastes. While some individuals enjoy coffee straight-up black, others find balance in adding cream and or sugar, and yet more adventurous coffee drinkers add a flavoring such as vanilla or hazelnut syrup. Wine brings the same ability to the table by contributing such elements as acid, fruit, sweetness, tannin, aromas, flavors, and spiciness, the same way that condiments or ingredients do to food.

When choosing a food to go with a wine, a relationship is created, just as when two people come together. As with most relationships, these can be happy and can work for different reasons. Sometimes, opposites attract; other times, people are attracted to one another because of similarities. Either way, the couple has found some complementary qualities that work, just as with a wine and food pairing.

Wine pairing can be considered within the same context. Matching wine and food to enhance the quality of a meal can be fairly simple if a few basic principles and a moderate degree of gastronomic experimentation are applied. It is important to note that pairings are highly subjective and there is no perfect match that is right for everyone, just as romantic relationships are made on the basis of personal factors. Some romantic relationships are blah, some are good, and some are great! Do not be frustrated because of the occasional lack of a great wine and food pairing; sometimes, it is just like finding that romantic partner—it takes time and practice at applying the basic pairing techniques. With all the intricacies of wine and food, it's understandable how it can be easy to become overwhelmed by the concept, because every dish is dynamic and can comprise thousands of food ingredients and infinite combinations, which contribute to difficult and somewhat subjective pairings. However, it is possible to generalize and reasonably predict what might work for most people.

What Is an Effective Wine and Food Pairing?

Applying and practicing the pairing principles presented in this chapter make it possible to greatly improve the overall consistent satisfaction found in wine and food pairings. At the very least, wine and food should be able to intermingle with one another. In an effective pairing, neither overpowers the other and yet each one contributes something to the table to enhance the other. Generally, a successful wine and food pairing is one in which the interaction of the wine and food does not diminish the pleasure of either partner, but instead enhances each one, to contribute to a more fulfilling whole.

The Quick-Fix Approach

The common phrases "Drink what you like" and "Serve white wine with chicken and fish, and red wine with meat" are fine basic rules that have been preached over the last 20 or so years. However, these *quick-fix* approaches are limiting, as well as gross simplifications of the nature of wine and food pairing. Of course, one may drink and eat whatever he or she likes, but for one who loves and appreciates food, the ultimate goal is to create the best gastronomic experience by finding a suitable wine to enhance the food.

The quick-fix approach is similar to the old adage, "Give a person a fish, and he will be fed for a day," as opposed to the more analytical long-term approach, which we advocate in wine pairing, "Teach a person how to fish, and he will eat for a lifetime." People get stuck in the belief that there is only one wine or one perfect match to pair with a food item. In reality, there are often several different options that can be paired for similar, or in some cases very different, reasons. The old rules don't take into account the complexity of today's multi-ethnic World Cuisine and menus or the wide range of wines available from around the world.

The Analytical Approach

Rather than relying on the quick-fix approach, we can create successful pairings that work in most situations. Making intelligent wine and food pairing decisions involves a bit of analytical thought beforehand, relying on the approach of "Teach a person how to fish, and he will be fed for a lifetime." By broadening the quick-fix perspective and approaching wine and food matching with some basic principles, we can make pairing less intimidating, less stressful, and less limiting. The methodical three-step analytical approach will lead to greater satiety at the dining table. A good match can bring nuances to, and enhance flavors and characteristics in, both the food and the wine.

The three steps in the *analytical approach* are as follows:

1. Mirror the body and weight (or overall intensity) of the wine and the food to ensure neither one overwhelms the other.
2. Connect bridge ingredients in the food with flavors in the wine.
3. Compare or contrast taste components between the wine and food on the basis of the desired emphasis of the match.

The analytical process can be applied to both complex and even the simplest of dishes. By applying the analytical approach, it is possible to show a connection between the wine and a food and point out possible wine pairings. Throughout the analytical process, there are many techniques for building flavor or bridging elements in the wine and food to ensure and solidify a more effective pairing.

THE ANALYTICAL APPROACH:

Principle #1

Mirror the body and weight (or overall intensity) of the wine and the food to ensure that neither overwhelms the other.

Principle #1 is the most significant step to forming the foundation of a successful wine and food pairing. It involves mirroring the body, weight, or overall intensity of a given food item with a wine at a similar level. Principle #1 is focused on creating an equal balance, or "mirroring effect," of the body of both the wine and food so neither will overwhelm the other. The like characteristics allow the wine and food to remain compatible, and they work to keep the meal grounded. For example, a light- to medium-bodied white wine such as Sauvignon Blanc would be overwhelmed by a heavy dish such as a grilled porterhouse steak with melted bleu cheese. Likewise, a full-bodied wine such as a bold, powerful Cabernet Sauvignon may overshadow a delicate dish of poached scallops.

The first principle to the analytical approach involves breaking down the plate of food and determining the primary food type(s) to match with a particular wine. Every food type has a certain body and weight (or overall intensity) that need to be assessed to determine a possible wine pairing.

Intensity can be described as a certain richness or concentration of aromas and flavors. The *intensity* of a wine's aromas and flavors can sometimes compensate for the wine's not having as much weight or body. For example, fatty, rich foods like roasted duck or goose can be partnered in some cases with lighter- to medium-bodied (yet intense) wines such as German Riesling (Spätlese or Auslese).

After considering the main food type and its relative body level, we should consider two additional factors used to judge the influence of the body and weight (or overall intensity)

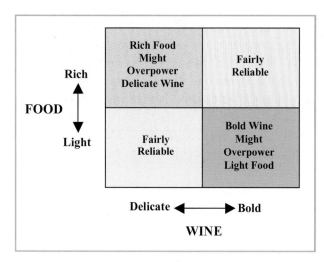

FOOD Rich ↕ Light

Delicate ◄───► Bold
WINE

FIGURE 5–1 Comparison of food and wine types
(John Laloganes)

of a food: method of cooking and type of sauce. These elements can collectively alter the body or weight of a food item and subsequently determine a wine pairing.

Figure 5–1 depicts food types and their relative level of body compared with wines and their level of body and weight (or overall intensity). In pairing wine, the goal is to seek fairly reliable matches between the wine and the food and to prevent one from overwhelming the other.

Type of Food

In each dish, there tends to be a core food type, or core ingredient, on display. Often, this is referred to as the *food type* or *center of the plate* item. This main item, on stage within the dish, is the determining factor in choosing an appropriate wine. The food type that is the main item in a dish is often a protein; however, it can certainly be a pasta (or other grain), vegetables, or some other item, depending on the course of the meal or, simply, the preference of the diner. The core ingredient will not necessarily point to one specific grape varietal, but it should help narrow the options to a small, workable list of potential ones. It will provide a direction to suitable wines and help rule out others.

Every food item can be loosely categorized into levels of body on the basis of its individual chemical makeup. Some food items, such as vegetables and pasta, do not have the fat or proteins that meat contains. Therefore, vegetables and pasta tend to be thought of as a lighter food type than meat, which is a full-bodied food type. Presented next are some generalizations of several common food types and their possible levels of weight or body.

Keep in mind that other factors, such as cooking methods and sauces, can significantly alter the body and weight of these food items. For the purpose of simplicity at this point, think of the food items in their unadulterated, somewhat uncooked forms.

☐ **Light-Bodied Food Items**—Vegetables, grains, pasta, chicken, turkey, mollusks, lean finfish
☐ **Medium-Bodied Food Items**—Veal, pork, crustacean, fatty finfish, duck, goose, game birds
☐ **Full-Bodied Food Items**—Certain sausages, game, lamb, beef

Some other factors to consider that will influence the weight and body (overall intensity), of a food type include age of the animal, skin on or off, bone in or out, dark meat or light meat, quality grade, method of aging, wild or farm raised. These factors are not always known to the wine drinker; however, they are questions that can and should be asked prior to continuing with principles #1 and #2 and committing to a particular wine.

Cooking Methods

The more familiar with the food type and cooking techniques the diner is, the more successful wine selection he or she can make. It is possible to understand flavors and textures and how these are modified to pair most effectively with wine. The way a food item is cooked will have a significant effect on how it tastes and what wine pairings will be suitable. Cooking methods can adjust and influence a food's weight and body (overall intensity), but also texture, aroma, and flavor. A food type can be neutral and light in texture and body (such as chicken), but powerfully flavored (because it has been grilled).

Cooking methods can be used to enhance and adjust the body of a food type. A certain method can manipulate a food type to work with an alternative type and style of wine

FIGURE 5–2 Poached salmon dish
(Edward Allwright © Dorling Kindersley)

FIGURE 5–3 Grilled salmon dish

(Ian O'Leary © Dorling Kindersley)

Moist-Heat Cooking Methods

that may have not been previously possible. Understanding basic cooking techniques can help improve the possibility of a good wine and food match.

Hearty, more robust cooking methods and food items demand fuller-flavored and fuller-bodied wines, whereas subtle, more delicate cooking methods and food items necessitate low-flavored, less intense, and light-bodied wines. Choosing a light cooking method such as steaming or poaching can preserve simple and delicate flavors in food. However, more intense cooking methods such as grilling and smoking create rich, robust flavors in food and assist in amplifying the natural flavors. The more aggressive the cooking style, the more body a food type will have. For example, poached salmon tastes dramatically different from grilled salmon. This in turn greatly influences the wine pairing.

Figures 5–2 and 5–3, illustrating salmon being cooked in two different ways, can inform the appropriateness of the wine pairing. Figure 5–2 shows salmon cooked through the poaching method. This method preserves flavor and provides a lighter body to the fish, therefore demanding a lighter styled wine. Figure 5–3 shows the salmon cooked by the grilling method, which incorporates additional flavor to make the salmon more robust. Salmon cooked by this method demands a more substantial wine.

Moist-Heat Cooking Methods

This method uses moist heat to cook food in water, steam, or the vapors of other liquids. Moist heat is used for tenderizing older or tougher cuts of meat by dissolving connective tissue, yielding a tender product. The goal of moist-heat cooking is to achieve the desired degree of doneness through cooking on low heat for a long period until doneness is indicated by tenderness (not by temperature, as is indicated in dry-heat cooking). In this cooking method, meat is cooked well done and beyond, but is still tender due to the breakdown of connective tissue.

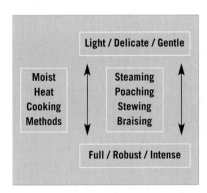

Steaming—Steaming involves lightly cooking small portions of food through the hot vapors of water or flavored liquid. A gentle, delicate process used mainly for delicate foods with fragile textures, steaming preserves a food item's natural flavors. Steaming is typically used for vegetables, dumplings, poultry, and seafood.

Poaching—This method involves submerging food in a simmering hot liquid. It is a slow, delicate cooking method for preserving delicate, tender foods (lean fish and poultry) or breaking down connective tissue in dense, tough meat (brisket). The poaching liquid can be as light and neutral as water or as distinguished as oil, butter, wine, or stock. Poaching is typically used for poultry and seafood.

♦ **En Papillote** (ohn-pop-ee-YOAT)—This is a unique moist-heat method that cooks food inside an individual enclosed pouch. It combines both the steaming and poaching processes, as the item is cooked both in a small amount of liquid in the pouch and through the release of vapors inside the pouch.

Braising and Stewing—These cooking methods produce foods with great dimension and layers of flavor. These methods are used for cooking tougher cuts of meat, older birds, and firm-fleshed fish. Braising involves browning larger pieces such as shoulders or shanks, and stewing involves browning smaller, bite-sized pieces on all sides in a small amount of oil and then simmering in a flavorful liquid until the meat is tender. The longer and slower the cooking process, the more tender the meat will become. The cooking liquid is critical and contributes significant flavor to the dish. The meats are often served with the sauce or gravy that they were simmered in. Braised and stewed food items include pot roast and coq au vin.

Wine Strategies for Moist-Heat Cooking

1. Poaching and steaming are the gentlest cooking methods used for delicate foods to preserve subtle flavors. These foods need an accompanying light- to medium-bodied white wine.

2. Sauces that accompany food items that have been poached or steamed often are emulsified or butter-based sauces that provide a touch of richness to the food item. But in some cases, the poaching liquid will replace these other sauces, thereby allowing a wine with a bit fuller body than what might normally be expected to be paired with the food item. Also, the sauce may play an interesting bridge, or compare–contrast element, with the wine. (See analytic principles #2 and 3, later.)

3. Braising and stewing are moist-heat cooking methods that incorporate significant body and weight to a dish. The cooking liquids usually coat the browned food to create a denser, more concentrated flavor. Food cooked in this manner calls for a medium- to full-bodied red wine, depending on the food type, which can range from seafood to poultry, sausage, or meat.

Dry-heat cooking comprises relatively quick cooking methods that use hot air, hot metal, or hot fat. This style of cooking is used for younger animals with less-exercised muscles that are naturally tender. The goal of dry-heat cooking is to achieve the desired degree of doneness (level of protein coagulation) while preserving the natural tenderness and juiciness. If a food item is uncooked or lightly cooked (from rare, to medium rare, to medium), it will be considered uncoagulated, with sufficient juiciness and internal fat content. In contrast, a food item that is overcooked (medium well or well done) will be drier, with less internal fat, because the item is considered coagulated. The level of protein coagulation is an extremely important consideration when pairing particular wines with food items. The less coagulation, the more fat, juice, and flavor are present in the meat. Generally, a bolder, more full-bodied wine that contains greater tannin would be an appropriate match with uncoagulated foods. When an uncoagulated piece of meat is paired with a tannic full-bodied wine, the fat in the meat can deactivate and soften the tannin to allow the flavors of both to meld together.

Dry-Heat Cooking

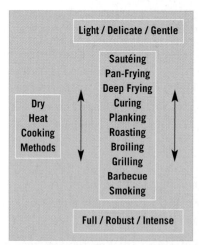

Light / Delicate / Gentle

Dry Heat Cooking Methods

Sautéing
Pan-Frying
Deep Frying
Curing
Planking
Roasting
Broiling
Grilling
Barbecue
Smoking

Full / Robust / Intense

Sautéing—Sautéing (saw-TAY-ing) is a quick-cooking method that uses high heat and a small amount of fat. It is usually reserved for cooking small pieces of food. Options for sautéing include shrimp, scallops, pasta, chicken breast, veal scallop or cutlets, and pork tenderloin. When cooked in this manner, the meat lends itself to a variety of flavors, depending on the pan sauces, which can be made from the addition of different types of wine or stock. The liquid can either be reduced down to make a syrupy glaze or finished with butter or cream for enrichment.

Pan-Frying—This method uses moderate heat with a moderate amount of fat and is used for more delicate items because there is less fat and the container is more shallow. The meat used in this cooking method is often tender and pounded (scaloppini) and may also be breaded or dredged in flour. The fat is needed to achieve a textured flavorful exterior while maintaining a juicy center.

Deep Frying—This method involves quick cooking small pieces of tender food product through immersion in a large amount of hot fat. The larger volume of fat is needed to crisp up the breading and allow the finished product to maintain a nice, crispy, flavorful exterior and a moist interior.

Curing and Planking—These are two of the more pronounced cooking methods used for seafood (mostly for finfish). The most common method of curing is a wet cure, otherwise known as picking. A wet cure consists of a brine solution of salted water possibly with the addition of sugar and spices. In some methods of brining, such as that used with the Latin American dish *seviche* (seh-VEE-cheh), a citrus acid solution is used to coagulate the proteins in the same manner that a pickling solution would.

Dry curing involves rubbing salt and perhaps other spices directly onto the fish, allowing the proteins to coagulate and the fish to lose some moisture content. The curing process can take place over a period of hours to weeks, depending on the desired predominance of flavor.

Planking is the technique of cooking meat, poultry, or seafood on a piece of seasoned wood in a dry-heat environment. The food absorbs the aromas and flavors of the wood throughout the cooking process.

Roasting—The roasting method involves cooking a food item on a suspended rack with the use of hot, dry heat within an oven. As the heat cooks and browns the outside of the roast, the flavors are concentrated by the creation of a slightly crusty, rich surface. (The chemical process by which this surface is created is called the maillard reaction.) The juices on the inside of the food item are intensified by the evaporation of moisture. Throughout the cooking process, the juices are released and collected into the roasting pan to become the foundation of a sauce.

FIGURE 5–4 Grilling method of cooking
(Dennis Lane/Photolibrary.com)

Broiling and Grilling—These methods use very high heat to cook meat quickly. If properly done, broiling and grilling will create a brown, flavorful, crusty surface on the exterior of the meat and maintain a juicy center. Grilling can be used successfully with steaks, chops, burgers, poultry with skin on, and fatty finfish such as tuna, salmon, and shark, that are meaty, full flavored, and oily, either with or without skin to assist in holding the fish together. This method works well for chops and steaks that are about 1 to 1½ inches thick. If the meat is much thinner, it will cook inside before there is enough time for a proper crust on the exterior to form. If the meat is much thicker, it will take too long to cook the meat through to reach a desired degree of doneness, risking burning and drying out the exterior in the process. Figure 5–4 illustrates the grilling process.

Barbecued/Smoking—True barbecuing is a long cooking process over a low, smoky heat to develop colorful, flavorful, and tender meat. It is often done outdoors, but can be done indoors, and is referred to as *smoking*. This cooking technique is used for tougher pieces of meat that can benefit from the long, dry-heat cooking process. Barbecuing is the process of cooking, preserving, and flavoring by exposing the food to burning or smoldering material such as wood. Smoking can be conducted by either the hot or cold method. The hot method is conducted over hot smoke (for several hours), often from burning hardwoods such as maple or oak (even from old whiskey or wine barrels), mesquite, and even tea leaves. Cold smoking is conducted at lower temperatures for an extended period, from days to weeks.

Wine Pairing Strategies for Dry-Heat Cooking

1. Most foods cooked by dry heat cooking methods (except for those which are deep fried) generally go well with oak-aged white and red wines because of the creation of caramelization on the food from sautéing, grilling, broiling, and roasting that mimics the flavor of the toasted oak barrel.

2. Sautéed and pan-fried foods (poultry and seafood) go well with medium- to full-bodied white wines that have been lightly or heavily oak aged.
3. Deep-fried foods contain an exterior coating that contains fat and some level of saltiness. Therefore, medium-bodied white wines or sparkling wines that have ample acidity are excellent at cutting through the fat content and providing a respite on the palate.
4. Because barbecued and smoked foods generally contain large amounts of fat and an intense smoke smell and flavor, they pair well with a medium- to full-bodied red wine that either is rich in fruit qualities or contains a qualities of earthiness and/or tobacco shop.
5. Broiling and grilling are robust methods (used commonly for steaks and chops) that can pair excellent with medium to full-bodied red wine that is medium to high in tannin.

Sauces

A sauce is a flavorful liquid that has been lightly thickened and is used to enhance foods such as meat, poultry, seafood, and vegetables by adding flavor, richness, and moisture. Most sauces act to provide a counterpoint of textural, visual, and flavorful dimensions to a dish. They can add a complementary or a contrasting flavor or structural component. Choosing a sauce with a base flavor similar to that of the main item tends to complement and intensify the flavor of the main item; a contrasting sauce, such as a red wine reduction, adds a contrasting acidity component to a rich fatty steak. Figure 5–5 illustrates sauce.

FIGURE 5–5 Sauce
(Richard Embery/Pearson Education/ PH College)

Sauces are an important consideration when attempting to construct an effective wine and food pairing. Understanding the nature of a sauce, such as its texture and flavors, can dictate a particular type or style of wine.

Classic Sauces

Having an understanding of classic base sauces can assist with a more effective understanding of derivative sauces and subsequent wine pairings. These sauces stem from classical French cookery and are still widely used today. The base sauces, sometimes referred to as *mother sauces*, include the following:

1. **Espanole** (ehs-pah-NYOHL)—Brown sauces derived from concentrated beef or veal stock.
2. **Béchamel** (bay-shah-MEHL)—White sauces derived from roux (a common thickening agent of equal parts fat and flour) thickened milk.
3. **Velouté** (veh-loo-TAY)—White sauces derived from roux thickened stock.
4. **Tomato**—Tomato sauces derived from cooking tomatoes.
5. **Hollandaise** (HOL-uhn-dayz)—These sauces are derived from an emulsion of clarified butter and egg yolks.

The base sauces are created from a base liquid with the addition of some sort of thickening agent. Then, additional flavorings may be added to create other variations of sauces known as *secondary sauces*. All classic base sauces have two major components:

Liquid (or the body of the sauce)—The classical base sauces (also known as mother sauces) use either clarified butter; chicken, fish, vegetable, or veal stock; brown stock (from beef); milk; or tomato.

Thickening Agent—Thickening agents are used to give the base liquid a certain amount of viscosity, which allows the sauce to adhere to the food. Sauces can be thickened

Liquid + Thickening Agent = Base Sauce

by a simple reduction of vinegar or cream (rapidly boiling to evaporate excessive liquid) or by the addition of starches (such as flour or cornstarch). Some sauces are emulsified (suspended as two unmixable substances) with egg yolks and butter, and other sauces are thickened through a puree of vegetables that gives a viscous consistency.

Additional Ingredients—The addition of seasoning and flavoring agents such as herbs, spices, fruit, and wine to the base sauces creates various derivatives known as secondary sauces.

Other Kinds of Sauces

With the popularity of world cuisine, sauces used in contemporary menus have expanded well beyond the classic sauces. The creative outlets for pan sauces, reduction sauces, salsas, vinaigrettes, and foams are endless. Here are samples of some of the more modern sauces that derive either from nouvelle cuisine or from other areas around the world:

FIGURE 5–6 Emulsified sauce
(SGM/Stock Connection)

- ☑ **Demi glace** (DEHM-ee glahs)—The base of many classic French sauces, demi glace derive from the reduction of espanole that can add a remarkable concentration of flavor.
- ☑ **Emulsified Sauces**—Some of the most popular sauces derive from this category of base sauce.
  - *Egg based:* Hollandaise, Béarnaise.
  - *Butter based:* Beurre blanc, compound butter, beurre noisette, and brown butter sauce.
  - *Mayonnaise based:* Aioli or garlic Mayonnaise, tartar sauce, and remoulade sauce. Figure 5–6 shows an emulsified sauce and some of its necessary ingredients.
- ☑ **Reductions**—Simmering a liquid (stock, vinegar, wine, or cream) evaporates part of the water and leaves a concentrated flavor in a sauce-like consistency.
- ☑ **Glaze**—Similiar to a reduction, but concentrated further, a glaze is made by simmering a stock to evaporate the water (to about one-fourth of original volume of the stock) and concentrate the liquid and flavors within it.
- ☑ **Salsa, Relish, and Chutney**—These are a mixture of chopped vegetables or fruit with the addition of an acid such as vinegar or citrus that provides a sweet, sour, or spicy element. They can be made in varying degrees of spiciness and intensity of flavor. Typically, salsas are uncoooked; relishes and chutney often are cooked.
- ☑ **Pure Oils and Flavored Oils**—Many oils in their pure form, such as olive, peanut, and walnut oil, can provide a hint of additional flavor. It is also possible to create a more substantial flavored oil by adding flavor agents such as garlic and herbs to enhance the base oil.
- ☑ **Coulis and Purees**—Cooked or uncooked pureed vegetables or grains, these creations have a sauce-like consistency.
- ☑ **Broths or Jus**—These are unthickened, natural juice from the item being served (often meat or poultry).
- ☑ **Pan Sauces**—The base of a pan sauce is the *fond* (FAWN), or browned bits, clinging to the bottom of the pan after a food item has been sautéed. Once the food item has been removed from the pan, the pan is *deglazed* through the addition of a liquid (stock, water, or wine) while the concentrated fond is scraped in order to be dispersed into the liquid. The sauce can then be reduced (by evaporating the liquid) and thickened further or even enriched with the addition of butter or cream. Figure 5–7 shows the beginning stages of what eventually will be needed to create a pan sauce.

FIGURE 5–7 Deglazing
(Ian O'Leary © Dorling Kindersley)

Pairing Strategies for Sauces

Sauces, just like wine, are meant to enhance the dish or meal. However, in some situations, the sauce is the overriding component in pairing a wine. One of the defining questions is, "To what extent is the sauce an integral part of the dish?" Here are some suggestions for the times when it has been determined that a sauce is a major factor in a pairing decision:

1. Emulsified sauces are based in egg yolks, which yield a mouth-coating quality. Light-to medium-bodied white (or sparkling) wines with ample acidity can pair well and keep the palate fresh.

2. Béchamel and Velouté sauces are based in milk- or roux-thickened stock. Each one provides a heaviness and richness to a food item. A full-bodied white wine with adequate acidity or alcohol can mirror the body (and often flavors and texture) of the sauce, while the taste components of acidity and or alcohol can keep the palate fresh.

3. Brown sauces have a beefy richness to offer. In some cases, the sauce may be light and brothy; in others, it may be extremely thick and concentrateed. A medium- to full-bodied red wine can be effective, depending on the item the sauce will be used for. Often, a brown sauce is used on red meat or game, which would be able to hold up to these recommended wines.

4. Tomato-based sauces have ample acidity. It is best to mirror acidity in the food with that of the wine. Light- to medium-bodied red wines with sufficient acidity and subtle tannin can pair effectively.

THE ANALYTICAL APPROACH:

Principle #2

Connect bridge ingredients in food with flavors in the wine.

After mirroring the body of both wine and food (see principle #1), the second principle involves finding a *bridge* ingredient or ingredients that the food and wine have in common. While bridges are not the most important matching considerations, paying attention to them can add an interesting dimension or validate the pairing experience.

Bridging Flavors

Bridge ingredients assist to connect the base ingredient (food type), cooking method, or sauce of a dish to a particular wine for a more effective pairing. Just as a bridge may create a connection between two bodies of land, a food-and-wine-pairing bridge uses the presence of certain ingredients in the food and wine to create a stronger association. Bridges can assist in linking complementary flavor components by mimicking or echoing an element found in both the wine and the food. Figure 5–8 illustrates how a bridge aroma and flavor are detected in both the wine and the food.

We begin by assessing the primary or even secondary flavors that are present in both the wine and the food. For example, when a primary flavor of herbs is evident in a food item, a wine that has some of those same herbal qualities may be paired with that item because they share a common bridge. However, it is important to stress that this is so, only assuming that the first principle of mirroring the body of the wine and food has been satisfied. Another example may include pairing a wine that has a buttery, creamy flavor and texture with a food item that has a buttery, creamy flavor.

Pairing based on flavor alone doesn't guarantee a successful match, but it helps to ensure a more effective one. The goal is to find a component to play off of in order to create a bridge.

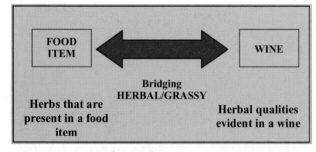

FIGURE 5–8 Bridging the ingredients in both the wine and food

(John Laloganes)

Example of the Bridging Approach

Following is an example of bridging ingredients in food with flavors in a wine:

Herbal Qualities

- **Food**—A lean fish placed in parchment paper with some fresh dill, lemon juice, and aromatic vegetables cooked en-papillote.
- **Wine**—Sauvignon Blanc sometimes has a recognizable grassy and herbal aroma and flavor associated with these seasonings.

An important reminder regarding principle #2, in order for a bridge to work, there need to be similar levels of body weight in the food as in the wine (as explained in principle #1). The Sauvignon Blanc often is considered a light- to medium-body, as the lean fish poached in its own juices, in essence, can be considered a light- to medium-body. The match can work without the bridge; however, the link makes it connect more effectively, providing a more complete dining experience.

Bridge Ingredient Categories

Pay attention to flavors, as they are considered accents to a dish. They can have a minor influence on the pairing; however, in a few cases, such as blackening spices or crusting of foods, they will have a major impact on the wine-and-food pairing. It can be helpful to think of flavors in terms of categories such as fruity, nutty, smoky, herbal, spicy, earthy, and meaty, as wines can sometimes have flavor categories that parallel these.

The following table shows particular flavors that may be detected by aroma or flavor within a wine and sometimes can be bridges, if used in the preparation of foods, to more effectively connect a wine and food:

CATEGORIES	EXAMPLES
Herbs/Spices	allspice, anise, basil, cilantro, dill, ginger, lemon grass, nutmeg, pepper, rosemary, mint, tarragon
Vegetables/Grains	beans, bell peppers, beets, corn, fennel, garlic, mushrooms, potatoes
Fruits	apples, bananas, cherries, coconut, figs, grapefruit, lemons, limes, lychee, mangoes, melons, oranges, peaches, pears, pineapples, plums
Dairy	butter, cream, milk
Nuts	almonds, hazelnuts, macadamia nuts, pecans, walnuts

Bridge Ingredient Possibilities

The following table does not present a complete list of bridge ingredients, but gives a small selection of potential possibilities, for purposes of illustration:

WHITE WINE	BRIDGE INGREDIENT POSSIBILITIES
Riesling	Fruits (raisins, pineapple, apricot, dried fruits), honey
Sauvignon Blanc	Herbs (dill, basil, oregano), vegetables (tomato, peppers)
Chardonnay	Nuts (pine-nuts, macadamia nuts, and almonds), dairy (cream and butter), vegetables (corn, potatoes)
RED WINE	**BRIDGE INGREDIENT POSSIBILITIES**
Pinot Noir	Vegetables/grains (garlic, beans, mushrooms, shallots, onions, bell pepper, mustard, fennel, lentils, potatoes)
Merlot	Fruits (dried cherries and cranberries)
Cabernet Sauvignon	Vegetables (black olives, mushrooms), herbs/spices (mustard, rosemary)

THE ANALYTICAL APPROACH:

Principle #3

Compare or contrast taste components between the wine and food according to the desired emphasis of the match.

Each taste component affects how a wine is perceived on the palate, and the slightest variation in the intensity of these components can drastically alter the interactions that occur. The components can heighten or diminish a particular characteristic in the wine or the food.

Comparing or Contrasting Taste Components

Assess the primary taste components of the wine and the food. Wine may offer components such as sweetness (residual sugar), sourness (from acidity), bitterness (from tannin), and spiciness (from alcohol). Food may offer such components as sweetness, sourness, bitterness, creaminess, smokiness, spiciness, saltiness, and bitterness.

It is possible to select any one of the taste components to play off of that may make the pairing better. One of two approaches can be used. One is to compare the "like" qualities (the brother and sister approach) that are found in both the wine and the food. The other approach is to contrast (having "opposite" qualities) the *cat and dog* approach in the wine and the food. Either approach can act to intensify or diminish the sensation of taste components suitable to the preference of the diner.

Example of Both Approaches

Provided are examples of a comparison and a contrasting approach.

- **Comparison Approach**—An acidic red wine (such as Barbera or Sangiovese) is compared to an acidic tomato sauce. This approach of matching similar taste components of acid works to achieve a complementary match.
- **Contrasting Approach**—The acid in an acidic white wine (such as Sauvignon Blanc or Unoaked Chardonnay) contrasts with the fatness or richness of a cream sauce. This approach can add interest to a dish, while some taste components in the wine are matched against an opposite of one found in the food. Even though it is an approach of contrasting opposites, each component brings something to the other in order to achieve a complementary match. This approach can be used as a counterpoint to provide interest or to diminish or intensify a particular quality.

Sweet Wines

Sugar is present in grapes prior to fermentation, after which many wines are fermented dry, removing most perceptible sugar from the wine. Any unfermented sugar left over from fermentation is known as RS (residual sugar) and is perceived as fruit. The sweetness in wine with some perceptible residual sugar can suppress the components of bitterness (think of adding sugar to coffee), spiciness, and acidity (think of adding sugar to lemonade). The perception of sweetness can be affected by a variety of elements, such as acid, alcohol, salt, and tannin, in both wine and food.

Wine must be as sweet as or sweeter than a food item (such as dessert). If the food is sweeter than the wine, there is a tendency for the wine to taste dull and flat. When pairing sweet foods with a wine, try to keep the dish less sweet than the wine. If necessary, sweetness can be diminished by adding an acidic component such as citrus juice or vinegar or adding spices such as black pepper and chili powder. The following table identifies the effects of a sweet wine when paired with foods containing various components:

PAIRING WITH SWEET WINES	
EFFECTS OF SWEETNESS ARE HEIGHTENED WITH...	EFFECTS OF SWEETNESS ARE DIMINISHED WITH...
☑ Sweeter foods	☑ Salty foods
	☑ Spicy foods
	☑ Acidic foods
	☑ Tannic foods

High sugar levels are more associated with white wines, sparkling wines, dessert wines, many rosés, but, rarely, red wines. Following are some examples of wines that may occasionally have some varying levels of sweetness:

White Wine—Riesling, Gewürztraminer, Chenin Blanc, sparkling wines from Italy (Asti, Moscato di Asti, Prosecco), dessert wines. (See Chapter 11, "BUBBLES: Sparking Wine" and Chapter 13, "NECTAR: Dessert Wines," for a detailed discussion.)

Rosé Wine—White Zinfandel, White Merlot, or, in general, some California rosé wines.

Red Wine—Sparkling wine from Italy (Brachetto and Lambrusco) and from Australia (Sparkling Shiraz), and varying dessert wines. (See Chapter 11, "BUBBLES: Sparkling Wine" and Chapter 13, "NECTAR: Dessert Wines," for a detailed discussion.)

Acidic Wines

Acid is fundamental to both a white wine's and a red wine's structure, making the wine taste crisp, fresh, and lively. Acid is perceived as sourness or tartness on the palate and causes salivation. Without an adequate level of acid, a wine is considered flabby or falls flat when paired with a food. Acidity has the ability to heighten or perk up flavors in food.

High-acid foods go well with crisp high-acid wines such as light- to medium-bodied whites, or light- to medium-bodied red with good acidity and low tannin. The following table identifies the effects of an acidic wine when paired with foods containing various components:

PAIRING WITH ACIDIC WINES	
EFFECTS OF ACID ARE COUNTERBALANCED WITH...	EFFECTS OF ACID ARE DIMINISHED WITH...
☑ Salty foods	☑ Salty foods
☑ Slightly sweet foods	☑ Sweet foods
☑ Fatty foods (from dairy fat)	
☑ Greasy/oily foods (from cooking methods)	

High acid levels are associated with white, rosé, and red wines from cooler climates, as well as with wines that either have been un-oaked or only lightly oaked. Examples of wines with ample acidity follow:

White Wine—Sauvignon Blanc, Pinot Gris, Pinot Grigio, Riesling, and most sparkling wine from around the world, particularly Champagne and Cava.

Rosé Wine—Most French or Spanish rosés.

Red Wine—Pinot Noir, Barbera, Gamay, Sangiovese, Dolcetto, and Cabernet Franc.

Tannic Wines

Tannin is a component that is fundamental to a red wine and can contribute to an increased level of body, weight, power, texture, and structure. Tannin is perceived as bitterness and causes a drying sensation.

High tannin in wine is subdued by the fat, protein, and heavy, chewy texture of meat. Meat that has been cooked to a rare, medium-rare, or medium degree of doneness is considered uncoagulated and has the ability to temper the tannin in a medium- to full-bodied red wine.

Meat that has been cooked medium well to well done is considered coagulated and does not temper tannin, but still has enough body and texture to pair well with a light- to medium-bodied red wine with low to medium tannin. The following table identifies the effects of a tannic wine when paired with foods containing various components:

PAIRING WITH TANNIC WINES	
EFFECTS OF TANNIN ARE HEIGHTENED WITH...	EFFECTS OF TANNIN ARE DIMINISHED WITH...
☑ Salty foods	☑ High protein foods
☑ Spicy foods	☑ Uncoagulated protein
☑ Tannic foods	☑ Fatty foods (animal fat)

Tannic levels are associated with red wines and are fairly undetectable in white wines. Examples of wines with moderate to high levels of tannin include the following:

Red Wine—Cabernet Sauvignon, Nebbiolo, Syrah, Grenache, Shiraz, Tempranillo, Zinfandel, Meriot, Cabernet Franc, and Sangiovese.

Fatty Foods

Fat adds richness, texture, mouth-feel, body, and weight to a dish. There are three basic types of fat: vegetable fat (olive oil, corn oil, peanut oil), dairy fat (cheese, butter, cream) and meat fat (beef, veal, pork, lamb). Fat can also be introduced from various cooking methods—primarily frying and sautéing—but it can be added as well in the form of a sauce. The following table identifies the effects of different kinds of fat and possible wine pairings:

PAIRING WITH FATTY FOODS
Vegetable fat–This type of fat contains mouth-coating qualities, but also a certain mineral flavor or other detectable flavor element. A white wine with substantial acidity or carbonation can counterbalance the oiliness, but bridge the flavor elements. These types of wines also work extremely well with fried foods because of the same ability to counter balance the fat and breading in the dish.
Dairy fat–This type of fat, rich and mouth coating, pairs well with full-bodied white wines that have significant weight, but also contain adequate alcohol or acid levels to counterbalance the richness.
Meat fat–This type of fat works best with a red wine that has substantial tannin. The tannin and fat can counterbalance and offset one another.

Salty/Smoky/Spicy/Highly Seasoned Foods (or SSSS)

Sometimes spices are a prominent factor in the flavor and texture of the dish. Spices can be categorized into three types: (1) sweet (cinnamon, allspice), (2) savory (curry, cumin), and (3) hot (curry, chili powder, horseradish, cayenne pepper). Heavy seasoning, spices or salts often take precedence over the type of food when a wine is chosen to match. These qualities can and often overpower food. Therefore, it may be best to match a wine to the cooking technique and spice level, instead of applying the typical pairing principle of matching a wine to the food type. The following table identifies the effects of salty, smoky, spicy and highly seasoned foods with various types of wine:

PAIRING WITH SALTY, SMOKY, SPICY AND HIGHLY SEASONED FOODS (SSSS)	
EFFECTS OF SSSS ARE HEIGHTENED WITH...	EFFECTS OF SSSS ARE DIMINISHED WITH...
☑ Oak-aging wine	☑ Residual sugar in wine
☑ High alcohol wine	☑ Acidity in wine
☑ Highly tannic wine	☑ Carbonation in wine
	☑ Fruit intensity in wine

White Wine—Youthful, acidic, fruity white wines with low to moderate alcohol, and with or without residual sugar, work most effectively. Examples are Sparkling wines, Rieslings, Chenin Blanc, Gewürztraminer, Pinot Grigio, and Pinot Gris.

Rosé Wine—Combines the fruitiness of a red wine with the crispness and lightness of a white wine. They are generally an appropriate warm-to-hot weather drinking option and work very well with full-flavored foods. spicy Asian, Latin American, or Cajun foods.

Red Wine—Young, acidic, fruity red wines with limited to no oak aging and with low alcohol and tannin work best. Examples are rosé, Pinot Noir, Gamay, Dolcetto, Tempranillo and Barbera.

OTHER TECHNIQUES USED TO ASSIST IN ACHIEVING AN EFFECTIVE WINE PAIRING

Food is easily adapted and altered by making minor adjustments to accommodate a wine pairing. There are many fine-tuning techniques that professional cooks use to build body, flavor, and texture into a food item. These methods can alter the appropriateness of a potential wine pairing. If a wine has been selected, applying these techniques can assist to connect a dish to a particular wine by either decreasing or building weight, body (or overall intensity) as well as flavors within the dish.

Adjusting food dishes, either intentionally or unintentionally, can alter a potential wine pairing. For example, linguine in a creamy Alfredo sauce is a simpler dish than sautéed jumbo shrimp, mushrooms, roasted red peppers, spinach, and spices with linguine in a creamy Alfredo sauce. Following are some possible adjustments that can be used to make a more cohesive match:

☑ **Skin On or Off**—Skin can be left on poultry (such as duck or chicken) to provide a heightened level of color, flavor, texture, and fat or taken off to lighten the intensity of a dish.

☑ **Bone In or Out**—Bones have a large amount of gelatine and flavor that contribute to the body of meat (porterhouse steak, pork chop, lamb chop), poultry (chicken), and seafood (finfish). Removing the bone or bones can slightly reduce the flavor and juiciness of a food item.

☑ **Combine Multiple Food Types**—Combining multiple foods can add dimension, change the flavor, and adjust the weight of the dish. For example, adding both sautéed shrimp and scallops to linguini pasta with olive oil and garlic alters the character of the dish.

☑ **Adjust Fat Content**—Leaving more external fat on a meat item adds richness and juiciness. Trimming away some external fat makes a food item leaner.

☑ **Adjust Cooking Method**—Altering a cooking method can be used to effectively match the intensity of a wine.

- ☑ **Alter the Type of Quantity of Sauce**—More or less sauce can adjust the weight or intensity of a dish.
- ☑ **Adding an Acid**—Squeezing a little lemon or vinegar over the food helps to liven the flavors and also may assist in bridging the flavor with the wine. In addition, the acid component in the food can be used to compare or contrast an acidic (or other) component found in a particular wine.
- ☑ **Using Infused Oil**—A splash of infused oil can heighten the flavors of any dish, from salads and soups to bread and pasta, and is great for sautéing or stir frying.
- ☑ **Dairy Fat**—Adding a pat of butter (or flavored butter) to melt over a finished food item can provide an additional bit of substance and weight and assist in bridging flavors that might be found in a particular wine. Finishing off a sauce or a risotto with a touch of cream can provide a similar effect.
- ☑ **Flavorful Poaching Liquids**—Using more flavorful liquids (wine, stock) than water when poaching can heighten the flavor of a dish.
- ☑ **Searing**—This is an important technique not only to seal the flavors and juices, but also to increase the flavors of meat prior to stewing, braising, or sautéing. Caramelization occurs on the surface and assists in adding complexity and in building aromas, flavors, and body in a food item.
- ☑ **Deglazing**—This method involves adding liquid to a pan over high heat in order to - remove and incorporate the dried brown bits left in the pan after the food item has been cooked. The liquid can be as simple as water or as complex as stock or wine.
- ☑ **Adjust Type of Fat**—Adjusting the type of fat (shortening, olive oil, vegetable oil, peanut oil) and what the item is coated in (batter or bread crumbs) prior to cooking will influence the flavor and intensity of the finished product. Also, a coating can cause a sauce to become absorbed into the food item, adding heightened flavor and richness.
- ☑ **Glazed or Crusted**—Food can be glazed or crusted with vinegar (balsamic vinegar) or wine (Madeira), condiments (honey, mustard, herbs) or bread crumbs. All of these coatings can act to heighten aromas, flavors, and the intensity of a dish.
- ☑ **Rubs**—A rub is a mixture of herbs and spices that are applied to an item, normally just prior to cooking or, in some cases, overnight. Since rubs lack liquid (as in marinades), a small amount can be extremely intense.
- ☑ **Marinade**—Marinading involves submerging a food item in a seasoned liquid (the marinade) of oil, acid, and flavorings for a short period. This method is used to tenderize a food item, and, more importantly, to flavor the product.
- ☑ **Brine**—This process involves submerging a food item in a ratio of salt and water (brine). It is used to enhance and season the interior of neutral flavored meats such as pork and poultry.

WINE AND FOOD PAIRING GUIDELINES

To achieve a happy marriage of wine and food, consider some general guidelines. These strategies have been preached for decades and certainly are useful to apply as loose, but reliable, guiding principles. Many of these guidelines follow the flow of the meal as each food course increases with intensity, body, and substance. An occasional palate cleanser (an intermezzo such as sorbet or a salad) may fall between a course or even each successive course. For example, many meals begin with an appetizer designed to be small and light so as not to overwhelm the palate, but instead to appease the hunger. Next, the soup or salad may follow, to provide another small source of nourishment and varying texture prior to the main event. Then the entrée—more substantial, heartier, and more filling—arrives. Finally, the dessert is consumed to provide satiety for the stomach and palate and to complete the dining experience.

Lighter Wines Before Heavier Wines

This approach runs parallel to the food courses—lighter foods before heavier foods. Most menus are designed to provide a diner with lighter courses first so as not to overwhelm the palate early in the dining process. Throughout the meal, the food courses increase in intensity, as do the beverages.

Dry Wines Before Sweet

This approach also runs parallel to the food courses—savory before sweet. A light, dry, crisp sparkling wine with an appetizer is a good example of a wine to serve with a beginning course. These kinds of wines cause salivation and do not overwhelm the palate too soon, whereas sweet wines tend to dull the palate and therefore are consumed at the end of the meal.

Seasonality, Occasion, and Mood (SOM)

There are certain moments, events, or times of year that can dictate a particular wine pairing.

Seasonality—Richer, heartier foods and beverages tend to be desired, sometimes unknowingly, with falling temperatures and crisp nights as fall and winter months approach. As fuller-bodied richer dishes are consumed, it is natural to pair richer, weightier wines that are compatible. Light, cool, and refreshing foods and beverages coordinate with rising temperatures, with long sunny days and warm evenings as the spring and summer months arrive.

Occasion—People drink different wines for different occasions. A customer might choose a wine with take-out food very differently than when dining at an upscale restaurant. A wine that might be appropriate for a summer barbecue could be quite different from wine that would be appropriate at a New Year's Eve festivity.

Not that people need a reason to drink other than for sheer enjoyment, but there is a certain correctness to selecting a particular type or style of wine for the given occasion.

Mood—This element is a free-for-all, as it really depends on the whim of the wine drinker. In some cases, the wine will be selected simply because a certain type or style of wine is desired or because a particular group of people may influence the decision. Sometimes, the time of day or day of week or amount of disposable income determines the choice of wine.

Regional Considerations

What would people drink if they found themselves in Burgundy, France? Local people usually drink the wines of their area with the cuisine of their region. Wine and food that evolve and grow together, go together. This guideline employs the classical approach to pairing wine and food.

Wine as a Main Ingredient

If a wine is incorporated within a dish, there is a natural partnership to pair the same or similar wine with the meal. This creates an obvious relationship between the wine and the food item; for example, when a Sauvignon Blanc is used as part of the sauce, it would seem appropriate to also serve it in a glass. The same care should be taken when using a wine in cooking as is taken with any other ingredients in the recipe. Most inexpensive wines (particularly the kind in jugs or bags) are low in alcohol, acid, and flavor. Therefore, an important philosophy to consider is, the dish will only be as good as the quality of the ingredients, including the wine.

FOUNDATIONS TO WINE AND FOOD PAIRING

NAME: _____   Score out of 20 points_____.

Use these questions to test your knowledge and understanding of the concepts presented in the chapter.

I. MULTIPLE CHOICE: Select the best possible answer from the options available.

1. A good guideline to follow when pairing wines with a food menu generally is

    a. Sweet wines are served before dry wines.

    b. Go from red to white wines.

    c. Progress from light- to full-bodied wines.

    d. Go from full- to light-bodied wines.

2. The first and foremost principle to follow when matching wine and food is to

    a. compare or contrast flavors.

    b. consider the mood, ambience, and occasion.

    c. contrast acidity with fat.

    d. balance the weight and intensity of the wine with the food.

3. A factor that can influence a food's weight and body is

    a. the cooking method.

    b. the sauce.

    c. the other ingredients (seasonings).

    d. all of the above.

    e. only answers a and b.

4. Which is a moist-heat cooking method?

    a. Grilling/broiling

    b. Smoking

    c. Deep Frying

    d. Poaching/Steaming

5. Coagulated protein (as in a pot roast) would pair best with

    a. Cabernet Sauvignon or Merlot.

    b. Merlot or Shiraz.

    c. Chardonnay or Sauvignon Blanc.

    d. Pinot Noir or Merlot.

6. Uncoagulated protein (as in a medium-rare T-bone steak) would pair best with

    a. Cabernet Sauvignon or Merlot.

    b. Pinot Noir or Merlot.

    c. Chardonnay or Pinot Noir.

    d. Riesling or Sauvignon Blanc.

7. A grilled wild king salmon would pair best with

    a. Cabernet Sauvignon or Merlot.

    b. Chardonnay or Sauvignon Blanc.

    c. Pinot Noir or Chardonnay.

    d. Sauvignon Blanc or Riesling.

8. Generally, medium-bodied acidic white wines can work well with

    a. acidic foods (lemon sauce).

    b. raw shellfish (oysters).

    c. light cream or butter sauce.

    d. all of the above.

    e. none of the above.

    f. only answers a and c.

9. Spicy foods have the ability to be paired with

    a. sweeter wines.

    b. fruity, low tannin wines.

    c. high-alcohol wines.

    d. all of the above.

    e. only answers a and b.

10. Fried foods have the ability to work well with

    a. sparkling wines.

    b. tannic red wines.

    c. high-alcohol red wines.

    d. fortified wines.

II. TRUE / FALSE: Circle the best possible answer.

11. A classic approach to wine and food pairing is where the food and wine have evolved together over a long period. **True / False**

12. The application of the analytical pairing approach can greatly increase the quality of a wine and food pairing. **True / False**

13. Generally, a wine's body should parallel that of the progression of the meal. **True / False**

14. Residual sugar in a wine can temper a moderately spicy food. **True / False**

15. Light-bodied red wines can pair effectively with coagulated protein. **True / False**

16. Light-bodied red wines go best with uncoagulated protein. **True / False**

17. Poached poultry and seafood work well with light- to medium-bodied acidic white wines. **True / False**

III. SHORT-ANSWER ESSAY / DISCUSSION QUESTIONS: Use a separate sheet of paper if necessary.

18. Provide some reasons that someone would pair wine with food.

19. Explain the difference between the classical pairing approach and the contemporary pairing approach.

20. Identify and describe the three principles of the analytical wine and food pairing approach.

FOUNDATIONS TO WINE AND FOOD PAIRING

ACTIVITY #1 FOOD TYPES

NAME _____

DIRECTIONS: Determine possible food types for each of the given Big Six grape varietals.

WHITE WINE VARIETALS	TYPICAL BODY AND WEIGHT	POSSIBLE FOOD TYPES
Riesling	Light-bodied	
Sauvignon Blanc	Medium-bodied	
Chardonnay	Full-bodied	

RED WINE VARIETALS	TYPICAL BODY AND WEIGHT	FOOD TYPE
Pinot Noir	Light-bodied	
Merlot	Medium-bodied	
Cabernet Sauvignon	Full-bodied	

FOUNDATIONS TO WINE AND FOOD PAIRING

ACTIVITY #2 PAIRING WINE TO FOOD TYPES AND COOKING METHODS

NAME _____

DIRECTIONS: Given a food type, expand on a possible cooking method for each and identify a possible wine pairing. Justify the reasoning.

FOOD TYPES	POSSIBLE COOKING METHOD	WINE JUSTIFICATION
Pork chop		
Salmon		
Oysters		
Whole chicken		
Chicken breast with skin		
Skinless chicken breast		
Beef stew meat		
Beef porterhouse		
Leg of lamb		
Risotto		

6

Advanced Wine and Food Pairing

The food types are the primary items analyzed in a dish to determine the wine match. The more familiar we are with base products, cooking techniques, and sauces, the more effective we can be at modifying food's weight, flavor, and texture levels to pair well with wine.

LEARNING OBJECTIVES

Upon completion of this chapter, the learner will be able to:

- Understand the typical progression of courses and the common styles of wine that may accompany each one.
- Comprehend basic knowledge about food types and their potential wine pairings.
- Provide a framework for wine and food pairing choices through detailed wine strategies.
- Develop analytical and decision-making skills by applying the three principles of the analytical approach.

FOOD TYPES AND COURSES

The food types are often the primary item analyzed in a dish to determine the wine match. They can be thought of as the particular "center-of-the-plate" item in a dish that is the main event or attraction. The primary food types typically tend to be protein based, such as meat, poultry, and seafood, but may include legumes, pasta, or vegetables as well. With a greater understanding of base products, cooking techniques, and sauces, it is possible to more effectively modify weight, flavor, and texture levels to achieve a more successful wine pairing.

Most meals outside the home (and inside, for those adventurous home cooks) consist of a set of courses. A course is a food or group of foods served in a single meal, normally served in a timed sequence. A common sequence of courses includes an appetizer, soup and/or salad, an entrée, and dessert. Some high-end fine dining restaurants serve meals that consist of 12 and even 20 courses. During the meal, there is the potential to serve a single wine throughout or a different wine for each individual course. Therefore, with each meal, a decision must be made as to which wine to serve with which course. The most memorable course tends to be the entrée. It is this course that the meal builds up to, as it is the main dish, or centerpiece, of the meal, and it tends to present the most substance or flavor of any of the other courses. Therefore, the entrée course generally calls for the most substantial and special wine of the meal.

Wine Strategies

When in Doubt?—Some components of certain styles of wine may be referred to as "user-friendly" or "wine friendly." User-friendly wines have a high probability of being paired successfully with many food types and dishes. Any or a combination of the following elements will be more likely to provide a more triumphant pairing for many food items:

- ☑ Carbonation (the bubbles)
- ☑ Moderate to high levels of acidity
- ☑ Dry to slightly off dry
- ☑ Medium bodied
- ☑ Moderate to low alcohol
- ☑ Low tannins to no tannins

FIGURE 6–1 Oysters on the half shell

(Ian O'Leary © Dorling Kindersley)

APPETIZERS
Pairing Wine with Appetizers

The role of the appetizer is to kick-start the appetite. Traditionally, the appetizer ("Hors d'oeuvre" (or DERV) in French, "Antipasto" in Italian, "Meze" (MEH zay) in Greek, and "Tapas" in Spanish) was offered as a greeting in anticipation to the beginning of a meal and to sustain the guests' appetite until the main meal was served. In some cases, there is no meal to be served afterward, and appetizers are to be a small offering in the case of a reception or cocktail party. Figure 6–1 shows freshly shucked oysters on the half shell, paired with a light, crisp sparkling wine.

The beverage drunk with the appetizer is known as the *aperitif* (ah-pehr-uh-TEEF). The term derives from the Latin word "aperio," meaning "open." An aperitif is a pre-dinner (or pre-lunch) drink designed to stimulate the appetite and can be thought of as an appetizer in beverage form. It is widely believed that aperitifs started out as medicinal beverages prepared from spirits that had been infused with herbs and spices. Over the years, the purpose of these beverages evolved, and the pre-dinner drink became fashionable in Europe both as a palate-primer and as a social tradition. This custom traveled to America at about the same time that cocktails were becoming popular in the 1900s. Figure 6–2 shows grilled prawns and melon appetizer salad.

The purpose of the aperitif is to offer a light, dry, crisp wine (Champagne, Sauvignon Blanc, Pinot Grigio, chilled Fino Sherry) or other beverage (vodka martini, gin and tonic) in order to cleanse the palate and get the gastric stomach juices flowing for the hunger pains to begin. The aperitif beverage typically is light because appetizers typically are light. The key is not to be too sweet. Aperitifs can be categorized in the following ways: (1) spirit based (the subject of which does not fall under the scope of this textbook) or (2) wine based. Figure 6–3 shows skewered chicken with peanut sauce appetizer.

FIGURE 6–2 Grilled prawn and melon salad
(Eliot Wexler)

Pairing Strategies with Appetizers

1. Dry white wines with ample acidity that work best with appetizers include Pinot Grigio/Gris, Dry Riesling (Alsatian Style), Muscat, Semillon, Chenin Blanc, or Sauvignon Blanc.
2. Dry fortified wines that may work with appetizers are Sherry (Fino or Manzanilla) and Madeira (Sercial or Verdelho).
3. Bubbles assist with refreshing the palate and are found in complex-style sparkling wines such as Champagne, Cava, or Blanc de Blanc Sparkling Wine.

SALADS
Pairing Wine with Salads

Salad has always been known as "unfriendly" when being paired with wine. This perception is mostly because many salads are drowned in a dressing with a strong acidic base. Also, while they have texture, many salads often lack weight and body. Traditionally, the salad provided a crisp, cool, and fresh respite from the rest of the meal. The role of the salad has served as a means of refreshment and rejuvenation for the palate by adding texture and acidity prior to the more heavy, filling, remaining part of the meal.

Over the years, salads have become much more than just a plate of lettuce with an acidic dressing. They now take all variety of forms, with elements providing weight and

FIGURE 6–3 Skewered chicken with peanut sauce
(© Renee Comet Photography/Stockfood America)

FIGURE 6–4 Walnut pecan blue cheese salad
(518 West Italian Café)

body that can more easily support a wine pairing. They are versatile and can be served as a first course or as an entrée. Whichever course they are served as, salads should always be well chilled in order to accentuate the crispness and freshness relationship with the wine. Figure 6–4 shows a walnut pecan blue cheese salad.

The traditional tossed, or green, salads consist of three parts: (1) the base (any variety of greens, from iceberg lettuce, to Romaine, to bibb), (2) complementary ingredients (including any varying combination of other vegetables, fresh or dried fruits, toasted nuts or seeds, cheese, pasta, and grains or protein), and (3) dressing (vinaigrette or dairy based).

Salad Dressings

A salad dressing consists of an unthickened or thickened liquid prepared for the purpose of applying flavor and moisture to a salad. There are two basic types of salad dressing: vinaigrette based and dairy based.

Vinaigrette-Based Dressings—Often, vinaigrette-based dressings are unthickened. Most salad dressings are an emulsion, which is a uniform mixture of two unmixable liquids that may be either temporarily or permanently held together. A basic vinaigrette dressing consists of oil, vinegar, and flavorings or seasonings. The types of oil and vinegar can range from neutral to flavorful (vegetable or corn oil, olive oil, walnut oil, peanut oil; plain vinegar, white wine vinegar, apple cider vinegar, red wine vinegar, balsamic vinegar).

Vinaigrette's base is vinegar and oil. The unfriendly ingredient is the vinegar, as it tends to clash with wine. However, the ratio of vinegar to oil can be adjusted to better accommodate a wine pairing or just for personal preference. A more effective wine pairing can occur by adjusting the ratio to cut down on the acidity. Normally, a vinaigrette ratio is three parts oil to one part vinegar (or other acid). Adjusting the ratio to four parts oil to one part vinegar or using a mixture of acid that is other than just vinegar—for instance, by adding fruit or citrus juice to replace all or part of the vinegar—helps the pairing. The vinaigrette may be emulsified with the addition of mustard or seasonings that create more flavor and mouth-feel, which can alter a wine pairing.

Dairy-Based Dressings—Sometimes, a vinaigrette is thickened with the incorporation of dairy products, as dairy tends to hold the dressing together and to calm the acid component. The dairy acts to create more of a pungent, creamy mouth-coating texture. Common dairy bases include sour cream, cream, yogurt, buttermilk, blue cheese, and mayonnaise.

Adjustments to a Salad and Its Dressing—Making adjustments can bridge a wine to the salad and create a more effective pairing.

☑ Using such ingredients as nut-based oils or olive oil, garlic, and herbs in the dressing, decreasing the vinegar-to-oil ratio, or adding dairy can adjust the wine pairing favorably.

☑ Protein (such as poultry, fish or beef) provides more texture, weight, and intensity to a salad; cheese helps to coat the palate from some of the acidity present in the dressing; and a garnish of nuts, seeds, or croutons likewise creates a bridge.

Pairing Strategies for Salads

1. Vinaigrette-based dressings work best with cool-climate white, rosé, or sparkling wines that are light- to medium-bodied with ample acidity, such as sparkling wine, Sauvignon Blanc, Pinot Grigio/Gris, Riesling (Alsatian Style), Grüner Veltliner, and unoaked Chardonnay (Chablis or New Zealand).

2. Dairy-based dressing or more substantial protein-type accompaniments such as grilled chicken or seafood increase the body of the salad and allow pairing with a warm-climate white wine that is medium to full bodied and oak aged white wine, such as Chardonnay, Viognier, or Fumé Blanc.

3. Some elements of sweetness or spiciness, such as honey, ginger, soy or hoisin sauce, and peanuts, in the ingredients either of the dressings or of the salad accompaniments, work well with white wines such as Gewürztraminer, Muscat, Chenin Blanc, Riesling (German Style), or Rosé.

4. A salad with elements of a strong type of cheese accompaniment or substantial protein should be paired with a full-bodied white wine or red wine with low tannin, such as Pinot Noir, Cabernet Franc, or Gamay.

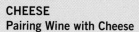

CHEESE
Pairing Wine with Cheese

Thousands of different varieties of cheese throughout the world are made from a single primary ingredient: milk. In essence, cheese is a concentrated form of milk, as it takes about 10 lbs of milk to produce 1 lb of cheese.

Cheese can be made from a variety and combination of different milks, primarily cow, goat, and sheep milk, with a small amount of buffalo milk. The aroma and flavor of milk can be influenced by varying climatic conditions and the type of grazing and feeding the animal was raised on. The fat content in the milk (skim, 2%, or cream), the type of mold or bacteria used, and the shaping and aging processes influence the texture, flavor, and color of cheese. Each step is crucial in determining the flavor and style of cheese.

There are various ways to categorize cheese, whether by style, type of milk, texture, aging (or ripening) process, or place of origin. Cheese can range across two broad categories: (1) fresh, young, and simple to (2) aged, mature, and complex.

The seven categories of cheeses described next have been arranged according to style and texture, and indicate the type of milk, and in some cases, place of origin.

1. *FRESH/SOFT CHEESE*—The term *fresh* is used to describe cheese that has not been aged or that is very slightly cured. Fresh cheeses may have a spoonable consistency, whereas other types may be slightly firm. They have a white appearance with high moisture content, usually are mild to tangy, and have a very creamy taste and soft texture.

Examples of Popular Fresh/Soft Cheese

Chèvre (Goat)—*Chèvre* is the French word for "goat" and refers to any cheese made from goat milk. *Banon* is a goat cheese wrapped in wine-soaked grape or chestnut leaves and having a bit of blue mold on the rind. *Cottage* (cow), *feta* (cow, goat, or sheep), and *mascarpone* (cow and cream) cheeses contain 70% milk fat, made by curdling heavy cream with citric acid to produce a highly moist, rich, and creamy cheese. *Neufchâtel* (cow) and *Ricotta* (cow) are made by heating the whey to create a new curd, which is then drained and becomes snowy white. Figure 6–5 shows a trio of soft cheeses.

2. *SOFT OR RIND-RIPENED CHEESE*—The term *soft or rind-ripened* is used to describe cheeses that are ripened from the outside in to the center. The most common soft-ripened cheeses have a white, bloomy rind. The rind is edible and is produced by dusting or spraying the surface of the cheese with a mold before the brief aging or ripening

FIGURE 6–5 A trio of soft cheese
(JONELLE WEAVER/Getty Images, Inc.-Taxi)

period. When fully ripe, the cheese will be resilient when pressed. If the cheese is under-ripe, it will be firm and chalky; if overripe, it will be runny when cut and will smell a bit like ammonia.

These cheeses are buttery and available in varying degrees of richness. For example, single cream is 50% butterfat, double cream is 60%, and triple cream is 70% butterfat.

Examples of Popular Soft or Rind-Ripened Cheese

Brie (goat's milk and, sometimes, cream), *Camembert* (raw cow's or goat's milk), and *Limburger* (cow's milk) have a brownish surface with an ivory interior. They are smooth and creamy with a pungent earthy aroma that intensifies with age. Figure 6–6 shows a soft or rind-ripened cheese.

FIGURE 6–6 Soft or rind ripened cheese
(Ian O'Leary © Dorling Kindersley)

3. *SEMI-SOFT CHEESE*—The term *semi-soft* is used to describe cheese that has a smooth, generally creamy interior, with little or no rind. These cheeses are typically high in moisture content and range from very mild in flavor to very pungent. Semi-soft cheeses are sometimes mixed with or coated in herbs, spices, or ashes.

Examples of Popular Semi-Soft Cheese

Edam (typically made with skim cow's milk) has a firmer texture. *Gouda* (typically made with whole cow's milk) has a pale yellow interior and a buttery, creamy, and nutty flavor. These types of cheese commonly have wax exteriors that are color coded to mean the following: Red = mild, Yellow = aged or flavored, Black or brown = smoked.

Fontina (cow's or sheep's milk) is ivory to light gold. *Havarti* (hah-VAHR-tee) (cream-enriched cow's milk) is pale yellow with a buttery, creamy, and slight acidic flavor. *Morbier* (mor-b-ay) (cow), *Monterey Jack* (cow), and *Muenster* (cow) all have an orange or white surface with a creamy white interior. *Port-Salut* (POHR-sah-LOO) (cow) is another example of a popular semi-soft cheese.

4. *SEMI-HARD*—The terms *firm* and *hard* are used to describe this broad category of cheese. Their taste profiles range from very mild and buttery, through nutty, to sharp and pungent. Most semi-hard cheeses consist of cheddars and Swiss types. This family of cheese has great melting properties for use in cooking.

Examples of Popular Hard Cheese

Cheddar Types—*Cheddar* (cow's milk) is probably the most well known and popular semi-hard cheese. *Colby* was invented in Wisconsin, and *Monterey Jack* was invented in Monterey, California. *Jarlsberg* (cow's milk) and *Manchego* (sheep's milk) are other often-used hard cheeses.

Swiss Types—*Emmenthaler* (EM-mawn-tahl or EM-mawn-tahler) (cow's milk) is the original Swiss cheese, which is characterized by its holes, or *eyes*, that form during the curing process as the CO_2 that is trapped in the cheese is released. *Gruyère (gree-YEHR), Beaufort,* and *Jarlsberg* are examples of Swiss types of cheese.

5. *HARD CHEESE*—In Italy, hard cheese is known as *grana,* meaning "grainy," because of its hard granular texture that develops through aging. It also has a firm consistency due to a loss of moisture through its considerable aging time. Hard cheeses often have been treated with a salt bath prior to aging to assist in drawing out additional moisture. Most are grated, or sliced and eaten in chunks.

Examples of Popular Very Hard or Grana Cheese

Asiago (cow's milk), *Parmigiano Reggiano* (raw cow's milk), *Grana Padano* (cow's milk), and *Pecorino* (sheep, goat, or cow's milk) are all examples of popular Italian Grana cheeses.

6. *PASTA FILATA CHEESE*—The term *pasta filata* is applied mostly to a cheese family of Italian origin and describes how that cheese is made. *Pasta filata* literally means "spun curd." The curds are dipped into hot water and then stretched or spun until the proper consistency, texture, and shape are achieved.

Examples of Popular Pasta Filata Cheese

Mozzarella (cow or buffalo) and *Provolone* (cow's milk). Provolone types are often smoked or aged for additional character and firmer texture.

7. *BLUE-VEINED CHEESE*—The term *blue* is used to describe cheese that has distinctive blue-green veins. These cheeses are created when a specific type of mold is added during the cheesemaking process and is exposed to air to encourage its growth. The mold provides a distinctive flavor to the cheese, which ranges from fairly mild to assertive and pungent. Needles are used to pierce holes in the cheese in order to allow gases to escape and oxygen to enter to support mold growth during the aging process. The cheeses are then salted or brined and allowed to ripen in caves or cave-like conditions. They are smooth and creamy to dry and crumbly, with a piquant, earthy, strong, and pungent flavor.

Examples of Popular Blue-Veined Cheese

Bleu or *Blue* (cow's or goat's milk with or without cream); *Danish Blue* (cow's milk); *Gorgonzola* (cow's or goat's milk), produced in Italy; *Maytag Blue* (cow's milk), produced in America (Iowa); *Roquefort* (sheep's milk), produced in France; *Stilton* (cow's milk), produced in England; and *Cabrales* (goat's milk, sometimes with cow and sheep's milk blended in), produced in Spain are all popular examples of blue-veined cheeses. Figure 6–7 shows a blue-veined cheese.

FIGURE 6–7 Blue-veined cheese

(Ian O'Leary © Dorling Kindersley)

Pairing Strategies for Cheese

1. The creamy, milky, and rich-mouth-feel cheeses such as fresh soft, soft or rind ripened; semi-soft; and pasta filata cheese can pair well with a medium- to full-bodied white wine with ample acidity and/or carbonation to assist in cleansing the palate.
2. Semi-hard and hard cheese can work well with medium- to full-bodied red wine such as Shiraz, Syrah, Sangiovese (Chianti Classico or Brunello), and Tempranillo (Reserva or Gran Reserva Rioja) Nebbiolo (Barbaresco or Barolo).
3. Blue-veined cheese has the ability to pair with robust red wine such as Cabernet Sauvignon or Port.

SOUPS
Pairing Wine with Soups

Soups have been known as wine "unfriendly," mostly because many soups are primarily liquid and lacking texture. Pairing a liquid (the soup) with another liquid (the wine) is simply, not very interesting. Although this wisdom makes sense, the days of the consommé or bowl of broth with every meal are gone. Nowadays, soups have more textural elements, such as chunks of meat, poultry, or seafood, in addition to beans, grains, pasta, or vegetables, and may be served with a large piece of crusty bread.

A soup can be described as a flavorful liquid of varying consistency, served hot or cold, that might contain pieces of other food (chicken, fish, beans, vegetables, and so on). All soups begin with a base or liquid—usually a flavorful stock based on chicken, beef, veal, or fish—but can also be water. Then they may be enriched with milk or cream. Figure 6–8 shows a cream-based soup.

Soup categories include the following:

1. **Clear Simple Soups**—Broths and consommés are in this category.
2. **Thin-Based Soups**—These soups are unthickened, with more of a broth-type consistency, but may have chunks of vegetables, grains, or proteins. Examples are French onion, Manhattan clam chowder, and minestrone.
3. **Thick-Based Soups**—These soups may be pureed or enriched with cream or milk. Examples are buttered squash, carrot ginger, New England clam chowder, cream of wild rice, and potato corn chowder.

Pairing Strategies for Soups

1. Clear simple soups work best with light-bodied acidic white wines such as Riesling, Pinot Grigio/Gris, and Blanc de Blanc Sparkling Wine.
2. Thin-based soups often have textural elements of vegetables, grain, and/or protein that allow a medium-bodied white or light- to medium-bodied red wine to pair well. Examples are as follows: whites—Sauvignon Blanc or unoaked Chardonnay; reds—Pinot Noir, Sangiovese, Gamay, Cabernet Franc, Barbera, or Dolcetto.
3. Pureed or cream-based soups such as New England clam chowder, corn chowder, and potato chowder work well with a weighty full-bodied white wine. Examples are Chardonnay, Viognier or Blanc de Noir Sparkling Wine, and vintage Champagne.

FIGURE 6–8 Cream-based soup
(© Dorling Kindersley)

VEGETABLES and GRAINS
Pairing Wine with Vegetarian-Type Dishes

Vegetarian or meatless food often lacks the weight and body of other foods such as steaks and poultry. Therefore, matching wine to vegetarian foods requires a bit more thought because they can be tricky to pair successfully. *Vegetarian food* is so broad and inaccurate a term that it can misrepresent the food it names. Some individuals perceive it to mean "without the use of animal products." Other individuals, technically called *lacto-pesco vegetarians,* consider themselves vegetarians because they don't eat meat, but they still consume seafood and dairy products. Others, called *lacto-ovo vegetarians,* consume no meat, poultry, or seafood, but will eat dairy products and eggs. Those who consume no animal products at all are called *vegans.* Wine pairings will be different, depending on the definition of *vegetarian-type food* that an individual is dining under. Figure 6–9 shows asparagus with a light citrus sauce paired with a crisp acidic white wine.

Often, the foundation of vegetarian cuisine is grain- or dairy-based, but a vegetarian dish may in fact be just a plate of vegetables. Such dishes may range from a bowl of steamed rice to a full-flavored, spicy Szechwan tofu or broccoli stir-fry. Pairing wine with vegetables is quite different from pairing wine with other types of foods. Vegetables lack the body and fat of meat. While it is possible to build flavor into vegetables, it is impossible to match a wine with vegetarian dishes with the same intensity that a wine is matched with a protein food.

Universally, vegetarian cuisine lacks weight and body, compared with protein-based food items. In vegetarian cuisine, there are ways to partially mimic the weight and body of those missing ingredients, with the use of tofu, tempeh, dairy, or mushrooms. Adjusting cooking methods to incorporate more caramelization—such as through broiling and grilling—can assist as well.

FIGURE 6–9 Vegetarian pairing with a crisp white wine
(Ian O'Leary © Dorling Kindersley)

Adjustments to Vegetarian-Type Food—Making adjustments can bridge a wine to the food and create a more effective pairing. Following are some suggestions:

- ☑ Accommodate wine pairings to vegetarian dishes by building body through using more robust cooking methods such as: roasting, grilling, or broiling.
- ☑ Use ingredients to create bridges. Butter, cream, mushrooms, and cheese can add texture and richness. Purees and sauces, such as reductions and emulsifications, can also be used to promote a fuller body in order to create a more effective pairing between the wine and food.

Pairing Strategies for Vegetarian-Based Dishes

1. Generally, light- and medium-bodied white wines, sparkling wines, rosés, or light-bodied red wines will pair best with foods that are free of any meat, poultry, or seafood.

2. Spicy ingredients such as curry and chilies work best with a wine that has a small amount of residual sugar, such as Gewürztraminer, Riesling (German Style), Chenin Blanc, or a fruit-driven Sparkling Wine (Asti, Moscato di Asti, and Prosecco) or sweeter Rosé (fruity and sweet style) or a light- to medium-bodied, fruit driven red wine with low tannin.

3. Vegetarian-type foods that include tempeh or tofu work well with a light-bodied red wine such as Dolcetto, Barbera, Pinot Noir, or Gamay.

4. Risotto or other grain-based dishes work well with light- to medium-bodied white wines such as Pinot Grigio/Gris, Riesling (Alsatian Style), or Sauvignon Blanc, Grüner Veltliner, or Pinot Blanc.

5. It is relatively simple to enrich and build flavors into a grain-based dish by adding cheese or cream. This can heighten a particular dish and allow for pairing with a medium- to full-bodied white wine such as Sauvignon Blanc, Chardonnay, or a light-bodied red wine such as Pinot Noir.

SANDWICHES and BURGERS
Pairing Wine with Sandwiches and Burgers

Sandwiches can consist of burgers, wraps, panini, or traditional sandwiches. The variations are endless, but they often consist of a protein element, cheese, vegetables, and sauce or dressing, with some form of bread. The bread acts to hold the protein and vegetables together and absorbs a large amount of the dressing or sauce.

Burgers—These essentially are made of minced-up meat, poultry, or seafood. When pairing a wine with a burger, consider whether the burger is beef, poultry, or seafood based. Traditionally, burgers are made from tougher cuts of beef with added fat. Therefore, most burgers veer toward being a beefy, fatty dish, often grilled or broiled, which adds another dimension of flavor and texture due to the browning or caramelization of the outside of the burger. A meat burger may consist of coagulated meat if cooked medium well or well done, or uncoagulated protein if cooked rare, medium rare, or to a medium degree of doneness. The degree of coagulation will influence the appropriateness of the wine to be paired.

Sandwiches/Wraps/Panini—Protein-based sandwiches made with "lunch meat" taste a bit different than those made with fresh, unprocessed meat. Processed meats such as ham, turkey, or chicken have a more prevalent amount of salt and will possibly dictate a different wine pairing than unprocessed meats. Figure 6–10 shows a turkey and cheese with mustard mayonnaise sandwich paired with a Chardonnay.

Pairing Strategies for Sandwiches and Burgers

1. Consider whether the item is a cold or hot sandwich. A cold sandwich works better with a cold and crisp Blanc de Blanc Sparkling Wine or white wine such as Riesling, Pinot Grigio/Gris, Pinot Blanc, Sauvignon Blanc, or unoaked Chardonnay.

2. Consider the sauces and condiments served on the burger or sandwich, as the bread holds a large amount of added ingredients besides the meat. A sauce such as

FIGURE 6–10 Sandwich with a glass of wine
(St. Supery Winery)

ketchup, mustard, or mayonnaise will work well with a medium- to full-bodied white wine such as Sauvignon Blanc, Viognier or Chardonnay.

3. Uncoagulated beef burgers need a more substantial medium- to full-bodied red wine, such as Merlot, Shiraz, Syrah, or Zinfandel. Adding such elements as bacon, cheese, or grilled onions or mushrooms can strengthen the pairing with these wines.

4. Coagulated beef burgers work better with a light- to medium-bodied red wine such as Pinot Noir, Gamay, Cabernet Franc, Pinotage, Merlot, Sangiovese, Dolcetto, or Barbera.

5. Whereas a medium- to full-bodied white wine can work with vegetarian, poultry, and seafood burgers, depending on the intensity of the sauce, light-bodied red wines can work as well. Whites wines good for this pairing are Sauvignon Blanc and Chardonnay; good red wines are Gamay, Dolcetto, Barbera, and Pinot Noir.

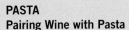

PASTA
Pairing Wine with Pasta

FIGURE 6–11 Pasta
(Ian O'Leary © Dorling Kindersley)

Selecting a wine to pair with pasta is dependent on several factors: (1) the shape of the pasta, (2) the type of sauce, and (3) other ingredients in the pasta. These elements should always be considered when pairing a wine, as they may alter the style and type of wine to be paired.

Shape of Pasta—Pasta can be made into various shapes and sizes. Certain types of pasta can influence sauce and ingredient adhesion, creating an effect of lighter or fuller pasta. For example, spaghetti does not allow for much sauce or ingredient adhesion; however, penne pasta is hollow and has ridges, which allow for greater sauce and ingredient adhesion and a potentially more robust pasta dish.

Some pasta shapes, such as jumbo shells, allow the pasta to be stuffed with ingredients like cheese, beef, chicken, or shrimp. Common fillable pasta shapes include manicotti, cannelloni, shells, ravioli, and tortellini.

Types of Sauce—Overall, pasta sauces tend to be the defining element in the dish. A wine is typically paired to the sauce and, possibly, to additional ingredients such as cheese or meat if they are part of the dish. Sauces can be based on five major styles: (1) oil based, (2) cream based, (3) cheese based, (4) tomato based, and (5) meat based.

Types of Ingredients—Ingredients that significantly influence a potential wine pairing often are added to pasta dishes. Common added ingredients include meatballs, sausage, shrimp, scallops, and bacon. Typically, meatballs and sausage will be added to pasta dishes with tomato- or meat-based sauces. Bacon, shrimp, and scallops will be more commonly added to oil- or cream-based sauces. Figure 6–11 shows pasta with red sauce.

Pairing Strategies for Pasta-Based Dishes

1. Ingredients such as shrimp, scallops, and bacon can work well with light- to medium-bodied white wine, such as Riesling, Pinot Grigio/Gris, Pinot Blanc, Grüner Veltliner, or Sauvignon Blanc.

2. Ingredients such as meatballs, sausage, or bacon can work well with light- to medium-bodied red wines such as Pinot Noir, Barbera, Dolcetto, or Sangiovese.

3. **Oil- and Cream-Based Sauces**—These add texture and mouth-feel to the pasta. Oil-based sauces add a subtle fat flavor that works well with light- to medium-bodied white wine such as Riesling, Pinot Grigio/Gris, Pinot Blanc, Grüner Veltliner, or Sauvignon Blanc. Common oil-based sauces are pesto and olive oil with garlic. Cream-based sauces add more weight and mouth coating to a pasta dish and work better with a medium- to full-bodied white wine such as Chardonnay or Viognier. Alfredo is common cream-based sauce.

4. **Cheese-Based Sauces**—These sauces are heavy and rich. They create a mouth-coating texture that pairs well with a medium- to full-bodied red wine such as Shiraz, Syrah, and Zinfandel. An example of this category is an aged cheddar cheese sauce, as may be used in a macaroni and cheese dish.

5. **Tomato-Based Sauces**—The acidity found in sauces such as a tomato-based sauce pairs best with wines that have ample acidity as well. Select a wine that has low to moderate tannin and body, such as Gamay (Crus Beaujolais), Pinot Noir, Sangiovese, Barbera, or Dolcetto. Common sauces in this category include marinara, Pomodoro, and Putanesca sauce.

6. **Meat-Based Sauces**—Meat-based sauces are hearty and meaty in texture and flavor. The making of these sauces usually begins by the process of browning ground or cubed and used as meat in a sauté pan to obtain caramelization on the exterior. Then the pan typically is deglazed with a wine or stock to increase additional flavor and ultimately is combined with the sauce. Meat sauces sometimes are combined with tomato-based sauces. These sauces work best with hearty red wines with good acidity and light to medium tannin and body. Examples are Sangiovese (Chianti Classico), Nero d'Avola, Barbera, Dolcetto, and Syrah. A common meat-based sauce is Bolognese.

Seafood consists of two subcategories: finfish and shellfish. Finfish can be broken down into round fish and flat fish. Shellfish can be broken down commonly into mollusks and crustaceans.

Finfish originate from either fresh water or saltwater and contain a backbone, gills, and fins. The flavor, color, fat, and texture of finfish are largely determined by how active they are and the type of water they live in (warm, cold, salt, or fresh).

Finfish meat has the same general composition as the meat of poultry, but is naturally tender, with varying amounts of fat and very little connective tissue. Therefore, finfish cook quickly and methods are generally based on fat content and size of fish. The amount of fat contained within a fish is a determining factor as to how a fish responds when cooked. High-fat fish yields a fatty or oily dish (salmon and mackerel), and low-fat fish yields a lean dish (cod and haddock). Figure 6–12 shows a stuffed fish.

Low-activity fish is often considered *lean fish* that has a delicate lean flesh with light flavor and texture. Lean fish usually respond best to lighter cooking methods that preserve their delicate flavor and texture. Although some have enough texture to be fried or baked. Examples of low-activity fish are sole, flounder, halibut, cod, pollock, monkfish, and tilapia. Sauces can be butter or egg based as a way to provide a bit of flavor and richness to the lean fish.

High-activity fish, often considered moderate to fatty fish, can be described as fatty or oily and has a darker flesh with more pronounced flavors and meaty texture. Fatty fish usually responds well and stands up to more intense cooking methods because of the higher fat content and often richer texture. This fish is most suitable for dry-heat cooking techniques such as grilling or broiling. Examples of high-activity fish are bass, grouper, salmon, tuna, mackerel, shark, swordfish, mahi-mahi. Sauces tend to be more acidic based (citrus, wine, mustard, tomato, or fruit) in order to balance the fattiness and richness of the fish. Figure 6–13 shows a poached salmon with herbed butter sauce.

Fish with a high fat content are often chosen for curing or smoking. These methods allow the fish to have sufficient flavor and fat left over after the cooking process. Common cured or smoked fish are sturgeon; salmon; tuna; whitefish; herring; and fatty finfish such as tuna, salmon, and shark. These fish are all are meaty, full flavored, and oily and are prepared either with or without skin to assist in holding the fish together.

FIGURE 6–12 Stuffed fish
(© Dorling Kindersley)

FIGURE 6–13 Poached salmon
(Edward Allwright © Dorling Kindersley)

Pairing Strategies for Finfish

1. Lean finfish goes well with light- to medium-bodied crisp acidic white wine with little to no oak, such as Chenin Blanc, Sauvignon Blanc, Pinot Blanc, Pinot Grigio/Gris, Grüner Veltliner, unoaked Chardonnay, Riesling, and Sparkling Wine.

FIGURE 6–14 Sushi
(David Murray © Dorling Kindersley)

2. Fatty finfish can pair most effectively with a medium- to full-bodied white wine with light or full oak that has undergone malolactic fermentation, such as Fumé Blanc, Chardonnay, or Viognier, or with light-bodied reds with low tannin, such as Gamay, Barbera, Dolcetto, Cabernet Franc or Pinot Noir.

3. Sushi can pair well with crisp acidic light- to medium-bodied white wines or sparkling wine. Sushi is pictured in Figure 6–14.

Shellfish have a soft body, which may be completely or partially enclosed in some form of a shell, and have no fins, vertebrae, internal skeleton, or skull. Overall, the meat of shellfish tends to be lean and on the tender side because of the fishes' low activity.

The two major types of shellfish are *mollusks* and *crustaceans*. Mollusks live within two external hard shells joined by a hinge. Within the shells, Mollusks contain tender to slightly resistant meat. Common types include clams, mussels, scallops, and oysters. Crustaceans maintain a segmented exterior hard shell as a part of the body, with jointed legs. The flesh is soft, sweet, and delicate. Common types include lobsters, crabs, and shrimp. Shrimp cocktail is pictured in Figure 6–15.

Less significant shellfish include cephalopods (SEHF-uh-lah-pod) that contain no external shell, but have cartilage in head (squid, octopus) and univalves (YOO-nuh-valv) are a mollusk with a single shell and single muscle (conch, snails).

Adjustments to Shellfish—Making adjustments in shellfish preparation can bridge a wine to the food and create a more effective pairing.

☑ Overall, shellfish are fairly neutral and can absorb the flavors of most sauces quite easily. Simple sauces can range from a squeeze of a lemon or a butter sauce to a mustard-garlic mayonnaise.

☑ Most shellfish do not need a lot of extra flavor and generally respond to most simple moist-heat cooking methods (if any cooking method). With some exceptions, shellfish can be cooked by dry-heat methods.

Pairing Strategies for Shellfish

1. Mollusks are often eaten raw or are lightly cooked through poaching or steaming. They contain a light flavor with a slight briny element that allows them to pair well with light- to medium-acidic white wines with either no or light oak aging. Wines such as Riesling (Alsatian Style), Chenin Blanc, Sauvignon Blanc (New Zealand, Sancerre and Pouilly-Fumé) Grüner Veltliner, Pinot Blanc, unoaked Chardonnay (Chablis or New Zealand), and Pinot Grigio/Gris can pair well with mollusks.

2. Crustaceans are often lightly cooked and contain rich, sweet, and delicate meat. They are often paired with a rich butter- or mayonnaise-based sauce to complement the richness of the shellfish. Crustaceans pair well with medium- to full-bodied white wines that have seen malo-lactic fermentation and slight or full oak aging, such as Fumé Blanc, Chardonnay, or Viognier.

3. In some dishes, crustaceans such as shrimp, and univalves such as snails are baked or broiled with garlic, breadcrumbs, butter, and fresh herbs. This preparation allow shellfish to be paired with a light, earthy red wine such as Pinot Noir, Cabernet Franc, or Gamay.

FIGURE 6–15 Shrimp cocktail
(Rob Melnychuk/Getty Images, Inc.-Photodisc.)

The term *poultry* describes domesticated birds often consumed young and referred to as *fryers* and *roasters*. Since the birds are less than one year old when consumed, they have not had much exercise and have developed limited amounts of connective tissue, yielding a tender, low-fat product. Pictured in Figure 6–16 is a roasted half chicken paired with Pinot Noir.

The two most popular types of poultry are *chicken* and *turkey*. They both contain white and dark meat, and little fat, flavor, and texture variation when prepared without skin. Chicken and turkey contain white meat both in the breasts and wings, which are lean and light in flavor. The dark meat is found in the drumsticks and thighs, which have higher fat, a denser texture, and a more pronounced flavor. Older birds known as *hens* and *roosters* are a bit tougher and need moist-heat cooking to become tender. Therefore, because of greater texture, more pronounced flavor, a more substantial wine is required.

Free-range poultry are allowed to roam in the outdoors, resulting in a more flavorful bird with greater texture variation.

Duck, goose, and *squab* all have dark, rich meat that contains substantial fat and are often cooked with their skin left on, which helps to increase fat and flavor content. Unlike chicken and turkey, duck, goose, and squab usually are cooked medium rare to medium doneness, for maximum retention of flavor and juiciness.

Foie Gras (FWAH-grah)—literally, "fat liver"—is the liver of a duck or goose that was force-fed a diet to fatten and enlarge the liver to yield a rich butterlike delicacy.

Game birds are generally juicy, with a distinctive flavor. Common examples of wild poultry are *quails*, tiny birds with sweet, juicy meat often stuffed and roasted, pan fried and finished in an oven, or grilled; and *pheasant*, a larger game bird of about three pounds.

FIGURE 6–16 Chicken
(Ian O'Leary © Dorling Kindersley)

Adjustments to Poultry—Making adjustments can bridge a wine to the food and create a more effective pairing. There are numerous variables that can be chosen to work with poultry to dramatically influence flavor and texture:

☑ Overall, chicken and turkey are fairly neutral, adapt to most cooking methods, and absorb the flavors of most sauces quite easily.

☑ Some options include whether to cook whole or fabricated into light or dark meat, with skin on or off, young (roaster or fryer) versus old (hen or rooster), or stuffed with additional ingredients. (The topic of adjusting food to more effectively pair with wine is discussed in greater detail in Chapter 5, "Foundations to Wine and Food Pairing.") Pictured in Figure 6–17 is a whole roasted and stuffed chicken.

Pairing Strategies for Poultry

1. Because most poultry is light and fairly neutral (particularly chicken and turkey), wine is often paired according to the cooking method and the sauce.

2. Whole poultry (because of the increased flavors associated with caramelization and fat on the skin) works with full whites such as Chardonnay or Viognier and light-bodied reds with low tannin such as Pinot Noir or Gamay.

3. Light meat poultry works well with light- to medium-bodied white wine such as a Pinot Grigio/Gris, Pinot Blanc, Riesling (Alsatian Style), unoaked Chardonnay,

FIGURE 6–17 Roasted Chicken
(© Dorling Kindersley)

Grüner Veltliner, or Sauvignon Blanc. Dark meat poultry works well with medium- to full-bodied white wine such as Sauvignon Blanc, Chardonnay, or Viognier; or light- to medium-bodied reds with low tannin such as Pinot Noir, Barbera, Dolcetto, Cabernet Franc or Gamay.

4. Free-range poultry has more flavor than traditional poultry (particularly if the bird has been roasted or stuffed) and can match with a light- to medium-bodied red wine such as a Gamay (Crus Beaujolais), Cabernet Franc, or Pinot Noir.

5. Older birds (hens and roosters) contain more distinctive flavor and often are prepared with an intense sauce derived from the cooking liquid. Thus, they pair well with earthy red wines with moderate tannin such as Syrah blends, Tempranillo (Reserva, or Gran Reserva Rioja).

6. Whole roasted duck or goose can work well with rich full-bodied white wines with some residual sugar because of the meat's higher fat content and rich meat. Wines such as Riesling (German Spätlese or Auslese) work well.

7. Squab, quail, and pheasant pair well with full-bodied white wines such as Chardonnay (from California or Burgundy), or light- to medium-bodied reds with low-to-moderate tannin containing some prevalent fruit qualities and slight earthiness, such as Pinot Noir, Merlot, Tempranillo (Crianza Rioja), or Gamay (Cru Beaujolais).

8. The richness associated with foie gras allows it to be paired with French "Rot" style wine such as Sauternes or other wine with residual sugar such as Riesling (German Beerenauslese (BA) or Trockenbeerenauslese (TBA)) ("Rot style" wine is discussed in greater detail in Chapter 13: NECTAR: Dessert Wines).

Difficult Pairings

In some cases, conservative wisdom has identified so-called *difficult food type(s) or courses* that do not pair well with wine. Perhaps in the past that was the case, but presently, there is a greater understanding of pairing and an abundance of different wine styles has come about that makes this perspective outdated. These difficult food types or courses just require a bit more thought or manipulation, such as adjusting the intensity of the food or using bridge ingredients to create a more effective connection between the wine and food item.

Traditionally, food items such as asparagus, artichokes, chocolate, and cheese have been considered difficult food items. Understandably, these items may not pair well with a wide range of different wines, but applying some of the previous guidelines can assist with an overall acceptable pairing.

MEAT COMPOSITION AND COOKERY

Meat is muscle tissue derived from the flesh of domesticated animals (cattle, lamb, and pigs) and wild game (deer and rabbit). The breed, feed, age, and amount of exercise the animal receives collectively influences the flavor, juiciness, color, and texture of meat. Meat has varying levels of fat from which the juiciness and some flavor derive and that plays an important role in defining the characteristics of meat and, therefore, a potential wine pairing.

The juiciness is what separates meat from other foods like pasta, vegetables, and fruit and allows meat to be paired with more robust, bolder wines. There are two types of fat: external and internal. Internal fat, referred to as *marbling,* consists of the streams of fat (known as intramuscular fat) within the layers of the meat. A well-marbled piece of meat comes from a younger animal and will maintain more juiciness, richness, tenderness and flavor that allow for quick-dry heat cooking. The parts of the animal body that get the most exercise, such as the shoulders or legs, tend to be tougher and require gentler, longer moist-heat cooking.

Tender versus Tougher Cuts of Beef

Meat is composed of long, thin muscle fibers bound together in a network of proteins called connective tissue. Meats high in connective tissue come from well-exercised animals or older animals and tend to be the tougher cuts of meat. Meats low in connective tissue are associated more with younger animals that tend to have more tender cuts of meat.

There are two kinds of connective tissue: collagen and elastin. When meat is cooked, gelatin, if present, is extracted from connective tissue and bones. Gelatin helps to maintain juiciness and also improves the texture and flavor of the meat. This is why a bone-in rib-eye will be juicier and richer than boneless rib-eye.

Coagulated versus Uncoagulated Meat

Since meat contains large amounts of protein, it becomes firmer and harder (coagulates) as it is heated. Through the heating process, the proteins contract and lose moisture and the meat becomes firmer. In essence, as the meat continues to cook, it dries out. The amount of cooking applied to a piece of meat is referred to as the desired degree of doneness.

Tougher pieces of meat contain a pronounced meaty flavor and more connective tissue. They are cooked by a moist-heat method that applies low heat for a long period. This cooking process breaks down connective tissue, yielding a tender product.

Tender pieces of meat contain less connective tissue and, consequently, less meaty flavor than tougher cuts. Tender cuts are cooked by quick dry-heat cooking methods. Meat also contains a small amount of carbohydrates, and cooking causes the sugars to caramelize and create a brown, slightly crisp, textured surface with concentrated flavor, on the exterior of the meat. Methods such as sautéing, roasting, broiling, and grilling cause the meat to brown and the "meaty" flavor to intensify.

To determine the ideal preparation and wine match, it is important to understand some of the major cuts of meat. Each cut of meat can be described as to whether it is a tough or tender cut, and this distinction should determine its cooking method and assist in identifying an effective wine pairing.

FIGURE 6–18 Sliced meat
(Ian O'Leary © Dorling Kindersley)

PORK
Pairing Wine with Pork

Pork has a distinctive and, in some cases, assertive flavor. But pork adapts well to other flavors and ingredients. Pork dries out very easily when cooking, which is why many cooks use a brine or dry rub to maintain flavor or add dimension to the internal section of the meat. Sliced pork loin over mashed potatoes is pictured in Figure 6–18.

The most popular pork cuts include the loin, which produces the loin roast, rib chops, and baby-back ribs; ham; and shoulder butt.

Pairing Strategies for Pork

1. Pork meat has a natural sweetness. Therefore, pork tends to work well with rich fruit-concentrated white wines such as Riesling (German Style), or fruit-dominant red wines like Merlot, Tempranillo (Crianza Rioja) or Pinot Noir.
2. The sometimes salty or smoky component in ham works well with white wines with moderate to high acid and some residual sugar for balance. Such wines are Riesling (German Style) or Rosé.
3. Pork chops that have been grilled, broiled, or barbecued have more intense flavor due to the caramelization on the exterior of the meat. A medium-bodied red wine

with low to medium tannin, such as Merlot Tempranillo, Cabernet Franc, and Syrah blends, works well. Grilled pork chops are pictured in Figure 6–19.

4. Pork ribs that have been smoked and barbecued work well with medium- to full-bodied red wines such as Shiraz, Zinfandel, or Merlot.

5. The shoulder butt is a tougher cut that is braised or stewed for hours over low heat. The meat is often pulled or shredded from the cut. It works well with light- to medium-bodied red wines that have an earthiness and dried fruit qualities associated with them, such as Tempranillo, Malbec or Pinotage.

Sausages, or *Würst* (VURSHT) as they are called in Germany, or *kielbasa* (kihl-BAH-sah) in Poland, are primarily made from pork, but can be made from beef, chicken, veal, rabbit, or turkey and varying amounts of fat. There are thousands of sausages produced around the world, and depending on the country of origin, sausages and names can mean different things. Figure 6–20 shows a cured sausage.

Typically, sausage can be classified in three ways: (1) *Fresh sausage* contains no preservatives and can be raw or lightly cooked. (2) *Smoked sausage* is cooked through either cold or hot smoke with a variety of different smoke flavors. (3) *Cured sausage* incorporates a curing agent (a combination of salt and preservatives), aging, and drying (often, in the air) process that renders them safe to eat.

Sausages typically have a rich, high fat content, a salty or spicy flavor, and possibly, a smoke flavor. Sausages are often garnished with assertive condiments such as onions (raw or caramelized), ketchup, mustard, and so forth.

Pairing Strategies for Sausage

1. Fresh sausage pairs well with a crisp acidic white wine such as Riesling (Alsatian Style), Pinot Grigio/Gris, Sparkling wine or Pinot Blanc to help offset some of the fattiness.

2. Cured and smoked sausages have an intense flavor because of the smoking, salting, and/or drying processes. They pair well with intense white wines with some level of residual sugar, such as Riesling (German Spätlese) or Gewürztraminer, or red and rosé wines that have ample acidity, intense fruit-forward qualities, and low tannin, such as Gamay, Dolcetto and Pinot Noir.

FIGURE 6–19 Grilled pork chops
(Ian O'Leary © Dorling Kindersley)

Veal comes from male calves generally two to three months old. Veal has delicate, tender meat with subtle flavor. A milk-fed (also called formula-fed) veal has been fed mostly milk or milk byproducts its entire life. The animal has been allowed minimal exercise in order to limit any tough muscles as much as possible.

FIGURE 6–20 Sausage
(Roger Phillips © Dorling Kindersley)

One of the most popular cuts of veal is from the shank. This cut is responsible for producing the dish called *osso buco* (AW-soh BOO-koh), which has immense flavor and body gained through the braising process. The scaloppini and cutlets from the leg are also very popular. They respond to dry-heat cooking methods such as sautéing and pan-frying.

Pairing Strategies with Veal

1. Because most veal cuts are often tender, with delicate meat, they work well with full-bodied white wines such as Chardonnay or Viognier and with light- to medium-bodied red wines such as Pinot Noir, Gamay, or Sangiovese.

2. Veal shank is a tougher cut that often is braised for hours to tenderize. Through the cooking process, the collagen melts into the meat and cooking liquid and flavors concentrate. Veal shanks can pair well with full-bodied red wines such as Nebbiolo, Syrah, Shiraz, Zinfandel or Cabernet Sauvignon.

LAMB
Pairing Wine with Lamb

Lamb is produced from the meat of young sheep less than one year old. Generally, lamb is tender, but has a pronounced pungent, earthy flavor. Its texture is a result of feed and age of the animal. Lamb can be either milk fed (which makes the meat more tender) or grass fed (which gives the meat a more pronounced flavor).

Some popular cuts of lamb include the leg of lamb, which typically is prepared by dry-heat cooking, such as roasting, and flavored with rosemary or mint and garlic. Crusting roasted lamb with a healthy dose of herbs and spices increases the flavor of the meat. Rack of lamb and lamb shanks use slow moist-heat cooking such as braising to produce a rich intense dish with a concentrated highly flavored sauce. Pictured in Figure 6–21 is an herb-crusted rack of lamb with red wine reduction sauce.

Pairing Strategies with Lamb

1. Lamb works well with medium- to full-bodied red wines that have savory and earthy flavors, such as Syrah, Merlot, Shiraz, Cabernet Sauvignon, Sangiovese, Tempranillo, and Grenache.

FIGURE 6–21 Herb crusted lamb
(Louise Goossens © Dorling Kindersley)

Game is the meat and poultry of animals that have traditionally been hunted in the wild. Most game nowadays tends to be farm raised. Game is lean and often tender, with a distinctive flavor.

Buffalo, or bison (somewhat richer than beef, but lower in fat); deer (often called venison); boar (wild pig); and rabbit (similar to the flavor of chicken, but more gamey) are fairly well known. Venison tends to be the most popular and should be treated like lean beef. The leg and loin are commonly cooked with the application of dry heat by such methods as roasting, grilling, and sautéing. Because venison is low in fat, it should be cooked to no more than a medium degree of doneness in order to maintain its juiciness.

Pairing Strategies for Game

1. Red wines with low to medium tannin work with game because of its low fat, yet distinctive flavor.
2. Game works well with both earthy red wines such as Pinot Noir, Syrah, Pinotage and Tempranillo, and ripe-fruit-forward red wines such as Merlot, Malbec, Zinfandel, and Shiraz.

Cattle used for beef consumption typically are castrated males (steers) and female cows (heifers) about one to two years old. The older a bovine is, the less tender the meat will taste. A specialty beef known as *wagu*—the most famous, called *kobe* (KOH-bay), is from Japan—is some of the most expensive beef in the world. The cattle used for this meat are forced to stand still for long periods in order to prevent the development of exercised muscles, yielding an extremely tender meat.

Aging Beef

Most beef is aged in order to enhance flavor, texture, and tenderness. There are two methods of aging: wet and dry. Dry aging is carried out in a controlled, cold and low-humidity environment. Dry aging gains maximum benefits within 12–14 days, during which time it brings about significant moisture loss, but also a concentration of flavor and denser texture. This high-quality method is expensive, but greatly desired by beef consumers. The majority of aged beef occurs with wet aging in vacuum packaging. This method does not allow for flavor development, but enzymatic activity improves the tenderness. Figure 6–22 shows a grilled steak with flavored butter.

FIGURE 6–22 Grilled steak with herbed butter
(Ian O'Leary © Dorling Kindersley)

Many popular, tougher cuts of meat derive from the round or rib primal cut that yield smaller subprimal pieces. Some popular subprimals include top round, bottom round, rib roast, and short ribs. These often are cooked by moist-heat cooking methods such as stewing or braising, with a few exceptions, such as rib roast, which can be roasted.

POPULAR STEAKS

The *loin* is one of the most sought-after primal cuts for its quality and tenderness. It yields many popular subprimal cuts know as *steaks*. With naturally tender meat, steaks can be cooked by quick-dry heat methods such as grilling, roasting, or broiling. Steaks that have more bite and texture (T-bones) work better with bigger red wines, whereas steaks that are more tender and delicate (filet mignons) work better with medium reds wines. Shown in Figure 6–23 is an example of an uncoagulated steak that has been grilled to a medium-rare degree of doneness.

Châteaubriand (sha-toh-bree-AHN)—This cut of beef is a large tenderloin steak, often marketed for two servings, with a mild, buttery beef flavor.

The *London broil* is an actual cut, but the term is also freely used for just about any cut that is broiled and served sliced. The true London broil is traditionally derived from the flank and contains a substantial beefy flavor and moderate texture.

The *tenderloin steak* (also known as *filet mignon* "fee-lay mee-NYOH" or *Châteaubriand*) is one of the tenderest cuts of beef, with a mild, buttery beef flavor.

Porterhouse Steak is sometimes called the king of steaks. It is a bone-in steak that is actually two different steaks in one because it includes the buttery tenderloin and the beefy strip steak.

The *T-bone steak* is similar to the Porterhouse steak, but is a smaller version with less of the tenderloin. The rib-eye steak (or *Delmonico steak*) is a boneless steak cut from the eye of the prime rib that maintains a smooth soft texture, with moderate beefy flavor and fat pockets throughout.

The *strip loin steak,* also called the *sirloin* or *New York cut,* can be purchased with or without bone and contains a strong beef flavor, with a desirable, slightly chewy texture and fat around the perimeter.

The *sirloin steak,* also called the *butt steak,* is cut from near the rump, so the meat, whereas a bit tougher, has a more beefy flavor than a cut from the loin or the rib.

FIGURE 6–23 Sliced steak
(Paul Poplis/FoodPix/Jupiter Images-FoodPix-Creatas)

Pairing Strategies for Beef

1. Naturally juicy and tender cuts of beef from the loin area (steaks, roasts) have substantial marbling (internal fat) and body, which allows them to work well with medium- to full-bodied red wines such as Zinfandel, Shiraz, Syrah, Cabernet Sauvignon, or Merlot.

2. Tougher cuts of beef that have been fully coagulated (stewed or braised) work well with lighter- to medium-bodied red wines such as Malbec, Pinotage, Pinot Noir, Syrah blends, Sangiovese, or Tempranillo.

3. Rare to medium-rare (with uncoagulated proteins) meat pairs excellently with medium- to full-bodied red wines such as Syrah, Shiraz, Touriga Nacional, Zinfandel, Sangiovese, Nebbiolo, Cabernet Sauvignon and Merlot.

4. Medium-well to well-done (with coagulated proteins) meat pairs excellently with light- to medium-bodied red wines.

THE STEP-BY-STEP PAIRING PROCESS, USING THE ANALYTICAL APPROACH

When pairing a wine with a food item, begin by pulling out the main components of the dish, and then analyze them to determine possible wine pairings. Following are the principles of the analytical approach, with the steps involved, for achieving a successful pairing. Throughout the process, each step leads to a group of possible wines to pair.

THE ANALYTICAL APPROACH:

Principle #1

Mirror the body and weight (or overall intensity) of the wine with the food to ensure that neither one overwhelms the other.

---

1. Break down a dish to determine the major components that will dictate a wine pairing.
2. Consider the food type, cooking method, and type of sauce and other ingredients and accompaniments.
3. Match similar levels of body and weight (or overall intensity) in the wine and the food.
4. If necessary, use food adjustment techniques that modify the dish to ensure a more effective pairing between the wine and the food. Apply knowledge of the dynamics of food and how to make adjustments to match a type or particular wine.

THE ANALYTICAL APPROACH:

Principle #2

Connect bridge ingredients in the food with flavors in the wine.

---

5. Use bridge ingredients to achieve compatibility by either contrasting or comparing elements in the wine and food.

THE ANALYTICAL APPROACH:

Principle #3

Compare or contrast taste components between the wine and the food according to the desired emphasis of the match.

---

6. Compare or contrast a wine's sweet, acidic, and tannic components with a food item.
7. Compare or contrast a food's acidic, sweet, and fatty and salty, spicy, and smoky components with a wine.

ADVANCED WINE AND FOOD PAIRING

NAME: _____ Score out of 20 points_____.

Use these questions to test your knowledge and understanding of the concepts presented in the chapter.

I. MULTIPLE CHOICE: Select the best possible answer from the options available.

1. Which element is *not* associated with a "user-friendly" wine?

   a. carbonation (the bubbles)

   b. moderate to high levels of acidity

   c. dry to slightly off dry

   d. high tannins

2. The purpose of the aperitif is to offer a light, dry, crisp wine or other beverage in order to

   a. cleanse the palate.

   b. provide a satiety effect.

   c. coat the palate.

   d. none of the above.

3. A simple salad with a vinaigrette dressing would pair best with

   a. a light- to medium-bodied white wine with good acidity.

   b. a light- to medium-bodied red wine with medium tannin.

   c. sparkling wine.

   d. answers a and c.

4. Spaghetti pasta with a tomato-based sauce served with a side of meatballs would pair best with

   a. a light- to medium-bodied white wine.

   b. a light- to medium-bodied red wine with good acidity and low to moderate tannin.

   c. sparkling wine.

   d. answers a and c.

5. Lasagna made with a cream sauce, chicken, and ricotta cheese would pair best with

   a. Riesling.

   b. Sauvignon Blanc.

   c. Chardonnay.

   d. Pinot Noir.

6. A medium-rare grilled Porterhouse steak would pair best with a

   a. light- to medium-white wine.

   b. medium- to full-bodied white wine.

   c. light- to medium-bodied red wine.

   d. medium- to full-bodied red wine.

7. Smoked pork sausage that has been lightly grilled would pair best with

   a. Chardonnay.

   b. Riesling with a slight amount of residual sugar.

   c. Cabernet Sauvignon.

   d. Red Bordeaux.

8. Veal shank that has been braised for several hours would pair best with

   a. Riesling.

   b. Sauvignon Blanc.

   c. Pinot Noir.

   d. Nebbiolo.

9. Poached chicken breast served with an herbed compound butter would pair best with

   a. Riesling.

   b. Sauvignon Blanc.

   c. Chardonnay.

   d. Merlot.

10. Grilled Ahi tuna would pair best with

    a. Sauvignon Blanc.

    b. Riesling.

    c. Pinot Noir.

    d. Cabernet Sauvignon.

11. Smoked and grilled barbequed baby-back ribs would pair best with

    a. Chardonnay.

    b. Nebbiolo.

    c. Cabernet Sauvignon.

    d. Shiraz.

II. TRUE / FALSE: Circle the best possible answer.

12. Soups and salads should never be paired with wine. **True / False**

13. If a food item is known to be considered one that is a "difficult to pair with wine", it means the item can never be paired successfully. **True / False**

14. Low-activity fish is also known as a fatty fish. **True / False**

15. Tougher pieces of meat contain little connective tissue and a more assertive beefy flavor. **True / False**

16. Generally, white wines or light-bodied red wines would pair most effectively with vegetarian-based food items. **True / False**

17. Soft-fresh cheese can pair most effectively with medium- to full-bodied red wines. **True / False**

18. Coagulated beef dishes generally work with lighter- to medium-bodied red wines. **True / False**

19. Mollusks that are eaten raw or are lightly cooked through poaching or steaming can pair well with light- to medium-acidic white wines that have light to no oak aging. **True / False**

III. SHORT-ANSWER ESSAY / DISCUSSION QUESTIONS: Use a separate sheet of paper if necessary.

20. Select a favorite food type and describe some potential food-and-wine pairings. Justify your selection with reasons.

ADVANCED WINE AND FOOD PAIRING

ACTIVITY #1 APPLYING THE ANALYTICAL APPROACH

NAME: _____

DIRECTIONS: Apply the analytical-approach process to each food item listed. Use a separate sheet of paper if necessary.

Food Items	Possible Wine	Justification
Tomato and red onion bruschetta		
Roasted corn and potato chowder		
Bacon-wrapped jumbo shrimp skewers with spicy mustard sauce		
Butternut squash ravioli with toasted pine nuts and a brown butter sauce		
Crab-, spinach-, and garlic-stuffed mushrooms		
Mixed greens, candied pecans, Gorgonzola cheese with a balsamic vinaigrette		
Steamed whole Maine lobster with drawn butter and boiled baby red potatoes		
Grilled rib-eye steak with red onion relish		

Unit 3
WINES OF THE NEW WORLD

"By prevailing over all obstacles and distractions, one may unfailingly arrive at his chosen goal or destination."

—Christopher Columbus

7

Wines of the United States and Canada

Throughout history...drought, inferno, world wars, depression and prohibition have all at one point attempted to either directly or indirectly handicap America's wine industry. But as of 2008, wine is produced commercially in all fifty states through 5,587 American wineries.

LEARNING OBJECTIVES

Upon completion of this chapter, the learner will be able to:

- Realize the significant wine producing areas within the United States and Canada.
- Understand U.S. labelling laws regarding grape, location, vintage, and vineyard.
- Comprehend the American viticulural area (AVA) concept.
- Recognize the most significant viticultural areas within the major wine-producing areas of the United States.
- Discern between the major grape varietals and styles of wine produced within each of the four significant wine-producing states.

UNITED STATES

Throughout history, drought, inferno, world wars, depression, and prohibition at one point have attempted to either directly or indirectly handicap America's wine industry. But as of 2008, wine was produced commercially in all fifty states through 5,587 American wineries, according to the Alcohol and Tobacco Tax and Trade Bureau (TTB). This is a dramatic increase; back in 1975, when the wine industry was in its adolescence, there were only 579 wineries throughout the United States.

The top four significant wine-producing states in America are California, Washington State, New York, and Oregon. In California alone, there are approximately 2,440 wineries that produce roughly 90% of all wine in America. There are also thriving wine industries in New York, with 271 wineries that manage 5% of U.S. production. Washington has 538 wineries, with 4% production, and Oregon, with 329 wineries, makes up less than 1% of the U.S. wine industry, in 2008, according to the TTB. Other states that produce a nominal amount of wine are not as well known outside their vicinity. These include Virginia, with 169, Texas, with 168 and Michigan, with 136 wineries.

American Viticultural Areas (AVA)

In 1978, the United States implemented *American viticultural areas*, or AVAs, as a way to set growing regions apart and to showcase their distinctions. These are unique grape-growing geographical areas, such as Napa Valley and Chalk Hill that have been officially designated as such by the TTB.

An AVA guarantees that, at a minimum, 85% of the grapes come from the location identified on the bottle. As of 2005, the TTB had recognized 170 AVAs throughout the United States. Lately, there have been an increasing number of sub-appellations designated to showcase even further distinction and specificity in a growing region. For example, there are approximately 14 sub-appellations within the larger Napa Valley.

American Labelling Information

Grape Name—To correctly label a wine with a grape name or varietal, the wine must contain at least 75% of that type. One significant exception to the 75% rule is that the state of Oregon requires a minimum of 90% for most varietals. States may always choose a stricter rule than the federal requirement, as in the case of Oregon, but never less.

Location—To identify a specific location or AVA on a wine label, at least 85% of the grapes must have come from that area.

If a wine is labelled with a broader country, state, county or multi county appellation on a label means that at least 75% of the grapes must have derived from the stated place of origin.

Vineyard—To identify an individual vineyard on a label, at least 95% of the grapes must have come from the vineyard specified on the label.

Vintage—If a vintage date is identified, then a minimum of 95% of the grapes within the bottle must have come from the year as specified on the label.

Marketing Terms—Terms such as *Reserve* and *Vintner's Reserve* are often used on U.S. labels. These terms do not have the legal meaning that they have in other countries, such as Italy or Spain. It is possible that the U.S. winemaker made a reserve or vintner's reserve with better-quality ingredients and production methods; however, there are no legal requirements to guarantee that this is so.

FIGURE 7–1 Map of California
(Thomas Moore)

BERINGER VINEYARDS

Since 1876, Beringer has been one of the oldest Napa Valley wineries in continuous production. Even during Prohibition, the Beringer family was granted approval to produce wine and brandy for sacramental and medicinal puposes.

CALIFORNIA

California produces the vast majority (approximately 90%) of wines in the United States and has grown from 150 wineries in 1960 to 2,440 in 2008 according to the TTB. In 2007, the state maintains over 480,000 acres of wine grapes and approximately 100 distinct *American viticultural areas* (AVAs) within California's five major wine-producing regions. Figure 7–1 shows a map of the significant wine regions in California.

The Famous Paris Wine Tasting of 1976

The Chardonnay and Cabernet Sauvignon grape varietals are historically significant to California, as they are the primary varietals that brought initial prestige and success to the state.

Up until 1976, France was generally regarded as the best producer of wines throughout the world. On May 24, 1976, everything changed. Nine of the most respected French wine judges participated in a 20-wine blind-tasting event held in Paris. Ten red wines were a mix of California Cabernet Sauvignons and red Bordeaux. In addition, a separate category of 10 white wines included a mix of California Chardonnay and white Burgundies.

The winners of first place for each category included a California red and white wine. The results caused a major uproar in France; to this day, many French people believe that the event was fixed. On the upside, this event encouraged the French to revisit their winemaking approach and make adjustments in order to remain competitive. Also, the results catapulted the United States to international fame as a world-class wine producer.

APPELLATIONS

The California climate is greatly influenced by the cool Pacific Ocean and the mountain ranges. Vineyards along the coast (and as far inland as 200 miles in some areas) are beneficially cooled from the ocean air. The impact of ocean waters creates ideal microclimates for grape growing in a way that sometimes reverses normal logic: For example, the farther north you travel in the North Coast wine region, the warmer it gets. Thus, the Napa Valley is warmer than many areas south of it, and some southern areas, such as the famed Carneros district of Sonoma County, are near the cooling influence of San Pablo Bay. The combination of these mesoclimates and microclimates, local soil types, and topography make the various wine regions of California ideal for growing an array of high-quality wine grapes.

California has roughly five primary wine-producing regions, with the *North Coast* and *Central Coast* known mostly for high quality. The Sierra Foothills, Central Valley, and Southern California regions are known mostly for quantity bulk production, with a few high-quality producers scattered throughout.

North Coast

North Coast is located in Northern California, just one hour's drive north of San Francisco. Its tradition goes back to the early nineteenth century in some of the oldest continuing vineyards in the country. The North Coast is recognized as the most prominent wine-producing region and contains some of the most successful AVAs in the United States.

FIGURE 7–2 Welcome to Napa Valley
(CLAVER CARROLL/Photolibrary.com)

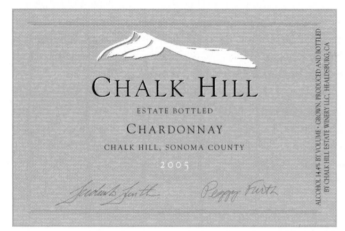

FIGURE 7–3 Chalk Hill Chardonnay label
(Chalk Hill Winery)

Napa Valley—This is California's preeminent wine production area and home of some 300-plus wineries. Napa is second only to Disneyland as the most visited American tourist destination, with over 4.7 million visitors annually. Napa Valley is 35 miles long and about 5 miles wide and is situated just the right distance inland from the cold northern Pacific Ocean. Hot, dry, sunny summer days (for ripeness development) and cool nights (for preservation of acidity) from the San Pablo Bay make Napa ideal for growing high-quality wine grapes.

Napa is most famous for high-quality (and some of the most expensive) Cabernet Sauvignon-based wines. In fact, about one-fifth of all vineyard acreage is devoted to Cabernet Sauvignon. Napa is also known for Chardonnay, Sauvignon Blanc, Merlot, and Zinfandel.

Napa Valley contains 14 different sub-appellations, or AVAs, including Atlas Peak, Howell Mountain, Oakville, Rutherford, Stags's Leap, part of Carneros, and others. Figure 7–2 identifies Napa Valley as the world's most famous wine growing region.

Sonoma County—Sonoma is a large appellation that is home to more than 250 wineries and 13 sub-AVA's, and growing. It is located west of Napa, closer to the ocean, with an overall cooler climate, but with a collection of microclimates that range from hot and dry to foggy and cool. Sonoma excels at Chardonnay, to which it has devoted to over one-fourth of vine acreage. But the vineyards of Sonoma County also produce quality Cabernet Sauvignon, Pinot Noir, Merlot, Zinfandel, and Sauvignon Blanc; and dozens of additional types of wine grapes can be found in this sprawling region.

Sonoma County contains 13 different sub-appellations, or AVAs, including: Alexander Valley, Chalk Hill, Dry Creek, Green Valley-Sonoma, Knights Valley, Russian River Valley, Sonoma Coast, Sonoma Mountain, Sonoma Valley, part of Carneros, and others. Figure 7–3 shows a Chardonnay label from the famous winery and appellation Chalk Hill.

Mendocino County—This is the northernmost wine-producing area and AVA in California's North Coast. It contains about 10 sub-AVAs. The most notable AVA is Anderson Valley, located near the Pacific Coast, which provides a cool, foggy climate that supports cool-climate grapes. Chardonnay, Pinot Noir, and Cabernet Sauvignon are the more dominate varietals.

Lake County—This AVA is north of Napa and east of Sonoma. It contains varying levels of altitude to make up for the lack of proximity to the ocean. The area features more temperature extremes between seasons and primarily focuses on warm-weather grapes such as Petite Syrah and Cabernet Sauvignon. Guenoc Valley is the largest AVA in Lake County and one of the older grape-growing areas in California.

Some Notable AVAs Throughout the North Coast

Alexander Valley—This large and densely planted AVA is located in the northern section of Sonoma County. Alexander Valley borders the Russian River, but experiences less fog and is located at higher elevations. The area is most noted for Cabernet Sauvignon, Chardonnay, Zinfandel, and Sauvignon Blanc.

FIGURE 7–4 Chalk Hill
Vineyards and Cabernet
Sauvignon
(Chalk Hill Winery)

Atlas Peak—This appellation is located in the southeast corner of Napa Valley. Atlas Peak takes its name from the highest point (about 2,600 feet) of the Vaca mountain range. The westward orientation of most vineyards provides maximum sun exposure. This, coupled with the gravelly and volcanic well-draining soil and high elevation, allows for a wide diurnal temperature range. This extreme in temperature range helps to preserve fresh fruit aromas and flavors, as well as acidity, in the grapes. Atlas Peak was originally planted with Sangiovese and Zinfandel, but now gives way to Cabernet Sauvignon, Merlot, and other Bordeaux-type varietals, in addition to Chardonnay and red and white Rhone-type varietals such as Syrah and Marsanne.

Carneros—This AVA is situated where the Napa and Sonoma Valleys meet in the south, just north of San Pablo Bay. The proximity to the bay yields a cooler maritime-type climate ideal for cool-climate grape varietals such as Pinot Noir and Chardonnay. Therefore, many of California's high-quality sparkling wine producers have been established there, including Domaine Carneros (by the French producer Tattinger) and Gloria Ferrer (by the Spanish producer Freixenet).

Chalk Hill—This Sonoma County AVA is a sub-appellation of the Russian River appellation. The name derives from its chalk-colored volcanic-ash soil, which promotes Chardonnay, Sauvignon Blanc, and Cabernet Sauvignon varietals. Figure 7–4 shows vineyards in the Chalk Hill AVA, as well as the Chalk Hill Cabernet Sauvignon.

Howell Mountain—This was Napa's first sub-AVA, with a small number of vine acres located in higher-elevation areas in the Vaca Mountains. Howell Mountain is most noted for producing Bordeaux varietals and Zinfandel.

Mount Veeder—This appellation encompasses 25 square miles of some of the steepest vineyards and most remote wineries in California. This viticultural area is located in the southeastern portion of the Mayacamas Mountains, which divide Napa and Sonoma Counties.

Oakville—An appellation located in the center of Napa Valley, Oakville contains many of Napa's prestigious wineries. It is positioned with the Mayacamas Mountains to the west and the Vaca range to the east. Oakville is famous for its gravelly well-drained soils, which contribute to well-structured Cabernet Sauvignons.

Russian River—This AVA is located in the northern section of Sonoma County. The climate of the Russian River is dramatically influenced by the cooling coastal-fog effect of the Pacific Ocean just a few miles to the west. The largely clay- and alluvial-based soils and cooler climate have allowed Pinot Noir and Chardonnay to become the signature varietals.

Rutherford— The majority of vines here are devoted to the premier grape of this appellation, Cabernet Sauvignon, with smaller amounts of Merlot and Zinfandel grown. The Cabernet is renowned for producing big structure; deep, complex fruit qualities; and richness and for expressing a terroir-like quality of "dirt and dust." Cabernets produced in Rutherford are known to have remarkable aging potential.

Spring Mountain—This Napa Valley AVA sits on steep terraces of the Mayacamas Mountains. It is dominated by the red varietals of Cabernet Sauvignon, Merlot, and Cabernet Franc. Chardonnay is the main white wine, with some plantings of Riesling and Viognier.

Stags Leap District—This Napa Valley AVA boasts volcanic soil, warm days that promote optimal ripening, and cool nights to maintain the grapes' acidity. The area is best suited to grow Cabernet Sauvignon and other Bordeaux varietals. Stags Leap District is one of the most historically significant of the AVAs, as it was Cabernet Sauvignon from Stags' Leap wine cellars that vanquished the top red Bordeaux's in the famous 1976 Paris tasting.

Central Coast

Central Coast is a large growing area along the Pacific Coast that extends from south of San Francisco to Santa Barbara. Over the last several years, California's Central Coast has matured into a region that produces world-class wines.

The Central Coast is a mega-AVA that includes many smaller sub-AVAs. The area is unofficially divided into northern and southern sections. Mountain ranges run throughout these areas in different directions, creating different pockets of microclimates that allow various grapes and styles of wine to be produced. The more common grape varietals are Chardonnay (with over half of the vineyard acreage), Pinot Noir, Viognier, Syrah, and Grenache.

Paso Robles—This area possesses a long growing season with a high diurnal range of temperatures between night and day—ideal for preserving a grape's acidity while still retaining its flavor development. Paso is known for Syrah, Zinfandel, and Cabernet Sauvignon grape varietals.

San Luis Obispo—A California wine region south of Paso Robles (although, technically, part of Paso Robles is located within San Luis Obispo County) and continuing south to Santa Barbara County, this large AVA produces many types of wine with varying quality levels. San Luis Obispo does grow the highest quantity of Syrah vines of all other California appellations.

Edna Valley—An appellation located south of San Luis Obispo, Edna Valley's location makes the region much cooler than surrounding growing regions and is ideal for growing Chardonnay and Pinot Noir.

Monterey County—This AVA is home to some of the best values in California wines.

Santa Ynez Valley—Located in Santa Barbara County, California, this AVA experiences cool ocean breezes that keep the valley temperate enough to grow world-class Pinot Noir, Chardonnay, and Syrah.

Santa Barbara—Located just south of San Luis Obispo, Santa Barbara is both a city and a county. Two of the main growing regions in Santa Barbara County are the Santa Maria and Santa Ynez valleys. Both of these valleys directly face the ocean, capturing the breezes that make these some of the coolest growing regions in California. For this reason, Pinot Noir, Chardonnay, and Syrah have done well. Other cool-climate varietals, such as Viognier and Riesling, thrive as well.

Santa Maria Valley—This is one of the cooler growing regions in California. Generally, the farther south in California you go, the warmer it gets. However, Santa Maria Valley is cooled by the Pacific Ocean, making it ideal for the cool-climate grapes that go into Pinot Noir and Chardonnay wines.

Sierra Foothills

Far to the east of the Pacific Ocean is home to California's original gold rush. Traditionally, this area is known for table grapes or low-quality inexpensive wine grapes. However, the Zinfandel grape varietal reigns supreme here, and new suitable grape varieties are slowly being planted as the region expands.

South Coast

This area is generally warm, with some spotty cooler areas, to produce wine grapes. One of the well-known appellations is in Temecula.

Central Valley

The Central Valley (also known as the San Joaquin) is a large, hot, fertile area that stretches almost 500 miles down the center of the state. San Joaquin is considered California's agricultural land, known for producing most of America's table grapes and raisins. The intense heat and sun overwhelms many grapevines, and production is mostly based on large quantities of grapes for mass-produced large wineries. The total acreage under wine grape cultivation in the Central Valley is massive and dwarfs all other California regions. The important appellations include Lodi and Woodbridge.

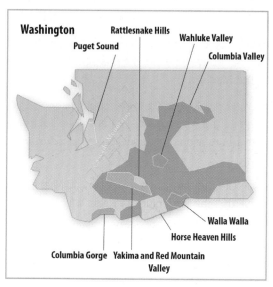

FIGURE 7–5 Map of Washington State
(Thomas Moore)

WASHINGTON STATE

Washington State is located in the northwest corner of the United States, just off the Pacific Ocean. According to the Washington Wine Commission, it's the nation's second-largest wine producer, with 31,000 acres of grapevines and over 530 wineries in 2007.

The climate offers sunny days, which allow the grapes to ripen through the long exposure to sunlight, and cool nights, which permit the grapes to maintain good acid profiles. Washington is significantly protected by the Cascade Mountains that cause a rain-shadow effect on the eastern side, which tends to be where the bulk of the wine regions are located. Figure 7–5 identifies the major wine-producing areas in Washington State.

The Varietals

Washington is a relatively youthful wine-producing region, with modern winemaking having begun in the 1960s with the emergence of Columbia Winery and Chateau Ste. Michelle. In the 1980s, Washington first established its reputation through the success of the Merlot grape varietal as its signature wine. Merlot eventually became the state's largest-selling red wine. As of 2007, Cabernet Sauvignon had surpassed Merlot, and Syrah had come in third for the most-planted grape varietal. Washington is also known for its white-wine grapes. Chardonnay, Riesling, Sauvignon Blanc, and Gewürztraminer are, in order, the top-producing white varietals.

APPELLATIONS

Washington maintains nine major viticultural areas, including Yakima (YAK-uh-maw) Valley, Walla Walla, Columbia Valley, Puget Sound, Red Mountain, Columbia Gorge, Horse Heaven Hills, Wahluke Slope, and Rattlesnake Hills.

Columbia Valley—Columbia Valley is the largest Washington wine region, with more than 17,000 vineyard acres that span from south-central Washington to Northern Oregon. The valley is protected from the Cascade Mountains, which act to shelter the region from the cool weather of the Pacific Ocean, making it one of the warmest growing areas in the Pacific Northwest. Columbia Valley's immense size yields several different types of sub-climates that encourage various grapes to prosper. Thus, Columbia Valley Cabernet Sauvignon and Chardonnay grapes can fully ripen in most years. Other grapes such as Merlot, Sauvignon Blanc, Semillon, Chenin Blanc and Riesling also prosper in the long sunny days and chilly nights of the Columbia River Valley's growing season. The wines tend towards rich, ripe flavors with lively acidity.

Columbia Valley is considered an "umbrella" appellation, as it contains several smaller sub-appellations, including Walla Walla Valley, Yakima, Red Mountain, and the newer appellations of Wahluke Slope and Rattlesnake Hills.

Puget Sound—Washington's only official American viticultural area on the west side of the Cascade Mountain Range is Puget Sound. More than 45 wineries are based in the Puget Sound appellation, but only a few of them actually use locally grown grapes to make wine. Most wineries purchase grapes grown in the warmer, drier wine regions to the east of the Cascade Mountain range. Puget is a cool-climate region with a maritime climate. The large body of water of the Puget Sound basin moderates temperature extremes. Puget Sound specializes in cool-climate varieties such as Pinot Noir and the more adaptable Pinot Gris grape.

Yakima Valley—Yakima Valley is located in south-central Washington along the Yakima River. This area has a very diverse climate that allows for various grape varietals, such as Cabernet Sauvignon, Chardonnay, Syrah, and Merlot.

Walla Walla—Walla Walla is a remote wine region located in the southeast corner of Washington and extending slightly into Oregon. This region is one of the older established wine-producing areas in Washington, with a reputation for Merlot, Cabernet Sauvignon, and Syrah.

Columbia Gorge—This appellation is located in the southern section of Washington and extends into northern Oregon. Its vineyards span the Columbia River, which provides a moist, cooler climate.

NEW YORK STATE

New York State is located in the northeast corner of the United States just below Canada. According to the New York Wine and Grape Foundation, New York State is the nation's third largest wine producer with approximately 32,000 acres of grapevines in 2007. The evolution of quality wine from the Vitis vinifera vine species is emerging here, with the majority of the wines deriving from the lesser-quality-producing American grapevine species *Vitis labrusca*.

The Varietals

New York State is mostly known for its Riesling and Cabernet Franc varietals, which are the most widely planted varietals in the Finger Lakes AVA. New York State is also a noted producer of dessert wines and ice-wines, primarily from the white hybrid *Seyval Blanc* (say-vahl-BLAHNK) and *Vignoles* (VIN-yoal) varietals.

APPELLATIONS

New York State has four growing regions, but the majority (about 90%) of the wine is produced in the Finger Lakes AVA.

Finger Lakes

Finger Lakes Region is located in northern New York State partly between Manhattan and Niagara Falls and is home to more than 100 wineries. Finger Lakes appellation is about 300 miles northwest of New York city and sandwiched among four main lakes and sub-regions: *Cayuga* (kay-YOU-guh), *Canandaigua* (can-in-DAYG-wah), *Seneca* (SEN-uh-kuh), and *Keuka* (Q-kuh). The lakes make it possible to grow quality wine grapes in the otherwise cold, northerly climate by moderating the temperatures, which extends the growing season to allow grapes to fully ripen. The lakes also assist in keeping the ground from freezing in winter and so help improve the conditions for the vines.

Lake effect is a term used around the great lakes area and other large lakes in cool regions to describe the climatic influence on wine grapes. In the spring, the lakes' cooling effect (due to the cooler temperatures stored from the winter) retards the vines from budding until the spring frost is over. As the season progresses, the lakes store daytime heat, which lengthens the growing season. The water's heat retention delays frost that might damage vineyards in the fall. In winter, the lakes also cause heavy, moist snowfall, which blankets the vineyards, insulating and protecting the vines from the frigid air. The lake effect influences the environment for many miles inland from the water, creating a viticultural environment that would not otherwise exist in such a cool climate.

Long Island

The Long Island region also encompasses North Fork of Long Island and the Hamptons. The maritime climate of this region is moderate and helps provide an extended growing season.

Cabernet Sauvignon and Merlot are the most common red grapes grown here, while Chardonnay is the main white grape. While the wines have been steadily improving over the years, no wine from Long Island has gained any worldwide reputation as of yet.

OREGON

Oregon is located in the Pacific Northwest, nestled between Washington State to the north and California to the south. According to the Oregon Wine Board, Oregon is the nation's fourth-largest wine producer, with approximately 15,600 vineyard acres in 2007. It has been only within about the last 40 years that Oregon has been acknowledged as a world-class wine-producing state. Because most of the wineries are small in scale, an impressive 23% of total vineyards are dedicated to some form of sustainable winemaking. Figure 7–6 identifies Oregon's significant wine-growing areas.

The Varietals

Oregon has gained most of its fame from successfully growing cool-climate varietals such as Pinot Noir (one of the premiere producers in the world and the most-planted variety in Oregon) and Pinot Gris (the second-most-planted variety), but it also produces warm-climate varietals such as Cabernet Sauvignon and Merlot.

Labelling Laws

The local wine laws of Oregon tend to be a bit stricter than those of other U.S. states. Labelling must include a minimum of 90% of the grape varietal as listed on the label, but many wines often are 100% of the stated varietal. Due to potential ripeness issues, the only exception is Cabernet Sauvignon, which is allowed to be at least 75% in order to encourage blending if necessary.

Oregon's growing regions can be broken down into three AVAs that contain several smaller sub-AVAs.

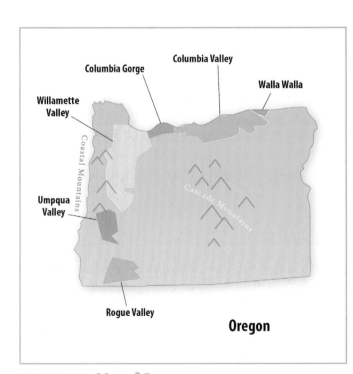

FIGURE 7–6 Map of Oregon
(Thomas Moore)

FIGURE 7–7 Adelsheim Pinot Noir label
(Adelsheim Winery)

APPELLATIONS

The winemaking regions are surrounded by natural barriers of the coastal range on the west, the Cascade Mountains on the south and east, and the Columbia River to the north.

Willamette Valley

Willamette (wuh-LAM-it) Valley is the largest AVA in Oregon (with over 10,000 acres of vines) and is named after the Willamette River that runs throughout the region. It boasts the majority (about 75%) of the state's wineries, with a concentration in the northern half.

The climate is relatively mild and moist, with warm, dry summers and cool, wet winters. The Cascade Mountains to the east and the coastal range to the west significantly influence and shelter the environment, creating a climate that somewhat mimics that of Alsace or Burgundy, France. The area tends to support cool-climate varietals such as Pinot Noir, Pinot Gris, Chardonnay, and Pinot Blanc.

The region has a large concentration of wineries and vineyards and contains six sub-appellations: *Chehalem Mountains, Dundee Hills, Eola-Amity Hills, McMinnville, Ribbon Ridge,* and *Yamhill-Carlton District.* Figure 7–7 shows an Oregon wine label from the Adelsheim Winery.

Eastern Oregon or Columbia Gorge

This AVA is known by both names and is located on both the Oregon and Washington sides of the Columbia River. The area is generally much warmer and drier than other Oregon appellations and supports such varietals as Cabernet, Merlot, and Syrah.

Southern Oregon

This area, with about 3,000 acres of vines, progresses from the southern point of Willamette Valley down to the California border. The climate is similar to Willamette, but is a bit warmer and drier because of the further southern influence.

Southern Oregon contains several major sub-appellations: *Applegate Valley, Red Hill Douglas County, Rogue Valley,* and *Umpqua (UMP-kwah) Valley.* Because of the region's warmer and drier climate, southern Oregon specializes in Bordeaux and Rhone grape varietals.

CANADA

Canada is not as large a producer of wine as it is a consumer. Canada is slowly moving away from the French hybrid grapes and making a serious effort to produce better-quality grapes from the more traditional international grape varieties. These newer wines have greater marketing potential and will continue to drive interest, particularly in the areas of southern British Columbia, with the Okanagan (oak-ah-NAH-gehn) Valley, and in Ontario, with the Niagara Peninsula. Figure 7–8 identifies the significant Canadian wine-growing areas within Ontario.

Ontario

Niagara Peninsula

Lake Erie North Shore

Pelee Island

FIGURE 7–8 Map of Ontario
(Thomas Moore)

The Varietals

Overall, Canada produces about 60% white wine (40% red wine), with Riesling leading the way. It also produces Chardonnay, Pinot Gris, Pinot Blanc and French hybrid varietals, and Vidal. Red wine varietals include Cabernet Franc, Cabernet Sauvignon, Merlot, Gamay Noir (also known as Gamay), Pinot Noir, and the French hybrid, Baco Noir.

Canada arguably is most known for its high-quality production of ice-wine. Grapes often are harvested in late December or January, yielding very small amounts of juice from each pressing of the frozen grapes. Common ice-wines are made from Riesling or Vidal grapes. Figure 7–9 shows frozen grapes on a vine.

APPELLATIONS

The Okanagan Valley and the Niagara Peninsula are the two prominent Canadian wine-producing areas. They are governed by the *Vintner's Quality Alliance*, or VQA, which is similar to other regulatory systems throughout Europe. The VQA is an appellation control system designed to authenticate the contents within the bottle through setting standards for viticulture and vinification practices.

Ontario

Ontario is Canada's largest wine-producing area, accounting for approximately 85% of production, with over 20,000 acres of grapevines. Ontario is considered a cool climate area similar to Germany or Burgundy, France. The VQA has recognized three viticultural areas, or VAs: Niagara Peninsula (the most significant of the three VAs), Lake Erie North Shore, and Pelee Island.

Niagara Peninsula

Niagara Peninsula is located in Ontario and most famous for its world-class *ice-wines*. For other grapes, the area is assisted by the lake effect from Lake Ontario in the North. The temperate climate allows for longer growing seasons by deterring damaging frosts, but the uneven ripening of red–wine grapes continues to make for huge vintage variations. Figure 7–10 depicts the famous ice-wine producer Inniskillin.

An increasing number of Pinot Noir, Cabernet Franc, Cabernet Sauvignon, and Merlot varietals are being produced, alongside Chardonnay and the more likely Riesling and Vidal Blanc grape varietals.

Okanagan Valley

Okanagan Valley is located just east of British Columbia, which is just north of Washington State. The valley is situated in a rain shadow between the coast and the Monashee mountain range. As of 2006, this area contained about 7,500 acres of vines and was the largest viticultural area in British Columbia. Okanagan Valley contains significant climate variations between its northern and southern sections.

In the north, the cold weather associated with Okanagan Valley is tempered by the lake effect. The northern section of the valley contains clay and gravel soil types. This area is most known for its Chardonnay, Pinot Noir, Riesling, and Pinot Blanc grape varietals.

In the southern section of Okanagan Valley is Canada's only desert, the northernmost tip of the Senora. Just as in the Columbia Valley, Washington, irrigation is the key to growing wine grapes. This southern end of the valley maintains a sandy soil type. The area is most known for its Cabernet Sauvignon, Merlot, and Syrah grape varietals.

FIGURE 7–9 Frozen Vidal grapes
(Inniskillin Wines)

FIGURE 7–10 Inniskillin Ice wine label
(Inniskillin Wines)

WINES OF THE UNITED STATES AND CANADA

NAME: _____ Score out of 20 points_____.

Use these questions to test your knowledge and understanding of the concepts presented in the chapter.

I. MULTIPLE CHOICE: Select the best possible answer from the options available.

1. In the United States, if a vintage date is listed on a label, at least _____ of the grapes must have come from that year.

   a. 75%
   b. 85%
   c. 95%
   d. 100%

2. In the United States, if a specific vineyard is listed on a label, at least _____ of the grapes must come from that vineyard.

   a. 75%
   b. 85%
   c. 95%
   d. 100%

3. In the United States, if a specific AVA or location is listed on a label, at least _____ of the grapes must have come from that location.

   a. 75%
   b. 85%
   c. 95%
   d. 100%

4. In the United States, if a grape name is listed on a label, at least _____ of the grapes must come from the specified varietal.

   a. 75%
   b. 85%
   c. 95%
   d. 100%

II. TRUE/FALSE: Circle the best possible answer.

5. American wines are governed by the Vintner's Quality Alliance (VQA). **True / False**

6. California produces more wine than any other U.S. state. **True / False**

7. Ontario, Canada, produces the most wine in all of Canada. **True / False**

8. Columbia Valley is a significant grape-growing area in California. **True / False**

9. Napa Valley is a significant grape-growing area in Oregon. **True / False**

10. Willamette Valley is a significant grape-growing area in Oregon. **True / False**

11. On an American wine label, the terms *Reserve* and *Vintner's Reserve* have specific legal meanings. **True / False**

12. The North Coast region is known as one of the most famous wine regions in all of the United States. **True / False**

III. MATCHING: Connect the grape varietals below with the significant growing location. No answer may be duplicated.

LOCATIONS

13. _____ Significant red wine grape from Washington State.

14. _____ Significant white wine grape in Washington State.

15. _____ Significant red wine grape from California.

16. _____ Significant white wine grape from California.

17. _____ Significant red wine grape from New York State.

18. _____ Significant red wine grape from Oregon.

19. _____ Significant white wine grape from Oregon.

GRAPE VARIETALS

A. Pinot Gris

B. Pinot Noir

C. Riesling

D. Cabernet Franc

E. Cabernet Sauvignon

F. Chardonnay

G. Merlot

IV. SHORT-ANSWER ESSAY/DISCUSSION QUESTIONS: Use a separate sheet of paper if necessary.

20. As a newly hired beverage manager (whether for a restaurant or wine store), you noticed the wine selections are *all* Old World focused. How would you justify to the owner the need for incorporating New World wine selections?

PINOT NOIR
NABOTH'S VINEYARD
THE MILLTON VINEYARDS
1995
PRODUCE OF NEW ZEALAND
1998
PRODUCE OF NEW ZEALAND
1997

8

Other New World Wine Countries

The most significant wine-producing countries of the New World include Argentina, Australia, Chile, New Zealand, and South Africa. These countries are perceived as dynamic, with enormous potential, and continue to gain immense popularity throughout the world. Overall, New World wines are reasonably priced and provide good value.

LEARNING OBJECTIVES

Upon completion of this chapter, the learner will be able to:

- Identify the significant wine-producing countries within the New World.
- Recognize the significant grape varietals and styles of wine produced within each New World wine-producing country.
- Recognize the most significant wine-producing appellations within the New World.

NEW WORLD

Since the early beginnings of winemaking, Europeans left their homelands to escape from political and religious injustice. A by-product of their flight was that they spread the influence of grapevine growing and winemaking around the globe. New societies came about through immigration, trade, exploration, and slavery routes as Europeans settled the New World countries. In various parts of the world, the immigrants wished to consume wine and other alcohol beverages that were comparable to those from their homelands back in Europe. Commodities markets for trading and selling products were created as a necessity as the settlers were faced with finding a source of earnings to support themselves. This led the immigrants to begin incorporating their knowledge and expertise of winemaking into the New World lands.

The most significant wine-producing countries of the New World are Argentina, Australia, Chile, New Zealand, and South Africa. These countries are perceived as dynamic, with enormous potential, and continue to gain immense popularity throughout the world. Overall, New World wines are reasonably priced and provide good value. New World wines use labelling practices similar to those of the United States, identifying the primary varietal, as opposed to labelling according to geography, as practiced by the Old World wineries.

In the Southern Hemisphere, the seasons are just the opposite of those in the Northern Hemisphere. Therefore, the autumn harvest occurs typically in the months of March and April, approximately six months earlier than the Northern Hemisphere harvest, in August and September. The term *flying winemakers* has become popular, as some winemakers (originally Australians) in the Southern Hemisphere have the luxury of working multiple vintages and contributing their skills and expertise as consultants to winemakers in the Northern Hemisphere. Some argue that this practice has led to a homogenization of wine and wine styles around the globe.

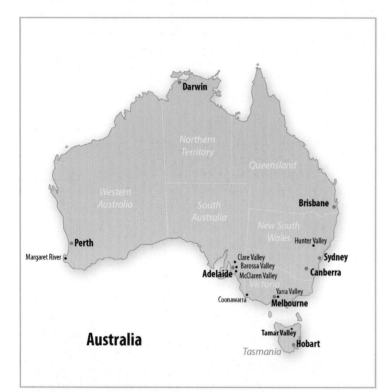

FIGURE 8–1 Map of Australia
(Thomas Moore)

AUSTRALIA

Australia maintains more than 1,300 wineries and 425,000 acres of vine. There are about 50 registered wine regions across Australia, and approximately 5 corporate-controlled companies make 75% of all the wine produced, which provides an economy of scale. These companies have also invested heavily in technology and mechanization, from vineyard to bottling, which contributes to the production of reasonably priced wines that offer great value. Australia has considerable success not only domestically, but also in the international market, due largely to the clever marketing approach of attaching playful characters and catchy names to the wine labels and selling wines at a desirable price point. Figure 8–1 identifies Australia's wine regions.

The Varietals

Australia produces wine from approximately 70 grape varietals, although most derive from only 5 key varietals (Chardonnay, Riesling, Semillon, Cabernet Sauvignon, and Shiraz). Shiraz was for a long time the predominant grape in Australia; now it rivals Chardonnay as the most widely planted grape variety, with more than 30,000 acres of vines. Semillon is the second most widely planted variety of white grapes, after Chardonnay.

Australian Wine Labelling

Australian wines are varietal based, similar to American wines. If wines are labelled by grape variety, at least 85% of the wine must be made from that grape. However, Australia has unique labelling requirements. If a wine comprises more than one variety and no single variety makes up 85%, then all varieties must be labelled in order of importance (by percentage used). For example, the label on a blend of Cabernet–Shiraz might state Cabernet 60% and Shiraz 40%.

If a place name is indicated on the label, then 85% of the grapes must have come from that region. Ninety-five percent of the grapes in vintage wines must have been harvested during the year listed on the label.

APPELLATIONS

Wine production in Australia is concentrated in cool valleys and coastal areas in the south or southwest.

Southern Australia

Adelaide Hills—This region contains several elevated vineyard sites and produces cool-climate varietals such as Riesling, Chardonnay, and Pinot Noir. Because of the large amount of these varietals (traditional grapes used to produce classic Champagne), these vineyards have been producing sparkling wine as well.

Clare Valley—Clustered near the city of Adelaide, this diverse region experiences both dry heat and cool sea wind. The vineyards are irrigated, because Clare Valley typically has the lowest rainfall of all the Australian wine regions. The cool higher-altitude vineyards allow the Riesling and Chardonnay grapes to ripen slowly throughout the growing season. Hearty reds such as Shiraz also are produced here.

Barossa Valley (bah-ROH-sah)—One of the most famous Australian wine regions and the first to become highly popular outside of Australia, the Barossa Valley has been producing wines longer than most other growing areas, with Shiraz vines dating back from the 1840s. The climate is ideal for growing legendary Australian Shiraz and other full-bodied red wines such as Cabernet Sauvignon and Grenache, as well as heartier whites.

Eden Valley—An area within Barossa Valley, but where the vineyards are at a higher elevation, Eden Valley boasts a cooler climate that is ideal for producing Rieslings.

McLaren Vale—The temperate maritime environment from the nearby ocean, coupled with rolling hills, creates a climate characterized by warm days and cool nights—perfect for maintaining the acidity balance that is vital for the rich, ripe fruit that is usually produced. The various microclimates of McLaren Vale allow many varieties to thrive, particularly Rhône varietals (Shiraz, Grenache, Mourvedre, Marsanne, and Viognier), but also Cabernet Sauvignon, Merlot, and Sauvignon Blanc.

Coonawarra—This is the most famous, highly recognized red wine district in Southern Australia, where vines were first planted in 1890. It is known primarily for its Shiraz and Cabernet Sauvignon, but also produces Chardonnay and Riesling. This key cool growing area is the home of the famous *Terra Rossa* soils (locally called "red earth"), which are composed of very old clay that is compressed until it resembles red brick. Figure 8–2 illustrates these famous soils.

FIGURE 8–2 Famous Terra Rossa soil

(RyMill Coonawarra)

Southeast Australia

Hunter Valley—Located about 100 miles northwest of Sydney, Hunter Valley is the most northerly of Australia's first-class vineyards. With long growing seasons, the area is traditionally known for its Shiraz and Semillon, but also produces a large amount of Cabernet Sauvignon and Chardonnay.

Yarra Valley—This is one of Australia's most picturesque and renowned wine regions, with its rolling, vine-covered slopes. A cool, inland region, Yarra Valley is known for the cultivation of Chardonnay and Pinot Noir. Cabernet Sauvignon and Shiraz also do well here.

Western Australia

Margaret River—Located in Western Australia, this area has perhaps the most maritime climate of any Australian wine district. It has a wide peninsula, around 60 miles cape-to-cape, and is bordered by the ocean on three sides. (Most Margaret River wineries lie only a few miles from the sea.) It produces a mere 2% of Australia's crush, yet represents around 20% of its premium bottled wines. It has excelled with varieties such as Cabernet Sauvignon and Semillon/Sauvignon Blanc, but Chardonnay has brought the most fame to this area.

Perth Hills—One of the newest and smallest wine-growing regions in Western Australia is Perth Hills. Many grapes are planted at higher and cooler altitudes here.

Swan District—This is the original wine district in Western Australia. Just north of the city of Perth, the Swan District is a very warm region and well suited for the fortified dessert wines.

NEW ZEALAND

FIGURE 8–3 Map of New Zealand
(Thomas Moore)

New Zealand is one of the southernmost wine-producing countries in the Southern Hemisphere. It comprises two large islands, called *North Island* and *South Island*, and a number of smaller islands. All of the islands are greatly influenced by the region's maritime climate, but still maintain a wide diversity in climate and terrain. New Zealand is a cool and damp environment, with cool nights even in the hot, sunny summers. This climate assists the grape varietals in maintaining their zesty acidity and fruit qualities. Figure 8–3 identifies New Zealand's wine regions.

The Varietals

New Zealand's success is a recent trend that has seen its greatest growth over the last 20 years, when it became one of the fastest-growing wine countries in the world. In 2006, New Zealand maintained over 57,000 acres of grapevines, dominated by 22,000 acres devoted to Sauvignon Blanc. Pinot Noir is the leading red wine varietal and trails Sauvignon Blanc in popularity. Chardonnay, Riesling, and Bordeaux varietals are other popular grapes found throughout New Zealand.

New Zealand is known mostly for wines that exude the pure personality of grape varietals. The pervasive use of stainless steel assists in preserving the grapes' acidity, the expression of the grapes' intensity, and the purity of the fruit. Oak aging is moderately applied in some areas, but, philosophically, doesn't overpower the expression of the grape's personality.

Screwcaps

A modern trend that New Zealand is noted for is the use of screw caps as the main closure to seal bottles of wine. This is a way to eliminate the concern of TCA, or cork taint. In addition, choosing the the screw cap is a natural progression for the winemaker, particularly if the wine has been stored in stainless steel prior to bottling. This practice supports the philosophy of pure essence of the fruit, youthfullness, and preservation of the acid qualities that oak aging and a cork would otherwise alter.

APPELLATIONS

North Island

Gisbourne—This region is located at the eastern tip of North Island. Gisbourne is coined the *Chardonnay Capital* of New Zealand because half of its vineyards are occupied by the Chardonnay varietal.

Hawke's Bay—Famous for its *Gimblett Gravels*, or rocky, stony soil, Hawke's Bay has been referred to as the *Bordeaux of New Zealand* because of the predominant Cabernet Sauvignon and Merlot- and Syrah-based wines.

Wellington—This area occupies the southern section of North Island, which includes the Wairarapa wine region. Martinborough, one of North Island's well-known subregions, is located within Wellington. Martinborough produces Sauvignon Blanc, but has become a leading Pinot Noir producer as well.

South Island

Nelson—This region is situated on the western side of the northern tip of South Island. Mountains to the west of the region provide a rain-shadow effect, while the coastline moderates the climate. Cool-climate grape types such as Chardonnay, Sauvignon Blanc, Riesling, and Pinot Noir thrive.

Marlborough—Possibly New Zealand's finest wine region and certainly the largest grape-growing area, Marlborough had over 29,000 acres of vineyards in 2006. Located on the northern end of South Island, Marlborough is a cool growing region with long, dry autumns that allow grapes to ripen. Sauvignon Blanc made the region well known, but it is Pinot Noir that is making great strides and has emerged as New Zealand's leading red grape varietal. Figure 8–4 shows a New Zealand vineyard.

Canterbury—A large wine region on South Island, Canterbury has many vineyards planted in white varieties, notably Riesling and Chardonnay.

Central Otago—This southernmost wine region in the world is characterized by varying levels of altitude. With a continental-type climate, Pinot Noir has become the leading varietal in Central Otago.

FIGURE 8–4 New Zealand vineyard
(Peter Bush © Dorling Kindersley)

ARGENTINA

Argentina is positioned in the heart of South America. Viticulture began during the Spanish colonization in the early 1500s and saw resurgence in the nineteenth century by a melting pot of European immigrants mostly from Spain, Germany, Italy, and France. In 2007 there were over 550,000 acres of vines, and until recently Argentina vintners were distributing most of their products domestically. Modern production techniques, greater vineyards

FIGURE 8–5 Map of Argentina
(Thomas Moore)

planted at higher elevations (in some cases, above 4,000 feet), and an influx in interest and talent from abroad have all helped to reshape this South American wine region. As the popularity of New World wine has increased, Argentina has successfully increased its wine exports, gained greater fame, and become a key player in the world wine market. Figure 8–5 identifies Argentina's wine regions.

The Varietals

Argentina has gained a reputation over the past decade for its signature grape *Malbec*. Orginally from Southwest France, Malbec has prospered as both a blending grape and a standalone varietal. Other popular red grapes produced are Cabernet Sauvignon, Syrah, Merlot, and Tempranillo. Figure 8–6 shows Argentina's most significant grape varietal: Malbec.

White grape varietals are not as prevalent as red grapes, but a standout grape unique to Argentina is *Torrontes* (tohr-RAHN-tez). Other recognizable international varieties include Chardonnay, Chenin Blanc, Semillon, Sauvignon Blanc, and Viognier.

APPELLATIONS

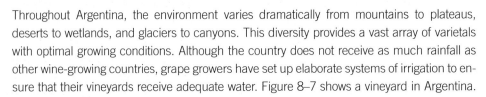

Throughout Argentina, the environment varies dramatically from mountains to plateaus, deserts to wetlands, and glaciers to canyons. This diversity provides a vast array of varietals with optimal growing conditions. Although the country does not receive as much rainfall as other wine-growing countries, grape growers have set up elaborate systems of irrigation to ensure that their vineyards receive adequate water. Figure 8–7 shows a vineyard in Argentina.

Mendoza—This is the largest and most vital wine-growing region in Argentina (with over 80% of the country's plantings) and is also the largest wine-growing region in all of the Southern Hemisphere.

Red wines produced include large amounts of Malbec, Bonarda, and Cabernet Sauvignon, with lesser amounts of Merlot and Tempranillo. The vineyards in higher altitudes yield excellent white varietals such as Chardonnay, Chenin Blanc, Sauvignon Blanc, and Torrontes.

Uco Valley (OOH-co)—Located in the southwest part of Mendoza, with some of the highest elevation levels in all of Mendoza, the Uco Valley has the ideal climate conditions for varieties such as Semillon, Chenin Blanc, and Malbec.

San Juan—The second-largest production area in Argentina, San Juan contains a set of valleys with varying levels of elevation.

La Rioja—Dry and windy, La Rioja grows Malbec, Syrah, and Torrontes varietals.

Rio Negro and Neuquen—The Rio Negro region in southeast Argentina is just South of Mendoza. Wine production has been taking place there since the early 1900s. The climate is dry and warm and yields old-vine Malbecs and other reds. Neuquen borders Mendoza in the North and Rio Negro in the South and is a developing wine region producing a mix of white and red varietals.

Salta—This region is the northernmost wine-growing area and showcases the highest vineyards in all of Argentina, reaching as high as 10,000 feet above sea level. The most

FIGURE 8–6 Malbec grapes
(Wines of Argentina)

FIGURE 8–7 Vineyards in Argentina
(Wines of Argentina)

planted white grape is Torrontes, while the most widely planted red grape varietal is Cabernet Sauvignon, with Tannat and Syrah as other significant grape varietals.

CHILE

Chile (CHEE-lay) is a long sliver of land located on the western coast of South America. It has a long history of winemaking dating back to the 1500s, but 1851 saw the arrival of French vine varieties. Chile has long been a country of isolation both geographically and climatically, with the Pacific Ocean to the west, the Andes Mountains to the east, and the Atacama Desert to the north. Since Chile has been free from the dictatorship of Augosto Pinochet over the past two decades, it has experienced an influx of foreign investment, particularly from Europe and the United States, which has assisted in modernizing the country's vineyards and wineries of Chile while broadening new markets. Chile's wine industry has been reshaped and has emerged from isolation with over 270,000 acres of vines. Figure 8–8 identifies Chile's wine regions.

FIGURE 8–8 Map of Chile
(Thomas Moore)

The Varietals

Chile features a mild Mediterranean climate that is warm, sunny, and moderated by the cooling influence of the Pacific Ocean and the moisturizing influence of the Andes Mountains. Several grape varietals thrive in this environment, including Merlot, Cabernet Sauvignon, Syrah, Sauvignon Blanc, and Chardonnay. A unique aspect of Chile is the Carmenere grape varietal, which is similar to Merlot. It was recently rediscovered in Chile through the DNA fingerprinting process. For years, Carmenere was mislabeled as Merlot, until it was properly identified as a completely distinct grape varietal.

APPELLATIONS

Most of the premium rootstock in Chile was imported from France in the 1800s, just in time to avoid the disastrous infestation of the phylloxera pest, which had devastated a large number of the vineyards throughout Europe. Chile was one of the few wine-growing places spared destruction from phylloxera, and it remains home to some of the few remaining strains of original vines. It was a combination of Chile's sand-based soil (phylloxera doesn't thrive in sand) and geographic isolation from the rest of the world that prevented the devastation wrought on other vineyards.

Aconcagua (ah-KOHN-kah-gwah)

Aconcagua Valley—Located just north of the Central Valley, Aconcagua Valley has a warmer climate that supports red grapes such as Cabernet Sauvignon and Syrah.

Casablanca Valley—Located closer to the coast, Casablanca Valley enjoys a cooler climate that produces white wines—notably Sauvignon Blanc and Chardonnay, but also some Pinot Noir.

Central Valley

The main growing area in Chile is collectively known as the Central Valley, which produces the vast majority of wines. The climate is dry, and there is little risk of springtime frost. The proximity to the Andés Mountains helps to create a wide diurnal range between day and night temperatures. Central Valley comprises the most important subregions from north to south:

Maipó Valley (My-POH)—The Maipó region, located just south of Santiago, is one of Chile's renowned, long-established quality wine regions. Cabernet Sauvignon is the core of the region, but Merlot and Carmenere are also prominent.

Rapel Valley (RAH-pell)—A large growing area with diverse soil, Rapel Valley successfully grows Carmenère as a significant varietal. Colchagua is an important sub-region of Rapel Valley.

Curicó Valley—This is one of the cooler regions in Central Valley, due to the influence of the Pacific Ocean.

Maule Valley—Many vineyards are located in the valley and on the slopes of the coastal mountains. White varieties flourish, predominantly Sauvignon Blanc and Chardonnay, and many red varieties including Merlot, Cabernet Sauvignon, and Carmenère.

SOUTH AFRICA

South Africa's wine-growing areas are situated in the Southern Hemisphere, with a largely Mediterranean climate. According to the *South Africa Trade Group*, the country had over 255,000 acres of grapevines in 2007. The South African winemaking heritage goes back to the seventeenth century; however, it was not until the government deregulated the wine industry and emerged from the shadow of Apartheid in 1994 that a renaissance occurred, allowing South African winemakers to compete with the rest of the wine world. Figure 8–9 identifies South Africa's wine regions.

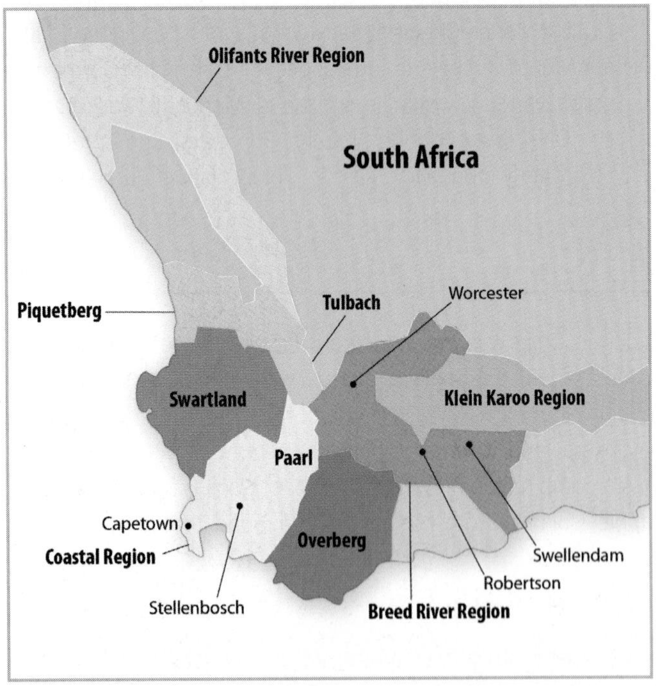

FIGURE 8–9 Map of South Africa

(Thomas Moore)

The Varietals

The climate associated with South Africa encourages a wide range of wine styles. Historically, Pinotage (a local grape that is a cross between Pinot Noir and Cinsault [SAN-soh]) had outperformed all other grape varietals. Now Cabernet Sauvignon has emerged as the leading South African varietal and currently surpasses all other red grapes. Syrah is the next major varietal, with the second-largest number of acres devoted to vines, followed by Merlot and then Pinotage.

White wine grapes include Chenin Blanc; known locally as *Steen,* it is the leading varietal of both white and red wine grapes. Chenin Blanc produces both dry and sweet styles. Other white wine varietals include Chardonnay, Sauvignon Blanc, and a small percentage of Viognier.

Over the last decade, producers have maintained a fairly rigorous uprooting and replanting process. This is largely due to the accessibility of new clones of existing varietals and a better understanding of site selection by the matching of the type of vine with a well-suited vineyard site.

Chardonnay is used for both table wine and sparkling wine. The South Africans produce a sparkling wine called *Méthode Cap Classique* by using the classic Champagne method of production.

APPELLATIONS

Depending on where the vineyard is located, it will be influenced by one of two oceans (Indian or Atlantic) that meet at the tip of South Africa and influence the vineyards by moderating the climate. South Africa has had the strictly legislated *Wines of Origin*, or WO, in place since 1973 to ensure the authenticity of its wines through the control of appellation areas.

The wine-producing areas are broken down into regions (the broadest-producing areas), then into district and wards (the smallest and most defined growing areas).

The four South African regions are Breed River Valley, Klein Karoo, Olifants River, and the Coastal Region. Most of the vineyards in South Africa are located in the southwest corner of the country called the Cape, or Coastal Region.

A wine that lists a name of a region, district, or ward on its label must contain 100% of grapes from that location. A wine is labelled according to its varietal (85% minimum as listed), similar to the European Union requirements.

Coastal Region

The Coastal Region is possibly the most recognized South African wine region throughout the world wine market. It contains many well-known districts and wards such as *Stellenbosch* (STELL-n-bahsh), *Paarl* (par-rl), and *Constantia* (kuhn-STAN-she-ah).

OTHER NEW WORLD WINE COUNTRIES

NAME: _____ Score out of 20 points_____.

Use these questions to test your knowledge and understanding of the concepts presented in the chapter.

I. MULTIPLE CHOICE: Select the best possible answer from the options available.

1. In Australia, if a wine comprises more than one grape and neither grape makes up at least 85%, then
   a. the grape that makes up the highest percentage is the only one which needs to be listed on the label.
   b. all grapes must be listed on the label.
   c. all grapes must be listed on the label in order of importance and by percentage.
   d. only one of the grapes needs to be listed, as determined by the winemaker.

2. Which New World country grows the most vines?
   a. New Zealand
   b. Argentina
   c. Chile
   d. Australia

3. Australia's Barossa Valley and Coonawara areas are best known for producing which grape?
   a. Chardonnay
   b. Merlot
   c. Riesling
   d. Shiraz

4. New Zealand's Marlborough area is best known for producing which grape?
   a. Chardonnay
   b. Merlot
   c. Riesling
   d. Sauvignon Blanc

5. The most significant wine region in Argentina is
   a. Salta.
   b. Rapel Valley.
   c. Mendoza.
   d. Margaret River.

II. TRUE / FALSE: Circle the best possible answer.

6. Most South African vineyards are located in the growing areas within the Coastal Region. **True / False**

7. All New Zealand producers use screw caps as closures for their wine bottles. **True / False**

8. In South Africa, another name for the Chenin Blanc grape varietals is *Steen*. **True / False**

III. MATCHING: In each of the following sentences, connect the grape varietal listed afterwards with the predominant location mentioned in the sentence: Answers may only be used once.

LOCATION

9. ____ significant white wine grape from New Zealand

10. ____ significant red wine grape from Australia

11. ____ significant white wine grape from Australia

12. ____ significant red wine grape grown in Argentina

13. ____ significant red wine grape from Chile

14. ____ significant red wine grape from South Africa

15. ____ significant red wine grape from New Zealand

16. ____ significant white wine grape from Chile

17. ____ significant white wine grape from Argentina.

18. ____ significant white wine grape from South Africa

GRAPE VARIETALS

A. Cabernet Sauvignon

B. Malbec

C. Chardonnay

D. Merlot

E. Sauvignon Blanc

F. Shiraz

G. Syrah

H. Pinot Noir

I. Chenin Blanc

J. Torrontes

IV. SHORT-ANSWER ESSAY / DISCUSSION QUESTIONS: Use a separate sheet of paper if necessary.

19. What is the philosophy behind the method, practiced by some New Zealand wine producers, of using screw caps to seal their wines?

20. Give a brief history explaining how New World wine countries started to produce wine.

Unit 4
WINES OF THE OLD WORLD

"Experience is the teacher of all things."
—*Julius Caesar*

OLD WORLD AND ITS NEW APPROACH

The major wine-producing countries associated with the Old World have been creating wine for thousands of years. Throughout the ages, the history of wine production has been entangled, on varying levels, with the political and sociological development of each country. Many of the bottle shapes, grape types, and styles of wine from the New World that have already been discussed in this text originated in the significant regions of France, Italy, Germany, or Spain.

The European Union (EU) was created just after World War II to bring peace, prosperity, solidarity, and stability to Europe. The EU is an economic and political partnership between 27 democratic European countries. The Union acts on a wide range of policies in order to benefit the member countries.

In the world of wine, the European Union organized a wine classification system consisting of two tiers, the bottom tier called *table wine* and the top tier called *quality wine*. The concept of the quality-wine level is based on a geographical-origin approach of wines produced from a specific place.

The EU has actively encouraged quality wine and discouraged the production of wines in the table wine category. In 2007, the EU and its member states agreed to uproot approximately 400,000 acres of grapevines in order to halt overproduction and government subsidies. This approach is being used to balance supply and demand, as well to encourage a focus on better-quality varietals and site selection.

9

Wines of France

French winemakers produce a variety of different wines in styles that may be a bit daunting to the novice wine drinker. However, by applying some generalizations on major varietals, regions, and appellations, it can become easier to solidify an understanding of French wines.

LEARNING OBJECTIVES

Upon completion of this chapter, the learner will be able to:

- Understand the significant wine-producing regions of France.
- Understand the French appellation control system and its levels of hierarchy.
- Know the major grape varietals and styles of wine produced within each of France's significant wine regions.
- Know the important subregions within Burgundy, Bordeaux, the Loire Valley, and Rhône.

FRANCE

France is one of the oldest wine-producing countries in Europe, with winemaking originating back to the sixth century B.C. It is also one of the largest producers and consumers of wine in the world. French wine has served as the standard of excellence of wine throughout the world for decades and is respected and often imitated by most major wine-producing countries.

The novice wine drinker may find that French wine selection can be intimidating, primarily because the labelling system is based largely on geography. Most French wines are labelled by the name of the place (which is registered and legally defined under French law) where the grapes are grown and the wine is made, rather than by major type of grape, as labelling is done in the New World. This is somewhat of a challenge for non-French speakers to have to read, understand, and pronounce French terminology, as well as to become educated in French geography and wine law.

French wines often are produced in a way that allows the expression of terroir to show through, with fewer overt fruit characteristics, and that allows the wine to gravitate toward more earth- and animal-oriented attributes. This wine paradigm associated with Old World France may not be as user friendly to the average wine drinker. For some, these expressions and attributes make French wines more dependent on consumption with food and less adaptable and drinkable by themselves, as many New World options are.

French winemakers produce a variety of different styles and types of wine. Applying some generalizations on major varietals, regions, and appellations makes it easier to solidify an understanding of French wines. The wine regions and appellations most commonly presented on American restaurant wine lists are outlined in this chapter. Figure 9–1 identifies the significant French wine regions.

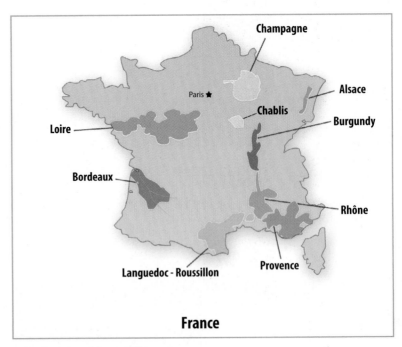

FIGURE 9–1 Map of France

(Thomas Moore)

An Introduction to French Wine

The regions of France can be divided into three broad areas on the basis of grape varietals and climate. Of course, these are generalizations, and there are obvious exceptions within each area. However, it can be helpful at this level of wine education to discuss the complexity of Old World wines more in generalities. There are seven significant wine regions in France that produce world-class wine. Each of these regions specializes in certain grape varieties for its wine, according to climate, soil, laws, local traditions, and so on.

1. The *northeastern* section of France (Champagne, Northern Burgundy, and Alsace) is subject to a continental climate that consists of four distinct seasons with short summers and harsh winters. This type of climate contributes to creating tart grapes with higher acid and the preservation of mineral qualities. The grapes produce low sugar and less ripe fruit, which ultimately yields a wine with lower alcohol content. Therefore, the technique of chaptalization (the addition of sugar to grape must) is frequently allowed in these regions according to appellation-controlled laws.

   Alsace (al-SASS)—This region produces mostly white wines from the Riesling, Gewürztraminer, Pinot Blanc, and Pinot Gris grapes. Alsace also produces sparkling wine and dessert wine.

   Burgundy (BER-gun-dee)—The Burgundy region produces both red and white wines. Red wine grape production is primarily from Pinot Noir and Gamay, while white wine production is from Chardonnay.

   Champagne (sham-PAYN)—Champagne is world famous for sparkling wines produced from varying blends of Pinot Noir, Pinot Meunier, and Chardonnay grape varietals. (This topic will be discussed in greater detail in Chapter 11, "BUBBLES: Sparkling Wine".)

2. The *western* section of France (Bordeaux and most of the Loire Valley) has a maritime climate of mild winters and cool summers, created from the moderating influence of the Atlantic Ocean.

   Bordeaux (bohr-DOH)—The Bordeaux region produces red and white wine and dessert wine. Red wine grapes are primarily blended in varying quantities of Cabernet Sauvignon, Merlot, Cabernet Franc, and others. White wines, whether dry table or sweet dessert wines, are produced primarily from varying quantities of Sauvignon Blanc and Semillon varietals.

   Loire (LWAHR) **Valley**—Loire produces mostly white wines, but also produces red wines, dessert wines, and sparkling wines. The white wines come primarily from Chenin Blanc and Sauvignon Blanc grapes and red wine dominated by the Cabernet Franc varietal.

3. The *midcentral* and *southern* sections of France maintain a Mediterranean climate. In hotter southern climates, grapes have less acid and higher sugar, which produces wine with higher alcohol levels, riper fruit and denser full-bodied wines.

   Rhône (ROHN) **Valley**—The Rhône Valley produces mostly red wines from Syrah, Grenache, and Mourvedre, with white wines produced from the Viognier grape.

   Languedonc-Roussillon (lahng-DAWK roos-see-YAWN) and **Provence** (praw-VAHNS)—In southern France, the majority of production is red wine from Syrah, Mourvedre, Grenache, and other varietals. In addition, produce some of France's most famous versions of fortified wine.

Useful French Wine Terms

- **Barrique** (bah-REEK)—Often refers to a barrel that holds approximately 60 gallons, used in Bordeaux
- **Blanc** (BLAHNK)—White wine

- **Cépage** (say-PAHZH)—Vine or grape variety
- **Château** (shah-TOH)—Often refers to a wine estate located on the land of the vineyard
- **Clos** (KLOH)—The term originally used in Burgundy to mean an enclosed vineyard
- **Côte** (KOHT) or **Coteaux** (koh-TOH)—Often refers to a slope or hillside
- **Cru** (KROO)—Refers to a ranking of a vineyard or estate; may also represent vineyard areas that are known for producing exceptional wines
- **Domaine** (doh-MAYN)—The term often used in Burgundy to refer to a single vineyard estate that may or may not derive from the location in which the grapes were grown
- **Piéce** (pee-YES)—Often refers to a barrel that holds approximately 60 gallons, used in Burgundy
- **Rouge** (ROOZH)—Red wine
- **Vendage** (vahn-DAHZH)—Grape harvest or vintage

THE FRENCH CLASSIFICATION SYSTEM

Created in 1935, the *Institut National des Appellations d'Origine* (an-stee-TYOO nah-syaw-NAHL dayz ah-pehl-lah-SYOHN daw-ree-ZHEEN), or INAO, is officially authorized to regulate the French wine industry according to standards that safeguard not only the consumer from fraud, but also the winemaker from unfair competition. The INAO guarantees that all appellation-controlled (AC) products hold to a rigorous set of standards. The creation of the AC system was designed to allow the consumer to distinguish between a wine with a simple name of origin and a fine wine with a "controlled" name of origin.

French wine is truly rooted in *terroir-based* laws, meaning that the wine has to be produced from specific appellations with permitted grape varieties, in suitable soils, and following defined procedures for viticulture and vinification. The French wine system is hierarchical, and theoretically, the wines should be better the higher they are up the rung, but in practice it doesn't necessarily work that way. The classification system defines four levels with varying quality standards. Figure 9–2 illustrates the French wine classification system.

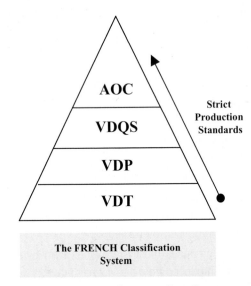

FIGURE 9–2 French wine classification system

(John Laloganes)

Appellation d'Origine Controlée (ah-pehl-lah-SYAHN daw-ree-JEEN kawn-traw-LAY) (AOC or AC)

AOC wines are held to the highest standard of the classification levels within the classification system. Vineyard growing areas, yields, varietals, blends of varietals, and alcohol content are highly regulated. In addition, all wines must be bottled within the region. The designation and regulations apply to all wines made from grapes grown in a designated AOC area of production.

Some AOC wines are further classified into *Grand Cru, Premier Cru*, or other designation. Each AOC has its own unique system of classification to determine this additional designation.

Vins Delimites de Qualite Superieur (van deh-lee-mee-TAY kah-lee-TAY soopehr-YUR) (VDQS)

Classified under a minor level of production with less strict, but similar, standards to the AOC level, VDQS wines hold great promise and are striving for recognition by the INAO for promotion to the AOC level. They can be thought of as virtually an AOC-in-waiting, or in transition, until they have a proven track record of consistent quality.

Vins de Pays (van-duh pay-ee) **(VDP)**

The vins de pays are regional wines whose broader growing area and grape varietal may be listed on the label. But the restrictions are more lenient than they are for wines at the previous two levels.

Vins de Table (van-duh-tab) **(VDT)**

The vins de table classification is at the lowest level with the loosest quality standards. These wines can be produced from grapes grown anywhere in France, with no regard for the level of yield per vine. The European Union actively discourages the production of wine at this level, and the vins de table classification is a declining category. These wines are most often consumed locally or used for distillation.

ALSACE

Alsace is a region located in the northeastern area of France, close to the German border east of the *Vosges* (vohzh) Mountains. Its location keeps this wine region relatively isolated from the rest of France. For many centuries, France and Germany had fought over the land of Alsace, which was ruled by Germany several times. The region's architecture, language, and grape varieties reflect this influence. Figure 9–3 identifies Alsace, France.

The Varietals

Alsace maintains some 35,000 acres of grapevines and is the largest producer of the nation's white wine (about 95%). With its vast soil types and cool, dry, and sunny climate, Alsace supports a variety of different white wine grapes. The Alsatians use the same grape varietals as the Germans, but, unlike the Germans who often leave varying amounts of residual sugar in the wines, the Alsatians ferment them mostly or even completely dry. It has been said, "Alsace uses German grapes, but makes them into a French style."

FIGURE 9–3 Map of Alsace

(Thomas Moore)

The primary grapes of Alsace are Riesling, Gewürztraminer, Pinot Gris, Muscat, and Pinot Blanc. Arguably the greatest wines of the region come from the Riesling varietal, and Gewürztraminer follows a close second.

APPELLATIONS

The region of Alsace contains two wine-specific areas: the *Bas-Rhin* (bahs-rine) and *Haut-Rhin* (oht-rine). Bas Rhin is located in the north and maintains a wetter, cooler climate. Many of the average-quality wines, or *edelzwicker* (ed-del-zvik-her, which means "blended wines"), derive from this location.

In the south, the Haut Rhin sustains many high-quality vineyards. They are often perched in the foothills of the Vosges Mountains. The mountains and nearby forests protect the area, creating a rain-shadow effect, which results in little rainfall and prolonged sun exposure to allow the grapes to ripen longer and gain maximum flavor development.

The minimum alcohol requirement of an Alsatian wine is 8.5%, but many are often much higher. In order to achieve a typical 12%–14% alcohol content, the wines can be chaptalized (the addition of sugar to grape must), because the region's cool climate may not always allow the grapes to produce enough sugar on their own.

FIGURE 9–4 Riesling Schlossberg Alsace Grand Cru
(Domaine Weinbach)

Alsace Grand Cru

Alsace Grand Cru require strict grape-growing and winemaking methods allowing four select kinds of grapes (Riesling, Gewürztraminer, Pinot Gris, and Muscat) from designated vineyards (although there are a few minor exceptions). Currently, 51 named vineyards are entitled to use the term *Grand Cru* (though many producers who earned the ranking choose not to use it because of a disagreement over the merit of the classification system). Figure 9–4 shows an Alsatian wine label from the famous Domaine Weinbach.

Bottle Shape and Labelling

Due to the German influence, most Alsatian wines are bottled in the typical German bottle. Alsace is also an AOC wine region that is allowed to label its wines by the grape name. When the wines are labelled with a grape name, 100% of the wine is made from the corresponding varietal.

Other Wines

The norm in Alsace is to produce dry white wines; however, a small amount of red and rosé wine is made from the Pinot Noir varietal. Alsace winemakers also produce small amounts of sweet and sparkling wine.

The terms *vendage tardive* (vahn-DAHZH tahr-DEEV), which is French for "late harvest," and *selection de grains nobles* (made from Botrytis Cinerea) are used to represent the dessert wine produced in Alsace. These wines can be made only from the permitted Grand Cru grape varieties. Figure 9–5 shows a Vendage Tardive Alsace Grand Cru wine label from the famous Domaine Weinbach.

Alsace also produces *Crémant d'Alsace*, a sparkling wine made from the local grapes, mainly from Pinot Blanc, but also from Chardonnay, Riesling, Pinot Gris, or Pinot Noir. Alsatian sparkling is made in the traditional bottle-fermented method, which is the same method used in the production of Champagne.

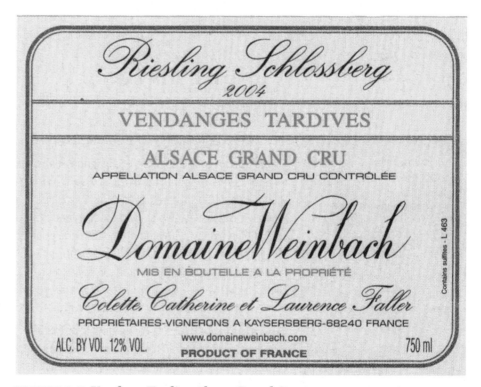

FIGURE 9–5 Vendage Tardive Alsace Grand Cru
(Domaine Weinbach)

LOIRE VALLEY

The Loire Valley is one of the world's greatest white wine regions. The Loire River extends the length of the Loire Valley, from far west of the Atlantic Ocean, inward some 634 miles through central France. With over 125,000 acres of vines, Loire produces various styles of wine, such as sparkling wine, dry table wine, off-dry table wine, and sweet dessert wine.

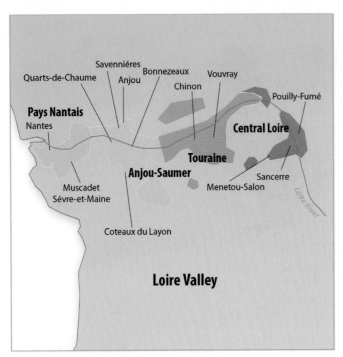

FIGURE 9–6 Map of Loire Valley
(Thomas Moore)

Figure 9–6 identifies the Loire Valley, France, and the significant wine regions.

Without the same level of prestige as that shared by other French wine regions, Loire has worked creatively to find notable ways to be recognized by the consumer. Some Loire winemakers have turned to organic or biodynamic farming and winemaking in order to add distinctiveness and marketability to their products. Nicolas Joly, a flourishing winemaker in the Loire, has often been referred to as "the father of biodynamics."

The Varietals

Loire is mostly known for its white wine grapes, Chenin Blanc, Sauvignon Blanc, and Muscadet, known locally as *Melon de Bourgogne* (meh-lohn duh boor-GAWN-yuh). But it also produces red wine from Cabernet Franc and Gamay varietals.

Wines are almost always unblended and are typically unoaked or lightly oaked. The philosophy of winemaking is to showcase the true nature of the grape, yielding its expression of terroir.

APPELLATIONS

The Loire Valley is divided into four main regions. Beginning at the east end heading west, they are (1) Central Loire, (2) Touraine, (3) Anjou-Saumer, and (4) Pays Nantais.

Central Loire—Unblended Sauvignon Blanc reaches its finest expression in the districts of *Sancerre* (sahn-SEHR) and *Pouilly-Fumé* (poo-YEE few-MAY). When Sauvignon Blanc is grown in this area, it is known as Blanc Fumé because of the smoky, or flintlike, aromas it possesses. Typically, Sancerre tends to be leaner than Pouilly-Fumé, but wines exhibit high acidity, with elements of mineral characteristics.

Other production areas of this region include *Menetou-Salon* (meh-neh-TOO sah-LOHN), *Quincy* (kan-SEE), and *Reuilly* (reuh-YEE), which produce other Sauvignon Blanc–based wines. Central Loire also produces red and rosé wines in Sancerre made from Pinot Noir and Gamay varietals. Figure 9–7 shows a Sancerre wine label.

Touraine (too-REHN)—The climate of Touraine offers good conditions for the cultivation of red and white wines. The best red wines are made from Cabernet Franc or Gamay in the distinguished production areas of *Chinon* (she-NYOHN) and *Bourgueil* (boor-GUH-yuh).

The most celebrated white wine in Touraine belongs to the *Vouvray* (voo-VRAY) appellation. Wines from Vouvray are produced from Chenin Blanc and made into many styles, from dry to sweet, from grapes affected by Botrytis Cinerea, as well as sparkling wines known as *Crémant d'Loire* (kray-mahn).

Anjou-Saumer (ahn-ZHOO soh-MYOOR)—The wine area of Anjou-Saumer produces a variety of styles. White wine is the most recognized, made from Chenin Blanc and produced in a dry style into a wine called *Savennières* (sa-veh-NYEHR).

Anjou-Saumer is also a famous area for the production of sweet wines. In favorable years, the development of Botrytis Cinerea produces a rich, luscious, concentrated flavor in the grapes. The best sweet wines are from the appellations of *Quarts de Chaume* (kahr duh SHOHM), *Bonnezeaux* (bawn-ZOH), and *Coteaux de Layon* (koh-toh deu leh-YAWN).

FIGURE 9–7 Bottle of Sancerre
(Kim Sayer © Dorling Kindersley)

Rosé d'Anjou (roh-ZAY dahn-ZHOO) and *Cabernet d'Anjou* (KA-behr-nay dahn-ZHOO) are pink wines produced from various red grapes such as Cabernet Franc, Malbec, Cabernet Sauvignon, and Gamay.

The Loire Valley's sparkling wine *Crémant de Loire* (kray-MAHN day LWAHR) is also produced in the Saumur area by the classic bottle-fermented method. These wines are made from Chenin Blanc, Chardonnay, or Cabernet Franc grapes.

Pays Nantais (pay-ee nahn-tay)—Located near the Atlantic Coast, Pays Nantais produces a prominent light dry white wine, sometimes with a light spritz, called *Muscadet* (muse-kah-DAY). Muscadet is named for the grape used to produce it rather than for its place of origin. Locally, the grape is called *Melon de Bourgogne* (meh-lohn duh boor-GAWN-yuh).

The best representation of this wine comes from the *Muscadet de Sèvre-et-Maine* area. Many producers age the wine on its lees by a method called Muscadet sur lie, which improves the wine by increasing the complexity and creating a full body.

BORDEAUX

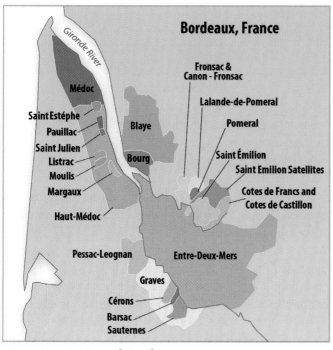

Bordeaux, France

Gironde River

Médoc

Saint Estéphe
Pauillac
Saint Julien
Listrac
Moulis
Margaux

Haut-Médoc

Blaye

Bourg

Fronsac &
Canon - Fronsac

Lalande-de-Pomeral

Pomeral

Saint Émilion

Saint Emilion Satellites

Cotes de Francs and
Cotes de Castillon

Pessac-Leognan

Entre-Deux-Mers

Graves

Cérons
Barsac
Sauternes

FIGURE 9–8 Map of Bordeaux
(Thomas Moore)

The Bordeaux region, located in western France, is naturally divided by the *Gironde* (zhee-RAWND) estuary and the *Garonne* (gah-RAHWN) and *Dordogne* Rivers into three broad zones with distinct geographical conditions. These zones form a left bank, a right bank, and an area between the banks to cover over 300,000 areas of vines. A variety of soils and maritime climate assist to provide wines with their unique character and connection to the land upon which their grapes are grown. Figure 9–8 identifies Bordeaux, France, and the major wine-producing areas.

This region produces some of the world's finest and most famous red, white, and dessert wines. *Bordeaux* has become synonymous with *quality* and *prestige* and is the source of the *chateau* concept (the French word for "castle," which has come to mean "wine estate"). Many of the world's most sought-after wines come from this region.

There are some everyday wines (vins de pays and vins de table) produced in the various locations of Bordeaux. The majority of the wines in the region are considered the best in the world and carry the *Premier Cru* designation. Wines in Bordeaux can be grouped into three appellation levels:

1. **Regional**—Bordeaux or labelled under a proprietary name, from a very generic, large appellation.
2. **District**—The district where the grapes were grown, such as Médoc or Entre-Deux-Mers. A fairly generic, but more specific, appellation designation than "regional."
3. **Village**—Where the vineyards are located, such as *Margaux* (mahr-GO), from a very specific point of appellation.

The "1855" Classification

In addition to their AOC rating, Bordeaux's thousands of acres are classified by the estate or chateau to which they belong. In 1855, several local wine merchants were commissioned by the Bordeaux Chamber of Commerce to group, or rank, the best estates (as opposed to

FIGURE 9–9 Chateau Lafite Rothschild—Pauillac

(SGM/Stock Connection)

Burgundy, where they rank the vineyards) of Bordeaux for the upcoming World's Fair. Figure 9–9 shows a Chateau Lafite Rothschild wine bottle.

The ranking took into account the sales history of Médoc chateaux since 1755. The top 61 estates were categorized into five different classes, or levels, in descending order of quality from the highest growth, or cru, called first crus, down through the fifth cru. This ranking became known as the famous "1855 classification." Only one significant change has occurred (believed to be politically based) in the classification: the elevation of Château Mouton Rothschild from second growth to first growth in 1973.

The Varietals

Bordeaux is mostly known for its long-lived ageable red and dessert wines and, to a lesser extent, its dry white wine. Bordeaux wines are almost always blended from varying amounts of the following possible grapes:

> **White Bordeaux or Dessert Wine:** (1) Sauvignon Blanc, (2) Semillon, and (3) Muscadet (in small amounts)
>
> **Red Bordeaux:** Primarily from (1) Cabernet Sauvignon, (2) Merlot, (3) Cabernet Franc, and (4) others in smaller amounts (Petit Verdot, Malbec, and Carmenere)

APPELLATIONS

The Bordeaux wine region is distinguished by its defining *Gironde* (zhee-RAHWN) estuary, which naturally separates the area into a left bank and a right bank. Within this region are numerous AOC districts and villages, but the six most significant growing areas are Médoc/Haut-Médoc, Graves, Pessac-Léognan, Sauternes/Barsac, St Émilion, and Pomerol.

On the *Left Bank,* or west side, of the river, the gravelly soil is mixed with pebbles and sand due to its proximity to the Atlantic Ocean and clay farther away. This area enjoys slightly warmer air temperatures, and the soil remains warmer as well. These factors allow for more slowly developing Cabernet Sauvignon grapes to reach optimal ripeness. The vines are old, strong, and hearty, and they produce wines with enormous power and aging potential. The notable appellations are as follows:

Médoc (may-DAWK)—Wines from Médoc are red, primarily from Cabernet Sauvignon, Merlot, Malbec, Cabernet Franc, and Petite Verdot. The wines are full bodied and tannic when young and more balanced and elegant when matured. Significant village appellations from Médoc and, more specifically, surrounded by the Haut Médoc, include *Saint-Estèphe* (san teh-STEHF), *Pauillac* (poh-YAK), *Saint Julien* (san zhoo-LYAN), *Listrac* (lees-TRAHK), *Moulis* (moo-LEE), and *Margaux* (mahr-GOH).

Pessac-Léognan (peh-SAK leh-oh-NYAHN) and *Graves* (GRAHV)—These areas produce some red wines, but most of the region is famous for its dry whites and the sweet wines from the areas of *Sauternes* (soh-TEHRN) and *Barsac* (BAHR-sak). Red wines from Pessac Léognan have a powerful bouquet, and white Bordeaux typically is made as well. The red wines of Graves are basically equivalent to those in the Médoc. But generally, reds contain slightly lower amounts of Cabernet Sauvignon and higher amounts of Merlot, compared with the wines of the northern appellations.

In the southern section of Graves, some of the most famous sweet wines in the world can be found in *Sauternes* and surrounding areas of *Barsac*, *Bommes* (BOME), *Fargues* (far-GAY), and *Preignac* (pray-NYACK). Sweet wine production is particularly sensitive to climate influences. Most of these areas are clustered in areas prominent in autumn mists, on high-mineral-content soils. The sweet white wines are made with noble rot, also called *Botrytis Cinerea*, a desirable mold that pervades the grapes. The two most notable sweet wine producers are *Chateau d'Yquem* (shah-TOE dee-kehm) in Sauternes and *Chateau Climens* (sha-TOE klee-men) in Barsac.

On the *Right Bank,* cool air and soil temperatures from higher concentrations of wet, compact clay and limestone soil coordinate with faster-maturing Merlot and Cabernet Franc, which are more suited for these conditions. The wines are approachable and young (with some notable exceptions), compared with those of the Left Bank. The prominent appellations are as follows:

Pomerol (POAM-ehr-all) and *Saint-Émilion* (sahn-eh-meel-YOHN)—These districts produce only red wines and are focused primarily on Merlot and Cabernet Franc, with lesser amounts of Cabernet Sauvignon and Malbec. Pomerol tends to be more structured than Saint Émilion. Notable in Saint-Émilion are *Chateau Ausone* (shah-TOE ow-zo-ney) and *Cheval Blanc* (shuh-VAHL blohng), two of the greatest wines of the region.

Unlike the Médoc's 1855 classification, Saint-Émilion reclassifies its wines every decade. The first classification officially took place in 1955. More recent reclassifications occurred in 1996 and 2006. Saint Émilion historically revises its list, or *crus*, of its top châteauxs every 10 years to keep the region dynamic and competitive, particularly at the top levels. The 2006 classification is in a current state of flux. A handful of winemakers who had their wines demoted from the classification brought charges against the system. The courts have instilled a three-year holding period to revert all wines back to the previous 1996 classification until the case can be resolved.

The estates of Pomerol have never been officially classified as the other wine-growing areas have. Instead, the reputation of each producer is generally known and trusted.

In the *middle*—Between the Left and Right Banks is the large *Entre-Duex-Mers* (ahn-truh duh MERR) district. This district focuses on dry white wines made from the traditional Bordeaux white wine varietals.

BURGUNDY

FIGURE 9–10 Map of Burgundy
(Thomas Moore)

Burgundy is one of the world's most famous wine-growing areas, located in Eastern France, southeast of Paris. Burgundy stretches from Dijon to Lyon, and the region is divided into five districts: Chablis, Côte d'Or (broken down into the Côte de Nuits and Côte de Beaune), Côte Chalonnaise, Mâconnais, and Beaujolais. The region consists of approximately 60,000 acres of vines that comprise over 100 Appellations d' Origine Controlee (AOC), or legally-defined producing areas—about twice as many as in Bordeaux. Figure 9–10 identifies the major wine regions of Burgundy, France.

Classification of Burgundian Wines

The combination of the end of the French Revolution in 1799 and the creation of the *Napoleonic Code* in 1804 removed the church from the vineyards and established that all heirs, regardless of age or gender, would share equal inheritance. This law has resulted in numerous individuals owning part of the famous vineyards in the Burgundy region. Historically, this movement led many vineyard owners to merely sell off their grapes to *négociants*, who would ferment and bottle their own wine. The situation is quite different from that in Bordeaux, where a single family or corporation owns each chateau.

In Burgundy, as in the rest of France, wines go by the name of the place they come from. In many ways, Burgundy is the most intensive *terroir*-oriented French wine region. In 1861, Burgundy classified its vineyards (in contrast to Bordeaux, which classified its estates). The top 33 Burgundy vineyards are classified as *Grand Crus*, and 570 are ranked second best, or *Premier Crus*. The vineyards are ranked according to several quality levels identified by level of specificity and quality of the appellation:

1. **Regional Wines,** or those labelled **Bourgogne** (BOR-gun-YAY)—These are made from grapes grown anywhere in the Burgundy region.
2. **Village**—These are wines with a hint of their origin (for example, Gevrey Chambertin or Puligny Montrachet). The village level can be thought of as a subregion.
3. **Premier Crus**—This labelling means "first-growth vineyards"; sometimes the term *1er Cru* may appear. The Premier crus are identified by the village name (for example, Gevrey-Chambertin), followed by the vineyard name, such as Clos Saint Jacque.
4. **Grand Cru**—Great-growth vineyards are wines that come from the best vineyards made in this region and are identified by the vineyard name alone (for example, Chambertin).

The Varietals

Burgundy maintains a continental climate that is best suited for cool-climate varietals such as Pinot Noir (known as Red Burgundy) and Chardonnay (known as White Burgundy). Farther south into Beaujolais, the soil and climate change and support a lesser-known Burgundian varietal known as Gamay.

APPELLATIONS

Chablis (shah-BLEE)—This is one of the five subregions and the northernmost part of Burgundy. It is located about 90 miles southwest of Paris (two hours by train). Chablis areas are ranked as one of four classifications ranging from *Grand Cru Chablis*, the most coveted, to *Premier Cru Chablis*, *Village Chablis*, and, finally, *Petit Chablis*, which is the most basic and simple of Chablis wines. Chablis is home to seven grand cru vineyards.

About 100 years ago, American winemakers borrowed the French name *Chablis* to label their nondescript low-quality white wine. For some Americans, therefore, Chablis went on to mean inexpensive, slightly sweet wine that comes in a box, although this has changed over the last decade. Authentic Chablis is named after the town central to the region that specializes in the Chardonnay varietals. Chablis has its unique interpretation of Chardonnay, as it often yields a style of citrus aroma and flavor, dry and fairly acidic, with a flinty, mineral style (because of its clay and limestone soils). In Chablis, the wine is delicate in aroma and flavor; therefore, most producers apply reductive techniques in which most wines are fermented and aged in stainless steel vats or in large, older wooden tanks or barrels that impart a subtle oak flavor. Application of these techniques allows Chardonnay to truly express itself. The Chablis style, in many cases, is almost the complete opposite of Californian and Australian Chardonnay, in which the liberal use of oak aging pervades.

Côte d'Or (koht-d-OR)—The vineyards of the Côte d'Or begin just 30 miles south of Dijon at the northern section of Burgundy. The Côte d'Or (hills of gold) produces some of the best Pinot Noir and Chardonnay in the world. The region is further divided into the *Côte de Nuits* (koht duh NWEE) in the north and *Côte de Beaune* (koht duh BOHN) in the south.

CHABLIS GRAND CRU VINEYARDS

1. Blanchot (blahn-SHOH)
2. Bougros (boo-GROH)
3. Grenouille (gruh-noo-yuh)
4. Les Clos (lay-KLOH)
5. Les Preuses (lay-PREWZ)
6. Valmur (vahl-MEWR)
7. Vaudesir (voh-day-ZEER)

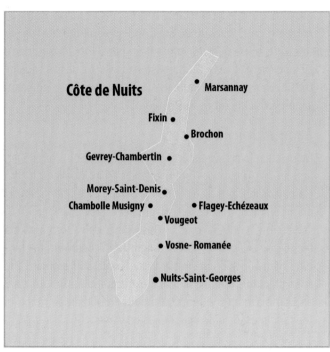

FIGURE 9–11 Map of Côte de Nuits
(Thomas Moore)

Côte de Nuits contains the highest-quality (firmest, longest lived) red Burgundy, but a small amount of excellent white Burgundy as well. It contains 24 out of the 25 red grand cru appellations.

Important Côte de Nuits villages that are surrounded by famous vineyards are as follows:: *Gevrey-Chambertin* (j hev-ray shahm-behr-TAN), *Morey-Saint-Denis* (maw-ree san duh-NEE), *Chambolle-Musigny* (shawm-bohl moo-sih-NYEE), *Vougeot* (voo-ZHOH), *Vosne-Romanée* (vohn raw-mah-NAY), and Nuits-Saint-George (nwee-san-ZHORZH). Figure 9–11 identifies the significant villages in Côte de Nuits.

Côte de Beaune (koht duh Bohn)—The Côte de Beaune area is located in the south of Côte d'Or and is considered the heart of White Burgundy country. This area is more diverse, offering great reds, but even greater legendary whites with a broader range of character and quality.

Important Côte de Beaune villages that are surrounded by famous vineyards are as follows: *Aloxe-Corton* (ah-lohx-kor-TAWN), *Beaune* (BONE), *Pommard* (pohm-MAHR), *Volnay* (vohl-NAY), *Meursault* (mehr-SO), *Puligny-Montrachet* (poo-lee-NYEE mohn-rah-SHAY), and *Chassagne-Montrachet* (shah-SAHN-nyah moan-rah-SHAY). Figure 9–12 identifies the significant villages in Côte de Beaune.

Côte Chalonnaise (koht shahl-oh-NEZ)—This subregion offers reasonably priced wines derived from Pinot Noir or Chardonnay. The wines can be compared to the wines produced from the Côte d'Or, but in minor-league versions. Some of the more notable wines from Chalonnaise consist mostly of grapes grown in vineyards on slopes or at higher elevation, from a collection of four smaller subdistricts: *Rully* (ru-YEE), *Mercury* (mer-cure-AY), *Givry* (gee-VREE), and *Montagny* (mon-tah-NYEE).

Mâconnaise (mah-kawn-NEH)—This large grape-growing area takes its name from the town of Macon (mah-KAWN). The climate becomes highly differentiated from the northern section of Burgundy and tends to produce less quality-oriented versions of Burgundian wines, but offers many affordable options.

White wine mostly made from Chardonnay or Aligoté yields the majority of production. Reds and rosés are made from the Pinot Noir and/or Gamay grapes. Several regional wines are produced, but also a few quality village wines, with their own appellations, such as *Pouilly Fuissé* (poo-YEE fwee-SAY) and *Saint Véran* (sahn-vay-RAHN). Both are known for producing Chardonnay wines of comparable style.

Beaujolais (BOE-zjoh-lay)—This region grows primarily the Gamay grapes (98%) rather than the Pinot Noir or Chardonnay grapes as in the rest of Burgundy. Beaujolais is located in the southern region of Burgundy. It is broken into

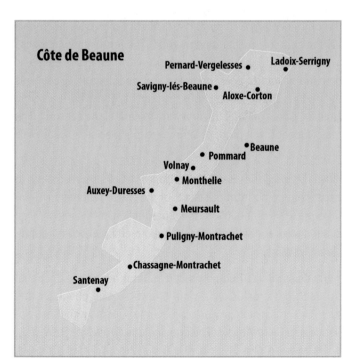

FIGURE 9–12 Map of Côte de Beaune
(Thomas Moore)

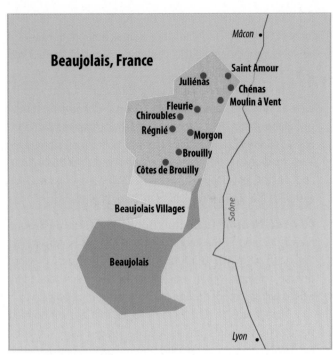

FIGURE 9–13 Map of Beaujolais
(Thomas Moore)

two broad areas: Haut and Bas Beaujolais. The Haut, or northern part, has granite soils and some of the best wines (the *crus* of Beaujolais) come from here. Bas, or southern, Beaujolais has clay and limestone soils for lesser quality (basic Beaujolais). Figure 9–13 identifies the significant wine-producing areas in Beaujolais.

Production Process

Many Beaujolais wines are inexpensive, young, refreshing, and fruity. They owe much of their fruity qualities to the Gamay grape, but also to the *carbonic maceration* method of production (discussed in greater detail in Chapter 3, "Viticulture and Enology"). This whole-berry fermentation technique is used to produce light red wines with low tannin, intense color, and fresh, fruity flavors and aromas. The strength of this method is that it extracts the maximum color and aroma from the grape without introducing as much of the tannin associated with other red wines.

Locations and Classifications

The 12 appellations of the region are divided into three categories, or levels of quality: Beaujolais (with Beaujolais Nouveau), Beaujolais Village, and the Crus of Beaujolais.

Beaujolais—The Gamay grapes produced here are grown in the southernmost region called Bas-Beaujolais. They produce very simple, flowery, and fruity wines that must be drunk young, as they are not intended for keeping.

Beaujolais Nouveau—The Gamay grapes produced are within the basic category and consist of about 50% of Beaujolais production. Young wines are produced in the Beaujolais region of France from the current year's Gamay harvest. After grapes have been harvested, they are fermented by the carbonic maceration method. The fermentation process takes about three to four days. The wine, only about nine weeks old when it is released, is full of the fresh, lively aromas and flavors of pear, cherries, and bubble gum. Beaujolais Nouveau shot to popularity in the 1970s and 1980s through the clever marketing approach of promoting the urge to "Come and get the first wine release of the season". The creator and promoter, Georges Duboeuf, still produces the most popular of all Beaujolais Nouveau wines.

Beaujolais-Villages—Wines bearing the Beaujolais-Villages label are restricted to being made from Gamay grapes that come from at least 2 of the 39 communes in Haut-Beaujolais and account for about a 25% of the total annual production of this region. Due to the better growing conditions, these are better wines with more complexity and depth. They can be kept from one to a few years.

Crus of Beaujolais—The highest-quality Beaujolais comes from one of the 10 major vineyard regions called *crus*. Each cru creates wine with its own special character and dimensions of aroma and flavor. The crus historically are named after villages with romantic-sounding names, such as Fleurie and Saint-Amour. The crus include *Brouilly* (BREW-yee), *Chenas* (shay-NAH), *Chiroubles* (shee-ROOB-luh), *Cote De Brouilly* (coat duh BREW-yee), *Fleurie* (FLUR-ee), *Julienas* (ZJOO-lee-ay-nah), *Morgan* (mor-GAHN), *Moulin à Vent* (MOO-lan ah vahn), *Régnié* (reh-N'YAY), and *Saint Amour* (sant ah-MOOR).

RHÔNE VALLEY

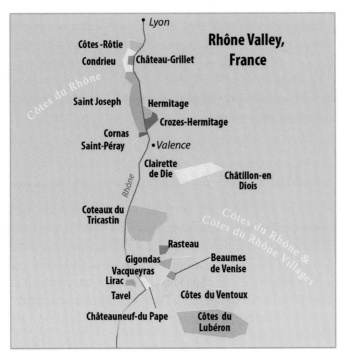

FIGURE 9–14 Map of Rhône Valley
(Thomas Moore)

Rhône is located in the southeast section of France, south of the Burgundy region. It is separated into two areas: the Northern Rhône and the Southern Rhône. While they both receive ample sunshine, the two are vastly different. The Northern Rhône terraine is steep and cooler, whereas the Southern Rhône is flatter, sunny, and warmer. The Rhône River runs southward for 120 miles through the valley, extending its way through vineyards. Nearly all Rhône wines are red (about 91%), followed by rosés and whites. Figure 9–14 shows the significant appellations in the Rhône Valley.

APPELLATIONS

Northern Rhône

Northern Rhône ranges from Lyon to the village of Valence. This northern section maintains a semi-continental climate and produces predominately single-variety red wines from *Syrah*, with small amounts of white wines from *Viognier* and others.

The classic wines of the northern Rhône reds are based on the Syrah grape in the renowned areas of *Côte Rôtie* (koht roh-TEE), *Hermitage* (her-mee-TAHZH), *Saint Joseph* (san zhoh-ZEHF), and *Crozes-Hermitage* (krawz her-mee-TAHZH). They can be cellared for as long as Bordeaux and sometimes continue to improve for decades.

White wines are based on a blend of *Viognier*, *Rousanne* (roo-SAHN), and *Marsanne* (mar-SAHN) grape varietals. Some of the red wine producers in the north use small amounts of these varietals to add fragrance and soften tannins in their wines.

The famous (but very rare) white wines of the region are from *Condrieu* (kawn-DREE-yuh), *Chateau Grillet* (sha-TOH gree-YEH), and *Saint-Péray* (san pay-REH).

Southern Rhône

Southern Rhône extends southward toward Avignon. The red wines of the southern Rhône tend to be blends of grapes dominated by Grenache, with smaller amounts of up to a dozen other red and white varieties. Some of the allowable blending varietals include Mourvèdre (moor-VEH-druh), Cinsault (SAN-soh), and Syrah.

Wines from anywhere in the northern or southern Rhône region can be labelled *Cotes-du-Rhône* (koht deu ROHN) or *Cotes du Rhône-Village* (coat-duh-RONE-vee-LAHJ). These are blended wines (with up to 13 permitted grape varieties) from anywhere in the region, but with a predominant Grenache base.

The most famous red wine appellation from the southern section is *Châteauneuf-du-Pape* (shah-toh-nuhf-doo-PAHP), or CDP. Predominantly, CDP is a red wine (a small amount of white wine can also be found) that is always blended, usually from a possible 13 different grapes, but dominated by Grenache, then Syrah, with smaller amounts of Mourvèdre, Cinsault, and others.

Châteauneuf-du-Pape means "Pope's new castle" and was named after the relocation of the Italian papal court to the French Rhone city, Avignon, in the fourteenth century to house the first French pope (Pope Clement V). Figure 9–15 depicts very old vines with rocky, stony soil.

FIGURE 9–15 Very old vines image
(Christophe Delorme)

Gigondas (zhee-gawn-DAH) is another southern Rhône appellation where Grenache with Syrah or Mourvèdre predominates, possibly along with a little of the 10 other allowable varietals.

Tavel (ta-VEHL) and *Lirac* (Lee-RACK) produce some of the most complex-tasting pink (or "rosé," as they say in French) wines in the world. This is a careful blending primarily of Grenache-based wine with a small amount of Cinsaut grapes that undergo partial maceration to gain pink color from the red-skinned grapes. According to French wine law, rosé wines may not be made from blending red and white wines together; instead, they must be made from the partial maceration of red wine grapes. Rosés of Tavel often produce medium-bodied wines with refreshing acid levels.

SOUTHERN FRANCE

Located in Southern France, these wine regions border the Mediterranean Sea with Languedoc-Roussillon to the west and Provence to the east. Southern France, is like a vast sea of drinkable, inexpensive, historical, and somewhat rustic wines. Languedoc-Roussillon is an enormous growing area with over 750,000 acres of vines; Provence has 50,000 acres of vines. Collectively, they produce about one-third of all French wine, but are largely categorized as either Vins de Table (DT) or Vins de Pays (DP). These classification levels have been somewhat appealing because they allow the winemakers the freedom to be quite creative and adaptable in their production processes.

APPELLATIONS

The Mediterranean climate is a key to the character of the grapes and wines of these regions. While it is hot and dry, with plenty of sunshine, the grape varieties planted must be quite hardy. When harvested, the grapes will be very ripe due to the existing climate.

Languedoc (lahng-DAWK)

The Languedoc wine region is the most extensive in France and represents 40% of the total France vineyard area. It produces the majority of France's table wines and Vin de Pays wines.

Languedoc produces about 90% of red table wine, with traditional varietals consisting of Carignan, Cinsaut, Grenache, Mourvèdre, Cabernet Sauvignon, and Merlot. The region is gradually losing its bulk-wine image, as many producers are incorporating greater amounts of the fashionable Syrah and Cabernet.

Coteaux de Languedoc—This large appellation contains several smaller wine-producing areas. Notable AOC appellations in Languedoc include *Corbieres* (coor-bee-EHR), *Fitou* (fit-OOH) and *Minervois* (mee-nehr-VWAH). Primarily, these red-wine-producing areas use partial carbonic maceration to preserve fruit and lessen the effects of tannin.

Roussillon (roo-see-YAWN)

Roussillon produces the majority of France's *Vin Doux Naturels* (or VDNs). VDNs are made by the addition of grape brandy to the wine during the fermentation process. The brandy kills the yeast activity and preserves the remaining sugar, yielding a sweet, fortified wine.

Two notable AOC appellations in Roussillon are *Côtes du Roussillon Village* and *Collioure* (kol-yoor).

Some Vin Doux Naturels (VDN) in southern France are *Banyuls* (bahn-YULES) and *Banyuls Grand Cru*. The latter is an appellation close to the Spanish border that produces France's famous red and white wine Vin Doux Naturels. The red wine is based on a minimum 50% Grenache, with the Grand Cru requiring 75%. *Maury* (moh-REE) produces both rosé and red Vin Doux Naturel from Grenache. *Rivesaltes* (reev-ZALT) produces red wine, mainly from Grenache, or white Vin Doux Naturel's from Muscat.

Provence (praw-VAHNSS)

The Provence region begins where the Rhône Valley has ended. Vineyards travel on hillsides and on flatlands exposed to extensive sunlight. Provence produces about half of the rosé wine made in France, and a majority of the wine made in Provence is rosé. The grapes predominately used in this region include Syrah, Grenache, Mourvèdre, Cinsault, and others.

Some AOC appellations in Provence are as follows:

Côtes de Provence (koht duh praw-VAHNSS)—Côtes de Provence is the largest area, a wide area covering the French Riviera from the cities of Marseille to Nice. This area is best known for its production of rosé wines, but red wines are also appealing, as they keep improving in quality.

Bandol (ban-DOAL)—Bandol is one of the best red wines from Provence. Mourvèdre grape is a strong base that contributes body and spice to any Bandol.

Bellet (behl-LAY)—This appellation maintains some of the smallest production (about 80 acres of vines) of wines throughout France, but offers whites, rosés, and red wines.

WINES OF FRANCE

NAME: _____ Score out of 20 points_____.

Use these questions to test your knowledge and understanding of the concepts presented in the chapter.

I. MULTIPLE CHOICE: Select the best possible answer from the options available.

1. The Côte d'Or is divided into

   a. Dijon and Lyon.
   b. Côte Chalonnaise and Mâconnaise.
   c. Côte de Nuits and Côte de Buenne.
   d. Médoc and Haut Médoc.

2. The best quality appellations in Beaujolais are designated as

   a. Beaujolais Nouveau.
   b. Gamay Beaujolais.
   c. Beaujolais Village.
   d. Crus of Beaujolais.

3. The most significant red wine grape in Northern Rhône is

   a. Gamay.
   b. Syrah.
   c. Cabernet Sauvignon.
   d. Grenache.

4. In the Loire Valley, the appellations of Sancerre and Pouilly-Fume are most famous for their white wine produced from which grape?

   a. Chardonnay
   b. Chenin Blanc
   c. Riesling
   d. Sauvignon Blanc

5. Sauternes is most famous for what style of wine?

   a. Dry white wine
   b. Dry red wine
   c. Sweet white wine
   d. Sweet red wine

6. The top rated vineyard in Burgundy is

   a. Grand cru.
   b. Clos.
   c. Commune.
   d. Premier crus.

7. The famous 1855 classification categorized the wines mostly of

   a. Médoc.
   b. Graves.
   c. Pomerol.
   d. Saint Émilion.

8. Alsace is unique in that it is the only AOC wine region that labels its wines with the

   a. vintage date.
   b. location.
   c. producer.
   d. varietal.

II. TRUE / FALSE: Circle the best possible answer.

9. Wines from Bordeaux are almost always blends. **True / False**

10. Burgundy is home of the famous Left and Right Banks. **True / False**

11. Alsace is known for its crisp, dry white wines. **True / False**

12. A white or red burgundy will come from anywhere in Burgundy. **True / False**

13. Chablis is known for producing full-bodied oaky Chardonnay. **True / False**

14. The Loire Valley is known for producing all different styles of wine, including dry white and red wines, dessert wines, and sparkling wines. **True / False**

15. Right Bank Bordeaux specializes in Merlot-dominated red wines. **True / False**

16. Beaujolais wines are generally made in a fruity, low-tannin style. **True / False**

17. Southern France collectively produces a large amount of Vins de Table (DT) or Vins de Pays (DP). **True / False**

18. Northern Rhône is noted for producing white and sparkling wines. **True / False**

19. The red wines of the southern Rhône tend to be blends of grapes dominated by Grenache, with smaller amounts of up to a dozen other red and white varieties. **True / False**

III. SHORT ANSWER ESSAY / DISCUSSION QUESTIONS: Use a separate sheet of paper if necessary.

20. Identify some reasons that can make French wine intimidating and challenging for the novice to the intermediate wine drinker.

10

Other Old World Wine Countries

Along with France, the countries of Italy, Germany, and Spain have nurtured and developed many of the vines and winemaking techniques that have formed the foundation of wine culture and enjoyment throughout the world.

LEARNING OBJECTIVES

Upon completion of this chapter, the learner will be able to:

- Understand the wine classification systems associated with Italy, Germany, and Spain.
- Comprehend the meaning of significant label terminology associated with Italy, Germany, and Spain.
- Discover Italy's, Germany's, and Spain's most significant wine regions with their corresponding grape varietals and wines.

ITALIAN WINES

FIGURE 10–1 Map of Italy
(Thomas Moore)

Inhabitants of Italy have been making wine for thousands of years. Today, Italy is one of the largest producers of wine in the world and yet, as a country, is only three-fourths the size of California. Italy is well suited for the vineyard, with over 80% of the land being mountains or hilly and having close proximity to the ocean. Figure 10–1 identifies Italy's 18 (out of 20) significant wine regions.

The vineyards throughout Italy have vastly different soils, altitudes, grape varieties, and climates. Italy's span is as far north as the Alps (bordering Austria, Switzerland, and France), which have a cool, alpine, continental climate, to the warmth of Southern Sicily (near North Africa), which has more of a Mediterranean-type climate. Overall, the soils can vary from volcanic, to limestone (or tufa), to clay.

There are over one million vineyards, 94 provinces, and 8,090 communes throughout Italy's 20 major wine-growing regions. Italy is one vast vineyard that produces a variety of grapes of both international and indigenous types. It has been noted that Italy has well over 400 authorized grape varieties. The abundance of grapes contributes to a huge range of flavor and style options, but also to confusion on the international markets.

Wine is produced throughout Italy, but many of the finest, best quality, and most prestigious wines come from the northern half. *Piedmont* is in the northwest, *Tuscany* is in the north–central, and *Veneto, Trentino* and *Alto-Adige* are the three regions in the northeast part (called Tre Venezie) of Italy.

In Italy, the culture of food and wine are inseparable. The wine and food have evolved together over thousands of years. An important feature that stands out in Italian wine is the preservation of the grapes' high acidity, with no excessive overt fruit or oak, making them very compatible with food.

Useful Italian Wine Label Terms

- **Bianco** (bee-ahn-koh)—"White," as in white wine in Italian.
- **Classico** (KLAH-see-ko)—The designation on a wine label indicating that the grapes and wine come from the original classic growing area rather than the expanded zone. Example: Chianti Classico as opposed to Chianti Rufina.
- **Passito** (pah-SEE-toh)—A dry or sweet wine made from partially dried grapes.
- **Ripasso** (ree-PAH-so)—A winemaking technique that allows a wine to remain in contact with the lees from a previous passito wine through re-fermentation.
- **Riserva** (Rih-ZERVA)—The designation on a wine label indicating that the wine has additional barrel aging, but the duration of aging varies by region. Example: Three years for Chianti Riserva, but five years for Barolo or Brunello Riserva.
- **Rosso** (RAWH-soh)—"Red," as in red wine in Italian.
- **Superiore** (soo-payr-YOH-reh)—The designation on a label indicating that the wine has a slightly higher alcohol content.
- **Vendemmia** (vayn-DAYM-myah)—Vintage or grape harvest.
- **Vino** (VEE-noh)—"Wine," in Italian.

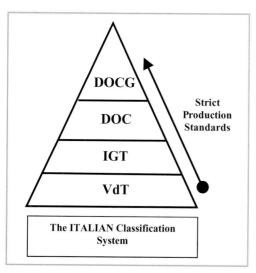

FIGURE 10–2 Italian wine classification

(John Laloganes)

Italian Classification System

Italy adopted a comprehensive, nationwide, regulatory quality-control system in 1963. The purpose of the Italian system is to regulate the production of wine, protect the defined wine zones, and guarantee the authenticity and consistency of style by defining boundaries, maximum yields, grape varieties, and production methods. Each wine-producing area is governed by the laws according to its quality level as granted by the Italian government.

The system was loosely modeled after the French AOC system; however, the Italian system has been highly criticized for its overgenerous awarding of high classification levels to wine areas that, arguably, are not necessarily deserving of it. Figure 10–2 illustrates the Italian wine classification system.

1. Denominazione d'Origine Controllata e Garantita (DOCG) (deh-NOH-mee-nah-SYAW-neh dee oh-REE-jee-neh con-traw-LAH-tah eh gah-rahn-TEE-tah)—Wines classified in this manner are produced according to the strictest standards of any of the other classification levels. Vineyard growing areas, yields, varietals, blends of varietals, and alcohol content are highly regulated.

The designation and regulations apply to all wines made from grapes grown in a designated region and must be approved by a government tasting panel. All wines at this category are given an identifiable paper strip just below the lip of each wine bottle.

There are approximately 32 DOCGs throughout Italy. On the left-hand side there is a list of the first wines granted the DOCG classification.

2. Denominazione d'Origine Controllata (DOC) (deh-NOH-mee-nah-TSYAW-neh dee oh-REE-jeh-neh con-traw-LAH-tah)—The second-highest classification level in the Italian system, this level requires that wines be produced with specific grape varietals in delimited geographical areas, by defined methods and quality standards in grape growing and wine production. There are approximately 350 DOCs throughout Italy.

3. Indicazione Geographica Tipica (IGT) (in-dee-kat-tsee-OH-nay jay-o-GRAF-ee-cah TEE-pee-cah)—This category was introduced in 1992 as a solution to the strict limited allowance for experimentation being required in the upper two levels of the Italian classification system. At this level, grape varietals can be identified on the label; however, specific places of origin are not allowed.

The regulations under this Italian quality level are often called the *Goria laws*, in reference to the Prime Minister Giovanni Goria. He designed this level to encourage Italian wine producers to still create wine within the existence of the Italian wine law system, yet have some flexibility to experiment. Some of Italy's most famous and prestigious wines are found at this level. *Sassicaia* (sahs-ih-KY-yah) and *Tignaello* (tig-ny-YEHL-low) are two examples.

4. Vino da Tavola (VdT) (VEE-no dah TAH-voh-lah)—The VdT designation is positioned at the lowest level, with the greatest amount of freedom. The producers are not allowed to label the grape varietal or specific location.

Major Wine-Producing Areas

Italy can be divided into four major wine areas, each containing several regions (communes), subregions (provinces), and appellations (zones) known for certain wines or features:

1. **Northwest Italy**—Sparkling wines and firmly structured red wines from indigenous grapes such as Barbera, Dolcetto, and Nebbiolo.

2. **Northeast Italy**—Mainly single-varietal white wines, often of French or German origin. However, there are some famous expressions of blended indigenous grape varietals and bold red wines from indigenous grape varietals (Corvina, Molinara, and Rondinella) made through the recioto process.
3. **Central Italy**—Premier red wines usually dominated by the Sangiovese grape varietal.
4. **Southern Italy and the Islands**—Rustic red wines made from a mix of different indigenous grape varietals, such as Aglianico, Primitivo, and others. In addition, the fortified wine Marsala is made in Southern Italy.

Northwest Italy

Northwest Italy encompasses the wine-producing areas of Piedmont, Lombardy, Liguria, and Emilia-Romagna.

Piedmont (PEED-mawnt)—Piedmont is located in Northwest Italy and remains one of the two greatest wine regions in the country. It has a high number of DOCGs, and while it is home to remarkable red wines, it also produces a range of wines (whites and sparklings) that are usually labelled with the varietal names and are frequently of great quality. The most important wine zones are centered near the towns of Asti and Alba.

Nebbiolo (neh-b'YOH-loh)   Barolo and Barbaresco are the two most famous and important appellations. The wines of the Nebbiolo grape ("nebbia" in Italian means "fog," and the grapes are so named because of the fog that rolls into the region) are intense, powerful, and, often, lightly colored wines. The common aromas and flavors include prune, tar, licorice, black cherry, and dried flowers. This grape is quite temperamental, low yielding, and late ripening. It also requires long aging to tame its fierce tannins. Even though Barolo and Barbaresco are made from the same grape, the grapes are grown in different microclimates and are processed differently. By law, Barolo must be aged a minimum of three years (at least two years spent in a barrel), and five years with a minimum increase in .5% of alcohol if labelled as a riserva. Barbaresco is aged two years (at least one year spent in a barrel), and four years with a minimum increase in .5% of alcohol if labelled as a riserva.

Other Good Nebbiolo-Based Wines—*Gattinara* (gah-tee-NAH-rah) and *Ghemme* (gehm-MEH) are both located in Northern Piedmont and offer reasonably priced alternatives to Barolo and Barbaresco. In Gattinara, the Nebbiolo grape is known locally as *Spanna* (spahn-NUH).

Other Wines Produced in Piedmont—Piedmont makes other very interesting red wines, and younger winemakers are experimenting with new oak barrels and other New World techniques.

Barbera (bar-BEHR-ah)   Along with Sangiovese, Barbera is the most widely planted grape in Italy. Barbera is significant in the towns of *Alba* (AHL-bah), *Asti* (AH-stee), and *Monferrato* (mohn-fayr-RAH-toh). The wines are labelled with the grape name first, followed by the growing area. For example, *Barbera d'Asti* is a wine produced from the Barbera grape derived from the town of Asti.

Dolcetto (dohl-CHET-toe)   This red wine grape varietal is significant in the town of Alba, where the wine is known as Dolcetto d'Alba. Similar to Barbera, the wine is labelled by grape name, followed by the growing area. For example, *Dolcetto d'Alba* is a wine produced from the Dolcetto grape that derived from the town of Alba.

Brachetto (brah-KAY-toh)   Brachetto is a red grape that makes either red table wine or the more common sparkling wine. It is most famous as a *frizzante* (lightly carbonated) red sparkling wine found as *Brachetto d'Acqui* (dah-KWEE) in the southeast portion of Piedmont.

White Wines Produced in Piedmont—The red wine in Piedmont seems to get all of the international attention; however, some appealing white and sparkling wines from local indigenous grapes can be found. The three most famous local white wine grapes are as follows:

Arneis (ahr-NAYZ), from the Roero area; *Cortese* (kohr-TAY-zee), from Gavi (also known as *Cortese di Gavi*; and *Moscato* (mo-SKAHT-oh), from Asti. Moscato (the local term for Muscat) is used to produce the very popular sparkling wines *Asti Spumante* (ahs-tee spoo-MAHN-tee) and *Moscato d'Asti* (moss-CAH-toe duh-AHS-tee). (The subject of the sparkling wines of Piedmont is expanded on in Chapter 11, "BUBBLES: Sparkling Wine.")

Lombardy (LOM-barh-dee)—Lombardy is located in Northern Italy near the Swiss border. This region contains two significant DOCG areas that it is most celebrated for: *Franciacorta* (frahn-chah-KOR-tah) and *Valtellina* (vahl-teh-LEE-nah). Franciacorta is noted for white wines from Pinot Bianco (the local term for Pinot Blanc) and spumante (the Italian term for "sparkling wine"). Valtellina is noted for its red wines, dominated by *Chiavennasca* (KEE-ah-VENN-eh-scah), the local term for the Nebbiolo grape.

Liguria (lee-GOOR-ee-ah)—The Liguria region stretches along the Mediterranean from the French border of Provence down toward Tuscany. Unofficially known as *the Italian Riviera*, Liguria is possibly more famous for its resort area than its wine.

Emilia-Romagna (eh-MEE-lyah raw-MAH-nyah)—Emilia-Romagna is located in North Central Italy just north of Tuscany. This region is home of the famous red frothy sparkling wine *Lambrusco* (lam-BROO-sko), also named after its grape. It has a red-cherrylike aroma and a flavor that is lightly sparkling and, usually, sweet; however, dry versions are made as well.

In Emilia-Romagna, the capital city is Bologna, the center of gastronomic activity, which is widely recognized for its foods such as Parmesan cheese and Parma hams.

Northeastern Italy

Northeastern Italy encompasses the wine-producing areas of Veneto, Friuli-Venezia Giulia, and Trentino Alto-Adige.

Veneto (VEH-neh-toh)   The Veneto is an extensive region of Northeastern Italy that borders Austria and Yugoslavia and includes the towns of Venice and Verona.

Soave (SWAH-vay)   This dry white wine, made from primarily the *Garganega* (gahr-gah-NEH-gah) varietal, is occasionally blended with a small amount of the Trebbiano grape. *Soave Classico* comes from the smaller, more defined, and original Soave-producing area.

Valpolicella (vahl-paw-lee-CHEHL-lah)   This wine is made from a blend of three indigenous grapes: *Corvina* (kor-VEEN-uh), *Rondinella* (rahn-dun-EHL-luh), and *Molinara* (mo-lin-ahr-uh). It is a fruity, medium- to full-bodied red wine with moderate tannins and aromas suggestive of cherries, chocolate, and a hint of almond.

Bardolino (bahr-doh-LEE-noh)   This wine is made with the same blend of grapes as Valpolicella, yet is a lighter-bodied version occasionally served chilled.

Recioto della Valpolicella (reh-CHAW-toh deh-lah vahl-paw-lee-CHEHL-lah) or **Recioto della Valpolicella Amarone** (am-ah-ROH-neh)   This wine is made from the same blend of grapes as in Valpolicella, but the grapes have been partially dried prior to fermentation. Drying the grapes prior to fermentation is known as the *passimento process* and is a technique that is used to increase the body and mouth feel of the wine.

As the wine goes through fermentation, if the yeast stops leaving residual sugar, the wine is a Recioto della Valpolicella, or simply, Recioto. If the yeast consumes all the grape sugar, yielding a bold, dry wine with relatively high alcohol of 15%–16%, the wine is referred to as Recioto della Valpolicella Amarone, or simply, Amarone.

Prosecco (praw-SEHK-koh)   Prosecco is produced in the northeastern part of Italy's Veneto region. It is a sparkling wine made from the grape of the same name. The charmant, or bulk, method is used to create the carbonation. The degree of effervescence is often indicated on the bottle, by either the term *spumante* (spoo-MAHN-tay), which indicates standard bubbles; *frizzante* (FRIZZ-zahn-tay), meaning light effervescence; or *frizzantino* (FRIZZ-zanh-tee-noh), signifying wine that is slightly sparkling.

Trentino-Alto-Adige (trehn-TEE-noh AHL-toh AH-dee-jay)—Trentino-Alto-Adige is Italy's northermost region and borders Germany, Austria, and Switzerland. Trentino-Alto-Adige is split into two provinces: (1) *Trentino*, around the city of Trento to the south and influenced by Italy, and (2) *Alto Adige*, around the city of Bolzano to the north (known as the South Tyrol), with a prominent German and Austrian influence.

The climate of Trentino-Alto-Adige is perfect for a variety of cool-weather white wine grapes, notably Chardonnay, Pinot Grigio, and Pinot Bianco, as well as sparkling wines. Farther south in the Trentino region, Cabernets and Merlots also do well.

The Alto-Adige, because of its history, is bilingual, and the German and Austrian influence is sometimes reflected on the selected grapes and the wine label. Many of the vineyards are located on steep hillsides, emphasizing quality. Approximately half of all wines produced in this area are given the DOC status (the highest number of DOCs of any Italian region).

Friulli-Venezia Giulia (free-OO-lee veh-NEHT-zee-ah JOO-lee-ah)—*Friulli*, as this wine region is called, is located in the northeast corner of Italy. It is known primarily for high-quality white wine varietals such as Pinot Grigio, Pinot Bianco, and also the red wine varietal Merlot. Wines usually are labelled according to their grape varietal.

Central Italy

This location encompasses the wine-producing areas of Tuscany, Marche, Umbria, Latium, and Abruzzi.

Tuscany (TUHS-kuh-nee)—The Tuscany region, located in Central Italy, is the home of the most famous of all Italian wine, *Chianti*. Most wines from Tuscany are red and based primarily on the Sangiovese grape, which is predominant throughout this region. Some of the most famous wines (named after their place), where Sangiovese is the principle varietal, are as follows: Chianti, Brunello (a clone of Sangiovese) di Montalcino, Vino Nobile di Montepulciano, and Carmignano. Also, Tuscany grows some Cabernet Sauvignon and Malvasia, which is the local white wine grape.

Chianti (kee-AHN-tee)   Chianti is a large wine zone located in Tuscany around the medieval cities of Florence and Sienna. The region of Chianti has been recognizable since the Middle Ages and is still currently the most famous.

Chianti is made primarily from the red sangiovese grape and historically has been made with smaller amounts of the white grape *Trebbiano* (treh-bee-AHN-oh) or *Malvasia*

(MAHL-vah-see-uh) varietals to lighten the wine. Most often, Chianti consists of between 75% and 100% Sangiovese and can be blended with up to 20% of Cabernet Sauvignon and/or Merlot.

Chianti is produced in one of the eight distinct, adjacent zones surrounded by the original core area *Chianti Classico* (KLAHS-see-koh). The zones are very similar to subdivisions within a neighborhood, with the most famous called *Chianti Classico* and *Chianti Rufina* (roo-FEEN-ah), which are commonly seen on labels and sold in restaurants and wine shops.

Chianti Classico is the most famous region in Tuscany because it is one of the first zones of Chianti, having been identified in 1716 and expanded in 1932. *Classicos* are made with good length, body, and complexity. If a bottle is labelled *Riserva*, it must have at least 12.5% alcohol and be aged for a minimum of three years and three months. Riservas are more full bodied than a typical Chianti Classico, often worthy of aging for years, and typically rank among the best red wines of Italy. A comparable (though slightly lighter) type of Chianti Classico is *Chianti Rufina* (key-ahn-tee roo-FEEN-ah).

Other Chianti districts include *Chianti Montalbano* (mahn-tehl-BAH-noh), *Chianti Colli Fiorentini* (KAWL-lee fee-or-ehn-TEE-nee), *Chianti Colli Senesi* (KAWL-lee sehn-AY-zee), *Chianti Colline Pisane* (KAWL-leen-ay pee-ZAH-nay), *Chianti Colli Aretini* (KAWL-lee Ahr-ehn-TEE-nee), and *Chianti Montespertoli* (mohnt-ehs-PEHR-tohl-ee). A wine produced from any of these subdistricts can be labelled by the specific name or can simply go by *Chianti*.

Super Tuscan Wine—One of the most revolutionary movements and defining moments in Italian wine history came from the rise of the *Super Tuscan Wines*, an unofficial name given to a certain category of wines. Officially, these wines fall under the Italian wine classification system at the IGT level. The wines were declassified from their DOCG status because they are made from non-traditional blends of the local Sangiovese grape, with varying amounts of international grapes such as Cabernet Sauvignon, Cabernet Franc, Syrah, or Merlot. The explosion of Super Tuscans was an obvious sign of innovation in Tuscany. The orginal and most notable wines are Sassicaia and Tignaello.

Sassicaia (sahs-see-KAH-yah)   A Cabernet-Sauvignon-based red wine with varying amounts of the local Sangiovese varietal. This wine has forever changed the landscape of Italian wines. Even though it originally was declassified (because the laws at the time did not permit the use of Cabernet Sauvignon) and given the lowest classification of VdT, it was one of the most expensive and critically acclaimed wines of Italy.

Tignanello (tee-nyah-NELL-oh)   Made in the Chianti region, Tignanello is named after the Tignanello vineyard operated by the well-known Antinori organization. Like Sassicaia, Tignanello had broken tradition and the legally allowable blending of grape varietals since its inception in 1971.

DOCG Chianti Alternatives—South of the Chianti zone is the town of Montalcino, which has become famous for its *Brunello di Montalcino* (broo-NELL-o dee mawn-tahl-CHEE-noh). The sloped vineyards are devoted entirely to the Sangiovese grape, known locally as *Brunello*. Brunellos produce rich and bold wines that have the ability to age for decades because of Montalcino's warm climate and quality-oriented growing and production methods. These wines are required to be aged for four years (with a minimum of two years in oak barrels), or five years for Riserva.

Rosso di Montalcino (RAWS-soh dee mawn-tahl-CHEE-noh)   A lighter version of Brunello di Montalcino, this wine is made from the same grapes from lesser vineyards and requires less aging, as it is intended to be consumed in its youth while waiting for the Brunello di Montalcino wines to evolve.

Vino Nobile di Montepulciano (VEE-noh NAW-bee-lay dee mawn-teh-pool-CHAH-noh)   This is an Italian red wine from the Tuscany region made from the *Prugnolo* (proo-NYO-loh) grape (the local term for Sangiovese). It is produceed in and around the town of Montepulciano.

Carmignano (car-mee-NYAH noh)   This is a small growing area just outside Florence. Its wine must be made from predominant Sangioves with between 10% and 20% of Cabernet Sauvignon and Cabernet Franc.

MARCHE (MAHR-kay)—Marche is an Italian wine region that is best known for its white wine produced from the *Verdicchio* (vehr-DEEK-kyoh) grape. It is a simple, dry white wine.

UMBRIA (OOM-bree-uh)—Located in Central Italy, Umbria is known for a mix of red and white wines primarily made from local grapes. The white wine *Orvieto* (ohr-vee-YAY-toh) is made primarily from Trebianno grapes, and the red wine *Sagrantino di Montefalco* is made from Sagrantino and Torgiano grapes.

LATIUM (LAH-tyum)—The Latium region is located on the western coast of Central Italy. It produces inexpensive, neutral white wine from the *Frascati* (frahs-KAHT-ee) area, made from the Trebbiano and Mavasia grapes.

ABRUZZI (ah-BROOD-dzee)—Abruzzi is located east of Rome on the coast of the Adriatic Sea. The main grape variety used for white wines is the Trebbiano (otherwise known as *Ugni Blanc* in France). Montepulciano is the main grape, followed by Sangiovese for red and rosé wines. *Montepulciano d'Abruzzo* (mawn-tay-pool-CHAH-noh dah-BROOD-dzoh) is made from the Montepulciano grape.

Southern Italy and the Islands

This region encompasses the wine-producing areas of Campania, Puglia, Basilicata, Sicily, and Sardinia.

Campania (kahm-PAH-nyah)—Campania is located near Naples along the eastern coast of Southern Italy. The most well known wine is from the area of *Taurasi* (tow-RAH-zee), produced with mostly the red wine grape *Aglianico* (ah-LYAH-nee-koh). This grape is sometimes called *Barolo of the South,* as it is known for its boldness, as is Barolo from the Piedmont region.

Basilicata (bah-zee-lee-KAH-tah)—Basilicata is located in Southern Italy. The notable wines are produced from the red wine grape Aglianico.

Puglia (POOL-yuh)—Puglia is located in the southeast section (the "heel") of Italy. The primary red grapes are Primitivo (the local name for the Zinfandel grape) and Negroamaro.

Sicily (SIHS-uh-lee)—Sicily is an island off the coast of Southern Italy and is one of the oldest most historic wine-producing regions in the world. Yet this region suffers in comparison with the wine quality of Northern Italy. Besides the region's economic disadvantages, the grape varietals are often obscure and the wines are not well publicized.

Nero d'Avola (neh-ROH dah-voe-lah), the most widely planted grape, historically has been used in blending, but is being featured more as a stand-alone varietal. More recently, this grape is being blended with the international varietals Merlot and Cabernet Sauvignon.

Sicily is historically known most for *Marsala* (mahr-SAH-lah), Italy's most famous fortified wine. Today, it is often relegated to the kitchen.

Sardinia (sahr-DIHN-ee-uh)—This island off the coast of Italy historically has been known for its Cannonau (cahn-AH-now) (otherwise known as Grenache in France and the U.S.) based red wines. Cannonau typically makes fleshy, heady, very fruity wines in their youth. They tend to age rapidly, showing tawny colors and being prone to oxidation or maderization after only a relatively short time in the bottle.

GERMAN WINE

FIGURE 10–3 Map of Germany

(Thomas Moore)

Germany is located in the heart of Europe and borders Denmark, Poland, the Czech Republic, Austria, Switzerland, France, Luxembourg, Belgium, and the Netherlands. It is one of the northernmost (and coolest) wine-producing countries in Europe. As a result, most of the 13 wine regions, or *Anbaugebiete* (AHN-bough-geh-BEET-eh), are concentrated in the southwestern part of Germany. Figure 10–3 is a map identifying the significant wine-growing regions of Germany.

Useful German Wine Label

Terms

- **Anbaugebiete** (AHN-bough-geh-BEET-eh)—Wine region
- **Einzellage** (INE-tsuh-lah-guh)—Vineyard
- **Halbtrocken** (HALP-trawk-en)—An off-dry wine that never contains more than 18 grams of residual sugar per liter
- **Rotwein** (RAWT-vine)—Red wine
- **Trocken** (TRAWK-en)—A dry wine without perceptible residual sweetness. The wine never contains more than 9 grams of residual sugar per liter.
- **Wein** (VINE)—Wine
- **Weinberg** (VINE-behrk)—Vineyard
- **Weingut** (VINE-goot)—Wine estate
- **Weiss** (VICE)—White
- **Weissherbst** (VICE-hehrbst)—Rosé wine

German Classification System

The wine laws of Germany establish four levels of classification for their wines, starting with the strictest level of standards first. Figure 10–4 illustrates the German wine classification system.

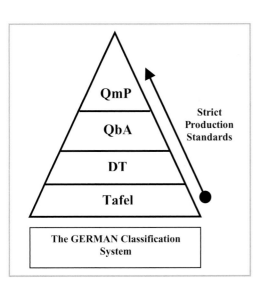

FIGURE 10–4 German wine classification

1. **Qualitätswein mit prädikat** (kvah-lee-TAYTS-vine meet PRAY-dee-kaht)—Often referred to as the *prädikat wines* or QmP for short, these wines make up the top level of German wine classification. The term "Qualitätswein mit prädikat" translates to "quality wine with special attributes." The growing of grapes and production of wine are held to a specific set of standards based upon the particular growing region. The wine must be made from its own natural grape sugar (with no chaptalization) or with the addition of the *süssreserve* (ZOOSS-ray-ZEHR-veh).

2. **Qualitätswein Bestimmter Anbaugebiete** (or QbA) (kvah-lee-TAYTS-vine buh-SHTIMM-ter AHN-bow-gah-BEET-eh)—This term translates to "quality wine." Wine that is classified into this category has come from one of the 13 approved wine regions and from approved grapes. The wine must have a minimum of 7.5% alcohol, and the winemakers are allowed to chaptalize their wines in order to increase sugar content.

3. **Deutscher Tafelwein** (DOY-cher TAH-fel-vine)—This wine is consumed mostly locally and is seldom exported. A wine labelled *Deutscher Tafelwein* (DTW) is a table wine of German origin.

4. Tafelwein (tah-fel-vine)—The lowest of the quality levels, with the least restrictions. If a wine is labelled simply as *tafelwein,* it may not be of German origin.

The Sussreserve

The way that the Germans devised to maintain some sweetness in their wine is known as the *süssreserve.* This method involves fermenting the wines fully dry, with low alcohol and high acid. Before fermentation, a small quantity of unfermented juice is held back. Later, this juice will be blended into the dry wine in order to adjust and balance the acid-to-sweetness ratio.

Label Indicators of Grape Ripeness

The grapes obtain greater ripeness by being harvested later (because they spend a longer time in the sun). These ripeness levels directly determine the natural sweetness of the grapes and the ultimate cost of the wine. At the prädikat quality level, all grapes must develop their own natural sugar content throughout the growing process, and no wine is allowed to be chaptalized, but the sussreserve is acceptable.

The sugar levels in the wine are ranked according to the *Oechsle* (UHX-leh) method at harvest. This method was devised by Christian Ferdinand Oechsle. The oechsle system maintains separate ripeness standards, depending on grape variety and region. The higher the ripeness of the grapes, the higher the wine will be categorized. The level will also translate to a wine that has a fuller body (from greater sugar) and higher concentration. The categories do not reflect whether the wine is sweet or dry; ultimately, the winemaker decides the style of the wine according to when fermentation is halted.

A wine eventually will be a sweeter style if the fermentation is interrupted before all sugar is converted into alcohol, therefore leaving residual sugar in the wine. If the fermentation continues until little or no sugar is left, the wine will be dry. Grapes for dessert wines (the Auslese level and above) have so much natural sugar that they often will not ferment completely (because most yeast strains die off at around 15% alcohol) and residual sugar (sweetness) will remain.

Generally speaking, the riper the grape or classification, the sweeter, more concentrated, and more expensive the wine will be. At the lower ripeness or sugar content level of the grapes, beginning at the Kabinett level, and as the grapes contain more sugar, they are placed in different categories, ascending toward the highest level of a TBA level. Figure 10–5 shows the graduating staircase of grape ripeness for the prädikat level of German wines.

Kabinett (kah-bih-NEHT)—Usually light (low alcohol that often hovers around 8.5% or 9%), these dry-to-sweet wines are made of grapes ripened at normal harvest. They usually have a delicate stucture and contain some minerality. Kabinetts often contain high malic acids, leaving an aroma and taste of tart green apples. They sometimes are spritzy with tiny bubbles from a touch of undissolved CO_2.

Spätlese (SHPAYT-lay-zuh)—These are *late harvest* wines made from very ripe grapes picked after the normal harvest. The later harvest lets the grapes dry and ripen on sunny autumn days, which increases the intensity of the fruit and the flavors. These wines are intense in flavor and concentration, which makes them compatible with richer food.

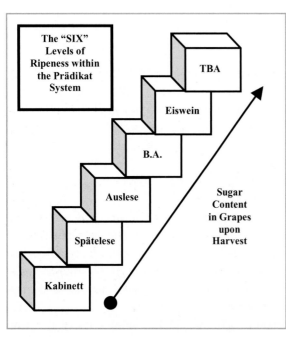

FIGURE 10–5 "Prädikat" Ripeness Scale

(John Laloganes)

Spätlese wines can range from dry to sweet. A good indication is the level of alcohol. If the alcohol is higher, the wine may be drier. If the alcohol is lower, there is a greater chance that the wine has considerable residual sugar.

Auslese (OWS-lay-zuh)—*Select picking* refers to selective hand harvesting of extremely ripe bunches of grapes, often with a touch of noble rot (called *Edelfaule* (ayduhl-FOY-luh) in German). These wines are intense in bouquet and taste and usually are sweet (although dry versions can also be found).

Beerenauslese (BA) (BEHR-ehn-OWS-lay-zuh)—BA is the German term for *select berries* that have been hand picked. BA is a rich, sweet dessert wine made of overripe, shriveled berries that are almost always affected by noble rot. The noble rot causes the water content in the grape to diminish and, therefore, all the flavors to be concentrated.

Eiswein (ICE-vine)—These wines are of at least BA sweetness intensity and have been made from grapes harvested and pressed while frozen. This is a unique wine with a highly concentrated aroma and intense fruit, acidity, and sweetness.

The production of Eiswein involves freezing the grapes on the vine at 32°F well into the winter time. During the process, the water inside the grapes freezes, but not the other components, of which sugar is the largest. When the grapes are crushed, the frozen water is not pressed out, but only the luscious, viscous, sugary nectar of the grape juice. Through this process, the water has been extracted from the juice, which doubles in sugar and acid and is highly concentrated in flavor.

Trockenbeerenauslese (TBA) (TRAWK-uhn-BEHR-en-OWS-lay-zuh)—TBA is the German term for *dry select berries* that are harvested individually. TBA berries have been affected with *Botrytis cinerea*, a fungus that causes them to dry up on the vine. These wines are rich, sweet, luscious, and honeylike in flavor and aroma.

The Varietals

Germany is located in the far northerly climate for grape growing. Because of the cool continental climate (except in small pockets), red wine grapes do not flourish to the degree that white wine grapes do. Therefore, the majority of wine produced derives from white wine varietals, predominately Riesling. Other white wine grapes include: *Müller-Thurgau* (MOO-lehr TOOR-gow), *Silvaner* (sihl-VAH-ner), Kerner, Gewürztraminer, *Grauburgunder* (GROUW-buhr-gunder) or Rulander (otherwise known as Pinot Gris), and *Weissburgunder* (VICE-buhr-goon-dair) (also known as Pinot Blanc) all prevalent grape varietals found throughout Germany.

A small fraction of red wine grapes are grown in Germany. The most notable is the up-and-coming *Spätburgunder* (SHPAYT-buhr-gunder) (also known as Pinot Noir), leading the way for red grapes.

Germany's marginal climate has led winemakers to cross-breed many grapes. Some reasons crosses are created is to allow the grapes to become late budding or early ripening, produce a higher yield, or of better disease resistance. Some popular German crosses and hybrids include Kerner, Muller-Thurgau, and many more white and red varietals.

Appellations

Many of the famous vineyards are established along the Mosel and Rhine Rivers and their tributaries. The tempering influence of the rivers allows high-quality wine grapes to grow this far north. Germany's unique microclimate creates a long growing season that allows the flavors within the grapes to mature slowly, the sugars to develop, and, yet, the acids to remain high. The harvest may take several weeks because the grapes rarely ripen in unison and therefore are harvested at different times.

FIGURE 10–6 Vineyards of the Mosel
(German Wine Institute)

Mosel-Saar-Ruwer (MOH-zel sahr ROO-vayr)—
The Mosel-Saar-Ruwer arguably is Germany's most famous wine-growing region. The Mosel River is the spine of the Mosel-Saar-Ruwer wine region, and the vineyards extend along the two small tributaries, the *Saar* and the *Ruwer*. The grapes are grown on steep hillsides (sometimes on 70-degree inclines) along the steep river banks. The Mosel region is widely known for its unique *slate* soil type that imparts a distinctive taste ranging from fruity to earthy, or *flinty*, sometimes with a hint of effervescence. Figure 10–6 shows the Mosel-Saar-Ruwer growing area.

The wines of the Mosel-Saar-Ruwer are nearly all from the Riesling grape, which makes a range of products, from light, richly fragrant wines to famous honeyed dessert wines. All of them are united by crisp acidity and generally low alcohol content. Other good wines are made from Gewürztraminer, Pinot Gris, Pinot Noir, Sylvaner, Müller-Thurgau, and several other grapes.

While some of the wines from the famous vineyards of the middle Mosel district can come with very high price tags, the best values often are from the upper and lower regions that lay claim to some excellent wines at fairly reasonable prices.

Rheingau (RINE-gauw)—Rheingau is arguably the second most famous wine-growing region in Germany and home to some of the world's oldest wine-growing families. According to the Wines of Germany trade group, of the small amount of vineyards that Rheingau maintains (7,500 acres), about 80% of it is ranked at the QmP level. This makes Rheingau more focused on overall quality than any other German wine region.

The region of Rheingau is one long hillside moving from east to west. The fairly flat, dimpled landscape evolves into progressively steep slopes bordered by the Taunus forest to the north and the Rhine river to the south. The southern-facing exposure, moisture from the river, the large amount of clay in the soil, and the Mediterranean-type climate combine to produce densely rich-flavored wines.

The popularity of this region's wines has driven prices upward; however, good values are still to be found if one seeks out the smaller producers. The main grapes are from the Riesling grape varietal, which yields elegant wines with a fruity aroma, pronounced acidity, and concentrated flavor. In addition to Riesling, a small amount of red wine is produced from the Spätburgunder varietal.

Vineyard Classification

Since 1994, the Rheingau was the first German region to have a semi-official vineyard classification, drawn up by the Charta (KART-ah) organization and the Verband Deutscher Pradikats (VdP Rheingau).

The best sites are allowed to carry the designation *Erstes Gewächs* (AYR-stess GUH-vehks), or first-growth vineyards. The use of this designation is optional, and the wine has to meet several criteria, such as the following: The wine must be made in dry style or at least in an Auslese, the grapes must be hand picked, and traditional techniques of winemaking must be used.

Rheinhessen (RINE-hehs-uhn)—Deep within a valley of gently rolling hills, bordered by the Nahe and Rhine Rivers, lies the region of Rheinhessen. This is the largest German wine-growing region, with over 63,000 acres of vines. In this land of varying climates and geography, many different types of grapes, both red and white varieties, are planted, producing wine that is delicately fragrant and fuller bodied than wine of the other regions, because Rheinhessen maintains a slightly warmer climate.

The rolling hills, varied soils, and favorable climate make it possible to grow many different grape varieties, both red and white. Silvaner is the predominant grape.

Rheinhessen is the birthplace of *Liebfraumilch* (LEEB-Frouw-MILCH), originally made from grapes grown in vineyards surrounding the Liebfrauenkirche. This wine is one of Germany's biggest exports to the United Kingdom and the United States. Liebfraumilch can originate from any of four wine regions: Nahe, Rheingau, Rheinhessen, or Faultz. The grape is dominately Muller Thurgau, and the wine is engineered to be sweet, with no true sense of place or personality.

Rheinhessen wines are often characterized as being soft, fragrant, medium-bodied, mild in acidity, and easy to drink.

Pfalz (FAHLTS) (Formerly known as Rheinpfalz)—Bordered by Rheinhessen on the north and France on the south and west, Pfalz is Germany's second-largest wine region in acreage, but often has the largest crop of all. Pfalz is second only to the Mosel in acreage planted with the Riesling grape. Here, it yields wines of substance and finesse, with a less sharp acidity than in Mosel.

The region boasts many small producers whose commitment to quality is beginning to renew the region's reputation for producing excellent wines. It has recently begun a trend back toward low-yielding high-quality vines.

Baden (BAH-den)—In this southernmost wine region of Germany, the famed *Black Forest* region of Baden is Germany's third-largest wine region, with over 65% of the wines ranked at the QmP level of quality. It is primarily a long, slim strip of vineyards nestled between the hills of the Black Forest and the Rhine River.

Baden's different soil types (gravel, limestone, and clay, to volcanic stone), combined with its warm climate, contribute to its multitude of different grape varieties. Nearly half of the vineyards are planted with Burgunder (Pinot) varieties:

Nahe (NAH-huh)—The Nahe River lends its name to one of Germany's dynamic wine regions. Bordered by Mosel to the west and Rheingau to the north, Nahe has diverse soils of slate, sandstone, clay, and loam. The region recently underwent a classification of its top vineyards. The designation given to the best sites is *Grosses Gewichs*, meaning "great growth." The wines given this designation must (1) come from the designated vineyard, (2) be of the Riesling grape varietal, (3) be made from grapes picked when the level of ripeness is high, and (4) be aged on the lees.

SPAIN

Spain has a long history of winemaking, possibly reaching as far back as 3,000 years. This country maintains more vineyards than any other country in the world, yet is only the third-largest wine producer (after Italy and France). This disparity exists because of the overall dry, warm air that reduces vineyard yields. Ever since the 1980s, Spain has been undergoing an economic revolution and has been in the process of rediscovering itself economically, culturally, and socially. Spain's renaissance has influenced technology in the vineyards, the winery, and the overall wine quality. New producers and labels are appearing annually, and great strides in quality and consistency are being made throughout the country. Figure 10–7 identifies Spain's significant winegrowing areas.

FIGURE 10–7 Map of Spain
(Thomas Moore)

Spain is located just south of the *Pyrenees* (pear-ah-nees) *Mountains* and contains two significant rivers, the Ebro and Duero, which maintain vineyards along their banks.

Traditionally, Spain has distinguished itself mostly for its red wines from *Rioja* (ree-OH-hah); fortified *sherry* wines from Andalusia (ahn-dah-loose-EE-yah); and *Cava* (CAH-vah), Spain's sparkling wine primarily from Penedes (pay-NAY-dayss) in the Catalonia/Barcelona area. More recently, the world is becoming aware of Spain's vast offering of every wine option imaginable due to its diverse climate and varying soil types. In addition to Spanish sparkling and fortified wine, Spain produces ranges of light crisp whites, to full-bodied whites and fruity rosés, to full-bodied red wines and more.

Local grape varietals such as Tempranillo and Garnacha (otherwise known as Grenache) are used predominantly for the red wines. Tempranillo is the most significant grape grown throughout Spain. It appears on many of the DO's/DOCa's by different names, showing many different expressions based on location.

The Spaniards classically have maintained a fondness for older, aged wines. Since the 1980s, groups of young, maverick winemakers have contributed an influx of new, more contemporary philosophies about, and techniques for, grape growing and winemaking. It appears that Spanish producers carry on two philosophies: The traditionalists practice longer oak barrel aging, where the emphasis is on oxidative qualities within the wine. The other perspective is one associated with the modernist style. This style emphasizes less aging and greater preservation of fruit.

Useful Spanish Wine Label

Term

- **Blanco** (BLAHNG-koh)—Refers to a white wine
- **Bodega** (boh-DAY-gah)—A generic term for a Spanish winery or wine cellar
- **Cosecha** (koh-say-chah)—Harvest or vintage
- **Doble Pasta** (DOH-blay PAHSS-tah)—A wine made with the addtion of grape skins to a fermenting wine. This technique adds heightened structure and body to a wine. Doble Pasta is similar to Italy's ripasso method.
- **Generoso** (heh-neh-ROH-soh)—A dry or sweet wine with high alcohol of 15% or more.
- **Pago** (PAH-go)—A classification created in 2003 to represent a single vineyard estate that performs all grape growing, winemaking, and bottling on the premises
- **Rancio** (RAHN-thyoh)—A fortified wine that has been deliberately oxidized or maderized
- **Rosado** (roe-SAH-do)—Refers to a rosé wine, made by allowing the juice to have only brief contact with the skin of the red wine grapes
- **Tinto** (TEEN-toe)—Referring to a red wine
- **Vendimia** (vayn-DEE-myah)—Vintage or grape harvest
- **Vino Joven** (VEE-no HOE-ven)—Young wine

Spanish Classification System

The Spanish government's Instituto Nacional de Denominaciones de Origen (INDO) (equivalent to France's INAO) guarantees the authenticity of its wine by designating each with a

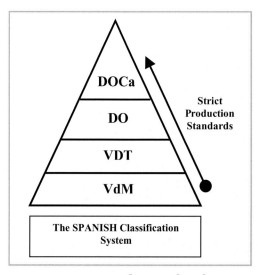

FIGURE 10–8 Spanish wine classification system

(John Laloganes)

region classification. The system is similar to those of France, Italy, and Germany, which divides the wine into two levels: quality wines and table wines.

The *quality wines* are required to maintain stricter standards and are equivalent to France's AOC and VDQS. The quality wines are classified according to a DO or a DOCa, in which each one is overseen by a *consejo regulador* (cohn-SAY-ho ray-goo-lah-DOOR), or administrative body. These agents ensure that each bodega acts in accordance with the individual DO quality requirements such as yield per hectare, aging requirements, and so on. Each individual consejo regulador within each DO/DOCa region issues *contraetiquetas* (con-trah-ett-ee-kAY-tahs), or back labels, as a stamp of approval.

At the *table wine* level, the standards are much looser and allow for more freedom with grape growing and winemaking. The table wine levels are comparible to France's Vin de Pays classification. Figure 10–8 illustrates the Spanish wine classification system.

Denominacion de Origen Calificada (DOCa) (deh-naw-mee-nah-THYON deh aw-REE-hen kah-lee-fee-KAH-dah)   This category is designed for winemakers that have a long, established track record of producing quality wines. Wines deserving this designation are produced in particular geographical areas by defined methods and quality standards in grape and wine production. As of 2008, there are 2 DOCas throughout Spain. The first DOCa was granted to the Rioja area in 1991 and Priorat in 2004.

Denominacion de Origen (DO) (deh-naw-mee-nah-THYON deh aw-REE-hen)   This category is the second level down from the DOCa. Wines are required to be produced in particular geographical areas according to defined methods and quality standards in grape and wine production. As of 2008, there are 65 DOs throughout Spain and constantly growing.

Vino de la Tierra (VdT) (VEE-noh day lah TYEHR-ah)   These are country wines with a hint of local origin. Their producers are allowed to use regional geographical names on the label.

Vino de Mesa (VdM) (VEE-noh day MAY-sah)   This is ordinary table wine made in bulk production from grapes that originate in a wide variety of regions. There is no designated vintage or location of origin identified on the label.

Major Wine-Producing Areas

As of 2008, there are 67 DOs and DOCas throughout Spain, and the number is constantly growing. Listed next are some significant DOs and DOCas that are becoming more available and popular in the marketplace.

Northwest Spain

Galicia (gah-LEE-thee-ah) and the Basque Country

Galicia is also known as *Green Spain*, which makes reference to its cool and misty climate with lush vegetation. Galicia's DOs include Rias Biaxes, Ribeiro, Ribeira Sacra, and Valdeorras, among others.

Most of Galicia's DOs rely heavily on indigenous white wine grapes, such as Albarino, Treixadura, Loureira, and Torrontes.

Rias Baixas (REE-ahs BY-shehs)—Rias Baixas is located in the northwest corner of Spain, just above Portugal. The cool, moist, maritime climate lends itself to aromatic white wine varieties. Eleven grape varietals are allowed in this DO, but about 90% of plantings are devoted to the Albariño (ahl-bah-REE-nyoh) grape varietals. This thick-skinned white wine grape is grown throughout Galicia and also is the dominant varietal in *Vinho Verde* wine, produced in neighboring Portugal.

Basque Country (Bask)—Basque Country is primarily known for producing a youthful, white, fresh wine known as Txakolina (Cha-co-LEE-nah). It is produced from an indigenous, aromatic, white wine varietal, Hondarribi Zuri (hahn-dur-ah-bee zoowr-ee), which comprises the majority of the plantings.

Northeast Spain

(The Mediterranean Coast)

Penedès (pay-nay-DESS)—This area is located in Catalonia, just south of Barcelona. Penedès produces both red and white wines, but is mainly known for being the region where *Cava* was first created.

Cava (meaning "underground cellar") is the term used to represent Spanish sparkling wine. Cava has been made on a large scale since 1872 and has since been required to be produced in the same way that classic sparkling Champagne is made. Cava wines can be made by several approved DOs throughout Spain, but Penedès remains at the forefront, contributing about 90% of cava production.

Most Cava is produced from the trilogy of indigenous grapes: *Macabeo* (mah-kah-BEH-oh), also known as Viura; *Xarel-lo* (sah-REHL-lyoh); and *Parellada* (par-eh-LYAH-duh). Chardonnay is also allowed to be blended in, but has been done so in small quantities. Outside of Catalonia, many Cavas use Macabeo as the dominant or even the sole grape in the wine. (Cava is discussed in greater detail in Chapter 11, "BUBBLES: Sparkling Wine.")

Costers Del Segre (koh-stehr del SEH-gray)—An increasingly wide range of wines is produced in this burgeoning DO. It showcases whites, rosés, and reds made from a mix of different grape varietals and sparkling wines made from Chardonnay.

Priorat (pree-oh-RAHT)—Priorat has a long history of winemaking, but has just begun to prosper, having gained DOCa status only in 2004. The area is of volcanic origin, which gives its *llicorella* (lyee-cor-EL-yah) soils unique features of reflecting and conserving the heat.

The influx of talented winemakers into Priorat brings a contemporary approach to wine production. The agable red wines often are dominated by Garnacha or blended with varying amounts of Carignan.

Jumilla (hoo-MEEL-lyah)—Monstrell (known as Mourvédre outside of Spain) is the dominant varietal, with over 85% of the plantings.

Duero River Valley

Castilla and León

Rueda (roo-AID-ah)—This area is home to Spanish white wines made primarily from *Verdejo* (vehr-DAY-ho), with smaller amounts of *Viura* (vee-YURE-ah), known as *Macabeo* in Catalonia and Sauvignon Blanc grape varietals. These wines often are made from single varietals, but are sometimes blended with each other.

Rueda also produces sparkling wine known as *Rueda Espumoso*, which must be made with varying percentages of the white grape varietal, Verdejo. Some traditional bodegas continue to produce oxidized Rancio and Generosos wines.

Cigales (see-GAHL-ess)—The Cigales DO produces many *rosado*, or rosé, wines from Tempranillo (known as Tinta del País) and Gamacha grapes. Some red wines are also produced by carbonic maceration. There are currently many experimental plantings occurring with several international varietals under vines such as Cabernet Sauvignon, Merlot, and Sauvignon Blanc.

Ribera del Duero (ree-BEHRR-ah del DWAY-rroh)—This DO is one of the most reputable wine regions of Spain, located north of Madrid and west of Rioja and situated along the Duero river. The region is best known for producing wines based on Tempranillo (also known as Tinta del País or Tinto Fino)—red wines that must contain a minimum of 75% of the varietal—with the liberal use of French oak.

The wines are fruity, with high preservation of acid, allowing for early consumption, but also are capable of aging into Gran Reservas. Permitted grapes include several international varietals such as Cabernet Sauvignon, Malbec, and Merlot.

Ribera del Duero is the home of some of Spain's most expensive and prestigious wines from the bodega *Vega Sicilia* (VAY-gah see-THEE-lyah). Created in 1864 from Bordeaux vines and French winemaking methods, this wine is unique and one of the most expensive wines produced in Spain, with a philosophy comparable to that of the Super Tuscans of Italy. This wine blends mostly the local Tempranillo grape with smaller amounts of the international Cabernet Sauvignon.

North Central Spain

(Ebro River Valley)

Rioja (ree-OH-hah)—This DOCa takes its name from the river *Rio Oja* and is located in north-central Spain between mountain ranges and along the path of the Ebro River. Rioja is one of the leading Spanish wine regions, most famous for its production of red wines. It remains the most recognizable of all Spanish wine-producing areas.

Rioja was the first Spanish wine region to receive the highest quality designation DOCa, in 1991, for consistent quality and authenticity of its wines.

A typical red Rioja is a blended wine made primarily from *Tempranillo*, with varying amounts of *Garnacha* and smaller amounts of *Graciano* (grah-thee-AH-no) and *Mazuelo* (mah-THWAY-low) (known as Carignan outside of Spain).

The Rioja wine region is divided into three distinct subregions: *Rioja Alta* (AHL-tah), *Rioja Alavesa* (ahl-lah-VACE-ah), and *Rioja Baja* (BAH-hah). These subregions are quite different in that they consist of varying levels of altitude, climate, and soil types.

- Rioja Alta is relatively dry, with high elevation. (*Alta* or *Alto* means "tall" in Spanish.)
- Rioja Alavesa has the highest elevation and is known for its chalky soil.
- Rioja Baja is the hottest and driest area of Rioja, with heavy stone soils. It is also the lowest in elevation; hence, it has the nickname *baja*, which means "low" in Spanish.

Classically, Rioja wines have been created from a blend of grapes from all three subregions, although single-vineyard wines have been gaining popularity as a way to illustrate their unique terroir differences. Figure 10-9 shows a bottle of Rioja.

Rioja also produces a lesser-known white wine that often consists predominately of Viura and, possibly, with varying amount of Malvasia and Garnacha Blanca. It is common to enhance the white Rioja with a touch of oak aging.

FIGURE 10-9 Marques de Caceres Rioja label

(© Dorling Kindersley)

Navarra (na-VAHR-rah)—This winemaking region, located in northern Spain, was once known only for its rosé wines. Increasingly, red wines of note have been coming out of this region.

Southern Spain

Andalucía—Jerez (heh-RAYTH)—Jerez is located in southeast Spain. The formal demarcated area was established in 1933 and was Spain's first Do. (Jerez is discussed in greater detail in Chapter 12, "BOLD: Fortified Wine.")

Aging Standards

Traditionally, the Spanish winemakers (more specifically, those in Rioja) have been loyal to the long aging periods required of their wines. They classically have not released wines until the wines were ready to drink. It was a way to differentiate themselves from Bordeaux, France, whose philosophy is to release wine early, which requires that the wine be cellared for an extended period before being consumed.

The Quality Wines are given aging categories that describe the durations of their aging period, as established by each DO and DOCa.

The styles range from youthful Joven, which have no aging requirements, to Crianza, Reserva, and Gran Reserva. Many of the old-school winemakers are obsessed with aging their wine. The labelling of age is purely voluntary, but also very traditional.

Vino Joven (Ho-vehn)   Vino Joven wines, translated as "young wines," are intended for early consumption and have no—or, at most, minimal—wood aging requirements. The period of aging is always shorter than that legally established for Crianza wines.

Vino de Crianza (Kree-AHN-thah)   Vino de Crianza wines are any DOCa or DO red wines that have been aged a minimum of 24 months, at least 6 months of which were in a barrel. The appellation areas of Rioja, Navarra, and Ribera Del Duero require 12 months in wood. White and rosé wines labelled as a Crianza must be aged for one year, at least six months of which are in wood.

Vino de Reserva (ree-SEHR-vah)   Vino de Reserva wines are any DO or DOCa red wines that have been aged a minimum of three years, one year of which was in wood. White and rosé wines labelled as Reserva must be aged two years, six months of which are in wood.

Vino Gran Reserva (GRAHN ree-SEHR-vah)   Vino Gran Reserva wines are any DO or DOCa red wines that have been aged a minimum of five years, of which at least one-and-a-half years were in barrels. The appellation areas of Rioja, Navarra, and Ribera Del Duero require a minimum of two years in wood. White and rosé wines labelled as Gran Reserva must be aged four years, at least six months of which were in wood.

The following chart identifies and summarizes each category's aging requirements:

SPAIN'S AGING REQUIREMENTS		
AGING CATEGORIES	**WHITE / ROSÉ WINE**	**RED WINE**
Crianza	At least 6 months in oak with a total aging of 1 year	At least 6 months (1 year for selected areas) in oak with a total aging of at least 2 years
Reserva	At least 6 months in oak with a total aging of at least 2 years	At least 1 year in oak with a total aging of at least 3 years
Gran Reserva	At least 6 months in oak with a total aging of at least 4 years	At least 1½ years (2 years for selected areas) in oak with a total aging of at least 5 years

OTHER OLD WORLD WINE COUNTRIES

NAME: _____ Score out of 30 points_____.

Use these questions to test your knowledge and understanding of the concepts presented in the chapter.

I. MULTIPLE CHOICE: Select the best possible answer from the options available.

1. The term *classico* refers to wine

    a. made in an old-fashioned style.

    b. made in the original production area.

    c. made to taste like an old vintage.

    d. made at least 10 years before released.

2. In Italy, the term *riserva* means

    a. the same period of aging for all wine.

    b. no legal requirement.

    c. that the wine has been aged with no restrictions.

    d. different things, depending on the appellation.

3. Barbaresco and Barolo are made from which grape?

    a. Dolcetto

    b. Sangiovese

    c. Pinot Grigio

    d. Nebbiolo

4. Barolo is considered

    a. medium-bodied and sweet.

    b. full-bodied, tannic, and robust.

    c. light- to medium-bodied.

    d. poor quality.

5. The most significant red wine grape found in Tuscany is

    a. Sangiovese.

    b. Nebbiolo.

    c. Barbera.

    d. Cabernet Sauvignon.

6. Super Tuscans often are created from a combination of the local Sangiovese and

    a. Riesling.

    b. Cabernet Sauvignon.

    c. Pinot Noir.

    d. Shiraz.

7. In German, *trocken* means

    a. ripe.

    b. acidity.

    c. dry.

    d. sweet.

8. The unique soil of the Mosel is

    a. chalk.

    b. slate.

    c. granite.

    d. clay.

9. The most significant grape varietal in Rioja, Spain, is

    a. Sangiovese.

    b. Riesling.

    c. Tempranillo.

    d. Garnacha.

II. TRUE / FALSE: Circle the best possible answer.

10. Chianti Rufina is generally better than Chianti Classico. **True / False**

11. The Trentino-Alto-Adige region in Italy is known for its Pinot Grigio. **True / False**

12. The Spanish historically have been in love with aging their wines for extended periods. **True / False**

III. MATCHING: Match the Old World country on the right with the wine region on the left.

13. _____ Priorat

14. _____ Piedmont

15. _____ Rheingau   A. Germany

16. _____ Mosel   B. Italy

17. _____ Rioja   C. Spain

18. _____ Veneto

19. _____ Chianti

20. _____ Trentino-Alto-Adige

21. _____ Tuscany

IV. MATCHING: Using the number 1 (lowest) through 6 (highest), place the German ripeness categories in order of lowest to highest sugar content upon harvest.

22. ____ Trockenbeerenauslese (TBA)   25. ____ Auslese

23. ____ Kabinett   26. ____ Spätlese

24. ____ Eiswein   27. ____ Beerenauslese (BA)

V. MATCHING: Connect each wine with its primary grape varietal.

28. ____ Chianti   A. Sangiovese

29. ____ Rioja   B. Tempranillo

30. ____ Barolo   C. Nebbiolo

Unit 5
OTHER TYPES OF WINE

"We do not grow absolutely, chronologically. We grow sometimes in one dimension, and not in another; unevenly. We grow partially. We are relative. We are mature in one realm, childish in another. The past, present, and future mingle and pull us backward, forward, or fix us in the present. We are made up of layers, cells, constellations."

—*Anais Nin*

11

BUBBLES:
Sparkling Wine

Sparkling wines are created in nearly every major wine-producing country. They can be found in a wide range of styles (from delicate to powerful, simple to complex, and dry to sweet), quality levels, and price points; but the most historic, prestigious, and reputable type of sparkling wine is Champagne.

LEARNING OBJECTIVES

Upon completion of this chapter, the learner will be able to:

- Explain the process of sparkling-wine production.
- Distinguish between bottle fermentation, transfer method, tank method, and méthode rural.
- Identify the two major styles of sparkling wine and potential food matches for each.
- Provide several strategies for pairing sparkling wine with food types.
- Identify several significant sparkling-wine-producing countries and other regions around the world.

BUBBLES: SPARKLING WINE

Sparkling wine is a generic term used to identify any table wine with the addition of its distinguishable effervescence, or CO_2. Along with climate and type of grapes, the method of incorporating the bubbles is one of the most important defining quality factors in what separates a poor-to-average-quality sparkling wine from an excellent one.

Sparkling wines are created in nearly every major wine-producing country. They can be found in a wide range of styles (from delicate to powerful, simple to complex, and dry to sweet), quality levels, and price points; but the most historic, prestigious, and reputable type of sparkling wine is Champagne. The terms *sparkling wine* and *Champagne* are often used interchangeably; however, although they can be similar, they actually are quite different. All Champagne is sparkling wine, though not all sparkling wine is Champagne. By understanding Champagne and how it is produced, we can understand almost all other sparkling wine in the world.

Champagne

Champagne is both a region and a type of wine. To be specific, Champagne is a sparkling wine that derives from the Champagne region of France and is made according to stringent AOC laws. Champagne in some form (not how we know the sparkling wine to be today), has been made for over 300 years.

The Location

The wines come from the northernmost vineyards in France, about 90 miles northeast of Paris. The most prestigious Champagne houses and vineyards are located near and/or within the city of *Rheims* (REEMZ) and the town of *Epernay* (ey-perh-NEH). Figure 11–1 identifies the Champagne region of France.

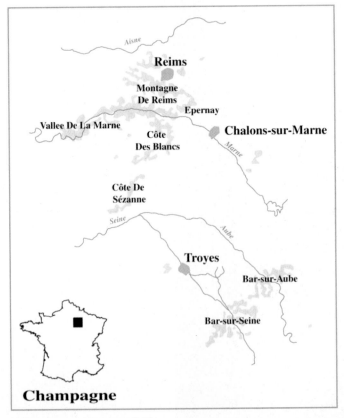

FIGURE 11–1 Map of Champagne

(Hoke Harden, CSW, CSS, Brown-Forman Corporation)

FIGURE 11–2 Chalk subsoil and roots of the vine

(Collection CIVC. Photographer: FION Alain)

The cold northerly climate and chalky soil (supposedly 60 feet deep in some areas) contribute to making the distinctive, crisp, and minerally taste of Champagne. The climate is so inconsistent that most Champagne (the wine, approximately 75%) is *nonvintage,* meaning that it is blended from multiple years in order to balance out quality variations to achieve a certain *house style* that is duplicated with every bottle. Figure 11–2 depicts Champagne's chalky soils.

Grape Varietals

Several different grapes can be used to produce a sparkling wine, but they often share a characteristic in common: substantial acidity. In Champagne, only three grape varieties are permitted for use in the Champagne blend:

1. **Chardonnay** is derived primarily from the areas of *Côte Des Blancs* (coat day BLANHG) and *Côte De Sézanne* (coat du say-ZAHN). This grape lends considerable acidity to the wine. When blended in higher amounts or as a solo varietal in the sparkling wine *Blanc de Blanc*, it produces a lean and crisp light-bodied wine. Figure 11–3 shows a cluster of the Chardonnay grapes.

2. **Pinot Noir** is found in the *Montagne de Reims* (mawn-TAH-nyuh) growing area. This grape provides considerable body and some fruit qualities to the wine. When blended in higher amounts or as a solo varietal (often with Pinot Meunier) in the sparkling wine *Blanc de Noir,* it produces a fuller-bodied, fruitier wine with some noticeable tannin. Figure 11–4 shows a cluster of the Pinot Noir grapes.

3. **Pinot Meunier** (muh-NYAY) is primarily from the *Vallee De La Marne* (vah-LAY duh lah MARN) area. This grape provides considerable fruitiness and some structure of tannin to the wine. Figure 11–5 shows a cluster of the Pinot Meunier grapes.

FIGURE 11–3 Close-up of a cluster of Chardonnay grapes

(Collection CIVC. Photographer: CORNU Alain)

FIGURE 11–4 Close-up of a cluster of Pinot Noir grapes

(Collection CIVC. Photographer: CORNU Alain)

FIGURE 11–5 Close-up of a cluster of Pinot Meunier grapes

(Collection CIVC. Photographer: CORNU Alain)

Production of Champagne or Other High-Quality Sparkling Wine

Winemakers can produce sparkling wine of excellent quality largely by using the classic *Champagne method* of production, known as *méthode champenoise* (may-TOAD

FIGURE 11–6 Harvest time in Champagne: porter of small picking baskets (full of Chardonnay clusters)

(Collection CIVC. Photographer: HADENGUE FREDERIC)

FIGURE 11–7 Harvest time in Champagne: basket full of Chardonnay clusters

(Collection CIVC. Photographer: HADENGUE FREDERIC)

cham-pen-WAHZ), or *MC method*. This production method creates a secondary fermentation within the bottle to create the carbon dioxide (CO_2).

Any producer of sparkling wine around the world may choose to use the classic Champagne method, but Champagne is one of the few sparkling wines that *must* use this technique. The steps outlined next are required in order to produce all Champagne. Producers around the world who choose to create high-quality sparkling wines in the style of Champagne generally will mimic these steps.

1. Harvest—The grapes are harvested early (typically in late September), to maintain their high, crisp, acid levels and low sugar content. Since Champagne undergoes two separate fermentations, grapes are harvested with low sugar levels in order to achieve lower amounts of initial alcohol. The first fermentation creates the initial base wine (basically, a table wine at this point), and the second fermentation produces and traps the carbon dioxide. Figure 11–6 shows a harvest taking place in Champagne. Figure 11–7 depicts a basket of Chardonnay grapes after being picked from the vine.

2. Pressing—Grapes are pressed gently with a wide device to prevent excess time traveling through skins, in order to limit juice and skin contact. The juice is then placed into stainless steel tanks where the first fermentation takes place in order to create the base wine.

The first pressing of juice, or *free run*, goes into the highest-quality sparkling wine; it is the only juice allowed in vintage Champagne. The second pressing, or *taille* (tail), goes into reserve for nonvintage Champagne.

3. First Fermentation—The first fermentation creates a *base wine* (known as vin clair) that is characteristically dry and acidic and near 10%–11% alcohol content. All Champagne and high-quality sparkling wine producers reserve some of this base wine for future vintages of their *house style* in the nonvintage wine they reproduce year after year. Figure 11–8 shows some stainless steel vats used for the first fermentation.

4. Blending—The *Cuvée Assemblage* (coo-VAY ah-sahm-BLAHZH) is a blending of multiple base wines from various years (often, dozens of different wines) to create a desired, consistent, house style. In a vintage year, a smaller percentage of reserve base wines can be blended. These wines may be aged in stainless steel tanks, wood barrels, or

FIGURE 11–8 Stainless steel vats for first fermentation
(Collection CIVC. Photographer: CORNU Alain)

FIGURE 11–9 Assembling
(Collection CIVC. Photographer: VISUEL IMPACT)

a combination of the two. Figure 11–9 shows several separate vin clairs being prepared for taste testing.

5. Second Fermentation (Incorporating the Carbonation)—This is a strictly controlled process called *Méthode Champenoise* that *must* be used to make all Champagne. It also may be used to make all other high-quality sparkling wines throughout the world.

The blended base wine is now bottled and combined with a dose of sugar and yeast, *Liqueur de Tirage* (lick-KYOOR duh tee-RAHZH), in order to induce a secondary fermentation. Through the secondary fermentation, a greater degree of alcohol (totaling around 12%) will be produced, along with carbon dioxide. The carbon dioxide will be trapped and create the characteristic bubble formation associated with sparkling wine. With the MC method, the sediment or dead yeast cells eventually will be removed, without the wine ever leaving its original bottle.

Champagne uses the labelling terminology, Méthode Champenoise to indicate the high quality production method. Other high-quality sparkling wine producers may use the identical production method, but may use alternative terminology. If the bottle lists *Traditional Method, Classic Method, Fermented in this Bottle,* or *Methodo Classico,* it is made by the Champagne method.

Alternative Methods of Incorporating Carbonation

There are other methods of incorporating carbonation into a sparkling wine, though Champagne is not allowed to use any of them. These alternative methods will dramatically influence the cost, labor, and style of a sparkling wine.

Transfer Method—This technique starts out as the traditional method of obtaining the complex aromas and flavors associated with Champagne. However, the entire contents of the bottle are emptied into a large pressurized tank for bulk clarification and transferred back into a bottle. This method increases efficiency and reduces production costs.

The transfer method is a great alternative to the Méthode Champenoise process because it has an advantage of producing a secondary fermentation within the bottle, which contributes some of the same complex flavors. But its disadvantage is that the resulting wine is slightly less intense, with shorter-lived bubbles.

If a sparkling wine is created in this manner, the label will state, *Bottle Fermented* or *Fermented in Bottle*. Note the distinction between the Champenoise method term "Fermented in *this* bottle" versus the transfer method's phrase "Fermented in *the* bottle." This latter terminology indicates that the wine has left its original bottle to be clarified of its sediment.

Charmat* or *Tank Method—The Charmat or Tank Method is a mass-producing technique in which the base wine undergoes secondary fermentation in a pressurized tank, or *autoclave* (AW-toh-klayv). After fermentation, the wine is filtered, sweetened, and bottled, all under pressure.

This method is inexpensive and is intended for wines that are not meant for long aging; therefore, it creates a light, easy-to-drink fruit-forward style of wine. Some of these types of wine may have varying amounts of residual sugar yielding a sweeter wine. Many sparkling wines are produced in this manner, including Sekt (Germany) and Asti, Moscato d'Ast, Prosecco, and Brachetto (Italy), as well as inexpensive sparkling wines around the world.

Pump Method—The pump method incorporates carbon dioxide (CO_2) into the base wine as it is being bottled. This method is similar to the creation of soda pop and is an inexpensive method often associated with producing a low-quality fruit-style sparkling wine.

Méthode Rural—By the *méthode rural*, the wine is bottled prior to completion of the first fermentation. The result is lighter, softer sparkle remaining in the wine, with a slight residual sugar. Asti, Moscato, and Prosecco may be made in this manner.

6. Aging—At this stage, the bottles are cellared and inverted into racks (called *pupîtres*) (pew-PEE-truhs) at a 45° angle in order to encourage the yeast to travel toward the neck of the bottle for eventual removal. The wine is stored a minimum of 15 months for nonvintage, and at least 3 years for vintage Champagne. Figure 11–10 identifies Champagne being cellared.

During this period of aging, yeast cells break down into what are known as *lees* and undergo the process of *autolysis* (aw-TAHL-uh-sihss). This decomposition of yeast cells

FIGURE 11–10 Champagne cellar with wooden racks called "pupîtres"
(Collection CIVC. Photographer: CORNU Alain)

FIGURE 11–11 Remuage Pupîtres
(Collection CIVC. Photographer: PIPER HEIDSIECK)

FIGURE 11–12 The sediment in the bottle neck (dégorgement)
(Collection CIVC. Photographer: JONKER JAN)

LEVELS OF DOSAGE

Extra Brut	→	Very dry (0%–.05% sugar)
Brut*	→	Dry (.05%–.5% sugar)
Extra Dry	→	Semi-dry (1.5%–2% sugar)
Sec	→	Slightly sweet (2%–4% sugar)
Demi-Sec	→	Sweet (4%–6% sugar)
Doux	→	Very sweet (6%–10% sugar)

* Indicates a very popular style of dosage

causes chemical changes that contribute a creamy texture and a toasty, complex aroma and taste. Autolysis contributes significantly to the character of a longer-aged sparkling wine, compared with a shorter-aged or non-aged sparkling wine.

7. Remuage (Reh-moo-ajh)—Remuage is a long, tedious hand-crafting process that takes place during aging. Over a period of six to eight weeks, each day the bottles are given a gentle shake, or *riddled,* a quarter turn in order to allow gravity to pull the lees toward the neck of the bottle. This step allows for the eventual removal of sediment without the wine being emptied from its bottle. Traditionally, the remuage was done by hand, but increasingly it is now being carried out in large, mechanized racks (known as gyro-palettes) in order to increase efficiency and decrease the labor expense. Figure 11–11 shows this more modern gyro-palette version of remuage.

8. Dégorgement (day-gorge-MAWN)—This is the process of removing the sediment (or lees) from the neck of the bottle. The neck of the bottle is dipped into an icy brine or glycol solution, which creates a small, frozen ice plug that contains the sediment. The bottle is placed upright, and the cap (or temporary cork) is taken off. Due to the internal pressure of the wine, the ice plug with the sediment shoots out of the bottle. At this point, the wine is completely dry, with no sugar remaining. Figure 11–12 shows the yeast sediment in the neck of the bottle.

9. Dosage (doh-ZAHJ)—Dosage is the sweetening syrup, or the *dosage d'expédition* (a mixture of sugar and wine), added to the wine to adjust the desired degree of sweetness and replenish the small amount of wine lost during dégorgement.

10. Bottling/Corking—Sparkling wines are distinguishing by their effervescence, or CO_2, which creates pressure within the bottle. This pressure is equivalent to 5–6 atmospheres or

FIGURE 11–13 Aging after disgorgement
(Collection CIVC. Photographer: CORNU Alain)

80–120 lbs per square inch (psi), approximately two to three times the pressure of a car tire. The carbonation is more stable at cold temperatures and unstable at room temperature. Due to the level of pressure, the sparkling wine bottle is made with thicker glass than that of other wine bottles. Each bottle also contains a *punt end*, or indentation, in the bottom of the bottle to help stabilize and secure the bottle. Figure 11–13 shows bottles being aged after disgorgement.

The bottle is sealed with a cork secured with a wire muzzle. Then the bottle is returned to the cellars for several months before being labelled for shipping.

Other Sparkling Wines

Champagne is made from a blend or, *cuvée,* of three grape varietals: Pinot Noir, Pinot Meunier, and Chardonnay. Most sparkling-wine-producing areas have the freedom to incorporate varietals that are appropriate (or indigenous) to their place of origin and to the desired style of the finished product. However, many high-quality California producers will duplicate (in a respectful way) the style of Champagne and incorporate the same or similar varietals.

France—Sparkling wine made outside the Champagne region is referred to as *Crémant* (kray-MAHN), such as *Crémant d'Alsace,* meaning a sparkling wine from the Alsace region of France. Many of the French (non Champagne) sparkling wines utilize local grapes associated with that region.

Spain—Spain is the largest producer of sparkling wine in the world. The Spanish sparkling wine *Cava* can be made in several authorized locations throughout Spain, but the vast majority (about 95%) is made in Catalonia. Cava typically uses three local grapes (completely different from those which Champagne uses) indigenous to Spain called *Macabeo* (mah-kah-BEH-oh), *Xarel-lo* (sah-REHL-yoh), and *Parellada* (par-eh-LYAH-duh). These grapes tend to be preferred by most producers, but currently there is experimentation with the addition of some classic Champagne-type grapes in the blend. Cava offers a good transition from Champagne to American sparkling, with reasonably priced wines and high minerality.

Italy—Mostly indigenous grapes are used to produce Italy's sparkling wines. *Asti* and *Moscato d'Asti* are produced from the Muscat grape, *Brachetto d'Aqui* (brah-KET-toe) is made from the *Brachetto* grape, and *Prosecco* (praw-ZEHK-koh) is produced in the Veneto from the *Prosecco* grape.

The generic term for sparkling wine in Italy is *spumante*, but the term has a dual meaning because it also can refer to a sparkling wine with a normal level of carbonation. The term *frizzante* (free-DZAHN-tay) is used to distinguish a sparkling wine with a less pronounced, softer sparkle and *frizzantino,* (free-DZAHN-tee-noe) indicate slight sparkling.

FIGURE 11–14 Champagne cellar

(Collection CIVC. Photographer: HADENGUE FREDERIC)

Nonvintages (NV or Multivintage)—A nonvintage is produced by most Champagne houses and all sparkling wine producers around the world. Nonvintage sparkling wine will not indicate a year on the label, because it is made from a blend of several cuvees from different years. These wines are made to achieve a *house style* that remains consistent in quality and taste from year to year. Nonvintage Champagne is released at least 15 months after harvest and often consumed within 5 years from harvest.

Vintage Champagne—Vintage Champagne indicates that a minimum of 95% of the grapes from the current year's harvest are within the bottle, though not every year is declared a *vintage*. The wine is released at least three years after harvest, after it has gained depth and complexity through the aging process. Vintage Champagne has the ability to be cellared for several years after purchasing, and even up to a decade before consumption. Vintage Champagne is expensive and considered to be prestigious. It is priced almost three times (and often even higher) more than nonvintage. Figure 11–14 shows a Champagne cellar, where the bottles rest until being released.

Blanc de Blanc—Blanc de Blanc roughly translates to "white from white." It is made from 100% Chardonnay (or other white wine grapes outside Champagne). The color is pale and light, and the wine has a certain delicate, lean, yet crisp style.

Blanc de Noir—Blanc de Noir roughly translates to "white from black." It is made from 100% Pinot Noir and/or Pinot Meunier grapes. The blend de Noir style is full bodied compared with Blanc de Blanc and traditional Champagne blend. The wine is likely to contain some perceptible levels of tannin and possibly a tinge of pink color because of the juice contact with black skins.

Pétillant (pay-tee-YAWN)—This sparkling wine contains less carbonation (around 3.6 atmospheres) than normal sparkling wines. Pétillant wines have less sugar added for the secondary fermentation, producing less gas pressure in the finished wine. This process can be comparable to the Italian *frizzante*.

Tête de Cuvée (tet duh koo-VAY)—An unofficial term, this often refers to a superior quality selection to identify a producer's best or most prestigious wine.

Dom Pérignon

Dom Pérignon (dohng pay-ree-NYOHNG), one of the most famous brands of Champagne, is named after an eighteenth century Benedictine monk. The monk is known to have perfected the blending of different grapes and created a durable bottle to withstand the carbonation present in sparkling wine. To the dismay of many, Dom Perignon is not responsible for creating Champagne (it happened quite by accident), but certainly, his contributions are numerous.

Dom Pérignon as a brand was launched in 1921 by *Moët et Chandon* (moh-eht ay shahng-DAWNG) as their premium level. It is similar to *Laurent-Perrier's* (loh-RAHNG peh-ree-ay) *Grand Siècle, Roederer's* (ROH-duh-rer) *Cristal,* and *Taittinger's* (tate-teen-ZHEHR) *Comtes de Champagne.*

Dom Pérignon is a *single-vineyard* wine made only from grapes in a single, exceptional year.

"Champagne" Used in Other Ways

In the past, the term *Champagne* in the United States has been used as a generic term to capitalize on the fame of the official and authentic Champagne. When the term is used in America or anywhere else that is not Champagne, it does not relate to place of origin, as it does in France. In 1927, representatives from Champagne asked countries to sign a treaty not to call sparkling wine *Champagne.* Most countries eventually agreed, except for the United States. The term *Champagne* is sometimes still used, and labels may read, "California Champagne" or "champagne" (with a small "c," which indicates that the wine does not originate from the authentic place). Beware of producers using this terminology; the products often are low-quality versions that resemble the Champagne style very little.

STYLES OF SPARKLING WINE

For simplicity, the vast world of sparkling wines can be understood better when the wines are categorized according to style. Two broad styles of sparkling wine are (1) complex and (2) fruit. Not every sparkling wine fits neatly into one of these categories, but some wines have more characteristics in common with one grouping than with the other.

Body of Sparkling Wine

Either style of sparkling wine can allow for various kinds of body. These styles can describe wines that range from delicate and light bodied (Blanc de Blanc) to bold and full bodied (Blanc de Noir) and from dry to sweet. The grapes and proportion of grape varietals, climate the grapes grew in, and winemaking techniques will largely affect the body.

STYLE #1 – Complex Style Sparkling Wine

A complex style sparkling wine is a sparkling wine that expresses the primary character of the grapes, but, more importantly, the complexity of the secondary winemaking techniques associated with bottle fermentation, oak aging, malo-lactic fermentation, and aging on the lees.

Aromas/Flavors—These include yeasty (brioche, biscuit), citrus fruit (lemon), tree (apple), bakeshop sauces (honey, vanilla, butterscotch, cream, butter), bakeshop nuts (toast, hazelnut, almond, popcorn).

Location—Some of the best and most noted places include France (Champagne, Loire), Spain (Penedes, Catalonia), and California (Carneros, Napa, Sonoma).

Types—Complex style sparkling wines include Blanc de Blanc, Nonvintage and Vintage Champagne, Cava from Spain, and high-quality sparkling wine from the United States.

STYLE #2 – Fruit Style Sparkling Wine

This style of sparkling wine expresses the primary character of the grapes. It characterizes a fairly straightforward, simple type of wine that preserves primary fruit qualities. Some of these types of wine have varying levels of residual sugar that results in a sweet wine.

Aromas/Flavors—These include fruit tree and candied (white peach, pear, apricot, watermelon, green apple, strawberry, Jolly Rancher), nuts, taffy, bubble gum, cream soda, cotton candy, and gummy bears.

Location—Some of the best and most noted places include Germany, Italy (Piedmont, Veneto), California (Napa and Sonoma), and Australia.

Types—Fruit sparklings include Asti and *Moscato di Asti* (from the Muscat grape), *Brachetto* from Italy's Piedmont region, *Prosecco* from Italy's Veneto region, *rosé* sparkling, *Sparkling Shiraz*, *Blanc de Noir*, and some inexpensive sparkling wines found throughout the world.

Pairing Strategies for Sparkling Wine

Overall, sparkling wines have several attributes that allow them to be one of the most adaptable types of wine to partner successfully with various types of food. Sparkling is a type of wine that works for most occasions, with or without food.

The combination of these factors (as identified on the left-hand side of the page) allows sparkling wines more successfully to partner with food than any other wine. Sparkling wine even has the ability to pair with so-called difficult ingredients and foods such as smoky, fried, spicy, salty, sweet, and mouth-coating food items such as chocolate and cheese.

1. **Complex Style Sparkling Wine**—This wine is often at the *brut* dryness level and contains enough richness to partner with cooked and smoked fish, white truffle risotto, steak tartare, beef carpaccio, and cheese (soft, rind ripened, semi-soft, and hard cheeses).

   Blanc de Blanc—These sparkling wines pair best with lighter, delicate food items and preparations such as assorted canapés, stuffed mushrooms, caviar, shrimp, raw shellfish, ceviche, and sushi. This style of sparkling wine contains generous acidity and effervescence that together stimulate the appetite and cleanse the palate.

   Vintage Champagne—This sparkling wine is made from a single, optimal season, from grapes of greater concentration, distinction, and a longer required aging period. These factors create a wine that is distinctive and rich on the palate and that pairs with bold foods (lobster, poultry with skin-on, grana or other heavily aged type cheeses) and preparation methods (roasting, broiling and grilling), with rich sauces (butter, milk and emulsified).

WHY SPARKLING WINE IS A VERSATILE FOOD PAIRING PARTNER

☑ It maintains lower alcohol than most wines.

☑ It contains ample acidity and effervescence that work together for more interesting sensations on the palate.

☑ Its ability to produce various styles, from dry, to sweet and light, to full bodied, accommodates various types of food.

FIGURE 11–15 Pouring of Champagne into a flute"
(Collection CIVC; Photographer: LECOMTE Jean-Marie)

2. **Fruit Style Sparkling Wine**—These wines are fruit forward (and, in some cases, contain residual sugar) and act to counterbalance the distinctive ingredients used in each cuisine. Fruit styles can partner well with cuisines that occasionally have spicy or pungent ingredients. Examples are Asian (which encompasses Chinese, Thai, Vietnamese, Japanese, and more) and African cuisine. This style of sparkling wine also pairs excellently with custard, fruit, and chocolate-based desserts.

   Blanc de Noir—This sparkling wine can pair with heavier, bolder food items and preparations methods. Blanc de Noirs contain fruity aroma and fuller body, with slight tannin from the higher proportion of Pinot Noir and/or Pinot Meunier grapes in the wine.

   Rosé—These sparkling are made from either a combination of red and white base wines or through the maceration process of red grapes bleeding some colored juice into the wine. Because of the higher proportion of influence of red wine grapes, Rosé sparkling offer a greater fruit aroma and flavor.

Serving and Tasting Suggestions

There are some definite signs that help determine whether one has chosen a low- or a high-quality sparkling wine. Some of the reasons may be associated with different methods of production or service techniques. Following is a list of visible signs that should be taken note of. Figure 11–15 depicts the pouring of a Champagne into a proper glass (the flute) that allows a sparkling wine to best express itself.

FIGURE 11–16 A glass of sparkling wine with a proper mousse

(Collection CIVC. Photographer: LECOMTE Jean-Marie)

☑ **Chilled**—Ensure that sparkling wine is well chilled (40–45°F), as chilling wine will accentuate its crisp acidity and preserve bubble life.

☑ **Pouring**—When pouring the sparkling wine into a glass, always proceed slowly so as not to create excessive foam, or *mousse*, in the glass. The mousse is the formation of bubbles that form on the surface of a glass after the sparkling wine has been poured. Any excess mousse will cause early dissipation of bubbles.

☑ **Size of Bubbles**—The degree of mousse refers to the way the bubbles of CO_2 feel in the mouth. A poor mousse may be described as coarse (large bubbles) and short lived, whereas a good mousse may be described as full, creamy, and fine, made up of numerous very fine CO_2 bubbles. The MC and transfer production methods have the ability to create a more condensed, finer bubble through fermentation in a tightly enclosed space.

- ☑ **Rate of Flow of Bubbles**—The MC and transfer production methods create a mousse that flows a bit more slowly and methodically than mousses created by other production methods.
- ☑ **Tasting**—When tasting, it is not necessary to swirl the wine in the glass, because the carbonation will assist to transport aroma and flavor molecules toward the surface of the glass and into the nose and palate. Excessive movement will cause the bubbles to dissipate prematurely. Figure 11–16 shows a glass of sparkling wine with a proper mousse.

COMPARISION OF COMPLEX STYLE VERSUS FRUIT STYLE SPARKLING WINE			
	Complex Style *Classic (Champagne)*	**Complex Style** *(High-quality Champagne impersonators)*	**Fruit Style**
VARIOUS NAMES and TYPES	Champagne (Vintage or Nonvintage), Blanc de Blanc, Blanc de Noir	Sparkling Wine, Cava, Blanc de Blanc, Blanc de Noir	Brachetto, Prosecco, Asti, Moscato d'Asti, Rosé, Sparkling Shiraz
Grapes Used	Permitted varietals include Chardonnay, Pinot Noir, and Pinot Meunier. They can be used individually or blended in various quantities.	Can use any grapes, but often respectfully imitate Champagne by using Chardonnay and Pinot Noir. Sometimes, completely different grapes may be used, but ones with qualities similar to the traditional grapes contribute.	Brachetto uses Brachetto grapes, Asti; Moscato d'Asti uses Moscato (or Muscat) grapes; and Sparkling Shiraz uses Shiraz.
Production Methods	Méthode Champenoise	Traditional method or transfer method	Tank Method Pump Method Méthode Rural
Aging	Longer aging produces more complexity due to effects of autolysis. Nonvintage – Minimum of 15 months Vintage – Minimum of 36 Months	No requirements, but often several months (in some cases, years) of aging. Cava requires aging a minimum of 9 months and 18 months for Reservas	Aging is typically avoided, because it would contribute undesirable complexity and mask fruit aromas and flavors.
Aromas/Flavor Emphasis	Secondary complexity from winemaking techniques	Secondary complexity from winemaking techniques	Primary fruit with fresh youthful taste
Bubble Perception	Small, less aggressive bubbles with a smoother mouth-feel	Small, less aggressive bubbles with a smoother mouth-feel	A bit larger, more aggressive bubbles with a fresh mouth-feel

BUBBLES: SPARKLING WINE

NAME: _____ Score out of 20 points_____.

Use these questions to test your knowledge and understanding of the concepts presented in the chapter.

I. MULTIPLE CHOICE: Select the best possible answer from the options available.

1. The soils in the best Champagne vineyards contain

    a. clay.

    b. gravel.

    c. chalk.

    d. sand.

2. Frizzante is an Italian sparkling wine that has

    a. normal sparkle.

    b. heavier sparkle.

    c. less sparkle.

    d. no sparkle.

3. Brut style of sparkling wine is

    a. dry.

    b. very dry.

    c. slightly dry.

    d. sweet.

4. Two styles of sparkling wine are

    a. smoky and sweet.

    b. salty and fruity.

    c. complex and fruity.

    d. complex and simple.

5. The process of collecting the yeast in the neck of the bottle during the Champagne production process is known as

    a. disgorging.

    b. remuage.

    c. dosage.

    d. riddling.

6. After the yeast is removed in the Champagne process, sugar is added to the wine to adjust dryness/sweetness. This is known as

    a. disgorging.

    b. remuage.

    c. dosage.

    d. riddling.

7. Champagne is allowed to use any or all of the permitted three grape varietals, including Chardonnay, Pinot Noir, and

    a. Pinot Gris.

    b. Pinot Blanc.

    c. Pinot Grigio.

    d. Pinot Meunier.

8. Descriptive aroma/flavor terms for complex sparkling wine would least likely include

    a. yeasty.

    b. creamy.

    c. nutty.

    d. fruity.

9. Descriptive aroma/flavor terms for simple sparkling wine would least likely include

    a. yeasty.

    b. berries.

    c. bubble gum.

    d. taffy.

10. Disgorgement is
    a. the process of cleaning the bottle before use.
    b. the process of cleaning the barrels before use.
    c. the process of removing dead yeast cells from a bottle of sparkling wine.
    d. the process of removing the grape skins from the wine after fermentation.

II. TRUE / FALSE: Circle the best possible answer.

11. The majority of Champagne is a blended wine that is aged several years in order to achieve a certain *house style*. **True / False**

12. *Blanc de Noir* sparkling wine roughly translates to a white wine made from black grapes. **True / False**

13. *Cava* is the name given to the most important type of sparkling wine made in Spain. **True / False**

14. The *MC* method is the name used for the production method to make sparkling wine in Champagne, France. **True / False**

15. It is important to swirl the sparkling wine in the glass in order to release its aroma. **True / False**

16. Lighter sparkling wine (Blanc de Blanc) can work best with more robust food items and heavier, weightier sparkling wines (Blanc de Noir) can pair better with more delicate food items. **True / False**

III. SHORT-ANSWER ESSAY/DISCUSSION QUESTIONS: Use a separate sheet of paper if necessary.

17. List and describe three reasons that Champagne is a unique type of sparkling wine. Explain the statement, "All Champagne is sparkling wine, but not all sparkling wine is Champagne."

18. Identify two examples of complex sparkling wines and two examples of fruit-driven sparkling wines.

19. Explain how, in Champagne and other high-quality sparkling wines, the dead yeast cells are removed from the bottle.

20. Identify at least two pairing strategies for sparkling wine. Why is sparkling wine considered to be one of the most adaptable food-friendly wines?

12

BOLD: Fortified Wine

A fortified wine usually consumed before a meal is known as an Apéritif (if dry), and the wine served after a meal is a Digestif (if it has some sweetness). Fortified wines also frequently are used in cooking, either as part of a reduction sauce or as a glaze for roasting meat.

LEARNING OBJECTIVES

Upon completion of this chapter, the learner will be able to:

- Understand the process of obtaining a dry versus a sweet fortified wine.
- Understand the basic styles of the more popular types of fortified wine.
- Identify some fortified-wine pairing strategies.

BOLD: FORTIFIED WINE

Table wine that has been enhanced with added alcohol (typically ranging between 15%–22%) is called *fortified wine*. Fortified wine styles can range from dry to sweet, depending on when the additional alcohol is added.

Fortified wines are also frequently used in cooking, either as part of a reduction sauce or as a glaze when roasting meat.

Apéritif (ah-pehr-uh-TEEF)—Apéritifs, if dry, are often consumed prior to or near the beginning of the meal, to assist with cleansing the palate. This beverage is served in a smaller portion size because of the higher alcohol content. This category can be grouped into two subcategories, depending on their base ingredient: (1) spirit based (such as vodka and gin) and (2) wine based (such as Port, Sherry, or Madeira).

Digestif (dee-zheh-STEEF)—Digestifs, if they have some sweetness, are often consumed after the meal to assist in satiety and aiding in digestion. This beverage is served in a smaller portion size because of the higher alcohol content.

SHERRY

Sherry is a fortified wine named after the town in which it is produced. Traditionally, Sherry is produced in *Jerez* (Heh-REHTH), located within *Andalucía* (ahn-dah-loo-THEE-yah) in southern Spain. The official Sherry-producing towns include Jerez de la Frontera, Puerto de Santa Maria, and Sanlúcar de Barrameda. These towns form what is known as the Sherry triangle because of their proximity to one another.

The Varietals

Sherry is made exclusively from white grapes such as *Palomino* (pah-loh-MEE-noh) (used in most Sherry) and *Pedro Ximénez* (PEH-droh hee-MEH-neth), which is often associated with many of the sweeter styles of Sherry.

The grapes are both fairly neutral white grape varieties that grow in a special chalky soil, rich in limestone, known as *Albariza* (ahl-bah-REE-thah). This unique soil contributes to these wine grapes growing successfully in an otherwise too hot and dry climate. The soil retains moisture and preserves high acid in the wine grapes, both of which would otherwise be lost in such a searing climate.

Production Process

Sherry contains between 15.5% and 22% alcohol. When the Sherry grapes are pressed, only the first 85%–90% of the liquid obtained is used to produce Sherry. The remaining 10%–15% is distilled to make brandy for the purpose of later fortifying the Sherry wine.

Sherry is one of the great expressions of the blender's art, made by the *solera system* (soh-LEH-rah), which is an intricate blending system involving a network of several wines of maturity levels ranging in tiers from the oldest (maybe 10–15 years) to the most recently produced. The system consists of drawing off one-quarter of the contents of the oldest barrels, from the bottom, for bottling. Wine is then emptied into the bottom barrel from the level of barrels above, and so on through the levels of the solera. With this process, the old wines incorporate character into the younger wines. Space is left in the barrels of the solera for yeast (called *flor*) to develop and thrive and impart its unique characteristic to the wine.

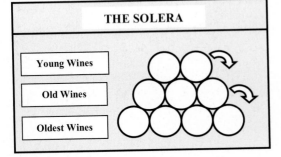

FIGURE 12–1 Solera system

The fractional blending system ensures a continuity of style quality from vintage to vintage. However, since the product is a blend from multiple years, the bottle will never carry a vintage date. The solera can be compared to a sourdough starter. Brandy is added after fermentation is complete. Figure 12–1 depicts the solera process.

TYPES OF SHERRY

All Sherry begins its life as a dry wine. The grape spirit is added only after fermentation has been completed. There are two general categories of Sherry: *Finos* (FEE-nohs) and *Olorosos* (oh-loh-ROAS-ohs).

STYLE #1 Fino Types

This category of Sherry produces light-colored, dry, and tangy fortified wines that include Fino, Manzanilla, and Amontillado. Finos are wines that have been affected and preserved by the *flor* and often are referred to as having been biologically aged (meaning the yeast has influenced the wine and protected it from the effects of oxygen).

The aromas and flavors of Fino and Oloroso Sherry tend towards bakeshop (yeasty), vegetables (olive), and fruit (apple press).

Fino Sherry (FEE-no)—This is the driest Sherry, with live flor yeast cells present in the wine during aging. Since the yeast never dies, its presence acts as a preservative against oxygen. Fino is a light, pale, dry, and delicate style protected by a layer of flor that grows spontaneously on the surface of the wine. Generally, it contains about 15.5% alcohol.

Manzanilla Sherry (man-zah-NEE-yah)—A light, pale, delicate, and the most pungent of the fino-style Sherries, a Manzanilla is a type of Fino that is matured in the cool seaside-influenced atmosphere of *Sanlucar de Barrameda*. Within this area, the flor grows with great abundance to give wines notable, fresh, crisp, and fragrant aroma with a slight salty tang. Figure 12–2 shows a wine label of Manzanilla Sherry.

Amontillado Sherry (ah-mone-tee-YAH-doe)—This Sherry starts as a fino, and if the flor dies, it becomes an Amontillado. Amontillado has been slightly affected by the passage of oxygen through the barrel aging process. This yields a light-brown-colored, nutty, and complex wine.

The aromas and flavors for an Amontillado tend to be bakeshop spice (root beer and butterscotch).

FIGURE 12–2 Manzanilla Sherry wine label

(© Dorling Kindersley)

FIGURE 12–3 Green olives stuffed with blue cheese

(Image by Steven Rimlinger)

Pairing Strategies

Fino-type Sherries are a great transition wine between summer and fall. They can be served at room temperature or slightly chilled. Their aromas and flavors are ideal for apéritifs with appetizers, soups, and even some types of entrees. Figure 12–3 shows green olives stuffed with blue cheese.

1. Fino and Manzanilla pair well with appetizers such as tapas (little plates) with olives, olives stuffed with blue or feta cheese, olive tapenade, various canapés, spicy or smoky sausage, nuts, grilled shrimp or shrimp cocktail, salty ham, crudités (croo-dee-TAYS) (raw vegetable platter such as carrots, bell peppers, and cucumbers) with a dip.

2. Fino and Manzanilla can pair well with gazpacho soup, whereas Amontillado can pair better with a more substantial beef

or veal-based soup such as French onion with melted Gruyére cheese, or beef barley.

3. Amontillados can pair with substantial beefy entrees, such as grilled or smoked beef tenderloin.

STYLE #2 Oloroso Types

The Oloroso styles maintain a deep color, a rich flavor, and an overall less dry style than Finos. Olorosos are not protected by a layer of flor, causing oloroso types to gain *oxidative* qualities from barrel aging and turn to a deep orange-brown color. These Sherries generally maintain 18% or more alcohol.

The aromas and flavors of Oloroso-type Sherries often contain bakeshop (maple syrup, caramel, butterscotch, brown sugar) and dried fruit (raisins).

Oloroso types also have varying levels of sweetness through the addition of a sweetening agent (the juice of dried grapes) after fermentation has been completed.

Oloroso Sherry (oh-low-ROAZ-oh)—This type of Sherry is sweet to taste because a small portion of sundried (for 12–24 hours) grape juice is added into a fortified dry Sherry.

Cream Sherry—This Sherry is even sweeter to the taste, because a small portion of sun-dried (for 10–14 days) grape juice is added to a fortified dry Sherry.

Pairing Strategies

Oloroso-type Sherries can pair well with desserts because they contain varying levels of sweetness, as well as high alcohol, which helps cut through the richness. In addition, the bakeshop aromas and flavors of the wine help to bridge the flavors in the desserts. Figure 12–4 shows chocolate pecan pie. Following are some desserts with which Oloroso-type Sherries pair well:

1. Custard or cream-based desserts, such as rice pudding, crème brûlée, crème caramel, pecan pie, and bananas foster.
2. Chocolate-based desserts, such as chocolate cake, truffles, and chocolate-chip-walnut cookies.
3. As a breakfast syrup (reduce the wine in a pan over a medium heat until it reaches a desired consistency) for French toast, waffles, pancakes and/or breakfast sausage.

MADEIRA

Madeira (muh-DEER-uh) is one of the three great fortified wines of the world and has played a role in connection with major historical figures and events since the seventeenth century. Madeira was a favorite of Thomas Jefferson and was held in high enough esteem to be used to toast the Declaration of Independence. Authentic Madeira comes from Portugal's Madeira Island, a Portuguese possession in the Atlantic about 625 miles from Portugal and 400 miles off the coast of Morocco.

Production Process

Madeira's success is attributed to the primitive shipping conditions of the seventeenth century. Madeira wine became fortified when British merchants on the island began to add grape spirit to preserve it on its long voyage to the Americas. This long voyage under the sun for months and even years ended up cooking the wine and yielding the beverage we call Madeira. The exposure to the elements assists in gaining Madeira its flavor—conditions that normally would ruin most typical table wine. The baking it received in the blazing tropical sun created a soft, deep flavor with a pleasant burnt quality and an oxidized, nutty taste. Nowa-

FIGURE 12–4 Chocolate and pecan pie
(Maas, Rita/Getty Images Inc.-Image Bank)

days, the wine is artificially heated in an *estufa* (es-TOO-fah) to mimic the long sea voyage. An estufa, Portuguese for "stove," is a heating room used to accelerate the maturation process. It exposes the wine to small doses of oxygen and allows the sugars to become caramelized.

Exposure to extreme temperature and oxygen accounts for Madeira's stability; arguably, Madeira is fairly indestructible, and an open bottle can last unharmed for months.

Types of Madeira

Madeira has aromas and flavors of bakeshop (oyster sauce, brown sugar, molasses, soy sauce, and cinnamon). The four major styles of Madeira are named after the dominant grapes that go into them. They provide a range of styles from dry to sweet.

STYLE #1 Sercial (ser-see-AHL)—*Dry* and light golden in color, delicate with a fresh acidity, Sercial makes an ideal apéritif beverage.

STYLE #2 Verdelho (vehr-DEH-lyoo)—*Semi-dry* and golden in color. There is a variation of the Verdelho style known as *rainwater*. The name is said to have come from the days when barrels left outside waiting for shipment would absorb rain through the wood and cause the wine to become slightly diluted.

STYLE #3 Bual / Boal (boo-AHL)—This style is *semi-sweet*, dark gold to brown in color.

STYLE #4 Malmsey (MAH'm-zee)—Malmsey is *sweet* and chestnut brown in color.

Pairing Strategies

1. A drier style of Madeira can serve as an Apéritif beverage and pair with appetizers that have a salty, nutty, or dried fruit component, such as a Prosciutto-wrapped fig.
2. A drier style of Madeira can be reduced in a pan to make a reduction sauce that can partner with savory-type entrees such as sautéed, roasted, or grilled pork or beef.
3. Sweeter style Madeiras pair excellently with *chocolate-based* desserts such as chocolate-chip-walnut cookies and chocolate cake; *nut-based* desserts, such as pecan pie and pumpkin pie; and other desserts, such as cinnamon rolls, bananas foster, and crème caramel.

Photo by Michéle Delvoie

PORT WINE

Authentic Port (also called Porto, Oporto, or Vinho do Porto) is a sweet, fortified red (sometimes white) wine with the addition of a grape spirit (unaged brandy) before fermentation has been completed. The brandy not only kills the yeast, leaving residual sugar in the wine, but also historically acted as a preservative to prolong the quality of the wine during its voyage at sea.

Vinho do Porto (Port wine) is named after Portugal's second largest city, *Porto* (PORT-oo), or *Oporto* (oh-PORT-oo), close to the mouth of the River Douro. Although most Port houses are based in Vila Nova de Gaia in Oporto, the vineyards lie along the river. Port was one of the first wine regions to be officially demarcated and recognized, in 1756. Figure 12–5 shows a boat shipping barrels of Port wine.

The Varietals

Port can be made from many grape varieties, most of which are red and must be grown in the Douro River valley. Primarily, varying quantities of five grape varieties are blended together to create Oporto: *Touriga Nacional* (tow-REE-gah nah syo-NAHL), *Tinto Cão* (TEEN-too cowng), *Tinta Barroca* (TEEN-tah bar-ROH-kuh), *Tinta Roriz* (TEEN-tah ROR-eesh), *Touriga Francesa* (tow-REE-gah fran-SAY-zuh), and, increasingly, *Tinta Amarela* (TEEN-tah a-mah-REH-lah).

The grape varieties grow mostly on the hillsides in schist soil, unique to the Douro River valley in northern Portugal. This type of soil is rich in minerals, but low in nutrients,

FIGURE 12–5 Boat in Portugal
(SGM/Stock Connection)

forcing the vines to dig deep. The grapes are picked almost entirely by hand, as the slopes are too steep for mechanical harvesters. Figure 12–6 depicts the steep hillside vineyards that predominate in Portugal.

Process of Production

Then the grapes are crushed (traditionally, by foot) in a process known as *treading*, which takes place in large, open, stone or concrete pits called *lagerns* (LAH-gehrns), which are also used for fermentation. This method is still used today, but has now been mainly replaced by fermentation in closed tanks (which gives better quality control and extracts the color from the skins equally well) until fermentation is partially completed. The fermenting grape juice is poured off into larger containers holding spirit, which kills the yeast and stops fermentation.

The young wine is then shipped from the vineyards to the Port houses in Oporto, where it stays in barrels for a year or two. For the most part, Port is blended and aged in the cellars at Vila Nova da Gaia, a city at the mouth of the Douro River, opposite the city of Porto.

Types of Port

Flavors/Aromas—The flavors are a harmonic ensemble, around a core of berry fruit, that includes compote, chocolate, coffee, cigar box, pepper, brown sugar, and pralines. While Port is in the cask, it can become increasingly refined and tends to taste of figs and other dried fruits, nuts, spices, and crème brulee.

Body/Style—There are numerous styles of Port, distinguished largely by the quality of the grapes and the method in which they are aged. Port is full bodied, high in alcohol, fruity, and tannic in its youth.

STYLE #1 Barrel-Aged Ports

Barrel-aged Ports have matured in a wood barrel, which allows the passage of oxygen. In the experience of *oxidative* aging, the wine loses its bright youthful red color and becomes tawnier or brick colored as it evolves.

Tawny Port—Tawny Ports are made from better, more concentrated grapes than ruby Ports. Tawny is aged in wood for up to six years and blends wines from other vintages. Tawny Ports gradually turn from bright red to reddish brown and begin to develop flavor nuances.

Aged Tawny Port—This type of Port is mellow and rich. Aged tawny Ports are made from top grapes from excellent years. They are usually bottled as 10-, 20-, 30-, or even 40-year-old wines, labelled according to the average age of the Ports in the blend. The younger wines add freshness, and the older wines add complexity.

Colheita (cuhl-YAY-tah)—Colheita is a tawny Port made of wines from a single year, with the date of harvest appearing on the label. A Colheita is essentially a vintage tawny, bottled after having aged in wood for seven years.

STYLE #2 Bottle-Aged Ports

Bottle-aged Ports have matured in sealed tanks or bottles, with limited exposure to oxygen, and experience *reductive* aging. This method preserves more of the youthful color, aromas, and flavors.

Ruby Port—Ruby is a young, bright red, sweet, and peppery wine meant to be drunk young. It is a blend of several vintages that are normally aged in tanks (often not made of wood) for two to a maximum of three years and then made into a house style. Ruby is simple and has the straightforward style of Port (as well as being most affordable). It is bottled in such a way as to limit as much oxidation as possible.

Late Bottled Vintage (LBV)—Late bottled vintage Ports are not blended, because they are from a single year, and they are bottled between the fourth and sixth year from

FIGURE 12–6 Terraced vineyard in Portugal
(Veiga, Luis/Getty Images Inc.-Image Bank)

harvest. They sometimes are referred to as "the poor man's vintage Port," not because they are lower in quality, but because of their accessibility to be drunk much sooner. These wines are softer, less tannic, and not as full bodied as vintage Port.

Vintage Port—Vintage Port is one of the rarest and most sought after of all Ports because it accounts for only about 2% of production. The wine is made with high-quality grapes declared to be vintage only when the crop is exceptional within a single year. In order for the wine to be called a vintage, the winery must seek approval of the Port Wine Institute.

Vintage Port is bottled between its second and third year from harvest. It spends the majority of its life (sometimes up to 50 years for the wine to reach its peak) evolving and maturing in the bottle to achieve great depth and complexity.

Serving Suggestions

Vintage Ports and LBV's should be decanted because they are unfiltered and develop considerable sediment as they age. Vintage Ports should be consumed within two to three days of decanting. In Portugal, this type of Port often is purchased when it first appears on the market, to celebrate a child's birth. It is matured throughout the life of the child and is finally opened upon the maturity of, not only the wine, but also when the child has become an adult.

Pairing Strategies

Port is sweet, rich, and high in alcohol, which provides a satiety effect. There are some possibilities if serving Port as an ingredient in food, but most Port wine is enjoyed after the entrée, with dessert, by itself, or with any form of tobacco such as cigarettes, cigars, or a pipe.

1. Port wine can add an interesting flavor as an ingredient in many dishes, both sweet and savory. Port can be used to plump up and macerate dried fruit, it can be reduced in a pan to create a thicker reduction sauce, or it can be combined with a bit of demi-glace.
2. Port pairs well with roasted or grilled game such as venison, poultry such as skin-on duck, pheasant and Paté de fois gras, or red meat such as grilled or smoked beef.
3. Port wine partners well with *chocolate-based* desserts such as chocolate-chip-walnut cookies, flourless chocolate cake, and chocolate truffles rolled in walnuts or dusted with cocoa. Figure 12–7 shows a chocolate souffle and bananas foster.
4. Port wine pairs well with dried or cooked *fruit-based* desserts such as pies, tarts, and cobblers. The taste of Port combines nicely with dried fruit (cherries) and Rhubarb or Berry Cobbler.
5. Aged tawny Port can partner well with salted, toasted or seasoned nuts (walnuts, cashews, and hazelnuts) or *nut-based* desserts such as pecan pie.
6. Rich, pungent *blue-vein* type cheeses, such as English Stilton, French Bleu, and Italian Gorgonzola cheese, work excellent.

FIGURE 12–7 Chocolate souffle and bananas foster
(Images by Ryan Michael)

BOLD: FORTIFIED WINE

NAME: _____ Score out of 20 points_____.

Use these questions to test your knowledge and understanding of the concepts presented in the chapter.

I. MULTIPLE CHOICE: Select the best possible answer from the options available.

1. The rich, chalky limestone soil in which Sherry grapes are produced is
   a. schist.
   b. sand.
   c. albariza.
   d. clay.

2. The area of production for Port is
   a. Dao.
   b. Vila Nova de Gaia.
   c. Bairrada.
   d. Douro.

3. A digestif is often consumed
   a. before or in the beginning of the meal.
   b. during the meal.
   c. after the meal.
   d. toward the end to after the meal.

4. An Apéritif is often consumed
   a. before or in the beginning of the meal.
   b. during the meal.
   c. after the meal.
   d. toward the end to after the meal.

5. A Sherry always *begins* its life as a
   a. dry wine.
   b. sweet wine.
   c. dry or sweet wine, depending on the style.
   d. medium-sweet wine.

6. Two main categories of Sherry include
   a. barrel aged and bottle aged.
   b. Ruby and Tawny.
   c. Fino and Oloroso.
   d. Fino and Manzanilla.

7. Two main categories of Port include
   a. barrel aged and bottle aged.
   b. Ruby and Vintage.
   c. Fino and Oloroso.
   d. Fino and Manzanilla.

8. The *Solera Method* is
   a. a style of Sherry.
   b. a style of Port.
   c. an intricate blending system used to produce a Sherry.
   d. an intricate blending system used to produce a Port.

9. In making Port wine, the fortification of alcohol is added
   a. before fermentation is completed.
   b. after fermentation is completed.
   c. any time during fermentation, depending on the style of Port being produced.
   d. never. No supplemental alcohol is added to a Port.

II. TRUE / FALSE: Circle the best possible answer.

10. Madeira is easily susceptible to spoilage. **True / False**

11. When making Port wine, fermentation is stopped by adding brandy to kill the yeast, which leaves residual sugar in the finished wine. **True / False**

12. Sherry wine will usually have a vintage date on the label. **True / False**

13. Aged tawny Ports are often labelled as 10-, 20-, 30-, or 40-year-old wines, indicating the average age of the Port in the blend. **True / False**

14. Ruby Ports are often aged for decades before they are consumed. **True / False**

III. MATCHING: Match the Style.

15. ＿＿ Malmsey   A. Dry

16. ＿＿ Sercial   B. Sweet

17. ＿＿ Boal   C. Semi-dry

18. ＿＿ Verdelho   D. Semi-sweet

IV. SHORT ANSWER ESSAY / DISCUSSION QUESTIONS: Use a separate sheet of paper if necessary.

19. Explain the similarities in, and differences between, Port and Sherry.

20. Provide some pairing principles with fortified wine.

13

NECTAR: Dessert Wines

Dessert wines have become a general category for wines that are rich, potent, and concentrated, with some varying level of sweetness. There are various types and styles of dessert wines that can be paired with dessert or served as stand-alone beverages in place of dessert.

LEARNING OBJECTIVES

Upon completion of this chapter, the learner will be able to:

- Discover the six methods used to produce a dessert wine.
- Identify some famous dessert wines found throughout the wine-producing world.
- Recognize the five dessert type categories.
- Comprehend some wine and dessert pairing strategies, depending on the type of dessert category.

NECTAR: DESSERT WINE

Dessert wines have become a general category for wines that are rich, potent, and concentrated, with some varying level of sweetness. They come from all over the world, and they can be made from many different types of grapes by various production techniques that yield numerous styles. The various types and styles of dessert wines can be used to make decisions about partnering the wine with dessert or instead choosing to serve the wine as a stand-alone beverage.

Dessert wines often are made from grapes that have been concentrated as a result contains high sugar content, less juice, and overall reduced yield. They frequently are labor intensive, as they demand more care and attention to detail in the harvesting and production processes. Therefore, it takes more grapes and manpower to produce a dessert wine, and this translates to a higher selling price. Because of both price and concentrated rich flavor, it is common practice to serve dessert wine in a small two-ounce portion in an undersized glass.

Dessert Menu and Dessert Wine List

For various reasons, dessert and wine pairings at the end of the meal all too often are treated with neglect. Few consumers order dessert wines, often because very few restaurants suggest them. Often, they are not promoted by service staff because of a lack of understanding and appreciation for these types of wines. Therefore, many servers take the safest action, which is no action. Service employees should be trained to clearly understand how dessert wines can enhance the dessert course and can act to satiate the consumer and provide him or her with a hedonistic experience at the end of a meal.

The dessert wine selections, just as the dessert menu, should be balanced and should offer plenty of options with various price points. A well-designed dessert menu should include a variety of types of different pastry and bakery products. A good balance is to include options from several categories, such as fruit, nut, chocolate, custard, pastry, and cookies. Various types and styles of dessert wines from various origins around the world should be offered to accommodate these dessert options.

Seven Methods of Marketing Desserts with Dessert Wines

1. Offer dessert wines in small portions of about 2–3 ounces. This is an adequate amount that does not overwhelm the wine drinker's palate and pocketbook. Be careful of glass size: If the 2–3-ounce portion is poured into a standard wine glass, the customer may feel shorted. Smaller-size dessert wine glasses should be used.

2. Ensure that various price points are met in order to accommodate customers with budgetary restrictions.

3. Clearly identify selling prices for both desserts and dessert wines on the menu. It is an inappropriate practice not to have selling prices listed.

   Some restaurants condone the practice of not including selling prices on products. This can be perceived as somewhat of an unethical business practice, and it ends up only frustrating or even potentially embarrassing the customer. It is a gamble for a customer to commit to purchasing products of unknown price.

4. Make a small, upfront investment in a preshift training session where service staff can sample the products and pairings, in order to instill in the staff confidence in and excitement about their selling ability. It is much easier for a server to sell desserts and dessert wines if the server has experienced the products firsthand.

5. Offer dessert platters with several miniature versions of the original-sized desserts. Each dessert platter can be paired with a dessert wine flight. A *dessert wine flight* is a small sampling of several (usually three to four) different dessert wines.

6. After each dessert selection on the menu, print the suggested wine pairing or wine flight for each one. List two prices, one for the dessert and a second for the dessert and wine pairing. Here is an example: Flourless Chocolate and Hazelnut cake, $6.95; add a wine flight that includes a small sample of a Tawny Port, Banyuls, and Malmsey Madeira for $14.95.

7. Other ways to incorporate dessert wines into desserts is to use wine as a poaching liquid; to macerate and plump up dried fruit; and in the creation of fruit sauce such as a compote, coulis, chutney, or sauce reduction. Dessert wines can also be used as flavoring agents in sorbet or ice cream.

Techniques for Producing Dessert Wines

There are several methods of creating a dessert wine. Each technique removes water content and concentrates flavors and sugars, while maintaining high acid levels and potentially high alcohol levels (in some cases) to prevent overpowering sweetness. Alcohol and or sugar levels are large contributing factors to a dessert wine's body, weight, or overall intensity. These wines can range from a consistency of light juice to heavy syrup. The combination of the components of concentrated sugar, acidity, and alcohol allows most dessert wines to have great aging potential and contributes to its great expense.

There are six techniques for producing dessert wines: late harvest wine, ice wine, rot wine, dried grape wine, fortification of wine, and enrichment wines. Each technique is unique to the country or region of origin of the wine.

1. LATE HARVEST WINE

Late harvest wine begins with leaving the grapes on the vine past the normal harvest. Through the extra *hang time*, the grapes begin to reduce in water content and increase in sugar content and in weight. The sugar content is measured in brix, which can equate to a desired level of alcohol content. Brix equals one-half of the projected alcohol content. For example, 24 brix equals 12% alcohol. Grapes used for table wine normally are harvested around 30 brix (depending upon grape type and other factors) or higher. Through a *late harvest*, aromas and flavors also become more concentrated.

Eventually, the grapes dry out and become raisins. During production, the fermentation process may stop naturally or intentionally before the yeast can consume all the sugar. This leaves varying amounts of residual sugar in the wine.

Late harvest wines are created in many environments around the world. They can be produced in both warm and cool wine regions. Figure 13–1 shows late harvest grapes.

Famous Late Harvest Wines

FIGURE 13–1 Late harvest grapes
(Domaine Weinbach)

Auselese, Beerenauslese (BA), and Trockenbeerenauslese (TBA)—These are considered three of Germany's greatest wines (mostly made from the Riesling varietal) in general, and late harvest wines in particular, in the world. These wines are produced from late harvest grapes and may even have varying amounts of noble rot.

Late Harvest Zinfandel—This wine is produced in various areas in California.

Late Harvest Shiraz—This is produced in various areas of Australia.

2. ICE WINE

Ice wine, or *Eiswein* (ICE-vyne) in German, is created in cold climates where the grapes are left on the vine into the late fall and winter to freeze. Once the grapes are sufficiently frozen, they are handpicked in the early morning or late evening and pressed while still frozen. Since the grapes have been left on the vine for a longer period, water content is decreased and sugar content is increased. Any remaining water is frozen, leaving a sweet, concentrated juice.

Most authentic ice wines are made in areas where the weather is cold enough to thoroughly freeze the grapes. Germany is the original ice wine producer, but Canada has become the world's leading producer in terms of both quantity and increasing quality. Figure 13–2 shows frozen grapes left on a vine.

Ice wines often are low in alcohol (9%–11%) and are rich and viscous, with a good balance of sugar and acid. Some wineries are producing sparkling ice wines and experimenting with nontraditional grape varieties such as Vidal Blanc, Merlot, Pinot Noir, and Cabernet Franc.

FIGURE 13–2 Frozen grapes
(Cosmo Condina/Stock Connection)

FAMOUS ICE WINE PRODUCING AREAS		
COUNTRY OF ORIGIN	**SPECIFIC LOCATIONS**	**COMMON GRAPE VARIETALS**
Germany	Mosel and Rhine	Riesling, Gewürztraminer
Canada	Ontario (about 90% of production), Niagara, and Okanagan	Vidal Blanc, Riesling, and Cabernet Franc (produces red ice wine)

Other locations around the world also produce natural ice wine, such as the Niagara region in Canada and New York State. Ice wine can be made vitually anywhere by an alternative method known as a *cryoextraction* in which the grapes are placed in a mechanical freezing device. Bonny Doon Winery in California uses this method to artificially create the same effect as freezing on the vine. Cryoextraction can produce less expensive versions than the traditional approach to making these wines.

3. ROT WINE

Noble rot, often referred by the more appealing Latin term *Botrytis cinerea* (boh-TRI-tis sihn-EAR-ee-uh), is produced from a so-called "friendly" fungus that grows on certain grapes, given the appropriate climatic conditions. It causes the grape skins to break, allowing the juice and pulp to become affected by the mold, and then extracts the water content by about one-third. This allows the remaining juice to concentrate into luscious, syrupy nectar consistency, maintaining natural acidity while imparting new flavors of honey and apricot with higher sugar content.

The ideal environment for the fungus is cool evenings and moist, foggy mornings, followed by sunny days. If the climate lacks the sun, the mold will turn into the undesirable *gray rot*. If the climate is too warm or lacks moisture, the *Botrytis* will never develop.

Noble rot goes by different names throughout the winemaking world. In France, it is called *Pourriture Noble* (poo-ree-TYUR NOH-bl); in Germany, *Edelfäule* (ay-duhl-FOY-luh); in Italy, *Muffa Nobile* (MOOF-fah NAW-bee-lay); and in Hungary, *Aszú* (AH-soo).

Rot wines are classically produced from thin-skinned grapes such as Semillon, Chenin Blanc, and Riesling varietals.

FAMOUS ROT WINE PRODUCING AREAS	
COUNTRY OF ORIGIN	**SPECIFIC LOCATIONS WITH COMMON GRAPE VARIETALS**
France	Bordeaux (Sauvignon Blanc and Semillon), Loire Valley (Chenin Blanc), Alsace (Riesling)
Germany	Mosel and Rheingau (Riesling)
Hungary	Tokay Aszú is rated by the amount of *Botrytis* grapes used to make the wine. It can range from 3 to 6 puttonyes. The sweetest and richest is Tokaji Eszencia.

Sauternes (saw-TEHRN) or (so-TERN)—Sauternes is arguably one of the best and most famous of all "rot" based dessert wines from the Bordeaux region of France. Sauternes is not a grape, but a blend of two grapes in varying percentages of Sauvignon Blanc and Semillon.

Other famous *Botrytis*-affected wines made in France are *Coteaux du Layon* (koh-toh deu leh-YAWN), *Quarts de Chaume* (kahr duh SHOHM), and *Bonnezeaux* (bawn-ZOH), all produced from the Chenin Blanc grape in the Anjou area of the Loire Valley.

Tokay (toh-KAY) or **Tokaji** (toh-ki)—One of the oldest and most renowned *Botrytis* dessert wines produced in the Tokaj wine region in northern Hungary, Tokaji wine is made from three permitted white grapes, but primarily from the *Furmint* varietal.

Tokay Aszú (toh-KAY AH-soo)—This Tokay style is made with a combination of wines from the *Botrytis*-affected harvests. The berries literally are harvested grape by grape in late October and November and sorted according to their degree of infection from *Botrytis*. The *Botrytis*-affected berries (called *Aszú* by Hungarians) are placed aside, and the uninfected berries are made into a dry-base wine.

The Aszú berries are mashed into a sweetened paste and placed into a basket called a *puttonyo* (PUH-tohn-yo). The *puttonyo* is capable of holding about 55 pounds and is used as a measure of sugar content. The sweet paste is now added to the dry white base wine in a cask called a *gönc* (GOON-ts), a 136-liter wood container. The exact number of *puttonyos* (PUH-tohn-yosh) (plural of puttonyos) determines the grade of the Tokaj Aszú (which can range from three to six) that will be identified on the wine's label.

Afterwards, the new Aszú wine is transferred into casks and matured in cool, damp cellars. These cellars are unique, forming tunnels up to 20 miles long in volcanic mountain rock. It is possible to find wines made over 300 years ago covered with the famous mold that allows them to age the minimum required three years. The wine will be aged a minimum of two years with barrel maturation, and an additional year in bottle for Aszú wines. The cellars maintain constant levels of temperature and high humidity, which provide ideal conditions for storing and aging Tokay wines.

Tokay Eszencia (toh-KAY EHS-sen-tsee-uh)—This is the most rare of all Tokay wines, made only from pressed, unblended Aszú grapes, with little or no base wine. It is the equivalent of seven puttonyos. Eszencia is the first-run juice of the Aszú grapes, which seeps from the press under the grapes' own weight. The sugar content is extremely high, and the wine will ferment at a very slow rate, often over many years.

This wine is even more concentrated and sweeter than Tokay Aszú. It is rarely made, because the small amount of juice extracted out of the dried, shriveled berries takes several years to ferment due to its high sugar concentration. Sometimes a small amount is bottled separately, after which it will develop for years in the bottle; more often, Eszencia enriches an Aszú blend.

4. DRIED GRAPE WINE

Dried grape wines often are produced in warm climates that allow grapes (either red or white) to be sun- or air-dried. The grapes are harvested and allowed to dry or raisin under controlled conditions, either hanging off rafters or laid on straw mats. This process evaporates water content, concentrates flavors and sugar content, and yields a rich, viscous wine.

This process of drying the grapes is known as *passerillage* (pah-seh-ree-LAHZH) in France and *passimento* or *passito* (pah-SEE-toh) in Italian. Dried grape wines are produced around the world into such wines as Vin Santo, Recioto, and Amarone from Italy; *Strohwein* (SHTROH-vine) from Germany; and *Vin de Paille* (van-duh-PIE) from France.

Famous Dried Grape Wines

Vin Santo (vin-SAHN-toe)—Vin Santo is a wine produced primarily in Tuscany, Italy, but it can be found in other areas of Italy as well. It often is made from white wine grapes *Trebbiano* (treb-ee-AH-noh) and *Malvasia* (mal-vah-SEE-ah) but also from the red Sangiovese grapes as well. The grapes are dried by being either being placed on straw mats or hung from rafters in the winery. The grapes are dried until they shrivel, which concentrates the grapes' sugar and flavors.

The very sweet grapes are then fermented in small barrels that allow oxygen in, which causes the wine to maderize (or oxidize). The result is a slightly brown wine that can be either sweet or dry.

Recioto (reh-CHAW-toh) and **Amarone** (ah-mah-ROH-neh)—These are dried grape wines produced in the Veneto region of Italy. When the grapes are fermented, the wine becomes either an Amarone or a Recioto, depending upon whether the yeast has consumed all the grape sugar or not. If the wine is left with residual sugar, it is known as Recioto; if it is fermented dry, it is Amarone.

5. FORTIFICATION OF WINE

Fortification is the process of adding a distillate (often, unaged brandy) during or toward the end of fermentation. The act of adding alcohol to the fermentation process kills the yeast and leaves residual sugar in the wine. Wines subjected to this process often are produced in hot areas where the original purpose of the added alcohol was used to preserve the wines while in transport.

Famous Fortified Wines

Vin Doux Naturel (VDN) (van doo nah-tew-REHL)—VDNs can be produced from either red wine based on Grenache or white wine based on Muscat grape varietal. VDNs are produced in Southern France, primarily in Languedoc, Roussilon and Southern Rhone Valley, such as *Banyuls* (bahn-YOOLS) in Languedoc and *Rastau* (rah-STOW) in Rhone Valley.

Port, Madeira, and Sherry are other famous versions of fortified wine. They are discussed in greater detail in Chapter 12, "BOLD: Fortified Wines."

6. ENRICHMENT WINE

Enrichment wines are table or sparkling wines that have been made by adding sugar either before or after fermentation. The purpose of enrichment is to produce a sweet wine, but of some varying degree of sweetness.

Famous Enrichment Wine

Champagne / Sparkling Wine—Most sparkling wine is fermented completely dry; then a *dosage*, or sugar mixture, is added to achieve the desired level of sweetness. Sparklings are fairly versatile in pairing with a wide range of desserts. The better options for pairing with desserts include *Sec* (semi-sweet), *Demi-Sec* (lightly sweet), and *Doux* (very sweet).

> Blanc de Noir ("white from black") often is created in the *Brut*, or dry, style, but may work with some desserts because of its fruit-forward aromas and flavors.
> Other sweet sparklings are Moscato, Asti, Lambrusco, Sparkling Shiraz, and Brachetto. Sparkling wines are discussed in greater detail in Chapter 11, "BUBBLES: Sparkling Wine."

MATCHING WINE WITH DESSERTS

An effective method of determining wine and dessert pairings is to categorize and divide the desserts into basic styles. Categorizing desserts is not straightforward, because a single dessert often is made from a combination of ingredients and thus can fall under several headings. Finding the primary base item within the dessert can lessen the challenge and assist in finding a more suitable partner. The five basic dessert categories are (1) fruit-based, (2) nut-based, (3) chocolate-based, (4) creams and custard-based, and (5) pastry, ice cream, and cookie-based desserts.

General Dessert Pairing Philosophies

1. A wine's sweetness needs to be equal to or sweeter than the dessert. Otherwise the wine will taste sour, tart, or bitter. The wine by itself needs to have enough sweetness, acidity, or alcohol to carry the weight of the sweetness of the dessert.
2. In pairing with some desserts, an intense concentration of fruit in a wine may work as a substitute for a lack of sweetness, even in a dry wine. This may work particularly in the case of red wine (Merlot, Shiraz) and chocolate, and certain white wine grapes such as Viognier and Riesling.
3. The basic elements that should be considered when matching are sugar content, acidity, alcohol content, and the intensity of the wine.

1. Fruit-Based Desserts

Fresh Fruit, Poached Fruit, Grilled Fruit, Fruit Pies, Fruit Cobblers, Fruit Compote, Fruit Tarts

Figure 13–3 shows some fruit tarts. Following are some principles on which wine may be paired with fruit-based desserts:

1. The higher the acid of the fruit, such as citrus or tree fruit (apple, pear, orange, lemon), the higher the acid of the wine will be, as found in cool-climate dessert wines such as *ice wine*.
2. Fresh fruit will pair more effectively with dessert wines such as *ice wine* or *enrichment wines*.

FIGURE 13–3 Mini raspberry fruit tarts
(Ian O'Leary © Dorling Kindersley)

FIGURE 13–4 Chocolate and pecan tarts

(Mira.com/Iris Richardson)

3. Dried and baked fruit desserts will pair more effectively with red-based dessert wines such as *dried grape* or *fortified wines*.

4. Hot or warm fruits such as tropical and dried fruits (pineapple, mango, melon) will pair better with *rot* and *enrichment* dessert wines.

2. Nut-Based Desserts

Nut Tarts, Caramel, Coffee, Toffee, Pecan Pie, Maple, Butterscotch, Toasted Nuts

Figure 13–4 shows a mini-pecan tart. Following are some principles on which wine may be paired with nut-based desserts:

1. Nut-based desserts pair best with wines that have an oxidative quality, such as *fortified* or *dried grape* wines.

2. A platter of toasted and lightly salted nuts such as cashews, walnuts, and pecans will pair well with *fortified* wines.

3. If nut-based desserts incorporate fruit (such as mango and pineapple nut tart), an *ice wine* or *rot* wine may work best.

3. Chocolate-Based Desserts

Chocolate Pot de Crème, Chocolate Bread Pudding, Chocolate Chunk and Walnut Cookies, Chocolate Soufflé, Chocolate Fondue, White Chocolate Mousse, Flourless Chocolate Cake, and Chocolate Truffles

Figure 13–5 shows a flourless chocolate cake. Following are some principles on which wine may be paired with chocolate-based desserts:

1. Consider the intensity and sweetness of the chocolate. There is white, milk, semi-sweet, and dark (or bitter) chocolate. All can be found in various forms, from flavored, to liqueur-filled, to soft chocolate (truffles)—and more—all possessing varying degrees of flavor.

2. The wine should be at least as sweet as, if not a touch sweeter than, the chocolate it is served with.

3. Match lighter-flavored chocolates with lighter-bodied wines; likewise, the stronger the chocolate, the more full-bodied (and dryer) the wine should be.

4. Dark and milk chocolate-based desserts have richness and mouth-coating qualities that pair best with fortified wines such as Banyuls or barrel-aged Ports.

FIGURE 13–5 Chocolate cake

(Ian O'Leary © Dorling Kindersley)

Dark chocolate matches well with fortified wines and table wines that have some body, richness, and moderate levels of tannin, such as Cabernet Sauvignon, Shiraz, Grenache, Merlot, and Zinfandel.

Milk chocolate partners best with fortified wines such as Banyuls, Port, and Madeira. Sweet red sparkling wines such as Brachetto and sparkling Shiraz are also good matches. Table wines such as Pinot Noir and Merlot (particularly when there are elements of caramel, butterscotch or toffee) may work, too.

White chocolate pairs well with late harvest Riesling and Gewürztraminer. Sweet sparkling wines such as Moscato d'Asti, Asti Spumante, noble rot wines, and ice wines also work well.

4. Creams and Custard-Based Desserts

Crème Brulée, Crème Carmel, Bread Pudding, Tarte Tatin, Tiramisu, Eclairs, Pumpkin Pie, Cheesecake, Pastry Cream, Ice Cream

Figure 13–6 shows a crème brulée. Following are some principles on which wine may be paired with creams and custard-based desserts:

1. Cream and custard-based desserts are rich and mouth-coating, making them difficult to pair with wine. Usually, *fortified* (because of high alcohol), rich *late harvest* (such as TBA or BA), or *ice wine* can work well.

FIGURE 13–6 Crème brulée

(Edward Allwright © Dorling Kindersley)

2. Ice cream typically is difficult to match, because the cold temperature can dull the body of most wines, leaving them tasting thin and watery. Pairing *fortified* wines (because of their density and sweetness), such as a PX Oloroso Sherry, or *Enrichment* wines (because of their carbonation), such as Moscato or Prosecco, can work fine.

5. Pastry, Ice Cream, and Cookie-Based Desserts

Baklava, Cookies (Macaroons, Madeleines, Ladyfingers), Cakes (Sponge Cake, Pound Cake, Angel Food Cake), and Banana Bread

1. The lighter airiness (yet sweetness) of cakes and ladyfingers can pair well with cool-climate dessert wines such as *ice wine* or *late harvest* and *enrichment* wines.
2. *Late harvest* and *rot wines* pair well with buttery, honeyed, or flaky pastries or cookies.
3. Spiced pastries or cookies can work well with *dried grape*, *late harvest*, or *rot* wines.

A CLOSER LOOK AT CHOCOLATE

Chocolate parallels wine in that it is a product of its origin and production process. There are hundreds of various flavors that can be associated with chocolate, which makes it quite a complex substance; and, like wine grapes, cacao beans draw aromas and nuances from the environment in which they grow. The pairing of chocolate and wine has always been thought of as one of the most sensual and hedonistic combinations; however, it has also been one of the least understood. The pairing of the two can become a bit easier with an understanding of the different kinds of chocolate available.

Production Process

Chocolate is made primarily of cocoa solids and cocoa fat derived from the *cacao* (kah-COW) tree, which grows in tropical environments near the equator in such places as Africa and South America. The cacao tree produces large pineapple-sized pods that contain cacao beans, which ultimately become the major ingredient in chocolate. The beans are hulled from the pod and allowed to ferment and dry for several days, during which time they become brown and rich, and are then often called cocoa beans.

Next, the cocoa beans are winnowed, a process in which they are roasted to cause the hard outer shell to crack and be separated from its interior known as the cocoa nib. The cocoa nibs contain both cocoa butter (a fat that provides melting properties in chocolate) and cocoa solids (to provide a rich chocolate flavor).

Then the cocoa nibs are placed in grinders to yield a thick, chocolate paste called the chocolate liquor. The liquor is combined with varying amounts of sugar; sometimes additional cocoa butter and milk are blended in, depending on the style of chocolate.

Now the chocolate proceeds to the conching phase of production, in which a series of heavy rollers grind the chocolate particles to a particular size that will largely influence the smoothness and mouth-feel of the chocolate. Smaller ground particles will result in a smoother chocolate, and a larger grind of particles will yield a grittier texture. The more expensive chocolates tend to be processed longer and thus have a smoother texture and feel on the tongue, whereas inexpensive, lower quality chocolates have detectable grittiness. Finally, the chocolate is tempered to give it a shiny, glossy appearance, and then molded into particular shapes.

FIGURE 13–7 Chocolate soufflé

(Sparky/Getty Images Inc.-Image Bank)

Type and Styles of Chocolate
White   Milk   Semi Sweet/   Dark   Unsweetened Chocolate Chocolate Bittersweet Chocolate Chocolate Chocolate
◄————————————————————►
Level of cocoa solids and cocoa **LOWER**   **HIGHER**
◄————————————————————►
Level of sugar and other ingredients **MORE**   **LESS**

The Meaning of the Cocoa or Cacao Percentage

Most high-quality chocolate manufacturers label their products with a *cocoa* or *cacao percentage*. This number refers to a combined amount of chocolate liquor and cocoa butter, with the remaining percentage making up everything else within the chocolate product. The cocoa percentage (which generally can range from 30% to 100%) represents the amount of ingredients directly derived from the cacao bean. Higher cacao percentages generally result in less sweet, slightly bitter, more intense chocolate flavor. In contrast, a lower cacao percentage indicates a chocolate with a higher proportion of other ingredients, such as sugar, milk, and vanilla, added to yield a lighter chocolate flavor.

Types and Styles of Chocolate

Many consumers believe that the cocoa percentage is a rating of quality, but it should be used instead as a general definition of the chocolate type and style. For example, 72% cocoa bittersweet has more cocoa and less sugar than 64% cocoa semi-sweet chocolate.

Dark chocolate offers unique and intense flavor aspects, but milk chocolate offers undertones of alternative flavor and a creamier mouth-feel. Which chocolate type is better is a matter of personal preference. But within each type, there are varying levels of cocoa percentages and flavors that alter the style. Figure 13–7 shows a chocolate soufflé.

The finest dark chocolate is referred to as couvertures (coov-er-CHURE), which is rich in cocoa butter and cocoa solids. Popular brands of couverture often used by pastry chefs and sold in gourmet and specialty food stores include *Valrhona* (French); *Scharffen Berger* (Californian); *Lindt, Callebaut,* and *Felchlin* (Felk-LIN) (Swiss); and *Guittard* (American). They all contain varying percentages of cacao with high amounts of cocoa butter, which allows the chocolate to melt at mouth temperature and the rich chocolate flavor to slowly be released during eating.

Unsweetened Chocolate—Unsweetened is pure chocolate liquor (also known as bitter or baking chocolate). It is unadulterated chocolate: The pure, ground, roasted chocolate beans impart a strong, deep chocolate flavor.

With the addition of sugar, unsweetened chocolate is used as the base for cakes, brownies, confections, and cookies.

Dark Chocolate—The term *dark chocolate* is used to describe any unsweetened or slightly sweetened chocolate that does not contain milk solids. The amount of sugar often is not regulated or is inconsistent from country to country. What one manufacturer calls *bittersweet* another manufacturer may call *semi-sweet*. If a company produces both bitter and semi-sweet, the bitter chocolate generally has a stronger chocolate flavor and the semi-sweet chocolate generally contains more sugar than the bittersweet.

Dark chocolate typically contains no less than 40% chocolate liquor (and often around 60% or higher), cocoa butter, some sugar, and, sometimes, vanilla. The higher the combined chocolate liquor and cocoa butter, the less sugar and more intense chocolate flavor will result.

Milk Chocolate—Milk chocolate is much sweeter and creamier and has a silkier taste and texture than dark chocolate. It is made from the same ingredients as dark chocolate, chocolate liquor, and cocoa butter, but has the addition of milk solids. The milk solids reduce the cocoa content a bit. Milk chocolate often has 38% cocoa content.

White Chocolate—White chocolate is mellow and buttery because it contains about 33% cocoa butter, with the rest made up of sugar, milk solids, and vanilla. White chocolate is different from dark or milk chocolate in that it does not contain cocoa solids.

FIGURE 13–8 Chocolate cookies

(© Dorling Kindersley)

Pairing Wine and Chocolate

The idea in matching chocolate to wine is to create a harmony that elevates both food and drink to the next level of taste experience. Sometimes the wine may take center stage; other times the chocolate may do so. In the ideal pairing, both wine and chocolate co-exist and create a more pleasant, hedonistic whole than each part alone. Through understanding the basics of chocolate, we can more easily understand how to pair the correct style of wine with the appropriate type of chocolate.

Most chocolate desserts are sweet—particularly, white and milk chocolate options. The wine must be gutsy enough (in terms of sugar content, alcohol, body, or fruit forwardness) to stand up to these types of chocolate. If the chocolate is sweeter than the wine, the fruit flavors of the wine will not come through. If the chocolate is too dry and the wine is too sweet, then the two will clash. Figure 13–8 shows chocolate cookies.

Wine must always taste as sweet or as fruity as its accompanying dessert, or it will fail to measure up. The drier and more intense the chocolate, the drier the wine will need to be. The sweeter the chocolate, the more fruit or sweetness will be needed in the wine. Use the flavors and dryness levels in the chocolate and the wine to bridge the pairing successfully. Pair a wine that is as sweet as or sweeter than the chocolate.

Characteristics of dark chocolate are an intense cocoa aroma, hints of bitterness, low sugar content (but not too low), slight acidity, tannins, and a persistence of flavors. Dark chocolate can work well with a young, fruity red wine. The dryness of a wine should balance the dryness of the chocolate.

Suggested Wines with Dark Chocolate—Dark chocolate (around 70%–100% cocoa) can pair well with big, bold, and dry wines such as Cabernet Sauvignon, Shiraz, Merlot, and Zinfandel. Since dark or bittersweet chocolate is intense and dry, it needs a wine that offers a dry sensation, with aroma and flavor components of roasted, smoke, spice, and chocolate or cocoa notes.

Suggested Wines with Milk Chocolate—Desserts based on milk chocolate (around 50%–69% cocoa) and any combination of caramel, malt, or toffee can pair well with fruit-forward Pinot Noir (from Sonoma Coast or New Zealand) or Merlot (from Washington State). Also, red-based enrichment wines such as Brachetto or sparkling Shiraz can work extremely well.

Suggested Wines with White Chocolate—Late harvest (such as Riesling or Gewürztraminer), rot, ice wine, and enrichment wines (such as Asti, Prosecco, or Moscato d'Asti) go well with white chocolate-based desserts.

NECTAR: DESSERT WINES

NAME: _____ Score out of 20 points_____.

Use these questions to test your knowledge and understanding of the concepts presented in the chapter.

I. MULTIPLE CHOICE: Select the best possible answer from the options available.

1. A good general guideline to follow when pairing wines with items on a food menu is to

   a. put sweet wines before dry wines.

   b. go from red to white wines.

   c. go from light- to full-bodied wines.

   d. go from full- to light-bodied wines.

2. The first and foremost principle to follow when matching wine and food is to

   a. compare or contrast flavors.

   b. consider the mood, ambience, and occasion.

   c. contrast acidity with fat.

   d. balance the weight and intensity of both the wine and the food.

3. Nut-based desserts include

   a. crème brulée.

   b. chocolate truffles.

   c. blueberry cobbler.

   d. pecan pie.

4. Chocolate-based desserts include

   a. crème brulée.

   b. chocolate truffles.

   c. blueberry cobbler.

   d. pecan pie.

5. Fruit-based desserts include

   a. crème brulée.

   b. chocolate truffles.

   c. blueberry cobbler.

   d. pecan pie.

6. *Botrytis cinerea* is also known as

   a. a sparkling wine.

   b. ice wine.

   c. noble rot.

   d. both b and c.

7. Which item is *not* associated with Eiswein (ice wine)?

   a. The grapes are frozen.

   b. an extremely late harvest wine

   c. dry-tasting dessert wine

   d. produced in Canada

8. Dark and milk chocolate pairs best with

   a. rot wines.

   b. ice wines.

   c. fortified wines.

   d. dried grape wines.

9. Dark chocolate can pair well with

   a. white wine.

   b. red wine.

   c. ice wine.

   d. none of the above.

10. White chocolate pairs best with

   a. ice wine.

   b. rot wines.

   c. enrichment wines (sweet sparkling).

   d. all of the above.

II. TRUE / FALSE: Circle the best possible answer.

11. Dessert wines are commonly consumed before and during the meal. **True / False**

12. Vin Doux Naturels are fortified wines that come from France. **True / False**

13. When making a dessert wine in cold climates, grapes can be allowed to be dried in order to heighten sugar content and flavor concentration. **True / False**

14. Pastries and cookies can pair well with fortified wines such as Port and Madeira. **True / False**

15. Vin Santo is an example of a famous dried grape wine found largely in Tuscany, Italy. **True / False**

16. Nut-based desserts match well with wines that have an oxidative quality. **True / False**

III. SHORT-ANSWER ESSAY / DISCUSSION QUESTIONS: Use a separate sheet of paper if necessary.

17. What is the number-one principle to consider when pairing desserts with dessert wine?

18. List the six methods used to produce a dessert wine. List the five dessert categories.

19. List one typical dessert wine that might be appropriate for each dessert category.

20. What kind of weather is needed for *Botrytis* to grow on the surface of a grape and penetrate the skin, enabling water to evaporate during a certain period?

Unit 6
WINE MANAGEMENT

"If you can't describe what you are doing as a process,
you don't know what you are doing."
—W. Edwards Deming

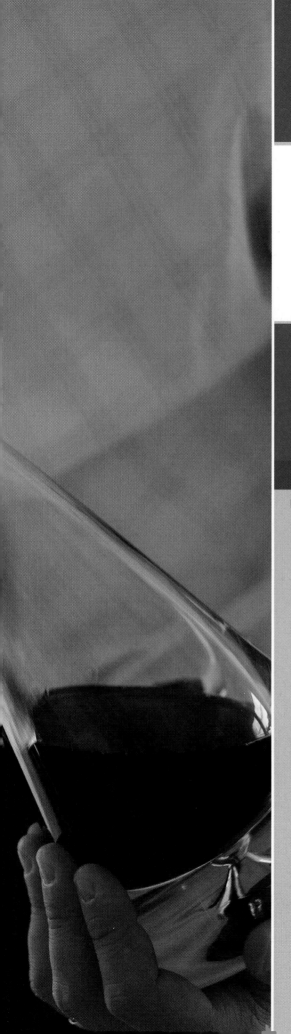

14

The Flow of Wine

In order to effectively manage beverages, the beverage manager must stimulate revenue and control expenses. Therefore, it is imperative that the manager clearly understand the concept, or image, of the establishment.

LEARNING OBJECTIVES

Upon completion of this chapter, the learner will be able to:

- Understand the role of the beverage manager throughout the flow of food.
- Describe some techniques that can influence wine sales in a restaurant or retail store.
- Cost-out wine by the case and by the glass.
- Identify procedures associated with the proper cellaring of wines for both short and long term.
- Recognize the stages of alcohol consumption on the basis of the behavioral signs of the consumer.
- Recall intervention techniques at each stage of alcohol consumption.
- Identify different methods of merchandising wine in a beverage establishment.
- Perform key steps and etiquette in table wine service.
- Perform key steps and etiquette in sparkling wine service.

THE WINE MANAGER

POTENTIAL RESPONSIBILITIES INVOLVED IN MANAGING BEVERAGES

- Source out beverages and related products appropriate for the restaurant concept.
- Order wine and related products in the appropriate quantity.
- Receive products; compare the physical shipment against the invoice and purchase order.
- Maintain the organization of the beverages within selected storage areas.
- Communicate and coordinate with the chef about wine and food pairings.
- Train the staff in product knowledge, wine and food pairing, and service etiquette.
- Design and maintain beverage menus.
- Cost-out and set beverage selling prices.
- Suggest appropriate wine and food pairings to both service staff and consumers.
- Market beverages and promotions within the restaurant.
- Sell, open, and serve wine tableside.

In every beverage establishment, whether restaurant or retail store, there is accountability for the success or failure of the beverage program. The accountable party, whether one individual or a group of people, may be entirely responsible for the revenue and cost control of beverages, as a primary responsibility of the job; or the role may be part of the accountable party's secondary duties, while the principal duties involve managing the entire operation. The beverage manager's title may be bar manager, assistant manager, or even *sommelier* (saw-muh-LYAY). Whatever the designated title, the person or persons responsible for managing beverages will influence revenues, expenses, and, ultimately, profit or loss in the restaurant or retail store.

The Role of the Sommelier

The sommelier, or wine steward, is a trained professional who specializes in all aspects of wine service and, in some cases, beer, spirits, water, and even cigar service. Sommeliers are often associated with high-end fine-dining restaurants, where they contribute value and prestige to the consumers' wine purchases. The title of *sommelier* is more recently evolving to include individuals managing wine beyond the scope of a restaurant setting. Wine shops and grocery stores are incorporating sommeliers into key buying and selling positions as a way to provide a competitive point of difference for their establishments.

INFLUENCING REVENUE AND EXPENSES

In order to effectively manage beverages, the beverage manager must stimulate revenue and control expenses. Therefore, it is imperative that the manager clearly understand the *concept*, or image, of the beverage establishment. This concept is a combination of various factors that form the character and uniqueness of a particular type of business. Restaurant and retail owners can vary the combinations of these factors in order to tailor the needs to particular situations.

The most significant and defining factors that characterize a concept include

1. creating a clear vision and mission of the concept,
2. identifying a cuisine (having a food and/or beverage focus),
3. recognizing target customers who desire the cuisine,
4. determining a suitable location to obtain the target customers,
5. designing an atmosphere that reflects the needs of the target customers, and
6. providing a level and type of service that coordinates with the other components of the concept.

1. The Vision and Mission

Who You Are

The vision and mission of an organization can provide guidance and direction. A vision and mission consist of a set of values that help an organization to align its actions with its purpose. The vision identifies *who the establishment strives to be*, and the mission describes *how the establishment will get there*. The vision and mission work together to demonstrate the unique purpose of the organization and to capture the qualities that are most desired in the beverage establishment.

2. The Menu

What Will Be Sold

The menu is the foundation on which the other components of the concept are based. The beverage menu is just as integral to the success of an establishment as the food menu (and even more important in the case of a wine bar or wine store). The beverage and food menus should be designed to enhance one another.

The first task before designing a menu is to determine the type of *cuisine* the concept will feature. The cuisine, or menu focus, is the main factor that drives revenue. Cuisines and *food types* vary dramatically throughout the United States, whether in some of Chicago's 9,000-plus restaurants or the 936,000 food service establishments throughout the rest of the nation. From coast to coast, the options for different food and cuisine are endless, ranging from American regional to Tex-Mex. In all of these restaurants, beverages (whether wine, beer, or spirits) will play either a starring or a supporting role for the type of food cuisine.

Clearly, according to the definition, a cuisine (on the left hand column box) defines the type of food, but here we expand the notion to include wine as a food item. After all, wine does begin its life as an agricultural product.

When a concept is in the process of defining a particular cuisine type, it is advantageous also to define a corresponding beverage focus. In food establishments, beverages generally account for approximately 25%–35% of revenue, yet contribute to a greater percentage of profit than food does.

A restaurant's menu can range from limited food types, to a 15-course *degustation* chef's menu at some ultra-high-end establishments, to an *a la carte* menu with over 200 items at some chain-type restaurants. Some wine lists offer a similar range, from a modest wine list of four options to a multipage booklet of 1,800 different selections. Wine lists must provide choices that complement the food focus and cuisine of the establishment, as well as the price points of the varying clientele.

A cuisine is a significant factor influencing the composition of the beverage menu (which is discussed in greater detail in Chapter 15, "Developing a Wine Menu").

3. The Customer

Who Will Buy It?

Every restaurant seeks to identify and serve a specific target market, or group of people that support the concept. Market research is exhaustively done to determine who the customers might be and what they prefer in terms of food, beverages, service, price point, and so on. By analyzing the *trading area* (the area that the majority of customers will come from), an establishment can focus on the needs and expectations of the desired market segment.

To identify their similarities and differences, customer groups often are grouped or identified according to a combination of demographics and psychographics as listed on the left.

Knowing demographics and psychographics information allows an operation to more effectively understand the desired target markets. This enables the beverage manager to make more intelligent decisions regarding the vision and mission of the concept. Then the manager can select the appropriate type and styles of beverages, food, price point, and level and type of service.

"manner of preparing food: style of cooking" Merriam Webster

DEMOGRAPHICS

Demographics consist of statistical characteristics of people in specific geographic areas. Individuals concentrated in a given area may be grouped on the basis of age, gender, income level, marital status, traveling distance to and from work, type of household, employment, and so on. This information can be even further divided according to zip codes. Groupings of individuals may even be given titles to recognize and differentiate them from other groups. For example, *baby boomers* are generally identified as those born between 1946 and 1964 and represent about 40% of the population.

PSYCHOGRAPHICS

Psychographics are consumer characteristics that are based on people's lifestyles. Psychographics depict motivations of consumer behavior and include areas such as personality types, habits, leisure activities, ideologies, values, beliefs, and attitudes. A particular group may be lumped together because of their beliefs. For example, *achievers* have many wants and needs and are dynamic in the marketplace. Their image is vital to them, and they favor established, prestige products and services that demonstrate achievement to their peers.

4. The Location

Where It Will Be Sold

All restaurants attract customers from what is known as a *trading area*. This is the area around an establishment from which the vast majority of customers (or revenue) probably will derive from. The trading area encompasses a radius surrounding the location of the establishment that can range from a single building to a few blocks to several miles to across the country, depending on the type of concept.

Demand generators are places or events that cause people to be in close proximity to a particular establishment. When a demand generator causes a concentration of large groups of people (whether for single events or consistently throughout a day), a *population center* is created. Population centers may contain groupings of potential customers and include train stations, bus stops, concert venues, shopping malls, strip malls, the downtown of a city and convention center, and other places.

The characteristics of trading areas and the type of demand generators will likely define the type of customer who will be inclined to visit a venue with a particular concept. One type of trading area and demand generator may bring customers who desire a relaxed, informal atmosphere and drinking experience, while another type may encourage more sophisticated consumers and a more formal atmosphere.

5. The Atmosphere

The Way It Looks Where It Is Served

The atmosphere is a defining element in the creation of a beverage concept. The environment communicates and attracts a particular type of customer on the basis of the design, style, and impression of the atmosphere. The kind of environment created can determine whether the concept will be formal or informal, festive or intimate, bright or dim. Customers often mirror a style or feel based according to who they are and what they are seeking. They want to feel connected to the environment they are choosing to spend time in.

Several aspects can be used to create the atmosphere, such as the pictures, lighting, music, drapes, flooring, and tablecloths. Some operations have a noisy, energetic environment that targets younger consumers, whereas others offer a quiet dining environment designed to appeal to more mature patrons. Therefore, understanding the needs and motivations of the market segment is indispensable in creating the type of environment and concept appropriate for the target market.

6. The Service

How It Will Be Served

The level and type of service often are decided simultaneously while the other factors that define the concept are designed. If owners have decided to create a formal, fine-dining operation, then the level and type of service should adhere and be appropriate to that vision.

There are several broad types of service formats that can be modified with different levels of formality to fit an individual establishment. Consider the following basic styles of service:

1. **Counter/Self Service**—This extremely informal type of service requires customers to place and pick up their own orders. Many *quick casual* restaurants, such as Noodles & Company and Go Roma, incorporate this type of service format along with offering a modest selection of wine with their food options.

2. **Bar Service**—Bar service requires customers to sit at a counter to place an order, which a server or bartender will then bring to them. This type of service is somewhat informal and casual.

3. **American/Table Service**—This is one of the most common types of service formats. It allows customers to be seated and communicate an order to a waitperson. The order is then prepared and delivered to the seated customer. This type of service can be formal, semi-formal, or casual.

4. **French/Tableside Service**—French service involves partially preparing food in the kitchen, while final preparation and serving are completed tableside on a *guéridon* (gay-ree-DOHN), or mobile cart. This type of service is formal and is often combined with other service styles. Some high-end fine-dining restaurants have incorporated this type of service, with certain dishes such as caesar salad or bananas foster prepared tableside for presentation purposes.

5. **Family Style Service**—Family style service involves bringing food to the dining table on platters and bowls. The customers will then serve themselves and then pass the food around the table. This type of service is informal and sometimes is offered in combination with American/table style service. Restaurants such as Maggiano's Little Italy have experienced success with this format.

The type of service can dictate a level of formality that will match a particular beverage menu and the various other factors that form the foundation of the concept.

The Flow of Wine

The *flow of wine* is the path that wine travel throughout the establishment. This path consists of several *control points* that can identify where there is a possibility of something going wrong, through lack of control. The control points can identify an area that may result in increased expenses and a loss of revenue. Because of these concerns, it is important to create controls for each control point, building what is known as a *control system*.

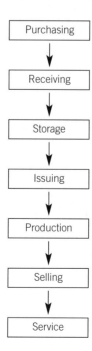

Control systems are a collection of all the *standard operating procedures* (SOPs) and measures used in a business. Successful cost control will depend largely on how well the control systems are applied throughout the flow of wine. When control systems are created, some considerations for effective results include cost effectiveness, ease of implementation and monitoring, consistency of results, and getting a return on investment.

To ensure success in any control system, four standard steps should be established throughout the flow of beverages:

1. **Create** SOPs for each area within the flow of wine. SOPs act as a means of communication of expectations between management and the line-level employees as they assist with maintaining the level of quality and encourage a consistent product and service. SOPs are needed to begin any kind of a training program and then are used as an evaluation tool by comparing the actual employee performance against them.

2. **Train** related individuals in SOPs. Establishing clearly defined and measurable learning objectives is necessary to have a quality training approach. Learning objectives are statements that describe what the learner should be able to do upon completion of training.

3. **Monitor** performance against the SOPs. Monitoring allows management to identify any gaps between communication with the employees and their performance.

   There are two methods of monitoring employee performance: direct and indirect. Direct monitoring involves management practicing *management by walking around* (or MBWA) to directly observe employee performance. Indirect monitoring involves management using indirect observation through the feedback of others, web-cam security, secret shoppers, and so on.

4. **Coach** by taking appropriate actions to correct deviations from the SOPs. An effective manager acts to quickly and consistently adjust employee performance when SOPs are not being met.

The Sand Theory

An interesting analogy known as the *sand theory* is that food and beverage products are like sand, and a manager's hands are like the efforts, techniques, and procedures (or control systems) used to manage the sand. Imagine picking up sand with a hand that has fingers spread apart. Most of the sand would fall through the hand, and very little sand would remain in the hand. This represents lack of, or low control of, products. By contrast, imagine a hand scooping up sand with fingers tightly held together. Most of the sand would remain in the hand. Great effort was exerted to maintain total control of the sand. This represents a high control of products.

Both approaches of picking up sand represent the extremes of exercising management control. Which one is the correct approach? There is no right or wrong answer, but merely a perspective to determine which would be appropriate for any particular establishment. In the first example, little effort is expended, but a higher loss of inventory occurs. The second approach exercises tight control through a constant time-consuming effort to control every product in inventory. Perhaps the best approach is one that can allow greater control over the products that are most susceptible to theft, rather than over all products.

PURCHASING CONTROL POINT

Purchasing is a generic term used to indicate the process of getting the appropriate products desired by the establishment. Three other terms used in discussing or performing purchasing responsibilities are *selection, sourcing,* and *procurement,* all of which play an important role in the purchasing process.

Selection

Purchasing involves making a selection regarding the kinds and types of beverages that are appropriate for a beverage concept. It entails choosing among alternatives such as New Zealand Sauvignon Blanc versus French Sauvignon Blanc. Most distributors provide wine samples and tasting notes in order to assist the buyer in making the selection. Another method that is helpful in the selection process is to attend distributor/producer trade tastings, which are available yearly in most larger cities throughout the United States.

Sourcing

The sourcing of alcoholic beverages can be somewhat challenging; certainly, it is not as easy as ordering food products. In most states, the laws allow middlemen the sole rights to a territory, with no form of competition. Therefore, the buyer will have to search various suppliers to obtain the desired products. For example, suppose that ABC distributor carries a particular brand of the New Zealand Sauvignon Blanc, and XYZ distributor carries a different one.

Procurement

Procurement is the process of ordering products and maintaining an orderly, systematic exchange between the buyer (the retailer) and the seller (the intermediary). Procurement defines (whether formally or informally) the procedures for obtaining the necessary products that were selected and sourced. For instance, deliveries may be made on Wednesday prior to 11:00 A.M., payment is by cash or check on delivery, and the manager must inspect and sign all invoices.

The Three-Tier Distribution System

Purchasing alcoholic beverages is a bit more complex than ordering other types of products. The sale of alcohol in the United States does not enjoy treatment under the free trade provisions of the U.S. Constitution. Instead, alcoholic beverages are governed by the 21st Amendment (the act that repealed *Prohibition*, established under the 18th Amendment), which gives each individual state the jurisdiction to regulate the sale and distribution of alcoholic beverages. Therefore, the distribution system consists of several levels, or tiers, that beverages are required to travel through. Overall, since state laws vary, the United States in effect has 50 distribution systems, each with its own rules and laws.

The *three-tier distribution system* consists of three levels: (1) primary sources (producers); (2) intermediaries (wholesalers and distributors); and (3) retailers (beverage establishments).

1. Primary → 2. Intermediaries → 3. Retailers

1. Primary Source—A winery is the primary source that employs a winemaker or vintner.

2. Intermediary—Intermediaries are also known as *middlemen* or *wholesalers*. One type of intermediary is an importer, who is legally licensed to bring alcohol into the United States. A distributor is the entity that transports alcohol from an importer or primary source for resale to a beverage establishment.

Throughout the United States, each state has some form of government control. The *Alcohol Beverage Commission*, or ABC, can exercise greater or lesser control, depending on the laws established within the individual state. The ABC (or some derivative) acts to control the licensing, purchasing, transportation, and sale of alcohol. Since the repeal of Prohibition, states have been allowed to classify themselves as either a *control state* or a *license state*.

In a control state, the state government actually sells some or all alcoholic beverages through its network of stores, thus exercising complete control over prices and distribution. Michigan, Oregon, and Maine are examples of control states.

Licensed states allow authorized wholesalers and distributors to sell alcoholic beverages directly to the retailer. California, Illinois, and Minnesota are among the licensed states.

In licensed states, *distributors/purveyors* are licensed companies in the business of transporting and selling products and/or services from importers to beverage establishments. Primary sources (producers) give the distributors *exclusive rights* to market and sell their products within a specified geographic area. In control states, the distributors/purveyors are government-operated entities.

3. Retailers—These are the beverage establishments that sell wine directly to consumers. The *selling* of alcohol can take place in an *on-premise* or *off-premise* type of beverage establishment.

On-premise is a term used to indicate a restaurant or bar. This is where the consumer will be coming to the premises to consume the alcoholic product(s).

Off-premise is a term used to indicate a grocery store or liquor store, where the customer will purchase alcohol and then consume the product off the premises.

Depending on the state, it is possible for individuals to personally order wine (often with some monetary limits) directly through primary sources. This process is known as *direct shipping*. However, licensed business establishments legally are not allowed to practice this method and must order directly through a middle tier.

Ordering Sizes for Wine

Wine is universally ordered by the case, which typically contains 12 bottles. Each bottle commonly holds 750 ml, equivalent to 25.4 oz per bottle. In some cases, an operation may choose to order an individual bottle of wine, or less than the standard 12 bottles per case. This means that a buyer is *breaking a case*. Most suppliers will charge a nominal fee (40 cents to $1.00 per bottle) if a full case has not been ordered.

Alternative bottle sizes have soared in popularity over the last decade. Half-bottles (375 ml, or 12.7 ounces) and splits (187 ml, or 6.3 ounces) have become more available, and these allow the wine consumer to purchase a good-quality wine without committing to a more expensive traditional-sized bottle.

Splits have become a great alternative for beverage establishments that may not offer a sparkling wine by the glass. Splits encourage the customer to buy a sparkling wine when the price of a full bottle may be cost prohibitive. Selling splits also lessens the cost to the restaurant if a sparkling-wine-by-the-glass program is not popular.

Ordering Techniques

There are several ordering techniques that are widely used in the beverage and food industry and that can be beneficial for a buyer to consider.

Optimal Ordering—Inventory control is vital to the success of any business. Therefore, ordering effectively can assist in maintaining optimal levels of inventory. There are two extremes of inventory control that may cause concern: The first is running out of product, referred to as *stock-outs*; and the second is having too much inventory, known as *surplus*. Either extreme jeopardize the success of any organization. Maintaining an optimal level of inventory is a constant effort that requires the full attention of the beverage manager.

When stock-outs occur, it is important to notify all service staff promptly in case a customer orders a stocked-out product. When stock-outs occur often, it reflects poorly on the buyer and may cause frustration on behalf of the staff; but more importantly, the repeat customer will experience repeated disappointment.

A surplus generally is caused by inadequate attention to ordering. Current on-hand inventory should always be known prior to placing an order for additional product. A constant surplus of items may lead to inadequate money management and cash-flow problems, which may destroy the financial stability of a company.

Purchase Order (PO)—A *purchase order* is a form that lists the products and quantities ordered, and possibly the current purchase price, with selected intermediaries. This form often is used to verbally place an order by telephone, fax the order, or send it electronically through the Internet. The purchase order creates a paper trail and communicates to other employees (both in house and out of house) the products that have been ordered and will be delivered to the establishment.

Opportunity Buys—An *opportunity buy* is a large quantity of a single product, or a large cumulative order, placed by the buyer, who is rewarded by the seller with some form of a discount. This type of strategic buying can enhance the operation because the purchaser buys a large quantity of product at a cheaper price.

Opportunity buys can also temporarily hurt the operation's bottom line because they require an outlay of money up front to pay for the product. Over the long term, the lower purchase price should offset the temporary cash outlay. This will cause the restaurant to have more money tied up in their inventory, but the savings per bottle can sometimes make it worth the effort.

Ordering Methods

Calculating the appropriate amount of product to order is a practice filled with a combination of both fluid and concrete factors. Some unknown elements include the peaks and valleys in business due to weather, time of year, neighborhood events, and so on. An important consideration that buyers can use as a basis for ordering is the *sales history*. Looking at historical information for previous trends in consumption, whether by day of the week or time of the year, can provide some solid data for future ordering references.

> **Par Stock** (amount needed until next delivery) − Subtract the **Inventory** (what is on the shelf)
>
> = **Amount to order**.
>
> **EXAMPLE**
>
> 24 bottles (ABC Chardonnay) − 12 bottles (ABC Chardonnay)
>
> = 12 bottles, or 1 case (ABC Chardonnay)

1. The *par stock order method* is used for determining what day-to-day quantities to order. This method is based on determining a pre-established par stock, which is the amount of product needed on hand to last until the next delivery date. Par stocks are created for each individual product within the restaurant and are based on sales histories. The par stock ordering method is not static, but fluid, and needs to be constantly reevaluated. During certain times of year, the par stock may need to be increased or decreased, as business volume dictates.

   In this example, the manager goes into the storage area to count the current on-hand inventory of wine. The quantities of bottles are summed up for each brand and written down on an inventory form to identify and document how much product is available. Then the buyer subtracts in predetermined par stock level from the current on-hand amount within the storage areas. The amount obtained is the quantity (in bottles) that needs to be ordered. Reality is not always as simple as the previous example (located in the left-hand side box) but it is possible to provide a guide.

2. The *other order approach* is another ordering method used for determining quantities to order for special one-time events such as banquets or catering. This technique is used when the number of guests is known. Once again, there is a certain level of subjectivity involved with using this approach to ordering. Deciding on the

$$\frac{\text{\# of Portions} \times \text{Portion Size}}{\text{Yield\%}}$$

= Quantity to Order

EXAMPLE

Step #1

$$\frac{100 \text{ portions} \times 5 \text{ oz portion}}{98\%}$$

(50 people with 2 drinks each)

= 510.2 ounces to order

Step #2

$$\frac{510.2 \text{ ounces (from answer in step \#1)}}{25.4 \text{ (amount of ounces in a standard bottle)}}$$

= 20.08 bottles, or 20 bottles.

The buyer may choose to purchase one full case plus eight additional bottles by breaking a case; or the buyer simply may order two full cases, yielding 24 bottles. Ordering the two cases allows the buyer to build in some inventory of extra bottles that can be used at other times if they are not consumed at the event they were intended for.

number of portions can be tricky, because no one will truly know how much a customer will drink at an event unless the drinks are actually restricted through a system of requiring chits or coins to obtain them. Yield is also subjective, because, ideally, the bartender will pour 100% of a product from the bottle into the glassware. However, allowing for spillage or overpouring assists in correctly moderating the amount to order.

Primary Factors That Influence the Frequency of Ordering

1. **Storage Space**—Storage space is usually limited for most organizations. Therefore, to maximize space, buyers may have to order smaller amounts of products more frequently. If an organization happens to have larger storage areas, some buyers will choose to take advantage of *opportunity buys*, in which they buy a larger amount of a single product to obtain a *volume discount*.

2. **Funds Available**—For control reasons, some organizations set price limits on the dollar limit of either single orders or total weekly orders on the basis of projected sales volume. This may be in order to adhere to certain budget or cash-flow constraints.

3. **Delivery Schedules**—Buyers are limited by the delivery schedule set by suppliers. Often, larger distributors deliver daily, except for Sundays, while smaller boutique-type distributors deliver only one or two days a week.

4. **Minimum-Order Requirements**—Distributors often set minimum-order requirements to discourage beverage establishments from ordering a single bottle or single case of product. Generally, requirements may be a $100.00 or a two-case minimum.

5. **Price Limits**—Beverage organizations may set maximum price limits per bottle of wine. This is a means of control which may limit buyers from purchasing or being tempted to purchase a high-priced product that may not fit the vision of the concept.

6. **Limited Supply**—Certain products have limited availability because they are either highly subject to seasonality, small-production items, or tightly allocated products for select sites in particular markets.

RECEIVING CONTROL POINT

Receiving is the act of inspecting products and either accepting or rejecting deliveries on the basis of whether they meet the predetermined set of standards. The criteria for standards are centered around the elements of quality, quantity, and price. The primary goal of receiving control is to ensure that deliveries received conform exactly to what was ordered from the previous purchasing control point.

Tools to Assist Us in Receiving Control Point

The primary purpose of standards in receiving is to ensure that the products ordered (quality, quantity, and price) conform exactly to what is delivered. All delivered products should be accompanied with an *invoice*. An invoice is a document that lists all products delivered, as well as the quantity, price, and, possibly, quality level of each product. An invoice alone cannot control received products; competent personnel and other elements in the receiving process are also necessary.

1. **Competent Personnel**—The personnel to receive alcohol products should be trained in the SOP's of the flow of beverages or, at the very least, in specific criteria associated with receiving.

2. **Appropriate Receiving Hours**—The best receiving hours are ones that are staggered (and not during peak service periods), to allow the order to be properly inspected and put securely away into storage areas.
3. **Invoice Receiving**—This is the most effective method of receiving control. It identifies where the physical products (the ones being delivered) are, compared against the invoice and the purchase order. It is not uncommon to have intentional or unintentional errors between the products ordered and what was actually delivered to the establishment. This process is vital to cost and product control.
4. **Daily Receiving Report**—The *daily receiving report* is a summary of all deliveries for the day. It is another form of paper trail that can assist with tracking orders if there is a future discrepancy.

The Receiving Process

1. **Once the delivery arrives, inspect products for quality, quantity, and price.**
   a. **Quality**—Ensure that the product ordered matches the product that is delivered in terms of producer, grape if appropriate, geographic region, level of quality rating, and vintage.
   b. **Quantity**—Ensure that the amount of the product as ordered on the purchase order (PO) matches the correct amount, not only on the invoice, but also on the physical product.
   c. **Price**—Ensure that the price stated either on the PO or supplier contact agreement matches the amount on the invoice.
2. **Acceptance or Rejection of Delivery**—Accepting or rejecting a product is not a simple black-and-white decision. If products do not meet the SOP's, reject the part of the order that is in question. When part of an order is rejected, it is vital that both the buyer and delivery driver initial the invoice. If a product is accepted that later turns out to be incorrect or not up to the SOP's, contact the salesperson immediately. Then, if merchandise is returned, ensure that the driver provides a credit memorandum when the product is removed from the premises.

STORAGE CONTROL POINT

Storage is the process of holding products under desirable conditions until the production and service control point. The main objectives of storage are to prevent loss of merchandise due to spoilage, theft, and pilferage. Storage management involves the active intention of maintaining (and in some cases, creating additional revenue from) the safe investment of the beverage operations, whether the stock being stored is a few cases of wine or a cellar containing 35,000 bottles. Keeping products safe from spoilage, theft, and pilferage, as well as maintaining the organization of product to allow for the efficient practice of conducting an inventory, are vital to the health of the business.

Managing the Storeroom

Optimal storage conditions entail that the items to be stored are protected from pilferage, theft, and inadequate environmental conditions that may cause spoilage or waste. Create the storage environment and cellar on the basis of the wine philosophy and the necessary specifics associated with the specific beverage establishment.

A constant concern in beverage establishments is *pilferage and theft*. Pilferage is often associated with inventory *shrinkage* by small-scale theft. However small, this type of theft can be damaging, particularly in the long term. For example, a bartender may drink a glass of wine while working and never pay for it. If the bartender does this during several shifts in a week over the course of months to years, the associated cost can be enormous.

Theft is predetermined and is considered large scale because of the greater cost associated with the loss of products. For example, employees may be giving away wine and not charging the customer. Or the employee may be charging the customer, but never ringing the sale into the cash register and then pocketing cash from the customer. Sometimes theft includes collusion, which may involve multiple individuals, perhaps a combination of various employees, employees and delivery drivers, or employees and customers. This approach to theft has become easier to carry out with the use of technology for text messaging, picture phones, and so on.

Solutions to Pilferage and Theft

Pilferage and theft are inevitable and probably never 100% stoppable. However, there are control measures that can be instituted to hinder the ease of execution and tame the temptation to behave in this inappropriate manner. Having the presence of an active management individual or team and practicing MBWA is important in keeping individuals honest and deterring bad motives. As discussed at the beginning of this chapter, setting up and implementing control systems throughout the flow of wine is important and can be helpful in reducing pilferage and theft.

Optimal Storage Conditions

To maintain optimal conditions, wine must be stored according to some basic guidelines. In rough order of importance, there are five primary ways that wine can be damaged as it is being stored: light, vibrations, temperature, humidity, and incorrect placement of products on the shelves.

Light—Ideally, wine should be stored in a dark location or, at the least, in minimal direct and indirect light. Over a period of prolonged exposure to light (weeks to months), chemical changes may occur and alter the aroma, flavor, and taste of wine.

Vibrations—Wine should be stored in a quiet location. Constant vibrations may have an effect by causing chemical changes that alter the aroma, flavor, and taste of the wine.

Temperature—Ideally, wine should be stored at a consistent temperature at a cool 55°F. Wine is relatively stable even if temperatures vary gradually within a small range. However, quick changes or prolonged warm temperatures may damage a wine. The temperature becomes more important the longer the wine will be stored. Wine evolves best at a consistent temperature between 55 and 65°F. The lower end of the temperature range slows down a wine's development, and the higher end speeds up development.

If wine is stored for a short period and used within a couple of months, then a room temperature of 72°F would be adequate. A basement, closet, refrigerator, or, even better, a wine cooler, will suffice, as long as it is away from extreme temperature swings.

Humidity—Humidity is an important consideration for wine that is sealed with a cork closure. Particularly in medium- to long-term storage situations, humidity may become a problem. A relatively high level of humidity of 70% would be best for wine storage. If wine is stored in an environment with lower humidity, there is a risk of corks drying out and allowing oxygen to enter and spoil the wine. If humidity levels are much higher than 70%, there are the risks of moldy cork and of the label on the bottle easily ripping or peeling away.

Placement—All wine that is closed through the use of a cork should be stored on its side or held upside down. This allows the cork to remain in contact with the wine and to maintain a moist, swollen state (forming a proper seal) at all times during storage. Wine stored in cold temperatures (that is, refrigerated) may survive unaffected while standing on its base for longer periods. For short-term storage (days to weeks), the cork won't dry out, but for medium- to long-term storage, placement of the wine on its base becomes more of a concern.

Inventory Management

Inventory management is vital to effective cost control. There are a few approaches that can be instituted based on the level of control and time commitment desired by the beverage manager. Each method involves conducting *physical inventories* (the counting and valuing of the beverage items in stock) on a regular basis.

Perpetual Inventory Method—The *perpetual inventory method* involves constantly recording the input of products in inventory from purchasing and the outputs of products being released or issued to production. The *IN's* and *OUT's* can be recorded manually on a simple clipboard (known as a bin card) that is maintained in the storage area, or the record keeping can be done electronically. Either method allows the beverage manager to know at any moment what the current inventory quantity and value are. Occasionally (maybe monthly), the inventory is manually counted to compare against the bin cards or electronic data in order to confirm accuracy.

Periodic Inventory Method—The *periodic inventory method* involves conducting a regular, or physical, inventory to communicate to the beverage manager the quantity and value of inventory. This method does not involve a constant tracking of inventory, as does the perpetual inventory method. By comparing inventory levels on a periodic basis (often monthly, but maybe weekly or even daily), the periodic method exercises less control, but consumes less time, than the perpetual method.

Hybrid Inventory Method—The *hybrid inventory method* combines the qualities of both of the alternative inventory techniques. The hybrid method conducts a perpetual up-to-date account of only the high-priced or most-sought-after inventory items that are susceptible to theft and pilferage. Then a periodic inventory is conducted for the other, less-susceptible items. The philosophy is to exercise greater control for the items that need control and apply less control on the items that do not need as much attention.

Hold or Drink

When is the optimal time to drink a wine? How long should wine be aged? The answers to these questions are baffling to the wine consumer, and the questions tend to be two of the most often-posed inquiries. Wine consumers have been led to believe that an older wine is always more precious and prestigious than a younger wine. Wine consumers have the mistaken belief that all wine is better with age, and that is simply not the case. Older is not necessarily better! Certainly, though, some wines may be aged and may improve dramatically with several years, and even decades, of aging.

The mechanics of aging can be somewhat complicated, because they are full of uncertainties and involve a lot of subjectivity. But all wine, just like food or even people, has a shelf life, and some wines are more perishable than others. Most wine is meant to be drunk at the moment of purchase or shortly thereafter. The peak time to drink a wine depends on many factors: grape variety, origin, grape growing practices, vintage, and so on. Some varietals just tend to be more age-able than others. A decision on whether or not wine should be cellared is based on wine type, wine quality, and personal preference. The wine purchaser will take into account the wine philosophy of the restaurant.

The reason that wine is aged is to allow the components of a wine (primarily acid, sugar, and tannin, but also alcohol and fruit) to assimilate and work together to create a complex, integrated wine. If wine is drunk too young or too old, the components can be off balance, yielding an angular, rough-tasting wine. Some defining components in a wine that assist in aging include tannin, sugar, alcohol, and acid.

Wine is a living, evolving product very much like an individual. A wine passes through its youth, adolescence, maturity, and, eventually, death. Ultimately, the goal is to know when the wine reaches its peak, which is when the components and molecules in the wine change to the correct degree to allow for the best, most enjoyable potential the wine can offer. For some wines, this could be a matter of months upon purchasing; for other wines, it could be a matter of decades. Just as individuals grow and change throughout their lives, changes in a wine occur until the wine is dead. Good cellar management means knowing when certain wines are ready to drink and which ones are likely to improve with age.

Several components contained in wine allow it to be aged. Tannins that are predominantly present in red wine are the primary reason these kinds of wine have the potential to age longer than white wine. During the aging process, tannin and color pigment precipitate (separate from the liquid) and form sediment, leaving a softer wine with greater complexity and, possibly, lighter color. This means that the wine will need to be decanted in order to remove sediment prior to service.

Effects of Oxygen on a Wine

Oxygen can be beneficial or disastrous to a wine, depending on how much oxygen the wine has been exposed to and for how long. As soon as a bottle is opened and exposed to oxygen, it begins to change. This change may be desirable or undesirable, intentional or unintentional. An entire range of chemical reactions occurs when a wine is exposed to the air, and the effects on wine can be categorized in two ways: through either *oxidation* or *aeration*.

1. **Oxidation**—Oxidation (or maderization) takes place when the wine is exposed to air for an extended period, causing certain components of the wine to change. When wine is exposed to air, it ages faster. If the wine is exposed too long, chemical changes cause the wine to be flawed or tainted. Occasionally, a bottle of wine will be opened that is *oxidized*. The effects of oxidation are generally considered undesirable and unintentional.

2. **Aeration**—Exposure to air can also be a positive influence. Through aeration, the wine breathes, a phenomenon that takes place when the volatile components of aroma and bouquet escape, either into the glass or into the air. Aeration is generally considered a desirable and intentional effect of oxygen exposure. The tannin, which, until this point, has acted as a preservative, now begins to soften, and the flavors and aromas are heightened. The benefits of aeration begin almost immediately and continue for hours.

If the wine philosophy dictates buying a certain quantity of wines for the purpose of *cellaring*, or aging in house, then proper storage is essential to protect the financial investment. Proper storage will allow the wine to mature properly, progressing in quality and value.

Tradition Associated with Red Wine

Tradition holds that red wine must *breathe* (or be aerated), or exposed to a small amount of oxygen before serving. Many wines are *tight*, or *closed* from their time in the bottle, and their aromas and flavors may not emerge immediately after the cork is pulled. The process of decanting helps to bring out the repressed flavor, which then evolves into a bouquet.

FIGURE 14–1 Decanting wine
(Ian O'Leary © Dorling Kindersley)

Young red wines seem to get the most benefit from breathing. An hour or two in the presence of air can give the impression of a slightly older, more complex wine. However, breathing too long will leave any wine tasting flat and as if it was beginning to turn sour. Very old wines are best opened just before drinking, as they can begin to *fall apart* almost immediately.

Very little reaction can occur on the square inch of surface exposed in the neck of an open wine bottle. To get the best effects of breathing, the wine needs more air. The fastest way to achieve this is through the *decanting* process (discussed in greater detail later in the selling and service control point subsection of this chapter). As the wine pours down the side of the decanter, it has plenty of chance to absorb oxygen, just as swirling the wine in the tasting glass helps to open up its aroma. (In fact, more *breathing* probably goes on in the glass than anywhere else.) It is safe to allow wine to breathe for an hour or two, though it is seldom necessary. Figure 14–1 illustrates the decanting process.

The decanter has another very important use, aside from allowing wines to breathe. Older red wines form sediment in the bottle. Decanting consists of slowly pouring the contents of a bottle of red wine into a carafe, while leaving the sediment at the bottom of the bottle. Classically, a candle (although any light source can work) is typically placed under the neck of the bottle to illuminate the contents to display any possible sediment. Figure 14–2 shows a wine decanter.

Cellar Management Philosophies

In cellar management, the type of establishment will largely determine the approach. Depending on the philosophy, the operation may purchase only wines that are ready to drink, buy only short-term-aging wines, or choose the opposite extreme of investing heavily in long-term-aging wines and storing them through the cellaring process.

Short-Term Aging (weeks to months)—These wines can be consumed at any time during a period of less than a year. The focus in short-term aging is on buying wines with a drink-it or sell-it-now philosophy. Occasionally, managers may purchase a volume order for the sake of gaining a discount. This approach results in a larger-than-normal quantity of wine sitting in storage for a short time.

Intermediate Aging (months to years)—These wines are consumed in a period of between one and three years. They have been moderately aged, and the wait will be rewarded by the components (acid, tannin, alcohol, and fruit) becoming more subtle; at the same time, the wine becomes more complex and refined through the cellaring process.

Long-Term Aging (years)—These wines are consumed after a period of three years or more of cellaring. Long-term-aged wines are from the best grapes and the best vintages

FIGURE 14–2 Wine decanter
(Bill Deering/Getty Images, Inc./Taxi)

The Flow of Wine **271**

that have the greatest aging potential. These wines need long aging in order for their personalities to truly be exposed. Optimal environmental conditions are needed to allow the wine to undergo its chemical and physical changes slowly and undisturbed. If stored properly and opened at their peak, these wines will have appreciated in value. It is possible for wine stores or restaurants to purchase *pre-aged* wines from someone or somewhere else, but the practice comes with a cost.

ISSUING CONTROL POINT

Issuing is the process of transferring products from storage areas to production. The issuing control point involves two elements: (1) the physical movement, and (2) the record-keeping aspect. The issuing control point is important, as it ensures a safe passage from one point to another and also acts as a means of inventory and financial accountability to the correct department within the operation.

Primary Objectives of Issuing—The main objectives are to ensure the appropriate release of products from inventory and to prevent the misuse of products from storage to production/service areas.

Tools to Assist in the Issuing Control Point

Requisition—A *requisition* is a form that is used in high-volume establishments (such as casinos, race tracks, hotels, and mega restaurants) in order to establish greater control. An employee who needs a particular type and quantity of product from the secured and locked storage area completes this form. Establishments that require this form use it to create a paper trail when service stations need to be stocked for each shift or day of production.

Transfers—Establishments may also require requisitions or other forms when beverage products need to be *transferred* between production areas. For example, suppose that the kitchen is making a sauce that requires a particular wine. The kitchen manager or other entitled employee will fill out an *intra-unit transfer* that documents the product. The product will be used in the kitchen, and the product cost will be moved and assessed to the kitchen. This process assists not only with accountability of product, but also with financial accuracy.

PRODUCTION CONTROL POINT

Production is the process of getting products ready to be sold and served to a customer. The objective of production is to ensure that all portions of any given beverage are identical to all other portions of the same item. This control point is important for both customer perception and cost control measures, and in order ultimately to set an appropriate selling price to create revenue.

Standards and Procedures in Production

For control and consistency purposes, it is necessary to develop standards and procedures for setting a *standard portion size*. Wine often is quantified according to volume. For example, the portion size at restaurant ABC is a 5-oz pour, meaning that each customer who orders a glass of wine receives a five-ounce portion. Quantities are stipulated in order to guard against excessive costs. Rarely do servers or bartenders measure the exact volume of wine when pouring a glass. However, the type and size of glassware are used as the means for obtaining a close approximation of the desired standard portion size. Service staff are trained to pour wine to *fill to the level* of some imaginary line on the glassware. With practice, it is possible to estimate pouring volume with surprising accuracy.

Once portion size standards have been determined, the customer is assured a drink of consistent quantity and quality each time he or she orders. Having a reliable standardized portion size leads to consistent costing for the establishment, or a *standard portion cost*—the dollar amount that a standard portion should cost each time it is served. Operating according to a standard portion cost is vital to cost control and achieving maximum revenue.

As Purchased (AP) versus Edible Portion (EP)

As purchased, or AP, is an indicator of the gross quantity of an item purchased "as is" from the supplier. It is the quantity of product before being opened, or poured, or otherwise manipulated within the beverage establishment. *Edible portion,* or EP, is an indicator of the amount or cost of an item as it is served to a customer. This indicates that processing or loss most likely will occur or already has occurred. In most beverage establishments (when full bottles are sold), the AP is identical to the EP. There is no loss of product quantity or value when a customer purchases an entire bottle. However, there often is a small degree of loss associated with pouring wine by the glass. Portion sizes may not be always 100% accurate, as some portions are a bit over and others a bit under. It is likely that the yield of actual, sellable product quantity is 95%–97% of the original 100% quantity.

COSTING-OUT WINE

The ultimate goal of *costing-out* beverages is to determine an appropriate *selling price*, or SP. The person pricing the wine assumes that bartenders and servers maintain the defined portion size, which should guarantee a portion cost that will result in determining an accurate selling price. If the portion size for a glass of ABC Chardonnay is five ounces and the portion cost yields $2.00, then an accurate selling price can be determined with reliable projected revenue that is easier to establish.

Cost Out "By the Bottle" and "By the Glass"

Step 1. To cost out a bottle of wine, the first step is to divide the cost per case by the number of bottles within the case. This will yield the cost per bottle, or bottle cost, as show in Step #1 on the left.

Step 2. To cost out a bottle of wine by the glass, take the bottle cost (as determined in the previous step) and divide it by the number of ounces contained in the bottle. This yields the cost per ounce, as show in Step #2 on the left.

Step 3. Multiply the cost per ounce by the standard portion size. (The typical portion size is five ounces, but it may vary by establishment.) This yields the standardized portion cost, as show in Step #3 on the left.

Practice Problem

WINE—A case of ABC Cabernet Sauvignon costs $345.67. Determine the bottle cost and cost per glass.

PRICING WINE

Establishing an accurate selling price is essential to producing a reliable estimate of revenue. The typical markup for wine from the wholesaler is about 35 to 40 percent and an additional 25 to 50 percent from the retailer (grocery stores, wine stores). Many independent retailers use a higher markup than chain operations, because they tend to sell a lower volume.

Determining Bottle Cost

$$\frac{\text{Cost per Case}}{\text{\# of Bottles in Case}} = \frac{\text{Bottle}}{\text{Cost}}$$

Determining Cost Per Ounce

$$\frac{\text{Bottle Cost}}{\text{\# of Ounces in Bottle}} = \frac{\text{Cost Per}}{\text{Ounce}}$$

Determining Portion Cost

$$\frac{\text{Cost per oz} \times}{\text{Standard Portion Size}} = \frac{\text{Portion}}{\text{Cost}}$$

Step #1

$$\frac{\text{Cost per Case}}{\text{\# of Bottles in Case}} = \frac{\text{Bottle}}{\text{Cost}}$$

$$\frac{\$345.67}{12} = \$28.80$$

Step #2

$$\frac{\text{Bottle Cost}}{\text{\# of Ounces in Bottle}} = \frac{\text{Cost per}}{\text{Ounce}}$$

$$\frac{\$28.80}{25.4} = \$1.13$$

Step #3

$$\frac{\text{Cost per oz} \times}{\text{Standard Portion Size}} = \frac{\text{Portion}}{\text{Cost}}$$

$$\$1.13 \times 5 = \$5.65$$

Beverage establishments (restaurants, bars, and so on) are able to purchase wine at wholesale prices, which is typically 30 percent below retail cost. For example, a wine that sells in a grocery store for $15 would be available to a restaurant for about $10. Then beverage establishments mark the wine up anywhere from 100% to 400% of the cost of the original bottle price they paid.

There are several methods and approaches to pricing wine, but the concept of the establishment is the major determining factor that drives selling prices. The concept defines who the customers are, what kind of wine they may desire, and the price they may be willing to pay. Therefore, the appropriateness of the pricing should match that of the customer, location, and type of food being served.

Pricing Strategies for Wine

Wine pricing is tricky because wine is one of the few products sold in a restaurant for which there is (in some cases) a comparable retail price. A customer is likely to perceive low value if he or she sees a price of $36 for a bottle of XYZ wine in a beverage establishment and the customer recently saw the same XYZ wine for sale at the local grocery store for $12. Many restaurants harm their wine revenue by actually discouraging some consumers with wine prices that are too expensive. On the other hand, selling the wine at too low of a margin may harm the restaurant because of a lack of revenue to pay for the expenses associated with operating the establishment.

Selling Price − Bottle Cost
= Markup
$30.00 − $10.00 = $20.00

There are different pricing strategies and philosophies that argue as to what is an appropriate *markup*. Markup is the difference between the bottle cost and the selling price. A wine that costs $10 and is sold for $30 has a markup of $20 as shown in the box on left.

The markup amount is used to pay other expenses associated with operating the establishment and possibly becomes a small percentage of profit.

The Fixed Markup Method

(Cost × Markup%) + Cost
= List Price

Example:
($10.00 × 200%) + $10.00
= $30.00

The *fixed markup method* is one of the most common pricing techniques. It applies a simple markup calculated on a percentage of the cost of the wine. The method assigns a predetermined markup percentage to the cost of each bottle. For example, all wines will be marked up a flat 200%, regardless of purchase price. The fixed markup method can be employed at all price points on wine lists as shown on the left.

The Flexible Markup Method

☐ The highest markups are on the lowest-priced wines. Markups may be three to four times the cost of the bottle.
☐ The lowest markups are on the highest-priced wines. Markups may be one to two times the cost of the bottle.

The *flexible markup method* (sometimes known as the *sliding scale method*) is a pricing system which uses a variety of markups that are flexible, depending on the price point of the wine. The markup is increased as the cost of the wine is decreased, and the markup is reduced as the cost of the wine is increased as shown on the left.

Granted, a lower markup may not be desirable, but in the larger picture, the restaurant produces greater revenue in the transaction of selling more expensive wine. This increases sales of wine and also encourages guests to buy more expensive bottles, possibly more often.

Cost Percent Method

The *cost percent method* uses a ratio of money spent to desired money earned. A cost percent of 30% means that 30% of the money earned from a wine sale is spent on its purchase.

Therefore, the markup is 70% of the wine's cost, or 100% − 30% (Bottle cost) = 70% markup:

$$\frac{\text{Cost per Bottle}}{\text{Desired cost\%}} = \text{Selling Price}$$

$$\frac{\$10.20}{30\%} = \$34.00$$

SELLING AND SERVING CONTROL POINT

During the meal, there are multiple opportunities to sell wine and enhance each food course, increase check average, and ultimately increase the service staff gratuity and the restaurant's bottom line. The wine manager should create opportunities to sell wine with each point of service, from the moment a guest enters the establishment, throughout the meal service, until the guest walks out the door.

SERVING ALCOHOL SAFELY

The form of alcohol found in wine is *ethanol*. In moderate doses, ethanol may have beneficial effects, but in large amounts, it is toxic and can be fatal. Alcohol relaxes inhibitions, impairs judgment, slows reaction time, and impairs motor coordination. All of these signs of overindulgence of alcohol can be identified through the observation and interaction of an attentive service staff.

Serving alcohol goes hand in hand with being responsible, making intelligent and appropriate decisions, and showing reasonable care for the safety and welfare of the customer and the public at large. A beverage manager's responsibility is to protect the reputation of the establishment and to limit personal and organizational liability by reducing the number of injuries and deaths associated with serving alcohol beverages irresponsibly.

Dramshop Laws—*Dram* (drink) and *shop* (where the drink is sold and consumed) laws have become significantly more rigorously enforced over the past 20 years. Beverage establishments that serve alcohol can be held partially or fully responsible for the effects of that alcohol on any individual who has been harmed in connection with it. There are no cut-and-dry type of situations in the eyes of the law. However, if an establishment has shown negligence in serving alcohol, it (and the individuals who served the beverages) can be subject to severe legal and civil penalties. These can range from fines (hundreds and thousands of dollars) and jail time (months to years) to lawsuits (thousands to millions of dollars).

The composition of a drink that is served consists of the following formula: 12 oz beer = 5 oz wine = 1.25 oz 80 proof spirit = 1 oz 100 proof spirit. Spirits are rated according to this equation: PROOF / 2 = Percentage; for example, 80 proof / 2 = 40% alcohol.

For the alcohol equation, multiply the number of ounces consumed by the percentage of alcohol to calculate the pure alcohol content of a drink.

Upon consumption, alcohol is quickly absorbed from the stomach into the bloodstream. Alcohol's path through the body can affect brain function in less than three minutes. Small amounts are absorbed into the mouth and excreted in breath, sweat, and urine, but 95% of the alcohol is metabolized by the liver. Depending on body size, weight, and

ROUGH GUIDELINES OF PORTION SIZE AND ALCOHOL CONTENT

12 oz beer → 16 oz × 4% = .64 oz of pure alcohol (approximately ½ ounce)

5 oz glass of wine → 5 oz × 13% = .65 oz of pure alcohol (approximately ½ ounce)

A mixed drink with 1½ oz of 86 proof spirit → 1.25 oz × 43% = .54 oz of pure alcohol (approximately ½ ounce)

metabolic rate, the liver can metabolize alcohol at a constant rate of about one standard-sized drink (one-third to one-half ounce of alcohol) per hour. Any additional quantity consumed in that time frame causes a buildup, with intoxicating effects.

Blood alcohol content, or BAC, is a common means of measuring how much alcohol someone has consumed. A BAC of .10 is equivalent to 1 drop of alcohol in 1,000 drops of blood. If a person's BAC rises to .30, there is a high risk of coma, and a BAC of .40 can be fatal.

Factors That Affect a Person's BAC

Factors that affect alcohol absorption include the amount consumed, the time taken to consume the alcohol, the type of food eaten with the alcohol (fatty, high protein, and so on), carbonation of the alcoholic beverage, and the body size of the individual drinker. Other factors that can cause rapid or erratic absorption are stress and depression, dieting, fatigue, altitude, tolerance, and medications.

Body size is one of the more influential factors that affect a person's individual blood alcohol content.

This information is only an approximate guideline and should not be used for legal advice.

Reading the Guest

Reading the guest involves recognizing behavior signs caused by the effects of alcohol. The process is expected to be carried out by service staff and goes along with responsible serving of alcohol. Identifying stages of behavior allows servers and bartenders to make a determination of the point at which the customer has had enough. The signs are categorized according to the lights associated at an intersection. Green lights mean "Go"; yellow lights mean "Slow down"; and red lights mean "Stop."

In the GREEN, the guest is relaxed, comfortable, and talkative.
Note: Servers could offer alcoholic beverages, food, other beverages, upsell, and count drinks.

In the YELLOW, the guest is talkative or laughing louder than normal, arguing, antagonizing, or careless with money.
Note: Servers should not avoid the guest, but offer water and high-protein food and, possibly, delay beverage service. Ensure that the guest does not reach the red level.

In the RED, the guest is making irrational statements, stumbling or falling down, or unable to sit up straight. Figure 14–3 is a visual of the stoplight approach to alcohol safety.
Note: Servers should stop serving alcoholic beverages—selling them when a customer is in the red is illegal. Drinking is a privilege, not a right, and that right can be taken away (by the management) at any point. Management's responsibility is to prevent a customer from ever reaching this level. Certainly, if a customer does happen to reach that level, he or she must be prevented from driving away.

Intervention Techniques

An intervention is never an easy situation, but there are some approaches that can make the process of "cutting off a guest" less hostile. Intoxicated customers never like being cut off, but as representatives of the beverage establishment, the manager and servers have an obligation to promote customer safety.

- **Wait Until the Guest Orders**—Refuse service before serving a drink, never after the drink has been delivered. Also, never take a drink away from a customer.
- **Alert a Backup**—Always inform at least one fellow employee when an intervention is going to take place. The coworker can assist by contacting police if any behavior by the intoxicated consumer becomes inappropriate.

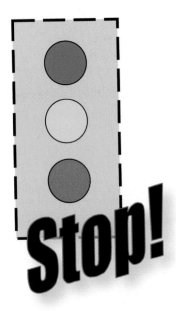

FIGURE 14–3 STOP serving alcohol
(Daniel Hollich)

GENERAL GUIDELINES FOR ESTIMATING BEVERAGE ALCOHOL LIMITS

- **The first hour:**
  - Small person: 1–2 drinks
  - Medium person: 2–3 drinks
  - Large person: 3–4 drinks
- **Subsequent hours**
  - One drink per hour, regardless of body size
  - One drink = ½ oz of pure alcohol

- **Isolate the Guest if Possible**—Isolating the guest helps him or her to avert possible embarrassment and may prevent a heightened conflict. Always speaking firmly and calmly, tactfully tell the guest that service is being stopped to avoid any miscommunication.
- **Do Not Be Judgmental**—Avoid using such phrases as "You are drunk!" This only heightens conflict. A more effective comment may be "Unfortunately, we won't be able to serve any more alcohol beverages this evening."
- **Contact the Police**—If the intoxicated person uses strong verbal abuse or violence or indicates that he or she is going to drive away or begins to drive away, contact the authorities immediately.
- **Don't Make Contact**—Do not touch or try to physically restrain an intoxicated guest. The natural reaction of the intoxicated customer may be to become aggressive and attack. Also, the contact may be perceived as sexual.

SET THE GROUNDWORK

Service Preparation

Many steps of wine service are founded in tradition. Depending on the style of the beverage establishment, wine service can be formal or informal. Formal service is identifiable through such practices as the use of high-end crystal stemware and decanting red wine with a ritualistic process of opening the wine bottle. Informal service uses a standard universal glass regardless of whether the wine is white or red wine and conveys the serving of wine in a more casual atmosphere.

TABLE SET-UP

A certain level of decorum is expected when one is sitting down in a restaurant for dinner. As with many interests or art forms, there is certain etiquette expected of the consumer in order to appreciate the experience. In restaurants, there is proper table set-up and the opening and pouring etiquette for the wine. Keep in mind that the level of table set-up and wine service formality should correspond to the sophistication of the restaurant and its customers. One possible table set-up is show in Figure 14–4.

FIGURE 14–4 Table setting
(Saint Supery Winery)

| 1. Bread and Butter Plate (B and B) |
| 2. Water Glass |
| 3. Red Wine Glass |
| 4. White Wine Glass |
| 5. Dessert Wine Glass |

Whether wine service is formal or informal, proper service involves *mise en place* (meez-on-plahs), a French term for "everything in its place." It conveys the philosophy of preparation, or the *four-P principle*: **P**reparation-**P**romotes-**P**roper-**P**erformance.

FIGURE 14–5 Wine key

(Frank Greenaway © Dorling Kindersley)

Proper Tools

Clean Glassware—Good-quality wine glasses (also referred to as *stemware*) allow a wine to show its best. Poor-quality stemware may mute or distort a wine's character. Even good-quality glassware may distort a wine if the glassware is not clean. The best glassware has a stem in order to prevent hands from warming the wine and also to minimize fingerprints.

Wine Key—A corkscrew is a crucial tool for opening up most bottles of wine. The most universal is known as the waiter's corkscrew, which comes equipped with a knife (to cut foil caps), a lever, and the worm (the part that screws into the cork). Figure 14–5 shows one of the more common wine openers.

The *ah-so* is a double-pronged cork extractor. It can be effective at removing a dry, crumbling, or broken cork, as might be the case with an older, more evolved wine.

Know the Menu—Before serving the customer, obtain a copy of the beverage and food menus. Become familiar with them and start to memorize the items. Look for possible wine and food pairings that are specific to the particular establishment. Ask friends or coworkers to provide quiz questions by asking the kinds of questions that an average customer would ask. Also, be familiar with the daily drink and food specials, and make sure that you know the items that are *86'd* (out of stock) for the particular meal period.

ON-STAGE

Serving the Guest(s)

First Impressions—The first 30 seconds to 1-minute of any customer encounter are crucial, as they will set the tone for the dining experience and may even set the percentage of gratuity.

Greet Promptly—If you do not have time to properly greet the table and take the beverage order, at the very least acknowledge the presence of your guests right away. Say something along the lines of "Good evening. I will be right with you." Make fast, meaningful connections, and approach with confidence and sincerity.

Establish a Rapport—This is the establishment of a common ground, a comfort zone where two or more people mentally join together. This will be established through

1. your presence (what you look like and how you move);
2. your attitude (what you say and how you say it); and
3. your ability (what you do to make them feel taken care of).

Read the Guest—Read the guests quickly and accurately to determine the kind of service the customer is seeking. Some customers prefer a self-guided approach, while others prefer a personal tour.

Utilize Sales Skills—Use key steps in the dining process as opportunities to sell more wine. These are great opportunities to increase the dollar amount of the guest check and thus increase the tip. The opportunities begin the moment the guest sits down—prior to

Proper Serving Temperatures

Medium to full-bodied red wine (60 – 65°F)

Light-bodied red wine (55 – 60°F)

Medium to full-bodied white table wine (50 – 55°F)

Light to medium-bodied white wine and rosé wines (45 – 50°F)

Sparkling wine (Below 45°F)

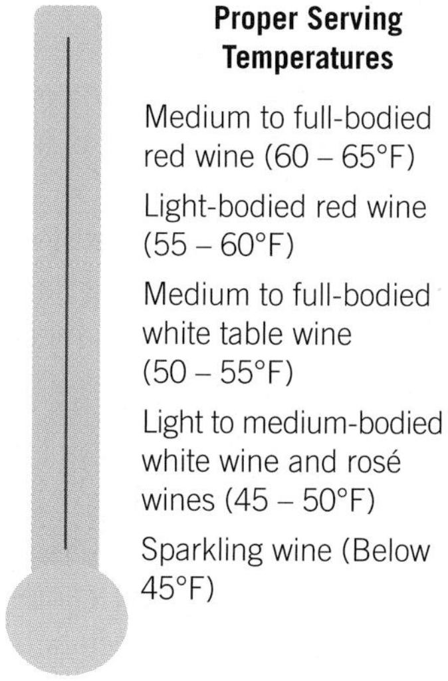

FIGURE 14–6 Proper serving temperatures
(John Laloganes)

Proper Serving Temperature of WHITE Wine

45°F ← → 55°F	
The colder a white wine is served, the more muted the aromas and flavors, but acid is perceived high.	The warmer a white wine is served, the more the acid is deemphasized and the more it tastes flat.

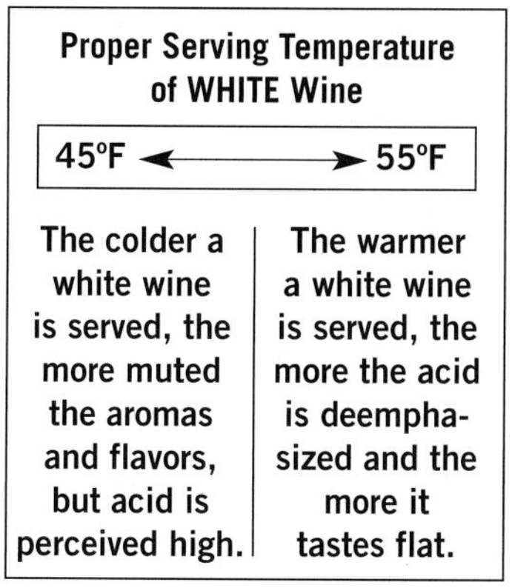

FIGURE 14–7 Proper serving temperature of white wine

serving the appetizer, salad, soup, entrée, and dessert—or after dinner. Each point of service allows the server to offer to enhance the meal experience by recommending a thoughtful and intelligent wine pairing.

Ask open-ended questions, as they force a customer to provide more than a simple yes-or-no answer. They are designed to encourage a meaningful answer through rapport building and to elicit information about the customer's needs and preferences.

Selling one additional serving or glass of wine can mean an additional $6–$12 (a common wine-by-the-glass price range) on the check. A server who persuades just two customers to have an additional glass of wine per shift adds $12–$24 in revenue and about $2.16–$4.32 (assuming an 18% gratuity) in tips. If this can be done for five shifts in a week, the server can earn an additional $10.80–$21.60 in tips each week, which adds up to $561.60–$1,123.20 in additional gratuities per year—all for simply encouraging a customer to order a glass of wine.

SERVING TEMPERATURE

The right serving temperature for a wine is the temperature that makes it taste the best. There are no rules, just guidelines and personal preferences. Some people enjoy ice water, while others prefer room-temperature water, and wine is no different. Generally speaking, in America, red wines are served too warm and white wines are served too cold. Improper serving temperatures have a significant impact on the wine's aromas and flavor, and the overall perception of components such as acid, tannin, and alcohol. As a general rule, a bottle of wine will chill at a rate of about 4°F every 10 minutes it is in the refrigerator, and it will warm at about the same rate when left at room temperature.

Overall Proper Serving Temperatures

The recommended temperature to serve wine varies greatly. Generally, service temperatures are as shown in Figure 14–6.

Serving Temperature for Sparkling Wine

Sparkling wines are best served and consumed cold, at a temperature between 40 and 45°F. At this cold, lower temperature, the crispness and acidity are emphasized and the carbonation levels are extended for a longer period.

Serving Temperature for White Wine

White wines and rosés are best served and consumed chilled, at a temperature between 45 and 55°F. At this temperature, the wine's crisp, refreshing acidity and aromas and flavors are emphasized.

White wines often are served too cold, as soon as they are removed from an ice bucket holding the wine at a temperature of around 32°F. Serving the wine at this temperature can mute the aromas and flavors of the wine. If the wine is too cold, remove it from the ice bucket and place the bottle on the table until it reaches a desirable temperature. If a white wine is served too warm, the wine's acidity is de-emphasized, and more evidence of alcohol gives the wine a flat and heavy taste. Figure 14–7 shows the proper temperature for white wine service.

Serving Temperature for Red Wine

Red wines sometimes are served too warm, as most consumers and restaurants store and serve red wines at actual room temperature (70–78°F). At this temperature, red wines will taste heavy, hot and spicy, or out of balance, because the excessive warmth emphasizes the alcohol content.

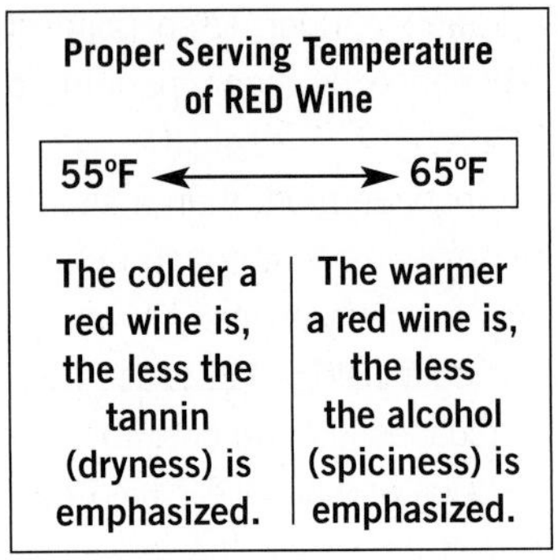

FIGURE 14–8 Proper serving temperature of red wine

(John Laloganes)

Red wines are best served and consumed at a cool room temperature between 55 and 65°F. At this temperature, the aroma, bouquet, and flavor elements are emphasized. Place a bottle of red into the refrigerator for 15 minutes, or into an ice bucket for several minutes, before serving.

If a red wine is served too cold, the tannins are emphasized and the fruit aromas and flavors become muted. Some very light low-tannin red wines, such as Beaujolais and Dolcetto, can be slightly cooler than other red wines to provide a bit more structure if desired. Figure 14–8 shows the proper temperature for red wine service.

PRESERVING WINE

When offering wine by the glass, it is critical to preserve the opened bottles of wine, to ensure that each customer receives the same level of quality of a given product. As discussed earlier, once a bottle of wine is opened, it begins a steady, often speedy decline due to its exposure to oxygen. This is not much of a concern if the bottle is consumed within a single meal period. However, the bigger fear is associated with less popular wines that do not sell very quickly and that will deteriorate before an entire bottle is sold.

Using a wine system that incorporates an inert gas (a nonreactive gas) has become an effective and popular method of preserving open bottles of wine. The type of gas used does not interact with and alter the wine, but instead, its purpose is to push oxygen out of the bottle, thus limiting oxidation.

Until the 1980s, it was rare to order wine by the glass. The *cruvinet* (a brand of a wine-preserving system) made it possible for beverage establishments to offer wines by the glass without such a significant loss of quality. There are two basic preserving options currently in wide use to protect open bottles of wine from rapid oxidation:

1. **Vacuum Pumps**—These systems, such as the widely available Vacu-vin, remove the air from an opened bottle and seal it with a reusable stopper. They may preserve an opened bottle of wine for several days.
2. **Nitrogen-Based Systems**—These preservation systems sold under brand names such as "Cruvinet" and "Winekeeper" hold opened bottles of wine in temperature-controlled cases. They fill the bottles with nitrogen or some combination of inert gas that displaces the oxygen and protects the wine. The cabinet systems fit the bottle with a tight rubber cork, with a siphon that feeds a spigot to release the wine without removing the gas. These systems have the capacity to preserve an opened bottle of wine for several days to weeks and are well suited for beverage establishments that extensively offer wines by the glass.

Current research from both formal and informal studies identifies only a negligible difference between either using the vacuum- or nitrogen-based system and sealing the bottle of wine and placing it in the refrigerator.

TEN STEPS OF TABLE WINE SERVICE

There are many methods for opening a bottle of wine, some more formal than others. Following are some universal steps:

1. Present the bottle of wine with full view of the label to the host (the individual who ordered the wine). Always confirm with the host that the bottle is correct, by stating

FIGURE 14–9 Opening a wine bottle

(Steve Mason/Getty Images, Inc.-Photodisc.)

FIGURE 14–10 Pouring wine

(Steve Mason/Getty Images, Inc.-Photodisc.)

SUGGESTED POURING ORDER

- First—Serve religious officials first.
- Second—Next, serve oldest to youngest women.
- Third—Then serve men.
- Fourth—Finally, serve the host.

the producer, grape varietal (or name of wine), and vintage date. Allow time for the host to respond as to the accuracy of the information.

2. Cut the capsule below the groove in the neck of the bottle and remove the upper portion of the capsule. Place the capsule in your pocket. Be careful not to remove the lower part of the capsule, as it is part of the bottle's decoration.

3. Insert the point of the corkscrew in the center of the cork and twist once clockwise, then continue to turn the corkscrew until almost fully into the cork. Do not turn the bottle.

   Note: Try not to pierce the opposite end or sides of the cork. Figure 14–9 shows the proper opening technique for a table wine.

4. Attach the lever onto the rim of the bottle.

5. With one hand, lift up firmly, but slowly, until the cork emerges, while holding the neck of the bottle and the lever together with the other hand.

6. Remove the cork from the corkscrew and place on a small plate next to the host. The purpose of this step is for the host to inspect the cork for moistness to indicate that the wine was properly stored on its side.

7. With a cloth napkin, clean the neck of the bottle to remove any remaining mold or cork.

8. Pour approximately 1 oz into the host's glass. Twist the bottle slightly before lifting away from the glass in order to leave the last drop in the glass, with napkin ready to catch any additional droplets. As the host tastes, hold the bottle with the label facing the host. If the wine is not approved, follow these three steps:

   - Listen carefully to the explanation as to why the wine is unacceptable.
   - Acknowledge the explanation and remove the tasting glass.
   - Ask whether you may bring another bottle or the wine list.

9. If the wine is approved, proceed with pouring wine into the glasses of all the guests, no more than one-half full; start with the guest to the left of the host, and continue clockwise, finishing by refilling the host's glass. Figure 14–10 shows the proper pouring technique.

10. Place the partially empty bottle to the right hand of the host (with the label facing the host). Offer the guest the option of having the wine chilled in the ice bucket (white wine) or left on the table.

Pouring Etiquette

In a table setting, wine glasses are placed on the upper right-hand side of the setting. Therefore, the server should pour wine with the right hand on the right side of the guest. (If you are left handed, then use common sense and adjust to the level of comfort.) It is important to leave the glassware on the table when pouring and never allow the wine bottle to touch the rim of the glass when pouring.

There are many approaches to, and beliefs about, what is deemed *proper wine service*. Certainly, in formal restaurants, wine service likely will be formal, and the converse will be true in casual restaurants. The pouring order can proceed (particularly in formal restaurants) as shown in the box on the left.

THE PROCESS OF DECANTING

Decanting can benefit both a young and an old red wine. Young red wine often needs some time for aging, or laying down, so that the components within the wine will assimilate with one another. Tannin often is higher the younger the wine is; therefore, the longer period of aging allows the tannin to naturally soften over time. Decanting a youthful red wine mimics the process of aging by dosing the wine with a large amount of oxygen.

An old red wine has color pigment and tannin particles that separate out from the wine, causing sediment and a loss of color. The sediment is harmless; however, etiquette dictates that the sediment be removed from the wine before the wine is poured into a glass to be consumed. Decanting is the technique used to separate the sediment, or solids, from the liquid.

Procedures Involved in Decanting a Wine

1. Stand the bottle up for a period of about 24 hours so that the sediment falls to the bottom.
2. After gently removing the foil cap and uncorking, position a lit candle (or other light source) next to the decanting vessel. The candle will illuminate the neck and shoulders of the wine bottle so that the sediment can be located.
3. Slowly pour the contents into a decanter, making sure to leave the sediment in the original bottle. If the sediment begins to float into the neck of the bottle, stop the process and let the bottle rest for about 10 minutes to allow the sediment to fall back to the bottom of the bottle again.

NINE STEPS OF SPARKLING WINE SERVICE

Opening a bottle of sparkling wine can be dangerous because of the natural high pressure from the carbon dioxide. Some sparkling wines contain pressures of 80–120 lbs/sq in. This is three to four times greater than the normal pressure of a car tire. Therefore, it is essential that a bottle of sparkling wine be carefully and properly opened. Ensure that sparkling wine is well chilled (40 to 45°F) in order to stabilize the carbon dioxide pressure when the bottle is opened.

There are many methods for opening a bottle of sparkling wine, some ways more formal than others. Following are some universal steps:

1. To open the bottle safely, slant or hold it at a 45° angle (being sure to not point in the direction of anyone), which increases the wine's surface area and decreases pressure. Some restaurants prefer that the bottle never be removed from the ice bucket as it is being opened.
2. Remove the top of the foil covering.
3. Holding onto the cork and wire hood, untwist and loosen the wire hood that covers the cork. Some prefer to remove the wire hood before progressing to the next step, while others choose to leave it on for safety reasons.
4. Hold the cork under a towel in one hand, and hold the bottom of the bottle in the other hand.
5. Twist or wiggle the bottle and ease the cork out slowly to subdue "popping." Keep a firm grip on the cork to prevent it from flying. Place the cork on a side plate in case the customer would like to inspect it.
6. Wipe the rim of the bottle with a cloth napkin.

7. From the right of the host, fill the host's glass with 1 oz. Let the host taste for approval.

8. If the host approves, pour one-third full, step back, and let the foam subside. Fill the glass three-quarters full. Start with the guest to the left of the host and continue clockwise, finishing by refilling the host's glass. Always serve ladies before gentlemen.

9. Place the bottle in an ice bucket and drape it with a towel.

Figure 14–11 shows Champagne chilling in an ice bucket.

FIGURE 14–11 Champagne being chilled
(Getty Images-Stockbyte, Royalty Free)

THE FLOW OF WINE

NAME: _____ Score out of 20 points_____.

Use these questions to test your knowledge and understanding of the concepts presented in the chapter.

I. MULTIPLE CHOICE: Select the best possible answer from the options available.

1. Decanting a wine is done
   a. to aerate the wine.
   b. for display purposes.
   c. to remove sediment.
   d. for all of the above reasons.

2. In the distribution system for alcoholic beverages, which of the following are considered intermediaries?
   a. distributors
   b. growers
   c. manufacturers
   d. processors

3. In the distribution system for alcohol beverages, which of the following transports alcohol into the United States?
   a. distributors
   b. wineries
   c. retailers
   d. importers

4. The amount of an item on hand that will carry an operation from one delivery date to the next is called
   a. par stock.
   b. blanket order.
   c. safety stock.
   d. purchase order draft.

5. The common title for the person in charge of managing wine in fine-dining restaurants is
   a. the server.
   b. the bartender.
   c. the chef.
   d. the sommelier.

6. The first step of the four-step control process is to
   a. monitor employee performance.
   b. coach performance.
   c. train employees.
   d. create standards and procedures.

7. Which is *not* an acceptable storage practice for wine?
   a. Lay it on its side.
   b. Keep it in cool temperatures.
   c. Keep it in fluctuating temperatures.
   d. The storeroom should have low humidity.
   e. All of the above.
   f. Answers c and d.

8. If ABC Chardonnay costs $120 per case, and there are 12 bottles in a case, then the cost per bottle is
   a. $12
   b. $20
   c. $10
   d. $13

9. If ABC Chardonnay costs $120 per case, and there are 12 bottles per case, determine the cost per oz.
   a. 39 cents
   b. $254
   c. $2.54
   d. $1.95

10. If ABC Chardonnay costs $120 per case and there are 12 bottles per case, the cost per glass (assume 5-oz portions) is

    a. $1.95.

    b. $1.50.

    c. 39 cents.

    d. 30 cents.

11. Under the same scenario as the preceding three questions, determine the appropriate selling price (assume a 200% markup).

    a. $3.90

    b. $5.85

    c. $7.80

    d. None of the above.

II. TRUE / FALSE: Circle the best possible answer.

12. Two methods of aeration are swirling the wine in a glass and decanting. **True / False**

13. Sourcing is the process of ordering the optimal quantity of product. **True / False**

14. Ultimately, it is the manager's job to ensure that the service staff is trained on responsible alcohol service. **True / False**

15. When purchasing wine, if less than a standard case is ordered, this is known as *breaking a case*. **True / False**

16. The perpetual inventory method allows the manager to know the exact amount of stock on hand at all times. **True / False**

17. For short-term storage, it is acceptable to store wine standing up. **True / False**

18. For long-term storage, it is acceptable to store wine standing up. **True / False**

19. If a guest is making irrational statements, stumbling or falling down, or unable to sit up straight, then he or she is in the *green*. **True / False**

III. SHORT-ANSWER ESSAY / DISCUSSION QUESTION: Use a separate sheet of paper if necessary.

20. Explain the importance of understanding and applying control techniques within the flow of beverages.

15

Developing a Wine Menu

The ultimate goal of the wine menu is to help generate revenue for the business. Just like a food menu, it is the controlling document and acts as a marketing tool to inform the customer what is available for sale, in order to produce revenue.

LEARNING OBJECTIVES

Upon completion of this chapter, the learner will be able to:

- Identify the components of an effective wine menu.
- Identify the key considerations of creating a wine program.
- Identify methods of arranging the layout of a wine list.
- Develop appropriate pricing strategies for wine-by-the-glass and wine-by-the-bottle programs.

WINE MENU

The ultimate goal of the wine menu is to help generate revenue for the business. Just like a food menu, it is the controlling document and acts as a marketing tool to inform the customer what is available for sale, in order to produce revenue. This is the driving force for how sales are gained and tells what costs need to be controlled.

The wine menu should emphasize that beverages are an integral part of the dining experience and should complement the cuisine. Each restaurant has different needs and different preferences—there is no one best type of wine list. More importantly, the wine list should create an identity. If someone asked, "What kind of food does your restaurant specialize in?" what would you say? What if the same question were asked about your wine list or wine program? The wine menu needs to provide as many options as are managable.

THE WINE PROGRAM

There are several basic concepts involved in creating a wine program and, consequently, a wine or beverage list:

1. **A clearly defined concept of the beverage establishment determines the wine philosophy**—The wine list can be as extensive as a book or as simple as a section on the food menu. A clear focus on the wine philosophy will dictate the design and format of the wine list. The basis of all sales control and cost control begins with *the concept*. A restaurant concept is a combination of various factors that form the foundation of that restaurant. The concept should be conveyed through not only the food, but also the beverage menu.

    Today's restaurant customers expect a wine list with variety and some depth. The most effective wine list will be designed with these very important factors in mind. Such factors can influence how a restaurant manages sales and costs. The major considerations that drive the design, content, organization, and price structure of the beverage menu are the cuisine (the food and beverage focus) and theme of the restaurant, the atmosphere and ambience, the target customer, the level and type of service, and the location of the establishment.

2. **Considerations in the List**—Some major considerations in designing a beverage menu are its composition, depth, and breadth.
    Composition—Categories of wine. Should there be a balance or an emphasis? Generally, more white wines would be offered in a seafood restaurant and more red wine selections in a steakhouse. Split the list into white, red, rosé, and sparkling wine. Seafood restaurants will emphasize white wines, and steakhouses will emphasize red wines.
    Breadth / Depth—Breadth is a having a wide range of alternatives or scope of wines being offered. Having wines represented from several different wine producing countries and regions around the world is having breadth.
    Depth is complete in detail and dimension; thoroughness. Offering wines from several producers and vintages from particular wine producing countries and regions around the world is having depth. Or it may be offering several different expressions of a particular grape variety or style of wine. How many selections are approriate? The answer is, anywhere from 1 to 25,000. The number is based on several factors, such as storage space, the amount of money that is available to invest in an inventory, and the type of restaurant. Pair two to three wines with each menu item.

Remember the type of restaurant and target market: A midscale family chain restaurant offers a completely different beverage program than a fine-dining restaurant.

A general breakdown of the list will consist of the 20/20/60 rule:

Inexpensive wines—(on the lower price end of your average guest check) will make up 20% of the wine list. Perhaps wines would be priced in the teens to 20-dollar range.

Expensive wines—(on the higher price end of your average guest check) will make up 20% of the wine list. Perhaps wines would be priced around $50 or slightly more per bottle.

The moderate range—making up the final 60% of the wine list, would incorporate the majority of wines priced between the low end and high end of the price range. Perhaps these would cost between $20 and $50 per bottle.

The terms *inexpensive, expensive,* and *moderate* are rather subjective. What may be expensive for one person is inexpensive to another. This is why the next step is crucial, as it involves developing a price point scheme.

3. **Determine the optimum price range of wines, and develop the product mix (types and styles of wine) that complements the cuisine**—Developing an appropriately priced selection of wine begins with establishing an *optimum* price range as a starting point. The optimum price range is a reasonable range of prices for most wines on the list. The factors that influence the selling prices and selections of wine include the restaurant concept, customer, service style, menu prices for food, the selections offered on the list, and the prices charged by the competition.

APPROPRIATENESS AND THE PSYCHOLOGY OF PRICING

Through understanding the appropriate selling price range of wines given a particular restaurant or retail concept, it becomes easier for the wine buyer to select the wine based on cost. Obviously, a particular concept may dictate French wines or primarily California white wine, but this process allows the buyer to focus on finding the French wines or California white wines at the appropriate cost in order to sell at the optimal selling price range.

Average Guest Check Pricing Method

The wine prices need to be set in relation to the restaurant's concept. Otherwise, the establishment runs the risk of either not obtaining enough revenue when a wine is sold or not selling any wines because they are too expensive for the particular concept. This method assumes that most diners are willing to spend a similar amount of money on a bottle of wine as they would on their collective food purchases.

The majority of wines ordered will consist of an optimal low and high end price range.

Formula 1
Average Guest Check × 2 = Lower End of Price Range
Formula 2
Average Guest Check + Lower End of Price Range = Higher End of Price Range

Examples of this procedure are located on the left hand side of this page.

In this example, by applying the 20/20/60 rule, at least 60% of the wine selections should be priced in the range from $40 to $60. The remaining 20% of wines will be priced below the optimum price range to provide economical wine options, and the other 20% of wines will consist of exclusive wine options.

LOWER END OF PRICE RANGE

Average Guest Check × 2 = Lower end of price range
$20 × 2 = $40

HIGHER END OF PRICE RANGE

Average Guest Check + Low end of price range = Higher end of price range
$20 + $40 = $60

Obtaining Economical and Exclusive Wine Pricing Options—It is important to realize that all wine lists have a few selections under and over the optimum price range.

Economical Wine Price point—Wines priced below the optimum price range are for consumers who desire thrifty options. Prices for these *economical wines* are obtained by using the low end of the optimum price range and subtracting $20.

Exclusive Wine Price point—Wines priced above the average bottle in the range are to provide higher-priced options for consumers who desire such options. These *exclusive wines* are priced by adding $20 to the high end of the optimum price range. Obviously, there are a number of restaurants and wine bars that offer a small selection of some extremely expensive, high end wine offerings that go beyond the exclusive price point. They may even be considered ultra-exclusive or token wines. In some cases, the restaurant or wine bar offers these options as part of portraying an image or for the occasional "buy-to-impress" type of customer.

Perceptions of Pricing

Certain wines have a sort of *luster,* as is seen with some of the *boutique wines* available in the marketplace. Not only do these types of wines benefit from the higher-quality growing and production methods, but also involved is the theory of *conspicuous consumption,* otherwise known as the *Veblen effect,* defined by economist Thorstein Veblen in the late 1800s. The theory states that people's preference for buying increases as a direct function of the price of the product. People acquire certain products (in the case of boutique wines and other expensive items) to display their income, wealth, or good taste. Status goods such as expensive or unique wines are perceived as exclusive and, therefore, more desirable. These wines may be perceived as adding an extra dimension of quality and prestige to the list. At some point, someone will want to buy such a wine. Exclusive wines have the psychological effect of making the one or two wines priced lower than them, but higher than those in the *hot zone,* look like a good buy.

MERCHANDISING TECHNIQUES

There are several techniques that can be used to sell wine and increase an operation's revenue. Having a wine-by-the-glass program, various bottles sizes, wine flights, wine dinners, and a trained and motivated service staff can work simultaneously to generate revenue and build repeat business.

Wine by the Glass (BTG)

Wines by the glass (also called *house wines*) remain very popular among wine drinkers and very profitable for restaurants. The BTG program will often consist of two price–quality tiers of wines by the glass. First is an entry-level price tier for those seeking value, and second is a premium tier consisting of better-quality and higher-priced options.

The initial level provides a reasonably priced alternative to paying for and committing to a full bottle of wine, which may be five times the cost and quantity of an individual glass.

The average profit on wines sold by the glass is relatively high, and this can help to offset the potential spoilage that can occur with serving wine by the glass.

A modest BTG program will include, at a minimum, two white wine and two red wine selections, but, more commonly, a selection of six to eight wines. A large selection provides greater options and adaptability when pairing with foods on the menu.

The standard portion size for wines BTG is approximately 5 oz (but can also be 4 oz. or even 6 oz. portion depending upon the desired standard). A typical bottle contains 25.4 oz of wine, which means that each bottle contains roughly five glasses of wine.

With a 4-oz pour, there are six glasses per bottle, and if the restaurant offers a 6-oz pour, then there are four glasses per bottle.

Glassware can significantly influence value perception. If a standard, 5-oz pour is served in an oversized 15-oz glass, it does not seem like a value to the guest, even if the amount of wine is the standard pour. Most guests are seeking perceived value, and a glass that is only one-third full does not seem like a value.

Various Bottle Sizes

Providing alternative bottle sizes can provide variety for the wine drinker. Gaining popularity is the half-bottle (equivalent to 375 ml/12.8 oz). The split (187 ml/6.4 oz) is also popular for sparkling wines. It allows the single-bottle portion to be sold to the consumer without any loss to the restaurant.

Wine Flights

A sampling of three to four smaller portions of wine are selected, with a theme or connection to each other. This provides variety, but potentially also a learning experience through making comparisions. For example, a sampling (often a depth of options) of four Chardonnays from around the world, perhaps from Sonoma, California; Clare Valley, Australia; Côte d' Beaunne, Burgundy, France; and Chablis, Burgundy, France, may be offered in the wine flight.

Wine Dinners

Wine dinners are a technique used to showcase a particular winery by offering a multi-course menu, each course being paired with a wine produced from the winery.

BYOB, or *"Bring Your Own Bottle"*

In some places, customers are allowed to bring their own bottle(s) of wine into the restaurant. Some customers do this because they have a special wine that the restaurant does not carry. But BYOB may also be offered because the restaurant's wine list may not have adequate options. Another reason is that the operation may not have a liquor license that allows it to legally sell alcohol. Most restaurants charge the customer a nominal service fee, known as a *corkage fee*, to compensate for the lack of revenue resulting from allowing this type of service.

Well-Trained Service Staff

The presentation of the list sets the tone. The server's manner will greatly influence the perception of the wine program and resulting sales and guest satisfaction.

- ☑ Assume that the customer has no wine knowledge by staying with the following basic questions: *Is there a particular price range in mind? What is everyone eating? Would you like red, rosé, or white? Any particular region? Would you like to be adventurous or traditional?* Then listen carefully, gauging the interest and knowledge level of the customer from the responses, and adapt the approach.
- ☑ Consider all the flavors, combination, and occasions of the food to be served.
- ☑ Present wine suggestions in an unpretentious manner. Offer several selections: expensive, moderate, and inexpensive.

ORGANIZATION AND FORMAT

There should be some method to organizing the wine list. Any of the following approaches creates a sort of distinction and should be chosen on the basis of the type and style of the concept:

1. **Organize by Category of Wine (and Color)**—This is a simple listing of the wine: Sparkling wine and table wine (White, Rosé, and Red).

2. **Organize by Grape Variety**—Organizing by the type of grape, such as Chardonnay, Merlot, and Cabernet Sauvignon, is the common denominator of what average restaurant customers are familiar with.

3. **Organize by Location**—Organize first by country, then by region: United States (Napa Valley, California), France (Bordeaux).

4. **Organize by Style**—Organizing by wine styles is an attempt to take the snobbery out of the process of buying wine. Unlike traditional wine stores that group wines by region (France, United States) or variety (Cabernet Sauvignon, Merlot), organizing by wine styles groups wines by taste—Crisp, Silky, Fruity, Bold, and so on. There is an international chain of wine retail stores called "WineStyles" that organize their selections in this manner at an effective attempt to de-mystify wine.

5. **Organize by Food Pairings or Course Titles**—Simply make the food pairings obvious: Shellfish Wines or Appetizer Wines.

6. **Organize by Body**—List the wines under such headings as Light-Bodied White Wines or Full-Red Bodied Wines.

7. **Organize by "Catchy Headings"**—Describe the wines in lighthearted terms: These sorts of categories are not very "wine serious;" however, they do convey a very specific style that the average consumer can associate with.

   - **Sparkling Wines**—Bubble up; or Foamy and Frothy, Fun and Fizzy
   - **White Wines**—Light as Spring, Aromatics, Barreled Whites
   - **Red Wines**—From the Spice Box, Powerful Reds.

8. **Combination**—Combine any of the aforementioned methods of organzing and formatting a wine list.

Information That Can Be Included on Wine Lists

Need-to-Know Information—*Need-to-Know Information* includes material that the customer would most likely want to know to assist him or her in making a purchasing decision.

    This includes significant information about the wine, such as: producer, varietal, geographical location, vintage date, and price of the wine. These items could be in any order, and any emphasis may be used. Some examples are shown on the left.

Nice-to-Know Information—*Nice-to-Know Information* includes material that the customer would most likely *not* need to know to assist him or her in making a purchasing decision. However, such information is useful or helpful.

    Some nice-to-know information that may be included on a wine listing is a description of the wine, food recommendations, or bin numbers. Some examples are as follows:

Example A
Sauvignon Blanc—Kim Crawford, Marlborough, New Zealand, 2007 $6 / $32
Refreshing, crisp, and acidic, with aromas and flavors of grapefruit and gooseberry.

Example B
Sauvignon Blanc—Kim Crawford, Marlborough, New Zealand, 2007 $6 / $32
Pairs well with our steamed and poached fish and poultry dishes.

Bin (identification) Numbers
These enable customers to order a wine without the fear of pronouncing its name improperly. Bin numbers also minimize mistakes made by servers and bartenders. The wines can be arranged in the storerooms according to the bin-numbering system.

POSSIBLE FORMATS FOR WRITING A WINE DESCRIPTION.

Example A
Kim Crawford, Sauvignon Blanc, Marlborough, New Zealand, 2007 $6 / $32

Example B
Sauvignon Blanc - Kim Crawford, Marlborough, New Zealand, 2007 $6 / $32

SAMPLE WINE LIST

White Wines

Fresh Unoaked: Light Bodied—These crisp and refreshing wines pair well with salads, soups, and appetizers.

Nautilus *Sauvignon Blanc*—2007, Marlborough, New Zealand, Gls$7 / Btl$28
Riff *Pinot Grigio*—2006, Alto-Aldige, Italy, Gls$8 / Btl$32
Bethel Heights *Pinot Gris*—2007, Oregon, Gls$8 / Btl$32

Aromatic and Fragrant: Medium Bodied—These aromatic wines can pair well with spicy and highly seasoned foods.

Bonny Doon Pacific Rim *Riesling*—2007, Santa Cruz Mountains, Gls$6 / Btl$24
Hirshbach and Sohne *Riesling* Kabinett—2006, Germany, Gls$7 / Btl$28

Earthy Whites: Medium Bodied—The earthy and mineral quality of this style of wine enhances salads, shellfish, and poultry dishes.

Tribut —2006, Chablis, France Gls$8 / Btl$32
Domaine Thibault, André Dezat—2006, Pouilly-Fumé, France, Gls$9 / Btl$36

Rich and Oaky: Full Bodied—These wines pair well with grilled poultry or full-flavored fish.

Rosenblum Cellars Viognier—2007, California, Gls$8 / Btl$32
Edna Valley Vineyard Paragon *Chardonnay*—2006, California, Gls$8 / Btl$32

Sparkling Wines

Bubbles are a perfect summer treat and work to jazz up flavors.

Paringa Sparkling *Shiraz*—Australia Gls$6 / Btl$24
Freixenet Cava—Spain (½ bottle) Gls$6 / Btl$24

Red Wines

Mild Mannered: Light-Bodied Reds—Light-bodied red wines pair well with full-flavored poultry and grilled fish.

David Bruce *Pinot Noir*—2005, Central Coast, California, Gls$9 / Btl$36

Vibrant and Spicy: Medium-Bodied Reds—The earthy and spicy flavors of these wines pair well with highly seasoned poultry and meat dishes.

Ostatu Rioja Crianza—2005, Rioja, Spain, Gls$6 / Btl$24
Santa Julia *Malbec*—2005, Mendoza Valley, Argentina, Gls$8 / Btl$32
Fairview *Pinotage*—2005, South Africa, Gls$8 / Btl$32

Robust: Full Bodied Reds—These robust wines pair excellently with grilled red meat and game dishes.

Yalumba Shiraz—2004, Australia, Gls$8 / Btl$32
Fife *Zinfandel*—2005, Napa Valley, California
(½ Bottle), Gls$8 / Btl$16

APPENDIX

WINE GLOSSARY: From A to Z

A

acetaldehyde (ass-ah-TAHL-duh-hide)—A compound that causes a wine to have oxidized qualities, caused by the unintentional and undesirable effect of oxygen.

acetic acid—Wines contain several types of acid, but acetic acid has the odor and taste of vinegar. If this acid is present at more than minimal levels, the wine would be considered faulty.

acidity—Present in all grapes and therefore all wines. Perceived as sourness and causing salivation on the palate, acidity is extremely important in determining the structure, shape, and life span (or backbone) of all wines, but particularly of white wines. Good acid levels make a wine crisp and refreshing, and prolong the aftertaste. Acidity also helps to preserve a wine, allowing it to be aged. Wines that are low in acidity are often described as tasting flat or flabby.

adaptation—A temporary loss in the ability to perceive an aroma, a flavor, or a taste.

aeration—The deliberate choice of incorporating oxygen into a wine, allowing it to "breathe" in order to soften the tannins and allowing the aromas and flavors to open up and integrate with one another. Young red wines benefit most from aeration, which is accomplished by decanting or by swirling the wine in a glass.

aftertaste—Also called the "finish," this is the taste that remains in the mouth after the wine is swallowed. A really great wine will have a long, complex, lingering aftertaste. The amount of aftertaste can be associated with how concentrated the wine is.

aging—The process of storing wine in either inert (stainless steel, concrete, etc.) or oxidative (oak, chestnut, etc.) containers in order to preserve or contribute additional flavors and allow the components of the wine to integrate.

alcohol—Derived from the fermentation of grape sugars by yeast, alcohol, affects the weight, strength, and overall personality of a wine. In U.S. table wines, the law allows a 1.5% variation from the level identified on the label.

alluvial—Highly fertile (said of soil). Alluvial soil is often located near rivers, floodplains of rivers, or the foothills of mountains.

american oak—Along with French oak, American oak is the most widely used wood in the world to build barrels in which to age wine. Because they contribute strong, intense elements of coconut, vanilla, etc., aroma and flavor to the wine, American oak barrels are most often used to age red wines. American oak varies with the forest and state of its origin.

American Viticultural Area (AVA)—A distinctive grape-growing geographical area, such as Napa Valley and Sonoma Valley, that has been officially designated by the Alcohol and Tobacco Tax and Trade Bureau (TTB). An AVA guarantees that, at a minimum, 85% (with some exceptions) of the grapes came from the location identified on the bottle.

amphora (ahm-FOR-uh)—A two-handled Greek vase with a swelled belly, narrow neck, and large mouth. Historically, an amphora was often used to transport wine or oil.

analytical approach—A methodical three-step approach to pairing wine and food. The method involves (1) mirroring the body and weight (or overall intensity) of the wine and the food to ensure that neither one overwhelms the other, (2) connecting bridge ingredients in the food with flavors in the wine, and (3) comparing or contrasting taste components between the wine and the food on the basis of the desired emphasis of the match.

antioxidants—These have recently been linked to reducing the risk of heart disease and certain types of cancer. Antioxidants have compounds in them that inhibit the formation of cancer cells and reduce the buildup of fat cells in the arteries.

anthocyanins—The name of the pigment found in red grape skins that provides the color to the finished wine.

appellation—A geographic designation of the place where a wine's grapes were grown, such as Napa Valley, Chianti, and Bordeaux. The regulations vary in coverage from country to country and region to region. The French and Italians also regulate what grapes can be grown where, winemaking methods, yields, etc. In America, the appellation references where the grapes were grown and does not specify grape-growing or winemaking methods.

Appellation d'Origine Contrôlée (AOC or AC) (ah-pehl-lah-SYAHN daw-ree-JEEN kawn-traw-LAY)—French term for "controlled appellation of origin" and refers to wine, cheese, butter, etc. The designation is given and controlled by the French governmental agency Institut National des Appellations d' Origine (INAO), and it guarantees that the products to which it pertains have been held to a set of rigorous standards. The appellation d'origine contrôlée is the foremost category in the French system and ensures the quality of a wine and that the wine meet quality criteria in several growing and production steps.

aroma—The scent of a wine; frequently used interchangeably with the word *bouquet*. Smelling the wine on the outside, as opposed to the inside. Some tasters apply the term *aroma* only to the fruit-like natural smells of a wine and refer to the more complex smells of bottle- or barrel-aged wines as *bouquet*.

aromatic—A wine-tasting term used to describe a wine that is highly fragrant.

astringent—The dry, mouth-puckering sensation caused by wines (usually young reds) that are high in tannin. Sometimes astringency can be appealing in a wine and favorably complement food. Astringency tends to decline with bottle age.

auslese (OWS-lay-zuh)—German for "select picking"; refers to the selective hand harvesting of extremely ripe bunches of grapes, often with a touch of noble rot (called *Edelfaule* in German).

autolysis (aw-TAHL-uh-sihss)—The process of decomposing dead yeast cells. Gives Champagne and other high-quality sparkling wines their distinctive character that occurs throughout the aging process.

B

backbone—Often used to describe wines with good acidity and structure.

balance—Describes a wine with harmonious components, in reference to the balance of acids, tannins, fruit, sweetness, and alcohol. Typicity (tih-PISS-it-ee) must also be considered in defining what the balance is for a particular varietal.

balthazar—A very large bottle that holds 16 standard bottles.

barrel aging—The length of time a wine spends in a barrel before being bottled. Barrel aging allows the wine to be exposed to the slow passage of oxygen and a small amount of evaporation, influencing the personality of the wine in several ways. Tannin in red wine softens; white wines become richer and more full bodied. Aging can add aromas and flavors of vanilla, spice, tobacco and wood.

barrel fermented—Indicates a wine that has been fermented in barrels. Will increase the wine's body and add complexity, texture, and flavor, but not to the degree that barrel aging will provide.

barrique (bah-REEK)—Barrel for fermenting or aging that holds approximately 60 gallons; used in Bordeaux.

Beerenauslese (BA) (BEHR-ehn-OWS-lay-zuh)—The German term for select berries that have been handpicked. BA is a rich, sweet dessert wine made of overripe, shriveled berries that are almost always affected by noble rot.

bianco (bee-ahn-koh)—Italian for "white," as in white wine.

big six grapes—Grapes from which Riesling, Sauvignon Blanc, Chardonnay, Pinot Noir, Merlot, and Cabernet Sauvignon wines are made. These grapes are arguably the most noble, as they are adaptable and produced around the world.

biodynamics—Philosophical viewpoint asserting that the land is a living system and vineyards are an ecological self-sustaining whole.

bitter—A sensation that may be caused by tannin. Slight bitterness in a wine may be a desirable trait; however, "overbitterness" is considered a fault and characterizes a poorly made wine.

blanc (BLAHNK)—French for "white," as in white wine.

blanc de blancs (BLAHNK duh BLAHNK)—Translates to "white from white," or a white wine made from white grapes. Most often used to describe sparkling wines made from Chardonnay or other white wine varietals.

blanc de noirs (BLAHNK duh NWAR)—Translates to "white from red," or a white wine made from red grapes. Most often used to describe sparkling wines made from Pinot Noir and Pinot Meunier or other red wine varietals.

blanco (BLAHNG-koh)—Spanish for "white," as in white wine.

blind tasting—A wine tasting that is conducted with no knowledge of the grape varieties or origins of the wine on the part of the tasters. In a double-blind tasting, the taster has no information about what he or she is sampling.

bodega (boh-DAY-gah)—A generic term for a Spanish winery or wine cellar.

body—Body is the feeling of a wine's viscosity, weight, or fullness in the mouth. It is usually the result of extract, alcohol content, or residual sugar. Wines are often described as light bodied, medium bodied, or full bodied, a spectrum comparable to skim milk vs. 2% milk vs. whole milk.

botrytis cinerea (boh-TRI-tis sihn-EAR-ee-uh)—Also called noble rot, a beneficial mold that may grow on wine grapes, causing them to dehydrate and shrivel resulting in the remaining juice becoming highly concentrated. This desired condition yields the honeyed richness of many classic dessert wines such as Sauternes, Trockenbeerenauslese, and Tokaji.

bottled by—Indicates the winery or group that bottled the wine, but did not necessarily grow, pick, or ferment the grapes.

bouillie bordelaise (Bwee-YEE Bor-duh-LEZZ)—An antifungal solution consisting of copper sulfate, lime, and water. Historically, commonly used in Bordeaux, France.

bouquet—The secondary smells of a wine. The term is used to refer to the addition of odors associated with winemaking methods, such as the odor of barrel-aged wine, which includes complexities beyond the fruit aromas.

breathing—Allowing a wine to come into contact with some oxygen for a short time. Breathing allows the components of the wine to integrate and is typically done when the bottle of wine is opened and the wine is poured into the glass.

brettanomyces (breht-tan-uh-MY-sees)—Often referred to as brett, a spoilage yeast that can grow on grapes and affect a wine during processing. Brett can add a horse-saddle aroma and flavor to a wine.

brilliant—A wine of high clarity. Highly filtered wines will always be brilliant—yet the process of filtration can strip some of the personality from a wine.

brix—A system used to measure the sugar content in grapes and wine. Brix at the time of harvest is normally in the range from 20° to 25°. After fermentation, brix can indicate how sweet a wine is as a measure of its residual sugar.

brut (BROOT)—Used in reference to sparkling wine; indicates that the style is dry.

buttery—Describes a rich wine with an aroma, flavor and texture like that of melted butter. Often referring to Chardonnay and often is the result of malolactic fermentation.

C

canopy—The foliage (leaves) that is produced from the grapevine.

canopy management—The practice of adjusting or positioning a vine's leaves, shoots, and fruit as the vine grows, in order to gain such beneficial advantages as increased exposure to sunlight and movement of air.

cap—The thick layer of skin, stems, and seeds that collects at the top of the tank during the fermentation of red wine.

capsule—The metal or plastic material that covers the cork and top of a wine bottle. Now used for decorative purposes, the capsule originally functioned as a means of protecting corks in old cellars from being attacked by insects. The capsule also limited moisture loss and mold growth.

carbonic maceration—Also called "whole-berry fermentation," the process of intracellular fermentation of whole grapes that allows the carbon dioxide which is produced to eliminate all oxygen. This fermentation technique is used to produce fruity, red wines with low tannin and an intense color. Often associated with Beaujolais wines.

cava—Spain's sparkling wine made by the traditional French method. Cava is produced mainly in the Catalonia–Barcelona area of Spain. The traditional méthode champenoise must be used.

cépage (say-PAHZH)—Vine or grape variety.

chaptalization (shap-tuh-luh-ZAY-shuhn)—The addition of sugar to grape juice before fermentation has been completed, in order to achieve a desired alcohol content with the finished wine. Chaptalization is common in cooler northern Europe, such as Burgundy, where grapes have to struggle to fully ripen, and is not allowed in warmer regions, such as Rhône.

charmat (shar-MAH)—Also known as tank or bulk process, this is an inexpensive way to create carbonation and limit complexity in sparkling wine. The wine undergoes secondary fermentation in a stainless steel pressurized tank, which results in coarse, large bubbles and simpler fruit flavors.

chateau (shah-TOH)—Often refers to a wine estate located on the land of the vineyard. In Bordeaux, a winery that has vineyards and that produces and bottles its own wine. This is the equivalent of the American terminology *estate bottled*.

chewy—Describes full-bodied, sometimes tannic wines.

claret—Historically, a British term used for red wines from Bordeaux.

clarity—A wine-tasting term used to indicate a wine's freedom from particles.

classico (KLAHS-see-koh)—A term used in Italy to signify the original or classic vineyard zone before an area was expanded.

clean—Otherwise known as healthy. A wine that is absent of any foreign and unpleasant odor and taste.

clone—A reproduction of a vine with distinctive traits of its parent vine. Usually produced through cuttings or grafting from the original vine, but may also arise through natural evolution.

clos (KLOH)—The term originally used in Burgundy to mean an enclosed vineyard.

condensed tannin—The tannin that is present in skins—particularly, the tannin found in seeds and stems; also referred to as unripe tannin because of its ability to taste bitter on the palate, especially if the grapes were harvested too early.

cooper—A barrel producer.

corked—Describes a faulty wine that smells and tastes similar to a musty basement or a wet newspaper or cardboard. Caused by a cork made defective by 2,4,6-trichloranisole (try-klor-ANN-iss-sahl), or TCA.

côte (KOHT) or **coteaux** (koh-TOH)—French term that refers to a slope or hillside.

coulure (coo-LYUR)—Condition that may occur when a flower has been improperly pollinated, resulting in insufficient fruit set and causing berries to abort or fall off the clusters.

crémant (kray-MAHN)—A term used to describe French sparkling wine made outside of the Champagne region, but employing the méthode Champenoise in its production.

crianza (kree-AHN-thah)—A Spanish wine-aging classification for any DOCa or DO. Applied to red wines aged a minimum of 24 months, at least 6 months of which were in a barrel. The appellation areas of Rioja, Navarra, and Ribera del Duero require 12 months in wood. White and rosé wines labeled Crianza must be aged for one year, at least six months of which are in wood.

criadera (kree-ah-DEHR-ah)—Spanish term that translates to nursery. Referring to a young wine used in the production of Sherry.

crisp—Wine-tasting term that denotes a desirable feature in white wines. The term indicates that the wine is firm and refreshing, meaning that it has adequate or ample acidity.

cross-pollination—Pollination that occurs between two different grapes of the same vine species, either naturally through evolution or intentionally within a vine nursery.

cru (KROO)—French term for rank or level (often translated as *growth*), used to define the hierarchy of vineyards within appellations. In Burgundy, France, the highest quality wines are given the Grand Cru term, and in Bordeaux they are called Premiere Crus.

crush—Usually late August, September, or October in the Northern Hemisphere, when grapes are harvested and crushed. In the Southern Hemisphere, the crush is usually in late February, March, or April.

crushing—The most common technique for extracting the juice from grapes, particularly in red wine.

crust—The name applied to sediment that forms in the bottom and sides of a wine bottle. Crust is commonly found in Vintage Ports or unfiltered or aged red table wine.

cuvée (koo-VAY)—An unregulated term that some wineries use to indicate a special blend or reserve batch of wine of various grapes or vintages blended together.

D

decanter—A glass vessel into which wine is decanted.

decanting—A technique used with either old red wines to remove sediment or young red wines to allow oxygen to soften the components. Decanting involves slowly pouring wine from the bottle into another container (typically a decanter) in order to separate the liquid from the sediment. The procedure also may be used to aerate the wine in order to soften the tannin and allow the wine to open up and the aromas and flavors to integrate.

dégorgement (day-gorge-MAWN)—French term for disgorging the removal of collected yeast that has settled in the neck of the bottle during Champagne production.

demi-sec (DEHM-ee SEK)—Literally "half dry," though, when referring to sparkling wines, it indicates a medium sweetness.

Denominación de origen (DO) (deh-naw-mee-nah-THYON deh aw-REE-hen)—The second-highest quality wine level of wines from Spain. DO requires that wines which are produced in particular geographical areas use defined methods and quality standards in their grape and wine production. As of 2008, there are 65 DO's that have been awarded this designation.

Denominación de Origen Calificada (DOCa) (deh-naw-mee-nah-THYON deh aw-REE-hen kah-lee-fee-KAH-dah)—The highest quality wine level of wines from Spain. DOCa requires that wines which are produced in particular geographical areas use defined methods and quality standards in their grape and wine production. As of 2008, only two DO's have been awarded the coveted DOCa designation.

Denominazione d'Origine Controllata (DOC) (deh-noh-mee-nah-TSYAW-neh dee oh-REE-jeh-neh con-traw-LAH-tah)—The second-highest quality level of wines from Italy. DOC requires that wines which are produced in particular geographical areas use defined methods and quality standards in their grape and wine production.

Denominazione d'Origine Controllata e Garantita (DOCG) (deh-NOH-mee-nah-SYAW-neh dee oh-REE-jee-neh con-traw-LAH-tah eh gah-rahn-TEE-tah)—The highest quality wine level of wines from Italy. DOCG requires that wines which are produced in particular geographical areas use defined methods and quality standards in their grape and wine production.

depth/deep—Wine-tasting term indicating a wine's intensity, complexity, and concentration, or aromas, flavors, and/or color.

dessert wine—Any type of wine that is sweet.

diacetyl (die-ASS-ih-tahl)—A chemical by-product of malolactic fermentation that adds a buttery aroma and flavor.

distillation—The process of heating a fermented mixture to separate the water by causing the alcohol to vaporize and then recondense with a higher strength and greater purity, whereupon it may be referred to as a spirit. The most common type of spirit used in fortified wine is brandy, which is made from grapes.

domaine (doh-MAYN)—French term for estate or property. Often used in Burgundy, France, where it refers to a single property that may or may not be made up of several vineyards from different locations.

dosage (doh-ZAHJ)—Denotes the addition of a small amount of wine and sugar to top off and adjust the sweetness of a bottle of sparkling wine.

doux (DOO)—French term for "sweet."

dry—A wine with no perceptible level of sweetness.

E

earthy—Used to describe an aroma of soil or mushrooms.

edelfäule (ay-duhl-FOY-luh)—German term for "noble rot."

eiswein (ICE-vyn)—A German term for "ice-wine," a wine

made from grapes that are harvested and pressed while frozen. The juice that is released is highly concentrated, fruity, acidic, and sweet.

elegant—A wine-tasting term that describes a beautiful, well-balanced wine.

enology (ee-NAHL-uh-jee)—Also spelled *oenology*. The science and study of winemaking.

enophile (EE-nuh-file)—Someone who enjoys and appreciates fine wine, also spelled *oenophile*.

esters—Compounds produced from the reaction between alcohol and acids. They may contribute to complexity in the smell of a wine. Esters contribute many of the fruit aromas in a wine, such as pineapple, strawberry, cinnamon, and apple.

extra-dry—The equivalent of semi-dry, a term used to describe sparkling wines that are not as dry as Brut.

extract—The components and concentration of a wine that contribute to its body, flavor, and color.

F

fat—A wine-tasting term that describes the mouth feel of wines that are full bodied because the wine is either high in alcohol, oak aged, or high in sugar. Most late-harvest dessert wines are luscious and fat.

fermentation—The process by which yeast metabolizes grape sugars, producing ethyl alcohol, carbon dioxide, heat, and other by-products that affect the aroma and flavor of wine.

field blend—It used to be a common practice to intersperse complementary grapevines in a vineyard; when all the grapes are harvested together, the resulting wine is often referred to as a field blend.

fill level—The amount of wine in a bottle that is gauged by its height in the bottle.

filtering—A clarification process done to wine before it is bottled. The purpose of filtering is to remove sediment, grape skins, dead yeast, etc., from the wine. However, it is increasingly being minimized (or avoided whenever possible) because the greater the degree of filtering, the more flavors and character are stripped from the wine. Many wineries are using the more labor-intensive, old-fashioned practices of fining or racking to clarify wines these days.

fining (FINE-ing)—A clarification process done to wine before it is bottled. A traditional technique for clarifying wines by adding egg whites or bentonite (clay) to barrels of wine. These agents cause the particles and sediment to slowly sink to the bottom of the cask, where the material is then removed. Fining is considered a less intrusive process for clarifying wines than filtering.

finish—Sometimes referred to as the *persistence*, it's the lasting impression, or aftertaste, of a wine on the palate after the wine has been spit out or swallowed. A long, complex finish is generally desirable, though it ultimately depends on the typicity of a grape varietal.

flat—Also called "flabby." A wine-tasting term that is often used to describe white wines that are low in, or lacking acidity and to describe red wines that are low in, or lacking, acidity and tannin. Sometimes said of a wine that has been open for too long and lost its vibrancy. Also may be applied to a sparkling wine that has lost its carbonation.

flavonoids—A group of chemical compounds found in grape seeds, stems, and skins that contribute color, aromas, flavors, and antioxidant benefits.

flavor—The word used to describe the process of smelling the wine on the inside as the wine aromas are forced up the nasal passages.

flight—A grouping of several (often three to four) small portions of different wines that have been selected for some comparision or for contrasting purposes.

flinty—A stone or mineral-like aroma or flavor character used to describe a wine.

flor (FLOOR)—In reference to Spanish Sherry, these are the live yeast cells that naturally develop on certain wines after they have been fermented. Flor contributes aromas and flavors, but also acts to preserve the wine from oxygen while it is barrel aged.

floral—A wine that has aromas or flavors of flowers.

flowering—A term used in the vineyard to reference when small flowers begin to appear on the vine. They occur typically about 2½ months after bud break.

flute (FLOOT)—A tall, slender stemmed glass that is ideal for drinking sparkling wine.

fortified added—A category of wine in which table wine is the base, with added alcohol (in the form of a distilled spirit—often an unaged brandy). Fortified wine typically contains between 15% and 22% alcohol, and it is possible to have white or red options that can be made into wines that are dry, sweet, or somewhere in between. Port, Sherry, and Madeira are the most common fortified wines.

free-run juice—The initial juice released from the grapes once they have been pressed or crushed. Generally, the initial juice is considered to be of the best quality, because it has less contact with seeds and stems that may cause bitterness.

French oak—The classic wood for wine barrels that imparts flavors of vanilla, cedar, or other spices. The oak from different French forests lends slightly different characteristics to the wine and is therefore named for the forest region from which it was harvested.

French paradox—In the 1980s, medical studies found a paradox in that French people who have a fatter diet also have a low incidence of heart disease. The study found that the higher amounts of wine consumed by the French lowered health risks. The study concluded that people who consume moderate amounts of red wine are less likely than nondrinkers to suffer from cardiovascular disease. This finding led Americans to increase their consumption of red wine.

frizzante (free-DZAHN-tay)—An Italian term for slightly sparkling wine. Equivalent to the French term *Petillant*.

fruit set—A term used in the vineyard to identify when the grapevine flowers evolve into tiny green grape berries.

full body—Said of a wine that is high in extract, alcohol, or sugar. Can be compared to the weight or viscosity of whole milk.

G

geographically based—Applied to European wine labels, this concept simply refers to wines that are produced from strictly regulated areas of the wine-growing country.

geographic indicators—Australia's term for appellation, geographic indicators are that country's control system of identifying where the grapes are grown. Australian winemakers are required to maintain a minimum of 85% of a grape varietal from the location identified on the label.

glycerin—A by-product of fermentation that is most noticeable in wines with a higher alcohol content and in late-harvested wines, giving a smooth, fuller tactile impression.

gönci (GOON-ts)—The traditional 136-liter containers or barrels in which Tokay wines are created.

grafting—A technique used in the vineyard whereby a vine is secured to a different vine or rootstock. Grafting is often used to attach *vinifera* cuttings to American *lubrusca* rootstock that is *phylloxera* resistant.

grand cru—Literally, "great site" in France, this term refers to top-tier vineyards and their wines. In Burgundy, this term denotes the highest classification of vineyard.

Gran Reserva (GRAHN ree-SEHR-vah)—Spanish wine classification indicating the time of aging. Gran Reserva wines are any DO or DOCa red wines that have been aged a minimum of five years, of which at least one-and-a-half years were spent in barrels. The appellation areas of Rioja, Navarra, and Ribera del Duero require a minimum of two years in wood. White and rosé wines labeled as Gran Reserva must be aged four years, at least six months of which were in wood.

grappa (GRAHP-pah)—Also known as *marc* in France. An Italian spirit distilled from the remains of the grape skins, seeds, and stems. These remains are also known as pomace (PUHM-ess).

grassy—A wine having aromas and flavors of grass or fresh hay.

H

halbtrocken (HALP-trawk-en)—German term for "half-dry," meaning that the wine is semi-sweet.

hang time—Delay in harvesting grapes, with the expectation of increasing flavor development. This practice produces very ripe fruit that yields a "jammy" quality in the finished wine.

heavy soil—Soil with a high ratio of clay with high water retention and nutrients. Tends to be colder than other types of soil.

hectare—A measure used in Europe to represent the size of vineyards or regions. 1 hectare is equal to approximately 2.47 acres.

herbaceous—A wine having aromas and flavors of fresh herbs or grass.

horizontal tasting—An evaluation of wines from a single grape variety from different locations, from a single region, etc.

hot—A wine that is high in alcohol and that causes a burning sensation in the back of the throat.

house style—Nonvintage wines (which are blends of multiple vintages) allow vintners to create a "house style" by blending for consistency and distinctive, recognizable aromas and flavors year after year. For example, Champagne producers create a house style with their nonvintage Champagne.

house wine—A wine offered by the glass in a restaurant, often as an inexpensive option, but sometimes found in several price tiers.

hue—The shade of color of a wine.

hybrid grapes—Grapes created from cross-pollinating two different vine species, such as American vine (to obtain hardiness) and European vine (to obtain complexity) varieties.

hydrogen sulfide—Chemical responsible for the off-odor of rotten eggs in a wine.

hydrolyzable tannin—The type of tannin extracted through oak barrels and often referred to as ripe tannin, as it benefits by softening from aeration during the aging process.

I

ice-wine—A sweet dessert wine made from grapes that have been frozen on the vine or in freezers. Because the grapes are pressed while frozen, they release the sweet concentrated juice and leave behind the frozen, slushy water content. An ice-wine is called an Eiswein in Germany.

Indicazione Geografica Tipica (IGT) (in-dee-kat-tsee-OH-nay jay-o-GRAF-eecah TEE-pee-cah)—This category of wine was introduced in 1992 as a solution to the strict limited allowance for experimentation required in the upper two levels of the Italian classification system.

inert aging—The process of storing wine in a container that prevents the passage of oxygen, therefore preserving the wine's natural aromas and flavors. An example of such a container is a stainless steel or concrete container.

Institut Nationale des Appellations d'Origine (INAO) (anstee-TYOO nah-syaw-NAHL dayz ah-pehl-lah-SYOHN dawree-ZHEEN)—The French governmental agency responsible for establishing and enforcing standards for the Appellation d' Origine Controlée system.

isinglass (Izing-Glas)—Used as a fining agent, this is a type of gelatin that comes from the bladder of fish.

J

jeroboam (jer-ah-BOME)—A large bottle that holds the equivalent of six regular bottles. However, with respect to sparkling wine, a Jeroboam holds four standard bottles of wine.

joven (HO-vehn)—Spanish term for *young*. A Spanish wine made with no or very little aging.

jug wine—An inexpensive generic wine that is of low quality. Often uses the place names of high-quality French wine regions and may be sold in 1-liter or 1.5-liter packaging.

K

kabinett (kah-bih-NEHT)—The lowest of the QMP levels indicating that the grapes from which a wine is made have been picked at normal harvest time with a standard sugar content of 17–21%.

L

lactic acid—An acid produced in high levels after a wine has undergone malolactic fermentation. This acid has an influence on the style of the wine by producing a softer, milky-type acid.

lake effect—Term used around the U.S. Great Lakes area and other large lakes in cool regions to describe the climatic influence on wine grapes. The lake effect retards early budding in the spring and allows for a longer growing season with a later harvest in the fall.

late harvest—Refers to wines made from grapes picked later than the normal harvest time and therefore with a higher sugar content (24% or above). Most late-harvest wines contain some residual sugar and would be appropriate for or with dessert.

late-bottled vintage port (LBV)—LBVs are an increasingly popular category of Port that is similar to, but less expensive than, Vintage Ports. LBVs spend an extra three to four years aging in a barrel before being bottled, which makes them more mature and easy to drink than Vintage Ports from the same year. Some LBVs are filtered before bottling; those labeled "Tradition" are unfiltered and will deposit sediment with further aging.

leathery—Said of a red wine that is rich with tannin.

lees—Sediment and dead yeast cells found in a barrel or tank during and after fermentation. "Sur Lie" is the French term for a wine left on the lees and denotes a winemaking technique used to increase complexities in the aromas and flavors during the aging process.

legs—The tears or sheets of wine that slide down the sides of the glass after it has been swirled. The more pronounced legs indicate a wine that has a higher alcohol or sugar content. Generally, the slower the flow and the more defined the legs are on the side of the glass, the fuller bodied is the wine.

light—Characterized by a low degree of alcohol and/or body.

light soil—Soil with a high ratio of sand with low water retention and low maintenance of nutrients.

Liqueur de Tirage (lick-KYOOR duh tee-RAHZH)—In Champagne, a blended base wine bottled and combined with a dose of sugar and yeast in order to induce a secondary fermentation. Through the secondary fermentation, a greater degree of alcohol (totaling around 13%) is produced, along with carbon dioxide.

loam soil—A mix of clay, silt, sand, and organic matter. Considered fertile and drains well.

M

maceration—The contact time between the grape skins (and sometimes stems) and the wine prior to and during the fermentation process in order to extract greater color, tannin, aroma, and flavor.

macroclimate—The general or broad climate in a large area such as Napa Valley or Champagne.

maderized—Said of a wine showing evidence of oxidation, including a brownish color and a bad Madeira-like flavor. Maderization is acceptable for certain types of wine, such as Madeira and Gran Reserva Rioja.

magnum—A bottle that holds two standard-size wine bottles.

malic acid—An acid found in large amounts in wine grapes and in some finished wines. Malic acid is responsible for producing a crisp, fresh feel and is also found in fruits such as apples.

malmsey (MAH'M-zee)—The richest and sweetest type of Madeira wine made from the Malvasia grape (though called Malmsey on the island of Madeira).

malolactic fermentation (ML)—Secondary fermentation (actually, a biochemical reaction) that converts the malic acid (fruit acids) in a wine to softer lactic acid (milk acids), so that the wine becomes softer, rounder, and more complex. Total acidity is also reduced. Most red wines go through this process, and so do some white wines, particularly Chardonnay.

mature—Ready to drink. All of the wine's components are in harmony.

meritage (MEHR-ih-tihj)—A term created by California wineries for Bordeaux-style red and white blended wines. A meritage wine must be made with two or more classic Bordeaux grape varietals. Producers may label the wines with the term *Meritage* or may use a proprietary name if they choose. Examples of wines that fall into this category include Opus One and Joseph Phelp's Insignia.

mesoclimate—The climate in a small area such as a vineyard or a portion of a vineyard.

méthode champenoise (may-TOAD cham-pen-WAHZ)—The traditional method for making Champagne and other high-quality sparkling wine. The method induces a secondary fermentation and traps the carbon dioxide within the original bottle. It is an expensive, labor-intensive process.

methuselah—The equivalent of eight standard bottles.

microclimate—The climate in a very small area, such as a row of vines within a vineyard.

micro-oxygenization—A winemaking technique that introduces the deliberate passage of a small amount of oxygen into the wine as it is being aged.

mildew—There are two main types of fungi that can cause damage within the vineyard. *Downy mildew* is associated with wet, humid growing areas. *Powdery mildew* (also called *odium*) is found in dry climates. Both can be treated with copper sulfate sprays.

millerandage (mill-lehr-AHN-dahj)—Condition in which grape bunches contain berries of varying sizes and maturity levels, causing a lower quality of wine.

mise en bouteille au chateau (meez ahn boo-TAY oh shah-TOE)—French term for *bottled at the winery*.

mousse (MOOSE)—A French term associated with the "foam" on the surface of a sparkling wine.

must—The unfermented juice of grapes before it is turned into wine.

N

nebuchadnezzar—A giant wine bottle holding the equivalent of 20 standard bottles.

negociant—A wine merchant who buys grapes or already fermented wines and then ages, blends, bottles, and ships them under their own label. Many famous French wine companies (particularly in Burgundy and the Rhône), such as Jadot, Duboeuf, and Drouhin, make wines from vineyards they do not own and thus are negociants.

noble rot—Also called *Botrytis cinerea*, a beneficial mold that may grow on wine grapes, causing them to dehydrate and shrivel resulting in the remaining juice becoming very concentrated. This desired condition yields the honey-like richness of many classic dessert wines, such as Sauternes, Trockenbeerenauslese, and Tokaji.

non-vintage (NV)—Said of a wine blended from multiple harvests; nonvintage wines are particularly common in sparkling wines, Sherries, and Ports. Blending allows the winemaker to create an individual "house" style that can be fairly consistent from bottle to bottle, year after year.

nose—The broadest term for the bouquet and aroma of a wine. The smell of a wine.

nouveau—A tradition started in Beaujolais, France, where a red wine is quickly fermented and then bottled and released within about eight weeks from harvest. Nouveau (or new) wines should be consumed within months of release.

O

oaky/oak—Describes the aroma or taste character of a wine that has interacted with an oak barrel. Most of the world's greatest red wines (and many of the world's greatest whites) are aged in wood before bottling and show some vanilla-spice-toast character and complexity contributed through the wine's interaction with oak.

Oechsle (UHX-leh)—A German method of measuring sugar content in unfermented grape juice.

off-dry—Said of a slightly sweet wine in which sugar is slightly perceptible.

old vines—"Vieille vines" in French. A wine made from old grapevines. Theoretically, old vines should produce better fruit, but they also yield less quantity.

oxidation—The chemical reaction whereby a wine is unintentionally exposed or overexposed to oxygen, causing the wine to become spoiled.

oxidative aging—The process of storing wine in a container that allows the slow passage of oxygen over time, therefore causing the wine's aromas and flavors to be enhanced. Oxidative aging can occur in oak or chestnut wood barrels.

oxidized—Said of a wine that has lost its freshness from exposure to oxygen, similar to an apple turning brown and losing its flavor once the skin is peeled. Oxidation causes chemical changes and deterioration that alters the colors, aromas, and flavors of wines. Oxidized wines are also referred to as "maderized." Using a wine preserver (which blankets the wine with inert gas and prevents contact with oxygen) can lessen or prevent oxidation. Oxidation is desired in certain types of wine, such as Madeira.

P

passito (pah-SEE-toh)—An Italian method of laying grapes on mats or hanging them to partially dry for weeks to several months. This process, which evaporates water content and concentrates flavors and sugar content, can produce a dry or sweet wine, depending upon when fermentation has ended.

peak—The time when a wine is meant to be drunk; the time when it attains its smoothest, fullest, most well balanced flavors and components. This time can vary from a few months for Nouveau or some white wines to decades for a Vintage Port or Red Bordeaux.

performance factors—Combination of aspects (color, aroma, flavor, acid, alcohol, tannin, body level, and so on) that cumulatively create the distinctive personality of a particular grape varietal. Performance factors can be used to identify the defining elements of a particular grape as it has been produced around the world by various viticulture and winemaking techniques.

pétillant (pay-tee-YAWN)—French term for slightly sparkling. Equivalent to the Italian term, frizzante.

phenolics—Chemical compounds found in grape skins and seeds and extracted from oak barrels. Phenolics are responsible for the tannins, color pigments, and flavor compounds in wine.

phenolic ripeness—Otherwise known as flavor ripeness, represented by a group of compounds that contribute color, aroma, flavor, and tannin to a grape. This kind of ripeness allows the tannins to become softer as the growing season progresses. Phenolic ripeness often trails sugar ripeness, but is important for allowing the maximum flavor of the grape to be obtained.

phylloxera (fil-LOX-er-uh)—The name of an insect that attacks and devastates the roots of grapevines. It spread from America to Europe in the 1860s and destroyed the vineyards of France, after which it spread elsewhere. Most of the world's vineyards are now grafted on American rootstock, which is more resistant to *Phylloxera*.

pièce (pee-YES)—Often refers to a barrel for aging or fermentation that holds approximately 60 gallons; used in Burgundy.

pierce's disease—A disease caused by a bacterium that is transferred through its insect host (the glassy-winged sharpshooter) and that kills the grapevine.

polymerize (PUH-lym-err-ize)—To separate or fall out of a liquid solution and form a sediment. Over time, a red wine's tannin (in combination with color pigment) will polymerize in the wine bottle.

pomace (PUHM-ess)—The solid remains left over after pressing grapes to extract juice. Pomace consists of the skins, seeds, stems, and remaining pulp of the grape. These remains may be fermented and distilled to create grappa.

prädikatswein (preh-dih-KAHTS-vine)—The highest quality category for wine made in Austria.

premier cru—This French labeling means "first-growth vineyards"; sometimes the term "1er Cru" may appear. In Burgundy the term denotes the second-best classified vineyard, but in Bordeuax it's the highest ranking of a classified estate.

press wine—The juice extracted after the initial pressing of white wine grapes and after fermentation for red wine grapes. Press wine has more color and, often, more tannins than free-run juice. Winemakers may blend a portion of press wine with the free-run juice for backbone.

private reserve—A term used to indicate a producer's best offering. Private Reserve has no legal definition and is applied to everything from $10 to $200 bottles of wine.

prohibition—A time in America when it was illegal to produce, transport, sell, and consume alcohol (with some exceptions, such as alcohol for sacramental purposes). Prohibition lasted from 1920 to 1933.

pruning—A viticultural practice of cutting back grapevines and related foliage in order to concentrate the vines' energies into the remaining grapes to make a high-quality crop.

pulp—The soft, succulent part on the inside of the grape, where the juice, acid, sugar, and flavor can be found. Approximately 75% of a grape by weight, pulp plays a major role in providing acid (which is present in the juice) and is pivotal in giving both red and white wine good structure.

pumping over—The aggressive process of pumping and circulating the juice of the grape (with a giant hose) over the cap during fermentation. Commonly used in Bordeaux in order to extract maximum color, juice, and tannin from grape skins.

punching down—The gentle process of pushing the cap (skins, seeds, and stems) down into the wine as it ferments. Commonly used in Burgundy.

punt—The indentation found in the bottom of most wine bottles and which is especially important in sparkling wine bottles, where it acts to strengthen the bottle.

pupître (pew-PEE-truh)—A French term for the "A-frame" rack in which bottles are placed for riddling for the production of Champagne.

puttonyos (PUH-tohn-yosh)—Name of the basket in Hungary which holds the aszú berries that were mashed into a sweetened paste.

Q

qualitätswein (kvah-lee-TAYTS-vine)—Term representing middle-quality wines in both Germany and Austria.

qualitätswein mit prädikat (QmP) (kvah-lee-TAYTS-vine meet PRAY-dee-kaht)—Term representing the highest quality wines in the German classification system. There are six subcategories within the QmP system, ranked in ascending order according to their sugar content upon harvest: kabinett, Spätlese, Auslese, Beerenauslese, Eiswein, and Trockenbeerenauslese.

R

racking—The practice of transfering wine from one container to another to rid the wine of sediment by leaving the sediment behind in the first container. Racking is essentially decanting on a grand scale by moving a wine from barrel to barrel. Racking is more labor intensive, but less disturbing to the wine, than filtration.

recioto (reh-CHAW-toh)—An Italian wine (speciality of the Veneto) made by the Passito method. If the wine is left with residual sugar, it is known as Recioto. If the wine is fermented dry, it is known as Amarone.

rehoboam—A large (rah-moo-ajh) bottle equivalent to six regular bottles.

remuage (reh-moo-ajh)—French term for riddling—that is, the process of shaking the Champagne bottles to encourage the lees to move towards the neck of the bottle.

reserva (ray-SEHR-vah)—A Spanish wine classification indicating the time of aging. Reserva wines are any DO or DOCa red wines that have been aged a minimum of three years, one year of which was in wood. White and rosé wines labeled as Reserva must be aged two years, six months of which are in wood.

reserve—This term may be found on American wine bottles and may mean a winery's top-of-the-line wine, but has no legal definition. It is used mostly for marketing purposes.

residual sugar—A measurement of the amount of grape sugar remaining in a wine after fermentation. Dry wines have little or no residual sugar (0.1–0.2%), whereas dessert wines contain as much residual sugar as 28–30%.

resveratrol (rez-VEHR-ah-trawl)—One of the phenolic compounds found in high amounts within grape skins and that have beneficial affects on cholesterol levels and prevention against certain kinds of cancer.

retronasal passage—Passageway connecting the throat with the nose and that enables a person to detect a wine's flavors inside the mouth.

riddling—The process of placing Champagne bottles upside down in a rack, in which they are shaken over a period of several weeks. The shaking allows the lees to collect at the neck of the bottle in order to eventually be discarded.

ripasso (ree-PAH-so)—A winemaking technique common in Italy that allows a wine to remain in contact with the lees from a previous passito wine through re-fermentation.

riserva (Rih-ZERVA)—Italian designation on a wine label indicating that the wine has additional barrel aging, but that the duration of aging varies by region.

robust—Full bodied, intense.

rosado (roe-SAH-do)—In Spanish, refers to a rosé wine, made by allowing the juice to have only brief contact with the skin of the red wine grapes.

rosé—French term for pink. Rosé wines range in color from pink to salmon and are made from red wine grapes through limited skin contact in order to extract only a slight amount of color. Sometimes, a small amount of red wine may be added instead.

rosso (RAWH-soh)—Italian for "red," as in red wine.

rotwein (RAWT-vine)—German for "red wine."

rouge (ROOZH)—French for "red," as in red wine.

round—Describes a smooth, well-balanced wine.

S

saignée (san-YAY)—A method of producing wine that allows some of the color from red grape skins to bleed into the fermenting juice, creating a pinkish color.

salmanazar—A large bottle that holds the equivalent of 12 regular bottles.

sediment—The color pigments and tannins that form together and naturally separate out from a red wine as it ages. The wine is removed from the sediment through the decanting process.

seeds and stems—Seeds are found on the inside, and stems are found on the outside, of a grape, and both may contribute a bitter component if crushed or used in excess. Stems and seeds contribute approximately 5% of the grape by weight.

sekt (ZEKT)—A German sparkling wine.

skin—That part of the grape found on the outside and in which reside the tannin, flavor, and color. Making up approximately 20% of the grape by weight, skin has an even greater influence on the style and structure of a red wine, which are achieved when the skins are allowed to ferment with the juice.

skin contact—The process of macerating the skins and grape juice together in order to extract flavor, tannin, and color.

solera system (soh-LEH-rah)—An intricate blending system used in Spain to produce Sherry.

sommelier (saw-muh-LYAY)—A French term for a wine steward. This individual is responsible for managing the wine program, which may include ordering and storing the wine, educating staff, making wine recommendations, and serving wines to customers. Sommeliers are often hired by fine-dining restaurants, but the term has been increasingly applied to wine experts in all forums (wine bars, retail stores, etc.) where wine is sold.

sparkling wine—A category of wine in which table wine is the base, with large amounts of CO_2 added for carbonation. Sparkling wine typically contains between 10% and 13% alcohol.

Spätlese (SHPAYT-lay-zuh)—The second ranking of the QMP levels, Spätlese indicates that the grapes have been picked after normal harvest and with a sugar content of 19–23% by weight.

spritzy—A pleasant, light sparkling sensation (sometimes found in young wines) caused by a slight secondary fermentation or the addition of carbon dioxide.

spumante—Italian term for sparkling wine with regular or standard levels of carbonation.

stainless steel aging—Method used primarily for white aromatic wines whose primary flavors and crisp acidity need to be preserved. Stainless steel doesn't truly age the wine; rather, it preserves the wine and prevents the passage of oxygen that would otherwise alter the wine's personality.

stemmy—Green, astringent character of wines fermented too long with the grape stems.

sticky—Australian term referencing a sweet dessert wine.

still wine—A term that applies to any wine that is not sparkling.

structure—A wine's texture, mouth feel, and balance.

struggling vine philosophy—Philosophical viewpoint which theorizes that the farther a vine's roots must dig to find nutrients, the fewer, but better quality, grapes will be produced, with thicker skins and more concentrated flavor.

sulfur dioxide—Sulfites are a derivative of sulfur and a natural by-product of fermentation. Most wines naturally contain very low levels of sulfites. However, winemakers have added sulfites to wine for hundreds of years to clean and sterilize equipment and barrels, to kill off bacteria, and to prevent browning and possible spoilage. Sulfur is also sometimes sprayed in a vineyard to prevent disease and pests. Under U.S. law, any wine with sulfites higher than 10 ppm must state "contains sulfites" on the label.

Super Tuscan—An unofficial name originally given to wines from Tuscany that are made from international varieties such as Cabernet Sauvignon or Merlot, rather than primarily local varieties such as Sangiovese. Because they are made outside the traditional Tuscan winemaking practices, these wines are labeled with the lower quality classification within Italy's system.

superiore (soo-payr-YOH-reh)—The Italian label designating a wine as having a slightly higher alcohol content.

sur lie (soor LEE)—A French term which indicates that a wine was aged "on the lees" (on sediment consisting mainly of dead yeast cells and small grape particles). This process is a normal procedure for fermenting red wines; Burgundian winemakers discovered that it often added complexity to their Chardonnays, and now the process is used in many white wines from around the world.

süssreserve (ZOOSS-ray-ZEHR-veh)—Winemaking method that involves fermenting the wines fully dry, with low alcohol and high acid. Before fermentation, a small quantity of unfermented juice is held back. Later, this juice will be blended into the dry wine in order to adjust and balance the acid-to-sweetness ratio.

T

table wine—This category of wine gets its name because it is made to be drunk at the table with meals. The alcoholic content of table wine generally is between 8% and 15%. Table wines are white, pink, or red wines that can be dry, sweet, or somewhere in between.

tannin—A natural chemical compound found in grape skins (mostly of red wine grapes), seeds, and stems, but also in oak barrels. Tannins produce an astringent, mouth-puckering sensation. Tannins are common in most fine young red wines and help form natural preservatives that allow wines to develop and age. Tannins soften in time, either naturally or with exposure to oxygen.

tartrates—Natural, harmless crystals that look like shards of glass and often form in a barrel, bottle, or cork. They may occur from the tartaric acids present in a wine if the wine gets very cold. Upon serving a wine, it would be proper practice to decant it if it shows evidence of tartrate crystals.

TCA—An acronym for 2, 4, 6-trichloroanisole (try-clore-AN-iss-all), a chemical that has a wet-cardboard odor and flavor commonly associated with tainted cork.

terroir (tehr-WHAR)—French term that encompasses all the environmental factors that affect the grapevine, such as the interactions among soil, climate, topography, and grape variety within a specific vineyard.

tête de cuvée (tet duh koo-VAY)—French term for a Champagne producer's best bottling.

thin—Lacking body; often used to describe a wine that tastes diluted.

tinto (TEEN-to)—Spanish for "red wine."

tirage (tee-RAHZH)—Method whereby, in Champagne production, the blended base wine is given a dose of sugar and yeast in order to induce a secondary fermentation.

toasty—A flavor imparted by oak barrels.

transfer process—The sparkling wine production process whereby the wine is removed from the bottle, transferred to a pressurized tank for filtering, and then rebottled.

trellis—An artificial support used to hold and train grapevines to grow off the ground.

trocken—German word meaning *dry*.

U

ullage (UHL-ihj)—The air space in the bottle between the top of the wine and the bottom of the cork.

V

varietal—A specific grape variety. Also denotes a wine made mostly or entirely from one grape variety.

varietal based—A concept applied to most non-European wine labels. The term simply refers to the grape variety used to make the wine.

varietal character—Sometimes referred to as "typicity," the varietal character identifies the aromas, flavors, and taste sensations typical of a particular grape variety.

vegetal—A word applied to wines that smell or taste like plants or green vegetables.

vendage (vahn-DAHZH)—Grape harvest or vintage.

vendage tardive—A French term for "late harvest."

véraison (vehr-ray-ZOHN)—Natural process whereby, near the middle to end of summer, the green berries begin to change color and become recognizable as grapes.

vin de pays—The name translates to "country wine." This is the third level of quality classification in the French wine laws. Varietals are allowed to be mentioned on the labels. These wines are predominant in the south of France.

vineyard—A grape-growing area that ranges in size.

viniculture—The science of growing wine grapes and making wine.

vino (VEE-noh)—"Wine" in Italian.

Vino da Tavola (VdT) (VEE-no dah TAH-voh-lah)—Lowest level designation of wine, with the greatest amount of freedom. The producers are not allowed to cite the grape varietal or specific location on the label.

vintage—Term that refers both to the year the grapes from which a certain wine was made were harvested and to the wine made from those grapes. To place a vintage on the label, most wine-producing regions now require that at least 95% of the wine contain grapes harvested from only that year. Historically, some wine regions were lax in requiring that vintage dates be accurate. Wines that are blended from more than one harvest are called non-vintage wines.

vintage ports—These wines are created from grapes deriving from a single year. The wine is bottled within 2½ years of the vintage and spends most of its life evolving within a bottle.

vintner—Wine producer or winery proprietor.

viticulture—The science or study of grape growing.

vitis vinifera—The classic European grapevine species most responsible for producing the world's best wines, including Pinot Noir, Chardonnay, Cabernets, etc.

W

wein (VINE)—German for "wine."

weiss (VICE)—German for "white."

weissherbst (VICE-hehrbst)—German for "rosé" (wine).

wood-barrel aging—A centuries-old tradition that uses wood vessels to store and age most red wines and many full-bodied white wines. The industry standard is to use French or American oak as the preferred wood. Oak from other places, such as Slovenian oak, is sometimes still used. In the past, different wine regions have used different kinds of wood, such as mahogany, chestnut, and pine.

world cuisine—In the broadest sense, food that has been created in present-day times and that may incorporate a combination of modern or classical practices, ingredients, and techniques.

Y

yeast—Important microorganisms that cause fermentation by converting sugar to alcohol. The predominant wine yeast, *Saccharomyces* (sack-row-MY-ceese) *cerevisiae*, is the same microorganism that ferments beer and makes bread rise. Two categories of yeast are cultured yeast and wild yeast.

INDEX

Pricing, of wine, 273–275.
See also Costing-out wine
average guest check pricing
method, 289–290
costing-out, 273
cost percent method,
274–275
exclusive wines, 290
markup methods, 274
perceptions of, 290
quality and, 5
strategies, 274
20/20/60 rule, 289
Primary aromas, 30
Primary source, 263
Primitivo grapes, 91, 200
Priorat region, 208
Procurement, of beverages, 263
Production control point,
272–273
as purchased (AP) versus
edible portion (EP), 273
standards and procedures,
272–273
Prohibition, 4
Proper wine service, 281
Proprietary wine blends labelled, 22
Prosecco, 198
Protein, as main food item, 100
Provence region, 175
Provence wines, 189
Pruning, 51
Psychographics, 259
Puget Sound wines of
Washington, 152
Puglia, 200
Pulp, 12
Pumping over, 58
Pump method, 220
Punching down, 58
Punt end, 222
Purchase order, 265
Purchasing control point,
262–266
order frequency, 266
ordering methods, 265–266
ordering techniques, 264–265
order sizes, 264
selection/sourcing/
procurement, 263
three-tier distribution system,
263–264
Puttonyo (basket), 245

Q
Quails, 131
Qualitätswein Bestimmter
Anbaugebiete (QbA), 201
Qualitätswein mit prädikat (QmP),
201, 205
Quality wine categories, 176
Quick-fix approach to wine and
food pairings, 98

R
Rabbit, 136
Racking clarification, 62

Rain, 53
Rapel Valley wines, 166
Reading the guest, 276
Receiving control point,
266–267
receiving process, 267
tools to assist in, 266–267
Receiving process, 267
Recioto, 246
Recioto della Valpolicella, 197–198
Recioto della Valpolicella
Amarone, 197–198
Red Bordeaux, 182
Reductive or oxidative process, 59
Red wines, 16. See also
specific wine
aroma and flavor categories,
83–84
berry size and, 84
Big Three grapes of, 82
body and, 83–84
climatic influence on, 83
color and, 29, 82
degree of extraction and, 82
fermentation of, 57
grape varietals, 82–83
improper storage conditions, 82
Italian, 196
oak aging and, 84
residual sugar and, 84
serving temperature, 279–280
traditions associated with,
270–271
Refermenting, 62
Refractometer, 54
Regional appellation, 181
Regional considerations of food
and wine, 96, 113
Regions, 13–14
Registered place names, 50
Riesling grapes, 45
Remuage, 221
Renowned wine-producing
regions, 21
Requisition form, 272
Reserve, and U.S. labels, 146
Residual sugar (RS), 32, 56
Restaurant guidance, 10
Retailers, 264
Retronasal passage, 30
Revenue and expenses, influencing
atmosphere, 260
flow of beverages and, 261
location, 260
menu and, 259
sand theory, 262
service, 260–261
target market and, 259
vision and mission, 258–259
Rheingau region, 204
Rheinhessen region, 204–205
Rhône Valley, France, 175,
187–188
Rias Baixas, 207–208
Ribera del Duero, 209
Riddled bottles, 221
Riedel Company, 19

Riesling grapes and wines,
73–75, 204
Rioja region, 209
Rio Negro and Nuequen wines, 164
Ripening process, 53–54
Roasters, 131
Roman Empire, 4
Rosado (rosé) wine, 208, 209
Rosé and Blush grape varietals, 81
Rosé wine, 11
Rosso di Montalcino, 199
Rotary fermenters, 58
Rot wines, 74, 244–246
Roussillon wines, 188
Roux (thickening agent), 104
Ruby Port, 236. See also Port wine
Rueda, 208
Russian River wines, 149
Rutherford wines, 149

S
Saccharomyces cerevisiae
yeast, 56
Safety
opening sparkling wine,
282–283
serving alcohol and, 275–277
Saignée method, 11
Salads and salad dressings,
121–123
Sales history, 265
Sales skills, when serving guests,
278–279
Salta wines, 164–165
Salt flavor, 31, 33
Salty/Smoky/Spicy/Highly Seasoned
Foods (or SSSS), 110–111
Sancerre, 75
Sand theory, 262
Sandwiches, 127–128
Sangiovese grapes and wines,
89–90, 198, 199
San Juan wines, 164
San Luis Obispo wines, 150
Santa Barbara wines, 150
Santa Maria Valley wines, 150
Santa Ynez Valley wines, 150
Sardinia, 200
Sassicaia, 199
Saucer glass, 20
Sauces, 104–106
Sausages, 134
Sauternes, 80, 245
Sauvignon Blanc grapes and
wines, 45, 75–77, 208
Screw caps/twist offs, 18, 163
Seafood, 129–130
Seasonality, occasion, and mood
(SOM), of food and wine,
113
Seasoning, 61
Sec, 247
Secondary aromas, 29–30
Secondary fermentation, 58
Secondary sauces, 104
Sediment in the bottle, 33
Seeds and stems, 12

Selection de grains nobles, 178
Select picking, 203
Selling wine, 10
Semi-hard cheese, 124
Sémillon grapes and wines, 80
Semi-soft cheese, 124
Semi-sweet chocolate, 250.
See also Chocolate
Sercial-style Madeira, 235
Service formats, 260–261
Service staff, perception of wine
program and, 291
Serving guests, 278–279
Serving size and alcohol
equation, 275
Serving temperatures, 279–280
Shellfish and wine paring
strategies, 130
Sherry
fino types, 233–234
oloroso types, 234
production process, 232–233
varietals, 232
Shiraz
late harvest, 243
name used in Australia, 90
Shiraz/Syrah, 90
Shortcuts in the barrel, 61
Shortcuts to aging process, 61
Short-term aging, 271–272
Sierra Foothills of California, 150
Sight, 14–15
Silvaner grape, 205
Single grape varietal, 11
Single-serve bottles, 5
Skin, 12
Skins to juice relationship, 57
Sliding scale pricing method, 274
Smell/taste, 14–15, 29–31
Smoked sausages, 134
Soave, 197
Soft/fresh cheese, 123
Soft/rind ripened cheese, 123–124
Soils, 47–50
Albariza, 232
gimblett gravels, 163
llicorella, 208
sand based, 165
schist, 235–236
slate- or clay-based, 74, 204
terra rossa, 161
types and influences of,
48–49
Solera system, 232
SOM, (seasonality, occasion, and
mood), of food and wine, 113
Sommelier, role of, 258
Sonoma County wines, 148
Soups, 125–126
Sourcing, of beverages, 263
Sour flavor, 31–32, 32
South African Trade Group, 166
South Africa wines, 166–167
Southern France, wines of,
188–189
Southern Rhône Valley wines,
187–188